*Frances Warde: American Founder of the
Sisters of Mercy*

W9-AXG-916

Frances Warde: American Founder of the Sisters of Mercy

KATHLEEN HEALY

THE SEABURY PRESS · NEW YORK

First paperback printing

Copyright © 1973 by Kathleen Healy
Design by Nancy Dale Muldoon
Printed in the United States of America

Library of Congress Cataloging in Publication Data
Healy, Kathleen.
    Frances Warde: American founder of the Sisters of Mercy.

    Bibliography: p. 509.
    1. Warde, Mary Frances Xavier, 1810?–1884.
2. Sisters of Mercy.
BX4705.W32H42   271′.92′024   [B]   73–6433
ISBN 0-8164-2430-6

Preface

NINETY years ago Frances Warde, one of the greatest servants of humanity who ever lived, died in Manchester, New Hampshire. Twenty-five years ago Roland Burke Savage, S.J., in his biography, *Catherine McAuley, the First Sister of Mercy,* wrote: "Frances Warde's work in America . . . would require a book in itself were the story to be told in any of the detail that it deserves." And just five years ago the Federation of Sisters of Mercy of the Americas decided that indeed it was time that the biography of the American founder of the Sisters of Mercy be undertaken. They commissioned the author of the present work to research and write the life of Frances Warde.

The biography now published is based on research in the archives of Convents of Mercy throughout America and Ireland, of archdioceses and dioceses in both countries, of the Propaganda Fide in Rome, and of the Irish College in Rome. Books, periodicals, newspapers, annals, archival collections, documents, letters, official records, and unpublished manuscripts have been consulted. The more significant of these are listed in the selected bibliography. The author has benefited from discussions with men and women of three continents who are knowledgeable about the history of the Sisters of Mercy. Any attempt to express gratitude here to the innumerable persons who offered information and suggestions for the biography would be clearly impossible. All of them know that the author thanks them sincerely.

It seems essential, however, to acknowledge the assistance and support of those who opened their archives so freely to the author: the Irish Sisters of Mercy in Dublin (Carysfort Park, Baggot Street, Coolock, and Dun Laoghaire), Carlow, Naas, Wexford, Westport, Cork, and Limerick; the American Sisters of Mercy in Albany; Auburn, California; Baltimore; Bethesda, Maryland; Burlingame, California; Burlington, Vermont; Chicago; Cumberland, Rhode Island; Dallas, Pennsylvania; Dobbs Ferry, New York; Merion, Pennsylvania; North Plainfield, New Jersey; Omaha; Orchard Park, New York; Pittsburgh; Portland, Maine; Rochester, New York; West Hartford, Connecticut; and Windham, New Hampshire.

The bishops of every diocese in which the Sisters of Mercy have served were most cooperative, and special gratitude is due for access to research materials in the Archdioceses of Baltimore, Chicago, Newark, Omaha, and Philadelphia as well as the Dioceses of Buffalo; Burlington, Vermont; Pittsburgh; Portland, Maine; Providence, Rhode Island; and Trenton.

The author is grateful for the continued kindness of successive Presidents of the Federation of Sisters of Mercy: Sister M. Thomas Aquinas, Pittsburgh; Sister Mary Clotilde, West Hartford; Sister Mary Kieran, Cumberland; Sister M. Eucharia, Burlingame; also, Sister Mary Regina, former Mother General of the Sisters of Mercy of the Union, and Sister M. Jerome, Executive Director of the Federation. Sister Mary Ellen, Windham, New Hampshire, in whose Congregation Frances Warde lived for twenty-five years, offered untiring assistance. Sister M. Bertrand, Albany, and Sister M. Ignatia, Baltimore, were supportive and helpful.

In Rome, indispensable aid was received from Rev. Joseph Metzler, O.M.I., Director of the Propaganda Fide Archives; Msgr. John Hanly, Irish College in Rome; and the Sisters of Divine Providence, Via San Giovanni Eudes. Special gratitude is due to the author's Irish friends: Most Rev. Patrick Lennon, Bishop of Carlow; Rev. Roland Burke Savage, S.J., Clongowes-Wood College, Naas; Rev. Peter Swayne, Kildare; Rev. Seán Swayne, Carlow College; Sister M. Gabriel, Carysfort Park, Dublin; Sister M. Carmel, Carlow; and Mr. R. C. Simington, Dublin.

Finally, the author is grateful to Justus George Lawler, her editor, and distinguished Professor of Humanities at Saint Xavier College, Chicago.

KATHLEEN HEALY

Easter Sunday, 1973

Contents

CONTENTS

Frances Warde: American Founder of the
Sisters of Mercy

1

Amazing Gifts: Abbeyleix and Killeany

AT the close of the first decade of the nineteenth century, a child was born in Abbeyleix, Ireland, who was destined in her zeal for Christ to travel more miles than St. Paul of Tarsus and to found more convents than St. Teresa of Avila. Frances Warde, the American founder of the Sisters of Mercy, was the youngest child of John Warde, a prominent merchant who lived at beautiful Bellbrook House, nestled among fresh greensward, hedgerows, and nooks of shrubbery beside a flowing stream in Abbeyleix. Her mother was Mary Maher[1] of Kilkenny, a member of a famous Irish family of ecclesiastics and political leaders. When their last child was born, John and Mary Warde had reached a peak of apparent good fortune. Every circumstance of their existence seemed to converge toward a happy life rare among men. But their joy was not to be lasting.

In the spring of 1789 John Warde had realized a dream when he secured the lease to the house and lands of Bellbrook, comprising fifty-one acres of Abbeyleix, the immense estate of the British John Viscount de Vesci. Abbeyleix was not only one of the most magnificent estates in the County then called Queens; it had a history which appealed to the cultural interests of John Warde.

The name *Abbeyleix* is derived from that of the Cistercian Abbey, *De Lege Dei,* founded on the site in honor of the Virgin Mary in 1183 by Conor O'More, Prince of Leix. The

3

Abbey of Leix, under the leadership of the famous Celt, St. Canice, became a monastery of first consequence in Ireland. Bordering the River Nore, Abbeyleix in the twelfth century comprised 840 acres, including the old town of Leix and four other tiny towns. In 1562, the British Crown granted the entire lands of Abbeyleix to Thomas, Earl of Ormond. Not only in old County Laois, the so-called Queen's County, but all over Ireland monastic lands were snatched from the Church under British Rule and transferred to members of the British nobility. The residents of the present town of Abbeyleix still recall the tradition that the old town of Abbeyleix was the scene of the martyrdom of three Franciscans under Queen Elizabeth. The estate of Abbeyleix was subsequently assigned to Sir John Vesey, ancestor of the present de Vesci family, who was the first Lord de Vesci. Toward the close of the eighteenth century, no trace of the old Cistercian Abbey could be found. The townspeople believed, however, that the mansion of Abbeyleix built by Lord de Vesci in 1774 occupied the site of the original monastery. It was architecturally a beautiful building, quadrangular in shape and faced with cut stone. In the early nineteenth century, the then Viscount de Vesci caused the old town of Abbeyleix which had sprung up around the Abbey to be razed, and laid out the present town of Abbeyleix on a more desirable site. Flour mills and woolen factories were established there. Although many large estates in Ireland have passed from the hands of the British nobility since the establishment of the Irish Republic in the nineteen-twenties, the descendants of Sir John Vesey are still the proprietors of the estate of Abbeyleix, now comprising hundreds of acres. The present Viscontess de Vesci is the daughter of the second wife of the Earl of Ross and the sister of Lord Snowden, husband of Princess Margaret of England.

When John Warde secured the house and lands of Bell-brook in 1797, he was granted a lease for thirty-one years or the lifetime of himself and his first and second sons, which-ever term should last longer.[2] A rent of over 110 pounds to be paid half-yearly indicated the comfortable financial status of John Warde. Two years later he had the good fortune to receive an annuity of 50 pounds to be paid half-yearly from the rent of two acres of the lands of Bellbrook.

Meanwhile, the family of John and Mary Warde contin-ued to grow. After the two oldest boys, Daniel and William, John and Helen were born, then Sarah, and finally Frances, about 1810. Fanny, the baby, was loved by all in the family. And it was a happy family, for John Warde was deeply in love with his wife, Mary Maher. He was described by those who knew him then as a tall, well-built man, with fair skin, deep blue eyes, and a calmness of expression which inspired trust. Yet there was a decisiveness about his mouth which implied that his serenity was not to be misunderstood. His character could have been dominating, but it was not. He was a contented man and a successful merchant, secure in the love of his family, the fortunate head of beautiful Bellbrook House.

Fanny Warde was never to remember knowing her fa-ther in these happiest of days. But she was to be closest to him in misfortune. Shortly after Fanny's birth Mary Maher Warde became seriously ill, and her death followed with frightening rapidity. John Warde was absent from Bellbrook when his wife died. On his return, his anguish was so in-tense that for a time his children feared for his health. A part of John Warde himself died with the person of Mary Maher. From now on he gave himself energetically to the task of caring for his children, but he never again revealed the joyful vigor that his life with Mary had created in him.

5

John Warde turned to a maternal aunt of his children to help in rearing his family. The two older boys were able to care for themselves, but John was no more than ten, and the girls—especially Sarah and the baby, Frances—needed a mother's love and support. And so the growing Warde children established a closer relationship with the Maher family. In his grief, John Warde could be glad for the personal associations thus offered to his children, for the Mahers were not only a distinguished, well-educated, and politically active family; more important, they taught the Warde children their father's own Christian values. Branches of the family were scattered throughout Abbeyleix, Mountrath, and Carlow, as well as Kilkenny.

Probably the most famous branch of the family was made up of the descendants of Patrick Maher and Catherine Moore Maher, of Donore, County Carlow, who later moved to Kilrush. They were cousins of Mary Maher Warde. Two years before the birth of Fanny Warde, Patrick Maher had died of exposure following upon an act of charity to a hungry poor man. His experience was symbolic of the benevolence of the Maher family which was legendary throughout three counties. Patrick Maher's son, also Patrick, was imprisoned four times in Kildare for refusing to pay tithes in protest of unjust demands upon the poor. His sister, Mary, married Hugh Cullen of Prospect, County Kildare, and was the mother of Paul Cullen, who became successively Rector of the Irish College in Rome, Rector of the College of the Propaganda, Bishop of Armagh and Primate of Ireland, and finally Cardinal Archbishop of Dublin.[3] In the troubled days of 1798, when the secret Society of United Irishmen under Wolfe Tone had sought to establish a republic through armed insurrection, Hugh Cullen had been tried in court for affording shelter to Irish rebels. His brother, Paul Cullen (uncle of the future Cardinal) was unjustly tried by court-martial and shot to death as a rebel leader at Leighlin Bridge, Carlow. Alicia, daughter of Hugh Cullen by a previous marriage, married Patrick Moran, the son of Honoria Maher, and their son became the famous Cardinal Patrick Francis Moran, of Sydney, Australia.

But the best loved of all the Maher family was Patrick Maher's and Catherine Moore's eldest son, James Maher, later parish priest of Carlow-Graigue, who was destined to be a dear friend of Mary Maher Warde's youngest child, Fanny. James Maher has been ranked with Daniel O'Connell and Bishop James Doyle of Kildare and Leighlin as one of the three most prominent men in the struggle for civil and religious liberty in Ireland between 1825 and 1875. Together they infused new life into the Irish people through the *Catholic Association* for abolition of the tithes system and for complete emancipation from England. All three of them were well-known political writers as well as orators, and through their unwearied efforts they did much to wring from a reluctant Parliament the historic *Emancipation Bill* of 1829. Though Father James Maher was twice offered a bishopric and also the rectorship of the Irish College in Rome, he chose to be a parish priest in Carlow-Graigue and to give all that he had in talents and possessions to the poor whom he loved. Often he was without a coat on his back or a coin in his pocket because he followed the Gospel command of charity quite literally. His sister, Mary Maher Cullen, devised the scheme of giving a friend money to buy food for him because she knew that if she sent her brother the money, he would give it to the first poor man he met. The only assignment outside of his pastoral work that James Maher ever accepted was a professorship in theology and Sacred Scripture at Carlow College which, as we shall see, he providentially assumed at precisely the time when his young cousin, Frances Warde, needed his help in Carlow. James Maher's great charism was to live for others and somehow to be always available at their moments of greatest need.

It was fortunate, then, that the Mahers assumed importance in the lives of the Warde children after the death of Mary Maher Warde. They lived happily with their father and their aunt at Bellbrook. The motherless little Fanny led a free and joyous life in Abbeyleix until she was nine. She was educated by private tutors, studying with her sister, Sarah, of whom she was especially fond. Her aunt assumed the full responsibility for the little girl's religious instruction and prepared her so well to receive the Sacraments that her knowledge of Christian doctrine startled her examiners.

What is most striking in Fanny Warde's response to the Christian faith is that she integrated it with the whole of her little life, making it one with her play and even developing a childlike habit of contemplation, the depth of which she was probably unaware. Each morning and night she prayed with her aunt, and then the two carried on a dialogue about God and the light of the Holy Spirit in the souls of men. It was the most natural thing in the world for the little girl to continue these thoughts throughout her day. Bellbrook House was located near a winding stream between two lovely elevations of green lawn. Not far away were the ruins of an old castle, hedged in by shrubbery of perhaps hundreds of years' growth. Fanny found a natural crypt behind the eastern wall of the ancient castle, and there she arranged a little altar, with a picture of Christ blessing children as the central figure. On one side was a print of the Virgin Mary. The child loved to go to her secret altar, and there her prayer and play became one.

An unusual insight into Fanny's character is revealed in

her relationship with her favorite brother, John, who was about ten years her senior. Despite the difference in their ages, "he was her constant companion in his leisure moments and, on account of her ardent, affectionate disposition, loved her more than all the world."⁴ He was delighted with her fondness for fun and amusement and her bright, lively traits of character. He often went with her at sunset to her castle crypt. There the more grown-up brother would join his little sister in a simple, spontaneous evening prayer, or read aloud from a small, well-worn volume on St. Teresa of Avila which had been among their mother's favorite books. Then the two would return hand in hand to Bellbrook House, happy to be together, Frances' little mind pondering the thoughts of St. Teresa on the love of God.

She received the Eucharist for the first time at an earlier age than most children of her generation, and she fully appreciated the joy of her communion with Christ. An unusual circumstance surrounded her reception of the Sacrament of Confirmation at the hands of Bishop James Doyle of Kildare and Leighlin, the great friend of her cousin, Father Maher. It was customary for the Bishop to examine the children who were to be confirmed in the church itself in the presence of the whole congregation. Fanny's answers were so expressive of spiritual depth that the Bishop lifted the little girl in his arms and said, "This child is destined by God for some great work in his service." Then he asked her why she chose "Teresa" for her Confirmation name. Perhaps through an instinctive sense of guarding her own spiritual secret, Fanny did not tell him of how she and John read and contemplated together the thoughts of the great Spanish saint. She answered simply, "Because I think it is a very pretty name."⁵

It is perhaps more remarkable that at a time when many Catholics read Scripture little or not at all, Fanny Warde not only read the Bible but memorized her favorite verses. After her Confirmation, she developed the habit of coaxing her aunt for food which she herself distributed to the poor children of Abbeyleix. When they had eaten, she would talk to her little friends about God just as she and her aunt talked when they prayed together. If the children were especially responsive in the discussion, she would show her delight by reciting verses from Scripture or singing sacred hymns. The children loved her because she was always lively and full of laughter. Yet her aunt and Sarah and John often found her in thoughtful moods which she did not share with everyone. Already the little girl was giving evidence that the life she would shape for herself would be unusual.

Fanny Warde was only nine when the first of an altogether unexpected succession of tragedies came to her and her family. The earliest disaster to strike was the loss in 1819 of the house and lands of their beloved Bellbrook, which John Warde had hoped to retain for his children's children.

In order to understand the extraordinary position of a Roman Catholic like John Warde holding a lease to an estate like Bellbrook and the precarious nature of his tenure, it is necessary to know something of political and economic conditions in Ireland in 1819, ten years prior to the passage of the *Emancipation Bill* of 1829. The little island was just beginning to emerge from a state of poverty, misery, and utter wretchedness in which it had lain for centuries under British domination. Penal laws had insured the continuation of the two greatest of evils—poverty and ignorance. Education was denied the masses, for there were no public schools except Protestant schools, and these the Catholics would not accept because in them the faith of the Established Church was taught daily to the children. No Catholic school teacher was permitted to open a school or to teach publicly in one.

If, in a very rare instance, a Catholic had financial means to send his children abroad to receive an education which was not a contradiction to his faith, he was fined 100 pounds for doing so. The child so educated was disinherited, moreover, and could possess no property in the land of his birth. Penal laws made poverty, as well as ignorance, an institution. No Catholic could hold an office of trust; he could achieve no higher position than that of serf to a Protestant master; he was not allowed even a decent remuneration for his labor. It was actually lawful for a Protestant to take possession of a Catholic's farm, evicting him simply on the plea that as a Catholic he had no right to possessions of any kind. If a Catholic failed to support a Protestant landowner's political persuasions, the proprietor could deprive him of his lease. If a Protestant desired a certain possession of a Catholic—his horse, for example—he could demand the horse by law simply by giving the owner five pounds for it, however valuable the animal might be. Toward the close of the eighteenth century, some relaxation was made in the penal code, granting Catholics the right to acquire freehold property for life or for inheritance. Only in 1829, however, was Catholic Emancipation forced from a hostile Parliament. Even then, because of both continued hostile legal measures and the long centuries of wretchedness and suffering of the people, at least another 125 years were required to establish the Irish people in even the minimum standards of freedom, education, and decent living which are the rights of all men. The state of degradation of the masses of the Irish people when Frances Warde was born in 1810 was still, with very few exceptions, almost unparalleled in the history of the West.

It is clear that John Warde's social and economic situation at Bellbrook was unusual. It was entirely extraordinary that a Catholic should hold a lease to such an estate at all. The penal laws had been a direct attack upon the Catholic faith, particularly through denial of land tenure and obstruction to education. As a successful merchant, John Warde was able to sustain his lease on Bellbrook for a time, but it is remarkable that he was able to secure it at all. One may conjecture that he was fortunate enough to have a good Protestant friend. That man seems to have been William Bird of Abbeyleix, who leased the house and lands of Bellbrook to Warde. It was also William Bird who two years later granted Warde an annuity of fifty pounds for the rent of two acres of Bellbrook—a large sum considering that the total rent for Bellbrook was 110 pounds half-yearly! Warde's loss of property seems to have been due to the influence of Sir Robert Staples of Dunmore, Baronet, who was so charmed with Bellbrook House that he desired to secure it for a select private school to be opened to the Protestant elite of England and Ireland. Evidently the usual tactics of the so-called "land-grabbers" of the era were used to secure Bellbrook. John Warde belonged to that sturdy class of Irish gentlemen who followed their own consciences in political matters, come what may. Up until now, no attempt had ever been made to interfere with his flourishing circumstances.

Now, however, John Viscount de Vesci found in politics an immediate pretext to seize on the leases of Bellbrook House.[6] The lease of the property was transferred to Sir Robert Staples, who, according to a deed of 1821, held it in trust for Lord de Vesci. The *Abbeyleix Institution for the Education of the Upper Classes of Society* was opened at Bellbrook with a gentleman named Matthew Eaton as headmaster. John Warde was paid 277 pounds for the lease, with part of which he paid a mortgage. He was morally compelled to go to Dublin to seek a new manner of livelihood at an age when he should have been long settled in life. And the Warde family sadly left the loved home which should have been theirs by lawful contract for the lifetime of John Warde and his two eldest sons. They had held the property for only twenty-one years. John Warde's contemporaries were wont to remark that if he had been as "wise in the ways of the world" as he was in the life of the spirit, he would not have signed the deeds by which he lost Bellbrook. He had a long-standing reputation for uncompromising Christian living. In Dublin, he continued to maintain the universal respect that was his as a scholar and a gentleman.

The loss of Bellbrook meant the breakup of the Warde family. Like his father, Daniel, the oldest boy, seems to have sought a career in Dublin, but no record of his future is extant. William, the second son, settled in Wakefield, England, where he married an English girl within a few years. John, Fanny Warde's favorite brother, had entered the seminary at Maynooth College at the age of nineteen three months before the family left Bellbrook in May, 1819. The girls—Helen, Sarah, and Fanny, then only nine—were to remain for several years under the care of their mother's family. The evidence that the girls went to live in the home of their uncle, William Maher, of Killeany, County Laois, seems to be conclusive. Early American records, written by persons who knew Frances Warde personally, indicate that she lived at Mountrath.[7] Not many miles west of Abbeyleix, the foundation of the present town of Mountrath, or Moynrath (meaning "the Fort in the Bog"), was laid in the seventeenth century by Sir Charles Coote, wealthy British landowner. Mountrath is situated on a tributary of the River Nore called the Shannon. By 1810, the year of Fanny Warde's birth, the town was a hive of busy industry, especially in the weaving of stuffs and tammies. It was in the *parish* of Mountrath, however, rather than the town, that Fanny Warde's Uncle William Maher and his family lived. Their home was in the town landing of Killeany, a part of the mensal parish of Mountrath established in 1788. Today Killeany belongs to the civil parish of Clonenagh and Clonagheen which contains three Catholic parishes—Ballyfin, Mountrath, and Raheen. The ecclesiastical parish of Mountrath was once called Clonenagh, or "Ivied Retreat," to honor the celebrated monastery founded there by St. Fintan in the sixth century. Abbeyleix, Mountrath, and Carlow—all closely associated with the life of Frances Warde—were part of the Diocese of Kildare and Leighlin.

Killeany is a lovely, lush townland in County Leix. Its farmlands are bright with a rich golden green emphasized by the sloping sweep of its hillsides, flanked by flowing streams and dotted with ancient stone ruins. Killeany was a serene countryside for a girl between ten and sixteen to grow up in—especially a girl like Frances Warde whose vivacity was not at all out of harmony with a profoundly contemplative character which she seldom revealed except to her closest friends. Her secret was her own, and the green slopes of Killeany were as congenial to her adolescent moods as the hidden crypt among the green shrubs of Bellbrook was to her childhood reverence for the sacred.

Externally, Fanny Warde's days in Killeany were given over chiefly to her studies. It was perhaps well that she was educated privately because her unusual creativity found expression quite early in her life, and probably she would not have responded with enthusiasm to a structured program of studies. Philosophy and mathematics held little interest for her. She did not like to deal in abstractions or conceptual thought. She delighted in literature and all the arts. Poetry she loved, and she read Scripture and continued to read it all her life not only because it was God's revelation to man but because it was the most beautiful book in the world. First among the beautiful things of earth that she loved were green hills and flowers and gardens. Wherever she went throughout life, in Ireland and in America, she never failed to plant a garden to which she could go quietly to pray. Always and everywhere she responded to natural loveliness. A yellow butterfly or a golden Killeany sunset captivated her more than a theorem in geometry or a question from Thomas Aquinas. The beauty of language stimulated her quick perception, and she began as a young girl to write the delightful letters whose simplicity of style and vitality of feeling charmed her friends. All her life, those fortunate enough to correspond with her were startled at the way in which her personality leaped up from her written words.

Sarah Warde sometimes supervised her younger sister's studies, and occasionally Sarah's mathematical turn of mind brought her into sharp disagreement with Fanny's literary tastes. One day Sarah determined to force her sister to master a slight intricacy in algebraic equations by locking away a book of Milton's poetry with which the younger girl was fascinated. But Fanny was not to be dissuaded. According to Sarah's account, she seized the algebra book she found on her desk in place of *Paradise Lost,* ran to her sister, and declared: "I can understand that x and y equal x plus y. I know that x plus y minus x equals y. I even know that x times y equals xy. But to go further into quantities expressed by letters and signs is for me time lost. Why spend hours in working out dry questions in Goff or Euclid when I can read beautiful words in Milton?"[8] Sarah stopped urging her sister, and from that day on Fanny had more to say about her personal curriculum of studies.

About five years after the loss of Bellbrook, tragedy struck the Warde family a second time in the death of young John Warde, Fanny's favorite brother. The young man was just completing his studies for the priesthood at Maynooth College when he became dangerously ill. He died on the day chosen for his ordination.[9] It is not difficult to imagine the grief of little Fanny Warde, then about fourteen. She had never known her mother. Her happy home had been uprooted when she was only nine. Now the brother dearest to her— John who had shared her secret thoughts and her prayers in her little castle crypt at Bellbrook, John with whom she had read and loved Teresa of Avila and who had chosen to be a priest of God—was gone from her life forever. And he had left her at a most sensitive age for a young girl. Her loneliness was intensified because her father no longer lived with his daughters. She had relied upon her older brother John as a strong support. Now she could no longer share her life with him in the frequent, familiar letters she loved to write. She could no longer share his happy holidays from the seminary with him.

Several months after the death of young John Warde, his sister Helen contracted tuberculosis. A beautiful young woman, and her father's favorite daughter, she died at the age of eighteen. This third tragedy was almost more than the elder John Warde could bear. As for Fanny, she had not been so close to Helen as to John, but the loss of her sister increased her frightful loneliness. Daniel, the oldest of the Warde children, had been in his teens when Fanny was born. Because of the difference in their ages, Fanny had never had so intimate a relationship with him as with her younger brothers and sisters. William Warde was in England. Now Fanny and Sarah would have to depend on each other. Their role was to console their father in his great grief.

But the earthly striving of John Warde was, in fact, ended. Not long after Helen Warde's death, he was invited one day by Robert Cassidy, somewhat of an Irish celebrity of the eighteen-twenties, to dine at his residence in Monasterevan with the poet, Thomas Moore. Shortly after dinner, John Warde became ill and died within a few hours. The account of his death seems to indicate that the tired and perhaps disillusioned man died of a heart attack.[10]

Perhaps it is not too much to say that Fanny Warde in her mid-teens was forced into maturity by a series of personal sorrows that converged into one completely overwhelming sense of loss and loneliness. Snatched from her loved Bellbrook, she suffered in rapid succession the deaths of her closest brother, her sister, and her father. At the age of about fifteen, she was too young to cope with the intensity of grief she experienced. She was compelled to make terms with depths of loneliness that come to most human beings either in later years or not at all. She learned to meditate and to pray alone. Indeed she had grown to love solitude at Killeany even before her great sorrow came to her. Her maturing experience was alien to that of most young girls of her age. Yet to the serene outsider she was the epitome of vivacity, joy, and grace. What would a girl like Fanny Warde, who had known so early the meaning of pain and loneliness, do with her young life?

Shortly after John Warde's death, Daniel and Sarah, now a high-spirited girl in her teens, endeavored more than once to regain their father's property, but without success. They had been advised in Dublin that the deeds executed between their father and Sir Robert Staples were worthless. They went to Abbeyleix to determine whether even some portion of Bellbrook could be recovered. The new lease holders denied being in any way indebted to the Wardes, spoke of their friendship for John Warde and his family, and offered to place the younger Wardes, Sarah and Fanny, in a first-class Protestant Academy. Whether the school was the one established at Bellbrook is not certain. When the offer was indignantly refused, the young Wardes "were spoken of at several evangelical tea parties as people who willfully closed their eyes to the light of the Gospel."[11]

Though she was so young, Fanny Warde's decisiveness in matters of personal values was already an evident part of her character. In later years, this quality became perhaps her greatest natural strength as well as her strongest support in the pioneering missionary life for which she was destined. One of her most intense sufferings in later life was to be the frustration of some of her wisest decisions by persons who lacked her own creativity of vision. In such disillusionments, her resolute determination was often to be the measure of her endurance. From childhood she had always given evidence of a strong will. Perhaps the early loss of her mother, followed by the extraordinary sorrows she experienced as a young girl, gave impetus to the development of initiative and individuality which were almost phenomenal in a teen-age Irish girl of the eighteen-twenties. It is not a romantic notion but a fact that young women of Fanny Warde's generation were expected to be docile and submissive. In her non-conformity to the code, Fanny was most attractive. When she went up to Dublin from Laois to live with friends at the age of sixteen, she faced an unknown future. But she had no fears. She had developed a maturity, a sense of personal security, and a creative centering of her individual talents that made her independent little person a delight to the more perspicacious of those older than she and a model to be imitated by her peers.

2

Encounter of Two Great Women: Catherine McAuley and Frances Warde

In the year 1827 in Dublin, Frances Warde met the woman whose influence was to change the whole course of her life. Like most persons destined to contribute much to humanity, neither of these two women had an awareness of the singular future awaiting her. Catherine McAuley, the future founder of the Sisters of Mercy, though now almost fifty years of age, had no more thought of a religious congregation than seventeen-year-old Fanny Warde, who had come up to Dublin from Queen's County to join wholeheartedly in the social life of the city.

The younger woman's fascinating personality had won her immediate favor among the youth of the well-to-do society of Dublin. Her sprightly, eager disposition added to her attractiveness, and she soon became the leader in her social group. Since Fanny Warde was not the person to do anything by halves, she threw all her energy into the party life of Ireland's capital. Balls, musical concerts, and theater parties filled her days. An early associate described her as "tall, well-proportioned, with a dignity of bearing and ease of manner that characterized her to her last day. She could have graced a court."[1] It is interesting to note how often the word "queenly" is used in her contemporaries' remarks concerning her. Though her personality was not completely formed, her expression and gestures revealed firmness and strength. Her forehead was high, her eyes the same deep blue as her father's. Their tone was forever changing with the sudden wit, droll repartee, or quick compassion that were characteristic of her. The searching quality of these eyes attracted others as much as her commanding presence. And yet the trait that, more than anything else, won her many young friends was an amalgam of utter sincerity and common sense. Her genuine honesty made them feel at home with her. They knew that she simply was what she was. They also knew that she was capable of deep feeling, that to seek understanding or sympathy from her was equivalent to receiving it. As her later life revealed, Fanny's weakness was to trust too much. When she erred, it was in trusting others beyond the bounds of prudence.

Among Frances Warde's young Dublin friends was Mary Macauley, the lovely sixteen-year-old daughter of Dr. William Macauley and Catherine McAuley's sister, Mary, who lived on the Military Road, Dublin, near the Royal Hospital at Kilmainham, where Dr. Macauley was a surgeon. Young Mary's Aunt Catherine lived at the time with her brother-in-law and sister, Mary, who was in the final stages of tuberculosis and whom Catherine nursed continually. It is not difficult to imagine the meeting of Catherine McAuley and Frances Warde at the house on Military Road and to understand why Fanny became a frequent visitor there. Catherine, about three times the age of her new friend, was all that a vivacious and idealistic young girl close to womanhood—especially a girl who had never known her own mother—would choose as an admired model. Everyone loved Catherine McAuley. A young woman who met her early in 1829, and who later became a Sister of Mercy and a well-known water color artist, has left a remarkable description of the founder of the Sisters of Mercy as she saw her for the first time:

> She was very fair with brilliant color on her cheeks, still not too red. Her face was a short oval but the contour was perfect; her lips were thin and her mouth rather wide. Her eyes were light blue and remarkably round, with the brows and lashes colorless. But they spoke. In repose they had a melancholy beseeching look; then they would light up expressive of real hearty fun, or if she disapproved of anything, they could tell that too. Sometimes they had the strange expression of reading you through, which made you feel that even your mind was in her power and that you could not hide anything from her. Her nose was straight but thick. She wore bands made from her own back hair, which were so well managed as to be quite free from the disagreeable look bands of the kind usually give; the color was pale golden—very fine and silky. She was dressed in black British merino, which according to the fashion of the time fitted tight to her shape. She was remarkably well made, round but not in the least heavy.[2]

Catherine McAuley was at once reserved and warmly affectionate. She moved quietly and spoke little. In Fanny Warde she perceived immediately the dignity and simplicity that always attracted her. From their first meeting these two became fast friends. Until Catherine's death, they were to share with each other, more than with any other, joys and sufferings of which they had now not even a vague intimation.

The story of Catherine McAuley has been told over and over again with reverent admiration. For Fanny Warde, to know Catherine was to become part of that story. Born at Stormanstown House, to the north of Dublin, about twenty years before the close of the eighteenth century, Catherine

McAuley lost her father in death when she was very young. Her mother, Elinor Conway McAuley, lived in Dublin for a time with her three children—Catherine, James, and Mary —before she too became fatally ill, leaving the children to grow up under the rather unstable guardianship of relatives. Catherine's superb heritage from her father, an architect, was a deep personal love of Christ manifested through an active care for the poor and suffering and an apostolate of mercy in which he gathered the poor children of the neighborhood about him to teach them the Word of God. James McAuley's influence was perhaps the strongest in his daughter's life. Elinor McAuley, an attractive and cultured woman, left to Catherine the wisdom gained from a child's observation of her mother's late remorse for having neglected her Christian faith. Despite her own laxity, however, Elinor McAuley had her children baptized and confirmed in the Catholic faith in Arran Quay Chapel, Dublin.

Destiny now brought Catherine under various influences which an indifferent witness might have calculated to foreshadow a rejection of her father's Catholic heritage. But not so. The guardianship of neither her Uncle Owen Conway, who like his sister neglected somewhat the practice of his faith, nor William Armstrong, a Protestant relative, detracted in the least from the girl's strong fidelity to the dynamic Catholicism of her father. Around the turn of the century, Catherine, then in her early twenties, went to live with William and Catherine Callaghan, a wealthy Protestant couple who had settled in Dublin after ten years of residence in India. Mrs. Callaghan, a deeply religious Quaker, became so fond of Catherine McAuley that the couple adopted her legally. Her pilgrimage from the McAuleys to the Conways to the Armstrongs to the Callaghans was altogether a checkered journey for a young woman—especially in terms of spiritual odyssey! Yet it is certain that despite many pressures and influences to the contrary, Catherine held firmly to her Catholic faith, seeking spiritual direction at times from some of the most scholarly theologians in Dublin.[3] She emerged from the conflict as a most unusual young woman—a deeply committed Roman Catholic devoted to few of the religious folkways of Irish Catholicism but attached to many of the cultural mores of Protestant Dublin of the early nineteenth century.

One of Catherine McAuley's significant spiritual advisers was Father Andrew Lubé, curate of St. Mary's, Liffey Street, who has been credited with contributing more than *any other* to the preservation of her religious faith. Father Daniel Murray, of St. Paul's, Dublin, later Archbishop, likewise directed her and was later associated with her in the foundation of the Sisters of Mercy. Also, the celebrated Dublin Jesuit, Father Thomas Betagh, was consulted by Catherine in her spiritual difficulties. Perhaps more influential than any of these in the establishment of her works of mercy were Father Michael Blake of St. Paul's, later Bishop of Dromore, and Father Edward Armstrong, of St. Andrew's, who became one of her intimate friends.

Catherine's close associations, beginning when she was a young girl, with many of Dublin's outstanding religious leaders, suggest that—like Frances Warde—she was destined for an extraordinary apostolate. While living in Dublin as a foster child of the Callaghans, she had already begun to reveal her singular charism—a loving, compassionate care for the sick poor which was to extend through her followers to thousands of persons for generations.

While Catherine was moving quietly toward a permanent commitment to the service of Christ in others, her sister Mary meanwhile had married Dr. William Macauley in

1804, and her brother James had chosen the career of physician. In 1809 William Callaghan and his wife secured a lease to beautiful Coolock House in the suburbs of Dublin, and Catherine McAuley went to live with them on this estate which was to serve, in effect, as a retreat in which she would grow in wisdom and grace for fully twenty years before returning to the urban center of Dublin to establish one of the largest religious congregations in the world.[4]

Coolock House, completely ivy-covered except for its high formal windows and its curve of white stone steps bordered by iron grillwork leading to a magnificent Georgian façade, was indeed dear to Catherine McAuley. She loved its walnut and copper beech trees, and she meditated in its gardens. There she instructed and cared for the poor children of Coolock as her father had done at Stormanstown House. Her charity to all—as well as to children—may be illustrated by one characteristic example. She used to visit the sick poor in the wretched alleys of St. Mary's Parish, Dublin, as well as in the village of Coolock. One day she found a poor old demented woman living alone in a shack in Liffey Street. Instead of committing her to an institution, Catherine took her home to Coolock House and cared for her until her death about five years later. The old lady died without recovering a gleam of reason. During the years preceding her death, she conceived, with the perversity of madness, an absolute hatred for Catherine, which she expressed in virulent and contemptuous language. Her habits were filthy, moreover, and her thievery was inveterate. But Catherine never relaxed her care of the old woman and would not even permit the servants to tease her.

In 1816 the more or less serene years at Coolock were interrupted when Catherine Callaghan became seriously ill. The younger woman devoted herself day and night to nursing her foster mother. It troubled Catherine McAuley that she could not give to the poor people of the town of Coolock the same care as she was accustomed to give them. Often when she fell asleep she dreamed of the sick, the suffering, and especially of young girls who were in need of care for any cause whatever. Meanwhile, she offered spiritual counsel as well as physical care to Mrs. Callaghan. When the latter died in 1819, Catherine was again free to give all her energies to works of mercy among the poor people of Coolock.

Three years later, on the death of William Callaghan, who had been spiritually instructed by his foster child and received into the Catholic Church by her friend, Father Joseph Nugent, Catherine McAuley was amazed to find herself the possessor of Coolock House and the sole residuary legatee of Mr. Callaghan. Misinformed biographers have spoken of her as a beautiful young "fairy princess," inheritor of a luxurious mansion, sought after by numberless handsome suitors eager for her favor. In truth, she was a beautiful middle-aged woman with only one dream—to serve Christ in others. Call it providence or destiny, she now possessed the means to make her dream a reality. Schools for poor children, relief for distressed women, nursing care for the sick— projects of mercy crowded one another in her imagination, and her heart sang with joy. She confided her desires to few. Father Blake, Dr. Murray, and Father Armstrong were her confidants. It was characteristic of her that, in all her works of mercy, she sought the advice of those in whose wisdom and integrity she trusted.

And now again it seemed that Catherine McAuley's personal charity would delay her more universal service to others. Her well-loved cousin, Anne Conway Byrn, had died three months before William Callaghan, leaving four young children. Without a thought of herself, Catherine went immediately to their aid. Ten-year-old Catherine Byrn went to Coolock House to live, and Catherine McAuley adopted the baby Teresa. The unfolding of time proved, however, that nothing was to interrupt the foundation of the Sisters of Mercy.

Father Michael Blake had listened with profound interest to Catherine's simple plan to establish a social service center in Dublin. He had become convinced that, in God's design, she was destined for a special work in the Church of Christ. From the moment of her first uncertain revelation of her dream, he did everything in his power to help her. Contrary to Catherine's plan, it would seem that Father Blake envisioned from the first a religious congregation with herself as its founder. But he did not tell her so. He allowed the plan of God to uncover itself as he believed it would. He consulted with Father Edward Armstrong, of St. Andrew's, Dublin, who agreed with him that the best site for the proposed house of social service would be somewhere in the residential section of St. Andrew's parish. The property chosen was on Upper Baggot Street. On June 20, 1824, it was leased at an annual rental of 60 pounds by the Earl of Pembroke, who did not harbor the hostility toward Catholic establishments rather common among the British nobility in Ireland in the early nineteenth century. The cornerstone for the "big house" on Baggot Street, planned largely by Dr. Blake, was laid in July, 1824. As Catherine watched the carpenters and masons at work, she listened to the ring of the hammer with expectant delight. Meanwhile she prepared herself for the management of a free school for the poor, studying school procedures and visiting the best educational institutions in Dublin, such as the Kildare Place Society.

Once again, sickness and death hindered her work. Word reached her that her good friend, Father Joseph Nugent, was seriously ill. Finding him in a sad state of neglect, she scarcely left him until he died on May 30, 1825. Father Nugent had baptized William Callaghan shortly before his death. He had been Catherine's adviser in legal proceedings that contested Callaghan's will. At his death, she lost a strong support. She was still living at Coolock House, keeping her intentions with regard to the proposed institution on Baggot Street more or less secret, for she had reason to believe that not only the enemies of her faith but many of her relatives and friends would disapprove of it.[5] She found it prudent to continue to live in good style, to keep a carriage, to dress well, to go into society occasionally, and sometimes to give parties at Coolock House. Most of her time, however, she gave to prayer, to visiting the sick poor, and especially to the instruction of poor children in the girls' school of St. Mary's, Abbey Street.

Her own brother, Dr. James McAuley, who had early accepted the Protestant faith of his foster parents, did indeed thoroughly disapprove of the new social service center. He called her venture "Kitty's folly," and both he and his Presbyterian brother-in-law, Dr. William Macauley, felt a kind of family shame because of their sister's seeming extremism. Opposition was intensified when Catherine moved to the Macauley residence on Military Road to care for her fatally ill sister, Mary. Catherine still retained Coolock House, but she now spent most of her time with her sister. Mary Macauley, like her brother, had long ago joined the Established Church. Catherine was now becoming accustomed to respond to the spiritual hunger, as well as to the physical suffering, of those she loved. Before her sister died, Catherine was to be—in secret, for fear of her brother-in-law—the reconciliation between Mary and the faith of her childhood. One truth about Catherine was beginning to emerge:

her suffering always related to her loving care for others, never to herself.

During the three years preceding the completion of the house of social service on Baggot Street, Catherine McAuley's closest companion in her charitable works was a young girl named Fanny Tighe, whom she hoped to have as an assistant in her new project. But precisely when Catherine needed her most, Fanny decided to enter the Presentation Convent in Galway. As providence would have it, however, just as the "big house" was nearing completion, a young girl named Anna Marie Doyle, who frequently passed by the new building, learned that it was the work of a charitable Catholic lady who planned a social service center for the poor of Dublin. Anna Marie had decided to enter a cloistered religious congregation, but feared to leave her elderly parents alone. Paradoxically, she had chosen the Presentation community, the very congregation which Fanny Tighe joined. Now Anna Marie became enthusiastic about a life of dedication in which she could serve both the poor of Dublin and her parents. She asked for an introduction to Catherine McAuley, and the two discovered to their joy that their goal of serving God's people was one. The difference between them was that Catherine had no intention of entering a convent! Anna Marie, however, was to become Catherine's first permanent recruit.

Mary Macauley died in August, 1827. It would have seemed to merely human wisdom that, with her new obligations to her sister's family, Catherine McAuley's plans for the Baggot Street establishment would come to nothing. But again the design of God was not to be obstructed. Anna Marie Doyle now expected that Catherine would remain at her brother-in-law's home on Military Road to care for her sister's children. With some anxiety, the young girl asked for definite plans. To her surprise, Catherine responded that the building on Baggot Street would be completed September 23 or 24 and that the free school for poor children would open then. Catherine's young cousin, Catherine Byrn, would go to Baggot Street to live and work with Anna Marie. Until further arrangements could be made, Catherine and her niece Mary would go daily to the new establishment to assist with the classroom teaching. Anna Marie responded immediately that she would arrive at Baggot Street on September 24. She added that this date was the Feast of Our Lady of Mercy and suggested that the new establishment be called the House of Our Lady of Mercy. Catherine agreed. Without knowing it, she had chosen the name for the Congregation of Our Lady of Mercy.[6]

The historic year of the opening of the first House of Mercy in the world was also the year that young Mary Macauley brought her friend Fanny Warde to her home on Military Road to meet her Aunt Catherine. This meeting was more significant in the history of the Sisters of Mercy than Catherine McAuley's encounter with any other woman. For Frances Warde was to found more convents, to spread the works of mercy farther, than any other Sister of Mercy. In the plan of God, each of these two women responded totally to the vision of the other.

Perhaps through her association with Catherine McAuley, perhaps through her own inward yearning for spiritual meaning in her life and for service to others, Frances soon became dissatisfied with the round of social life in Dublin. She recalled with a homesickness for union with God her childhood days at the castle crypt in Bellbrook where she and her brother John had pondered God's love for them, for the poor, and for all men. She remembered the happy days when she fed and taught and sang for the poor children of Abbeyleix.

Most of all, she relived in imagination her quiet days of meditation on the hills of Killeany. Frances voiced her restlessness
to her confessor, Father Edward Armstrong, who of course
had close personal knowledge of Catherine McAuley's work.
He suggested to her that she teach a few hours each day in
the poor school recently opened in Baggot Street.

While Frances deliberated on his advice, Father Armstrong became seriously ill. A pattern seemed to be developing
in the life of Catherine McAuley: one by one she was to be
deprived of her closest friends and spiritual advisers. Since
the summer of 1824, Catherine had relied upon Father Armstrong in matters temporal as well as spiritual. Now, in the
early months of 1828, she was experiencing financial problems in the maintenance of the House of Mercy. Coolock
House was not yet sold, and funds were not available to her.
And now Father Armstrong was soon to be lost to her. She
nursed him daily in his last days. This profoundly holy man
confided to her his desire that her work should result in the
foundation of a religious congregation. And he told her over
and over again the answer to her anguish at her repeated loss
of human support: "Place your confidence in no human help
but in God alone."

Edward Armstrong died on Ascension Thursday, May 15,
1828. Frances Warde came to the House on Baggot Street
on June 22—a gift of God to Catherine McAuley in her
grief. The spiritual pilgrimage of Frances Warde, the American founder of the Sisters of Mercy, had just begun.

3

Spiritual Growth: Dublin, Kingstown, Tullamore, Charleville

CATHERINE McAuley and Frances Warde both came to the House of Mercy on Upper Baggot Street in the early summer of 1828, Catherine to remain permanently and direct the work of the new Institute, Frances to reside there occasionally while she taught in the free school for poor children.[1] Catherine brought with her her godchild, Teresa Byrn, and her two nieces, Mary Teresa and Catherine Macauley. Since Anna Marie Doyle and Catherine Byrn were already living and working in the new house, the little community was beginning to grow.

Without their realizing it, the life of Catherine McAuley and her young friends soon became almost that of active-contemplative Sisters. A horarium was planned. The members rose early in the morning for community prayer and spiritual reading. They went daily to the Carmelite Church of St. Teresa, on Clarendon Street, for the Celebration of the Eucharist. At certain hours they assembled to pray together. During the day they taught the poor girls who applied in large numbers for instruction in the Catholic faith and in "various branches of industry." The sick poor in the neighboring lanes and alleys were visited and cared for. Young tradeswomen who could not afford safe lodging were welcomed to the House of Mercy as their home at night and were taught the practice of their religion. One day when Catherine McAuley brought home in her arms to Baggot Street a motherless child, it became evident that an orphanage would also be an essential work of the new Institute. Soon the numbers of poor children to be cared for began to increase. The days of the young women of the House of Mercy were indeed filled. At night, everyone in the Institute assembled for evening prayers and some for meditation before retiring. The "form of life was primitive Christianity."

The House of Mercy itself resembled a convent more than a social service center, much to the chagrin of Catherine McAuley, who was somewhat mystified by its architecture. She had explained her practical needs to Father Blake and the contractors during the planning of the building, but she was not aware that Father Blake was perhaps looking toward a future that she had not yet clarified for herself. Probably because of the strong Protestant influence in her background, she had felt from her youth an aversion toward convents. There is humor in the fact that the members of the community began not only to adopt a conventual manner of life but to wear plain black dresses with net caps and black muslin veils, and even to call one another "Sister." And all without a thought of becoming a religious congregation!

Fanny Warde was true to character in her association with the new Institute. Whatever she did, she did with complete involvement of her whole person. Perhaps the epithet least applicable to her during her entire life was "lukewarm." She soon confronted herself with the question of whether she should commit herself completely and permanently to the work that Catherine McAuley had initiated. Since the death of Father Edward Armstrong, her confessor had been Father Francis L'Estrange, Prior of the Carmelites in Dublin. Fanny consulted him, and he inquired of Catherine McAuley concerning the permanency of the new Institute and the attitude of Archbishop Murray toward it. On September 10, 1828, Catherine wrote to Father L'Estrange her first formal statement concerning the Institute of Mercy. The establishment had the full approbation of Archbishop Murray; it was open to ladies who preferred conventual life but who were prevented from embracing it because of property or connections; its objects were the education of poor girls, the instruction of young tradeswomen who boarded in the house, and the care and instruction of the sick poor. Five days later Catherine took another step toward the permanency of the Baggot Street house by negotiating the sale of Coolock House. And on September 24, 1828, Archbishop Murray confirmed his approbation by granting his approval to the "Institute of Our Lady of Mercy" as a title for the social service center at Baggot Street.[2] All doubts were now laid to rest, and Fanny Warde assumed the black dress and cap of a permanent member of the Institute in October.

Eighteen-year-old Fanny now entered with complete enthusiasm and fascination into the changes that were to transform her life. Day after day she learned with Catherine McAuley both the spiritual depth and the practical hard work of founding an Institute of Mercy. Above all, she learned from Catherine the mysterious secret of trusting completely in God alone, a way of life which was to be her spiritual strength in the long years to come. The two women were intimate in their dedication to Christ and his poor. Sometimes Frances and another young woman would rise with Catherine McAuley at an earlier hour than all the others in the house to recite the Psalter or to read a spiritual book together. A month after Frances' permanent entry at Baggot Street, she shared with Catherine the joy of the baptism of Mary Teresa Macauley, dear to both of them. The sacrament was received without the knowledge of the girl's father. Mary Teresa now spent most of her time at the new establishment, teaching in the poor school. At first her father, Dr. William Macauley, had objected strongly to her being so continually in a Catholic atmosphere.[3] But Catherine would send Fanny Warde, with all her winning ways, to the house on Military Road to coax Dr. Macauley to let Mary Teresa spend more time with her loved aunt and her friend. Since Catherine was a real mother to her favorite niece, it was difficult for Dr. Macauley to refuse Fanny's pleas.

The same day as Mary Teresa's baptism, Archbishop Murray formally approved the visitation of the sick poor as a work of the Institute. And on November 30, Catherine, Frances, and two other young women visited Sir Patrick Dunn Hospital in Dublin. Up until now they had visited only the sick poor in their homes. In order that they might not be rejected as proselytizers, Catherine and her young friends dressed carefully in the fashion of the day and drove to the hospital in style in her Swiss carriage. After permission for visiting the patients was granted, Catherine sold her carriage and she and her little community assumed a plain, distinctive going-out dress. From now on, their life "in society" was ended. Soon they were visiting patients in three Dublin hospitals daily.

Christmas dinner for the poor children was a beautiful closing to Fanny Warde's first year at the Institute of Mercy. The dinner was an annual event, but it was special in 1828. Daniel O'Connell, the great liberator, on the eve of his triumph in the Emancipation Act, attended and carved for the orphans. For years afterward, he maintained relations with the founders of the Institute of Mercy. His love for the poor and that of Catherine McAuley and Frances Warde were based on both a historical and an experiential knowledge of cruel persecution and an intense compassion for the suffering.

The year 1828, however, and the year that followed were not completely happy for the young community. Disapproval of the new Institute, both ecclesiastical and secular, had plagued them from the beginning. The so-called "new nuns" were not religious; yet they did not live like seculars. They followed a regular life of prayer and meditation; they practiced labor for the poor and mortification; they participated in the daily celebration of the Eucharist and received the sacraments frequently; they even had a chapel—not yet dedicated—in their new establishment. They seldom went abroad, except to do works of mercy. Yet they insisted that their Institute was not a convent, that they called one another "Sister" only playfully. Was their life not a kind of scandal to the somewhat rigid, conservative Catholics of Dublin? Indeed, who or what were they?

Catherine McAuley's pondering on the nature of her Institute was interrupted by the serious illness of her brother-in-law, Dr. William Macauley, who died January 25, 1829. As might have been predicted, his five children chose their loved Aunt Catherine as their guardian rather than their uncle, Dr. James McAuley. The girls—Mary Teresa, who was now eighteen, and little Catherine—could live at Baggot Street. But what of the boys—James, Robert, and Willie—who were twelve, ten, and seven years old? One wonders what Catherine McAuley would have done if her brother-in-law had died a few years earlier. Again, Providence seemed to have provided plans that could not be obstructed. The Institute of Mercy was now well established. Catherine's commitment was already made. She kept the girls with her at Baggot Street and enrolled the boys as boarders in the preparatory school at Carlow College. They would visit their Aunt Catherine and Uncle James on holidays. Fanny Warde, too, was their good friend. She had spent many happy days with them at their home on Military Road. She was to share their vacations at Baggot Street. She was to be present with Catherine McAuley when they would be baptized and receive the sacraments for the first time.

The new Chapel of Our Lady of Mercy at Baggot Street was dedicated June 4, 1829. Catherine was now suffering so much from open adverse criticism of her venture that she thought it best not to attend the reception. Dr. Blake preached the sermon at the Eucharistic Celebration and praised Catherine McAuley and the new Institute of Mercy in enthusiastic terms. At the reception which followed, a priest who was an officer of the Mass spoke in a most deprecatory fashion of Catherine and her work. Fanny Warde listened with mounting anger. At once another priest, Father William Young of Baldoyle, turned to her in her great consternation and asked her if she were a member of the community. Frances was delighted to have the opportunity to assert her loyalty to Catherine and the new Institute publicly and loudly so that all present could hear. Father Young responded by asking her to assure Catherine McAuley of his respect for her and his good wishes for the Institute.[4]

Now Catherine began to receive anonymous letters of harsh criticism. She was sneered at as an uneducated upstart. As opposition increased and gossip spread throughout Dublin, she became aware that she must decide in favor of a religious congregation or let her little community revert to a much more secular type of life. Her followers, meanwhile, were increasing in numbers. Five young women joined the Institute during the year 1829, two of them close friends of Fanny Warde. One was Catherine's niece, Mary Teresa. The other was the beautiful daughter of Captain John Harley of Dublin, a young girl who had greatly admired

Fanny Warde when she lived at the center of Dublin social life. Attracted by the intense devotion of Frances to the poor, Elizabeth followed her friend to the Institute of Mercy in October, 1829. In the early months of 1830, three more young recruits presented themselves. Catherine McAuley herself was to write later: "In a year and a half we were joined so fast that it became a matter of general wonder."[5]

Fearing the disedification arising from the differences of opinion which prevailed as to the religious status of her little community, Catherine consulted Archbishop Murray. He suggested that she either establish a religious congregation according to canonical regulations or go back to a definitely secular way of life. When she proposed the question to her followers, they unanimously agreed upon a religious institute. The Archbishop suggested that a few of the members prepare for the religious foundation by serving a regular novitiate in an established congregation. The Presentation Convent at George's Hill, Dublin, was chosen. On September 8, 1830, Catherine McAuley, Anna Marie Doyle, and Elizabeth Harley entered the novitiate there with the intention of returning to Baggot Street after their religious profession.

One may wonder why Catherine did not take her closest associate, Fanny Warde, to George's Hill with her. Yet one of Catherine's greatest concerns during her absence would be the management of the new Institute. Fanny Warde had already proved herself to be an excellent organizer. She had already acted as an assistant to Catherine in the difficult work of setting up the new establishment. Now Catherine would feel more confident about the community she left behind if Frances was in charge of household affairs. As one reads the memoirs concerned with the days of Catherine's absence, one wonders if the Institute would have progressed better during its leader's absence if Frances Warde had also been placed in charge of spiritual matters. Abuses crept in which would not have been tolerated by Fanny Warde, who was noted for her common sense. An early member of the Institute recorded the lack of spiritual discretion of some of the young women:

. . . Everyone mismanaged her own spiritualities in her own way. One took to fasting, another took the discipline, another slept in haircloth, while a fourth and fifth thought proper to remain up half the night at their prayers. To this last piece of perfection, however, Father O'Hanlon put a stop . . .[6]

Years later, Frances Warde, as Superior of a Mercy convent, was unjustly accused of "lacking discipline in the control of her Sisters." Perhaps she had learned at the age of twenty in Baggot Street the difference between unhealthy discipline and the responsible freedom of the children of God.

It is clear that, while Catherine McAuley's novitiate at the Presentation Convent was extremely difficult for a woman well over fifty, her suffering was increased by concern for the community that awaited her return. One young woman, Sister Caroline Murphy, died before the founder was professed. Another, Sister Anne O'Grady, was seriously ill when Catherine returned to Baggot Street in December, 1831. She died the following February. Indiscreet mortification and imprudent service in the apostolate seem to have been involved in hastening the death of both.

A different side of Fanny Warde's character is revealed in a lighter incident which occurred during Catherine McAuley's absence.[7] A few "lay Sisters," as opposed to Choir Sisters, had been admitted by the founder to do manual work in the Institute. The venture appeared to be unsuccessful in the beginning, for all were dismissed except one. Her

name was Hannah Fulham. She was gifted with a remarkably fine voice and musical talent as well as an attractive
personality. One day, according to an associate's account,
Hannah was detected in an attempt to steal some articles of
plate. She managed to interest Fanny Warde in her behalf.
It is likely that she pleaded remorse and Frances forgave her.
As has been stated earlier, Fanny Warde's weakness was too
great trust in others. Word of Hannah's misdemeanor
reached Catherine McAuley, who ordered her immediate dis-
missal. Hannah then resolved on a stratagem which she
hoped would insure her remaining at Baggot Street. She
appeared one morning with her head completely shaved, declaring that the action had been taken by supernatural
agency. With a great deal of questioning, she was finally led
to confess that she herself had executed what she wished to
be interpreted as a revelation of God's will in favor of her
vocation. The humor of the incident was lost on those members of the community who were devoted to the discipline
and the hair shirt. Frances Warde's "fault" of trusting others
often led her to err on the side of charity, but never on that
of harshness or cruelty. Nor did she ever trust herself to the
point that she imagined herself to be called to "heroic" virtue
which had its source in self-pride.

Catherine McAuley and her two companions were professed at the Presentation Convent on December 12, 1831.
So impatient were they to return to Baggot Street that they
left the Presentation Sisters immediately after the ceremony.
Nine postulants awaited them, eager to begin their novitiate
as Sisters of Mercy. Fanny Warde's joy was unbounded. All
her life she loved to recall the day of Catherine McAuley's
return to the first convent of Mercy, and she experienced a
childlike happiness in being "one of the first seven" Sisters
of Mercy. The following day Archbishop Murray appointed

Catherine McAuley as Mother Superior of the new Congregation. All was new and novel and exciting. A great adventure was beginning. How far-reaching its effects were to be, the new Sisters had no idea. Archbishop Murray suggested that work begin on a Holy Rule for the Sisters of Mercy, but that until it was completed the Chapter of the Presentation *Rule* on "Union and Charity" would more than suffice. A new conventual horarium was approved. The Office of the Virgin Mary was to be recited daily in English, for Mary was the patron of the Sisters. The new habit designed by Mother Catherine was to be the distinctive dress of the Sisters of Mercy for a century. Indeed, life was new, stimulating, and challenging for Fanny Warde, who had just turned twenty-one. She now looked forward to the great day of her reception into the Congregation of Our Lady of Mercy —January 23, 1832.

Archbishop Murray himself received the new members into the community in the Chapel of Mercy in Baggot Street. According to the convent register, Frances Warde was given her own name in religion: Sister Mary Frances Teresa. Her patron was to be Saint Francis Xavier. Those who knew her personally have pointed out that she desired to be always associated in spirit with Mother Catherine McAuley just as Francis Xavier was associated with the great founder of the Jesuits, Saint Ignatius Loyola; that just as Xavier turned in his missionary zeal to India, Japan, and China, Sister Frances Warde was to leave home and country for the new continent of America; that, like Xavier, Frances never lost the first fervor that she learned from the founder of her Congregation; and finally, that she loved her leader intensely just as Xavier did, neither time nor distance ever changing that love in the smallest degree. Francis Xavier knelt on the ground when he wrote letters to Ignatius Loyola; Frances Warde never spoke of Catherine McAuley without tears.

Mother Catherine always addressed her younger Sister as "Mary Frances," and this is the name she was called in Ireland. In later years, in America, she was called "Mother Xavier" or "Mother Warde." But even when she used the name "Frances Xavier," she never used the masculine form, "Francis."[8]

The new little community now set themselves seriously to the task of establishing a stable religious congregation. The spirit of Mercy established at Baggot Street by Catherine McAuley and her little band of followers in 1832 is the spirit alive in 25,000 Sisters of Mercy throughout the world today. Love and mercy toward all men, and especially for the poor and the suffering, was the founder's special gift from the Holy Spirit. She poured out her love upon Frances Warde and all her Sisters, and together they poured out loving mercy upon the sick, the poor, and the suffering of Dublin. And they shared personally in the suffering of the poor. Like St. Teresa, Catherine McAuley never refused a young girl entrance to the Congregation for want of temporal means when it was at all possible to provide what was essential. In order to do so, she insisted on the plainest meals and accommodations for all. When she later founded new convents, she never waited for comfortable arrangements, but relied upon Providence to supply necessities for the Sisters. Bishop John Murphy of Cork used to call her the "Sister of Divine Providence" because of her trust in the future as planned by God—a future which Murphy preferred to provide for himself in temporal matters!

The continued source of love, Catherine taught her Sisters over and over again, is the Holy Spirit alone. The spirit peculiar to her new little Congregation, she insisted, was the union of a life of prayer and contemplation with a life of the service of Christ in others.[9] Unlike the Carmelites, the Sisters of Mercy were not to be a purely contemplative congregation; nor were they to be a secular institute concentrating solely on service. In the life of the Sister of Mercy, prayer and service flow together reciprocally. A true Sister of Mercy can never abandon service for contemplation, nor can she abandon prayer for service or substitute a purely humanistic devotion to mankind for union with Christ and his people. A Sister of Mercy is never narrow in her concept of service. She is always ready to respond to the needs of Christ's Church in the particular age and society in which she lives. A Sister of Mercy respects the inspiration of the Holy Spirit in each Sister with whom she lives and in all of God's people. She has profound trust and confidence in her Sisters and in all Christians. A Sister of Mercy is a witness to Christ in her daily life: man learns by witness rather than by precept.

All of these values young Frances Warde learned by word and by witness from Catherine McAuley in the beautiful years between 1832 and 1837, years of her life that she was never to forget. These Christian and conventual ideals which the young girl made a part of herself in these priceless days of spiritual intimacy with the founder of the Sisters of Mercy cannot be overstressed as influence in her later life. Her naturally passionate character found strength and stability in living the spiritual message of Catherine McAuley with the grace of the Holy Spirit. To make the spiritual formation of the founder peculiarly her own, Frances Warde now needed only to leave Baggot Street and try her wings. In the minds of both women, the necessity of Frances' going forth to new leadership in the Spirit was always present. Both of them, humanly speaking, dreaded the day when zeal for Christ's Church would demand their separation. But both of them were filled with holy desire to spread the Good News; both believed that the works of mercy to which they were called were God's works and not their own. They had not chosen to found the Congregation of Mercy; God had chosen to found it.

From the beginning, Catherine McAuley and her followers had responded to spiritual forces outside themselves which moved their inmost lives. They did not see themselves as initiators; Providence had guided them. God would therefore grant them the grace to develop the Congregation which was His own. Frances Warde now responded to the unfolding of her own life with the fascination of a faith which held firmly to the belief that a personal God guided her personally to do His will. Her role was that of response. Her work was that of complete cooperation. She emerged from her apprenticeship with Catherine McAuley in the Spirit with an unshakeable faith which was never once to waver through fifty years of love and suffering so closely interwoven that the two became one.

The works of mercy served as a practical training ground for young Sister Mary Frances. Two months after her ceremony of reception into the Sisters of Mercy, the first victim of an epidemic of Asiatic cholera died in Dublin. Mother Catherine immediately offered the services of the Sisters to the Townsend Street Hospital. Panic among those Dubliners who were ignorant of the disease caused the plague to be an extreme threat to the poor. Rumors spread hysterically that the hospitals were death traps in which the sick poor were poisoned or marked to be buried alive in order to halt contagion. The response of the poor was concealment of the cholera which promised greater disaster. Precisely at this point the Sisters were of greatest service. The poor people, who had learned to love the new "walking nuns" when they visited their homes before the epidemic, now learned that these same Sisters served in the hospitals every day, all day, and would remain as long as the cholera lasted. Trust was restored. The Sisters went to the hospitals in relays of four every four hours to care for the cholera victims. The regular works of mercy were short-staffed, but the Sisters managed. They learned the meaning of personal physical suffering and extreme exhaustion. They were doing God's work. At least one of their number was later to serve with other Sisters of Mercy and Florence Nightingale in the Crimea.

While the cholera epidemic was at its height, sorrow came to Sister Mary Frances from another source. Sister Elizabeth Harley, one of her dearest friends who, attracted by the zeal of Frances, had entered the community at Baggot Street in the early days and had made her novitiate with Mother Catherine at George's Hill, died of tuberculosis on April 25, 1832. Sister Elizabeth was the daughter of Captain John Harley of the Forty-Seventh Regiment, Dublin. The Harley family was prominent in Dublin society. Elizabeth's older brother, Lieutenant John Harley, had been killed at the Battle of Vitoria. Her three-year-old brother, later Sir Robert Harley, was destined to serve in Africa and British Honduras. Fifty years after Elizabeth's death, as Governor of British Honduras, he was to welcome the Sisters of Mercy from Mobile, Alabama, to their first foundation in Belize. When Elizabeth had informed her father that she wished to follow Fanny Warde to the Institute of Mercy, he had advised her, in military terms, "to be no cowardly soldier of the crucified Christ."[10] And she was not. As a very young Sister, she was regarded by her companions as a saint among them. Unfortunately she was not physically strong, and her novitiate at the Presentation Convent was severe. Frances Warde remained with her friend until the last moment of her life. Sister Elizabeth Harley was the first of innumerable young women that Sister Mary Frances attracted to the religious life, and she was the first Sister of Mercy to die.

The care of the cholera patients offered some distraction to Sister Mary Frances in her grief. In August the epidemic subsided and the Sisters participated in their first annual retreat at Baggot Street, then returned to their regular duties. And now further personal suffering came to Frances Warde. Illness of many of the young Sisters, caused no doubt by fatigue and over-work, struck her dear friend Mary Teresa Macauley, now Sister Joseph Teresa. Mary Teresa became consumptive and her health deteriorated rapidly. To complicate matters, she decided that perhaps she should be a contemplative rather than a Sister of Mercy precisely when she, together with Frances Warde, approached the day of profession.

On January 24, 1833, Sister Frances Warde became the first Sister of Mercy to be professed by Mother Catherine McAuley in the first Convent of Mercy in the world. The beautiful ceremony for the consecration to celibate life and service of God's people was prepared by Catherine McAuley and was used, substantially unchanged, for the profession of hundreds of Sisters of Mercy throughout the world for well over a century. Frances' three companions in profession did not include Mary Teresa Macauley. In late summer she broke a blood vessel in an attempt to rescue one of the orphans who had climbed to a dangerous position on a roof top. Her health became steadily worse. On November 3, she was professed on her death bed and on November 12, she died. Mother Catherine and Sister Mary Frances suffered her loss intensely. But the year 1833 also brought great joy to Frances when her older and well-loved sister, Sarah, decided to enter the convent at Baggot Street.

After Fanny Warde had left Queen's County to go to live in Dublin, Sarah had continued to live with her aunt in Killeany. Like Frances, she considered the possibility of becoming a religious. She visited a Presentation Convent in Kilkenny, her mother's old home, and then went to Dublin to visit several convents, but she was attracted to none of them. Several years older than Fanny, Sarah was a tall, graceful girl, popular because of her delightful disposition. The story is told that Sarah was pursued by a young country gentleman who sought permission from her Uncle William Maher, according to the custom of the time, to court her.[11] One evening the young man was invited to dinner, and Mr. and Mrs. Maher contrived to leave the two young people alone, so that Sarah might give the young man a definite answer before the next day, when she was to go to Dublin. Later that night she told her uncle that she had given her suitor a kind but firm refusal. Her decision was disappointing to her relatives, who felt that the young man's excellent financial status might make up to her for the loss of Bellbrook House. He, meanwhile, instantly called for his horse in great disappointment and dashed away without waiting for dinner. The autumn evening was dark and unusually warm in Killeany, and a sudden storm arose, so that the Mahers sent a messenger after the young man to beg him to remain with them for the night. He refused, dashing blindly on in the torrents of rain until horse and rider fell suddenly to their death in a nearby lake.

The incident was said to be decisive in Sarah Warde's decision to waver no longer in choosing the religious life as her vocation. Whether the account was truth or legend, it created a romantic aura about the life of the young Warde girl. She attended her sister Fanny's profession in January, 1833, and entered the novitiate at Baggot Street in April. Her sister's consecration sealed her choice of the Sisters of Mercy. Sarah, who was received into the Congregation in December, 1833, was destined to go on the foundation to

Cork and, as Mother Josephine Warde, to be the Superior of that community for almost fifty years. The very next month, Teresa Macauley's little sister Catherine, whom Frances Warde had known since her childhood, entered the novitiate at Baggot Street. To date, sixteen young women had been received and seven professed!

In June, 1834, Catherine McAuley drew up a petition to the Holy See, explaining the work of her little community and asking for approval of two Chapters of the Holy Rule on the visitation of the sick and the protection of young women, to be added to the Chapter on charity which Archbishop Murray had approved as a temporary Rule for the Congregation.

Frances Warde, acting as confidential secretary to Catherine McAuley, continued to share in all the plans and works of the Institute. She shared, too, in the founder's sorrows. Laborious duties, fever, and tuberculosis brought death to many of the young Sisters. Six died in one year. Sister Mary Frances' grief was equal to that of Mother McAuley. The younger woman's relationship with the older not only helped to mature her personally; she also acquired a practical knowledge of religious administration and government. Impatient and fiery by nature, she became a real genius at "getting things done."

. . . In energy and organizing ability she was undoubtedly the most gifted of the early nuns; with them she shared that deep interior spirit that gave life and meaning to her many activities and that was to sustain her in the rebuffs and disappointments that would keep pace with her ever increasing foundations. All through her life she preserved a spirit of constant prayer and tender piety. Yet she was a woman of steel . . . She was so obviously a great woman that she inspired immense loyalty and drew people to follow her eagerly by the very strength of her personality. Years later, when she had begun her American career, a Cork magnate often expressed annoyance at the number of young girls attracted to the religious life by Sister Mary Frances' sister, Mother Josephine Warde, at that time Superior in Cork. "That woman," he said, "will not leave a bright girl in the county for a man." "True," one of his friends replied, "Mother Josephine is bad enough, but she had a sister who was deported for it."[12]

It was almost inevitable that the close association between the founder and Sister Mary Frances would create some feeling of envy among the young Sisters, all of whom idolized Mother Catherine. One Sister in particular, who suffered a nervous ailment, caused unpleasantness in the new community. Fortunately, another Sister who wrote down her memoirs of early life at Baggot Street set the record straight.[13] Sister Mary Ann Doyle, who had been appointed Mother Catherine's Assistant in the spring of 1832, was extremely timid, so that she hesitated to join Mother Catherine in the convent parlor to interview young women for admission to the House of Mercy. Sister Frances Warde, who was far from timid, helped the founder in her work, with the result that she had less time for domestic duties in the convent. The "nervous" Sister criticized Sister Mary Frances for "not sweeping the floor," despite the fact that the latter managed the financial business of the house in addition to teaching in the school, visiting the sick, and sharing Mother Catherine's duties. This resentment against Frances Warde was to continue until the death of Mother Catherine and to precipitate, as we shall see, one of the most unhappy experiences of Frances' life.

Joy came to the Sisters of Mercy on March 24, 1835, with the approbation of Pope Gregory XVI, granted to the Congregation through Cardinal James Philip Fransoni, Prefect of the Congregation for Religious.[14] To the Sisters and their Dublin friends, it seemed almost a miracle that the little Congregation received approval from Rome within three years of its foundation. Catherine McAuley and Frances Warde, with grateful and characteristic faith, regarded the *Decretum Laudis* as the blessing of God upon the Institute. Authorization was granted to complete the adjustment of the Holy Rule to the needs of the new Congregation, and work was begun on a draft of the Rule for final approval by the Church.

Catherine McAuley, meanwhile, had sought medical advice in her deep concern for the health of her young Sisters. She was advised to secure a house close to the Irish Sea to which she might send Sisters who "needed a change of air." At this precise moment Providence intervened with the request of Father William Walsh, later Archbishop of Halifax, to establish a school for the poor children of Kingstown, now Dun Laoghaire, a beautiful town facing the calm blue waters of the Irish Sea in Dublin Bay. The "long-fronted house in Sussex Place" near Dun Laoghaire Harbor, still one of the loveliest seaside resorts in Ireland, was purchased by Catherine McAuley. Providence also offered funds brought to Baggot Street by a wealthy widow, Mary McCann, who had become Sister de Chantal in 1832. The branch house, opened March 24, 1835, was named St. Patrick's Convent and School. The poor of Kingstown were cared for, over 200 children were enrolled in the school, and the instruction of adults became a chief apostolate of the Sisters there. Today St. Michael's Mercy Hospital, School for Nurses, and Nursing Home in Dun Laoghaire are among the finest in Ireland, and Glasthule School is served by Sisters from the Mercy Convent. Mail Steamers daily cross the Irish Sea to Holyhead in Wales from this beautiful seaport town which was the site of the second Mercy institute in the world. Financial problems were to make the new convent a difficult establishment for several years, but it was destined to prosper. Catherine McAuley was also to use it as a training ground for young Sisters to be sent as Superiors to new foundations.

The *Irish Catholic Directory* of 1836 recorded the amazing expansion of the works of mercy of the new Institute: excellent day school for 300 children in Dublin; visitation and care of the sick poor; care of cholera patients in hospital; protection and instruction of young women; and already a new branch house in Kingstown.

On a beautiful April day in 1836, the first independent foundation outside Dublin was led by Catherine McAuley to the town of Tullamore, close to the Irish midlands, in the Diocese of Meath. Today this market town is famous for the production of an internationally known liqueur, "Irish Mist." The Sisters of Mercy, in 1836, knew Tullamore for historical reasons. In the same County of Offaly, St. Patrick, according to legend, first preached the Gospel 1400 years before. And Tullamore itself originally formed part of Durrow, the site of the Holy Well of St. Columba, which still attracts pilgrims today. True to her love for the poor, Mother Catherine chose Tullamore as her first foundation because of its extreme poverty. "If we do not take Tullamore," she said simply, "no other community will."[15] Mother McAuley with Sister Mary Ann Doyle as Superior of the new foundation and three other Sisters took the "Grand Canal" at Portobello harbor for Tullamore, passing through the cornfields and meadows of Dublin, Kildare, and King's County to Meath. The Sisters took possession of St. Joseph's Convent, Tullamore, toward evening of April 21. Within four decades, foundations of Sisters of Mercy were to go from Tullamore to Kells, Londonderry, Drogheda, Clara,

Rochfort Bridge, Trim, and London. The Londonderry Convent was to send a foundation to Dundee, Scotland, in 1859, and Tullamore was to open a branch convent in Orange City, California, as late as 1959. Of these and numberless convents of Mercy to spring up throughout the world, Catherine McAuley knew nothing on that pleasant spring evening cooled by April showers when she took possession of the holy ground at Tullamore.

On that very day, before she left Dublin, she appointed Sister Frances Warde as her new Assistant. It became Catherine McAuley's custom to remain at each new foundation for a month until the convent was in order and then return to Baggot Street. Now Sister Mary Frances was to be in charge at the parent house in Dublin until the founder's return. Though neither of the two alluded to the future, both were painfully aware that the time must soon come when they could no longer remain together. Leaders would be needed for new foundations. And Frances Warde, the most capable as well as the best loved, was the most promising leader of all the young women who had consecrated themselves to Christ at Baggot Street as Sisters of Mercy.

One more foundation was to be sent from Dublin before the inevitable parting between Mother Catherine and Sister Mary Frances. In October, 1836, Catherine McAuley set out by canal packet for the town of Charleville, County Cork (now Rath Luric), with Sister Angela Dunn as the Superior of the new foundation. Like Tullamore, Charleville appealed to the early Sisters of Mercy because the poor of the town were in such severe need of care. Two attempts by other Congregations to establish convents there, moreover, had failed.[16] A vague impression was held by the townspeople that no religious foundation could succeed in Charleville. The challenge to help the poor and instruct the unfortunate won Mother Catherine's heart: let others choose more thriving towns for their labors. Charleville proved to be as difficult a mission as the Sisters expected it to be. Poor schools, a pension school, and industrial schools were established gradually, and visitation of the sick was soon a daily work of mercy there. But not for thirty years did Charleville venture to send out a new Mercy foundation. Rich blessings came in the end. The Charleville community finally established a convent in Bathhurst, New South Wales, which sent missions to numerous Australian towns, including Carcoar, Mudgee, Dubbo, Orange, Parkes, and Forbes. Irish colonies were sent out from Charleville, too, in the seventies, to Buttevant in Cork and to New Inn, in Tipperary.

But the days of the Irish winter of 1836 were often bitter trials to the Sisters in the poor convents of Tullamore and Charleville. As requests to make new foundations multiplied, Catherine McAuley had chosen those invitations which she believed to come by the providence of God for the love and care of the poor and needy through the works of mercy. She felt the approval of Providence and was confirmed in her intention to maintain the Convent of St. Joseph in Charleville despite intense suffering and hardship when a peasant woman in the town suddenly declared to her one day: "Oh, it was the Lord Himself that drove you in among us!"

When Catherine McAuley returned to Dublin from Charleville on November 30, 1836, she was faced with a request to begin a new foundation by Bishop Edward Nolan of Carlow, "the most Christ-like man she had ever met." This invitation was the call of Providence to Sister Mary Frances Warde.

4

Spiritual Maturity: Carlow

CARLOW, the Episcopal See of the Diocese of Kildare and Leighlin, had perhaps closer connections with the new Institute of Mercy in 1837 than even Dublin itself. Catherine McAuley had more intimate friends in Carlow than in Dublin, and Frances Warde's birthplace at Bellbrook as well as her later home in Killeany and her relatives in Carlow made Kildare and Leighlin dear to her. The Carlow Mercy foundation was to become one of the most beautiful in Ireland; St. Leo's was to be the first Mercy institute built as a convent and the best loved by the founder and the early Sisters of Mercy.

If Carlow had witnessed its brightest days in the age of St. Brigid, credited with the appointment of St. Conlaeth, first Bishop of Kildare, it was in its lovely second spring in the eighteen-thirties. The town of Carlow, or "the City on the River," lies at the meeting of the Barrow and the Burren Rivers. Its earliest charter on record, dated 1209, grants the town to William Marshall, Earl of Pembroke. Sixty years later, William le Gros was appointed Governor of Carlow as Deputy of the Earl of Norfolk. From the twelfth century until the nineteenth, Carlow withstood a long history of attacks and counterattacks between the British armies and Irish insurgents. One of the most memorable uprisings occurred in the spring of the historic year 1798 when a band of rebels marched on the town and the castle. Unfortunately, the British garrison had been warned of the insurrection, and 600 Irish farmers and laborers were slaughtered. Some who sought refuge in hovels near the town were burned to death by the soldiers who set the cabins on fire. On the County Laois side of the Barrow River, 417 victims were buried in a sandpit, called "Croppie Hole" to this day.

A small but sturdy town, Carlow survived its long history of suffering. So did the famous Carlow Castle, boldly seated on a hillside overlooking the Barrow. Originally it was an oblong square structure, flanked with round Norman towers, probably erected by Hugh de Lacy in the twelfth century. The castle was in an excellent state of preservation until the nineteenth century. In 1814 an eccentric physician named Middleton secured possession of it and conceived the idea of converting it into an asylum for the insane.[1] Alterations interfered with the foundations of the castle, and the greater part of this historic fortress, which had withstood centuries of siege and assault, fell to the ground. The two towers and one wall which remain today are still a magnificent stronghold overlooking the town.

It was Carlow College, however, and not the castle, that provided the link between the town and the Congregation of Mercy. With the relaxation of penal laws in 1782, Bishop Luke Keeffe of Carlow had determined to establish a college in Ireland to educate young men for the priesthood. St. Patrick's College was begun by Keeffe in 1787 and completed under Henry Staunton, Dean of Kildare and Leighlin and President of the College until his death in 1814. Staunton was succeeded by President Andrew Fitzgerald, a Dominican who came to Carlow as a Professor of Philosophy by way of the Universities of Louvain and Lisbon. He incorporated Carlow College with the University of London, with the power to grant baccalaureate degrees.[2] Refusing appointments to other institutions of higher learning, including Maynooth College, the scholarly Fitzgerald made Carlow "the best college in Ireland"³ under his leadership. Nor was she purely academic in his involvements. In 1832 he was thrown into prison in Carlow for refusing to pay what he considered unjust tithes to the British government.

For years Catherine McAuley had been a friend of President Andrew Fitzgerald, of Edward Nolan, Vice-President and Professor of Theology at Carlow College and later Bishop of Kildare and Leighlin, and of Father James Maher, Professor at Carlow in 1837, truly great parish priest of Carlow-Graigue after 1840, and cousin of Frances Warde. Dr. Fitzgerald was a true friend and counselor to Catherine McAuley beginning in the eighteen-twenties when many clergymen distrusted or persecuted her because of her nonconformist works of charity among the poor of Dublin. When she assumed the guardianship of her three nephews in 1829, she naturally placed them under the guardianship of Fitzgerald in the lay secondary department of Carlow College. In 1834, the year that Dr. Nolan became Bishop in Carlow, Fitzgerald traveled to Dublin several times to attempt to induce Mother Catherine to introduce her Congregation into Carlow. She had given Tullamore and Charleville preference, however, because of the perhaps more pathetic situation of the poor in those towns.

But when Bishop Nolan himself came to Baggot Street in 1836, the people of Carlow could be refused no longer. Catherine McAuley "never knew any other ecclesiastic who brought Christ so forcibly to her mind."⁴ Unlike some of his confreres, Bishop Nolan was affectionate and unassuming as well as profoundly learned. As a spiritual guide, he revealed the simplicity of sanctity. Recently Edward Nolan had received a bequest of 7000 pounds from a hard-working Carlow man named Michael Nowlan who had kept a delft shop in the town for years. The Bishop believed that the legacy could serve no better purpose than to establish care for the sick poor, to protect young women in need, and to educate the children of Carlow. No one could perform these tasks better than the Sisters of Mercy.

Early in 1837, the possibility of a Carlow foundation was much discussed at Baggot Street. Catherine McAuley had now become aware in an experiential way that new foundations meant parting with her most beloved associates at the Dublin convent. Kingstown, Tullamore, and Charleville had required the services of her earliest and best trained Sisters. Up until now she had managed to retain her dearest friend, assistant, and secretary, Frances Warde. Another member of the Institute who was especially close to her was Sister Veronica Corrigan, an orphan whom she had reared from infancy and who had been her personal maid at Coolock House. While Catherine debated the question of whom she should send to Carlow, Sister Veronica was stricken suddenly with virulent typhoid fever in February, 1837, and died after four days of agony. With her profound faith in a personal Providence, Mother Catherine at once made a resolution which she never retracted: no matter how dear and valuable to herself, she would never "reserve" a Sister from an apostolic work requested by the Church of God. Frances Warde was immediately appointed as the first Superior of the Carlow foundation.

Sister Mary Frances had matured considerably since entering the Baggot Street convent in 1828. Now twenty-seven, she was more dignified, animated, and attractive than ever. She had developed her administrative ability considerably, but though businesslike in manner, she knew how to unbend with ease. With her keen sense of the incongruous, she could always spot a ridiculous situation, and she laughed so heartily at every droll occurrence that everyone around her shared her infectious joy. Indeed, she was to remain youthful in her spirit of fun always. As a witty conversationalist, she fascinated young and old, thus winning considerable influence over others wherever she went. Frances Warde was obviously an ideal choice for the town of Carlow, with its intellectual center under the patronage of Andrew Fitzgerald and its loved poor under the guidance of Bishop Nolan and Father Maher.

On April 10, 1837, Mother Catherine and Sister Mary Frances left Dublin for Carlow in "Purcell's Mail Coach," chartered for the purpose. Sister Cecilia Marmion, later Mistress of Novices at Baggot Street, and the third Mother Superior of the Congregation, went to Carlow as Mother Catherine's companion. Two others, assigned temporarily to Carlow, accompanied them: Sister Ursula Frayne, destined to found the first Australian Mercy convent in Perth, 1845, and Sister Teresa White, who was to go on the first English foundation to London in 1839 and to be the first Superior in Galway in 1840.[5] Only Sister Frances Warde and Sister Josephine Trenor, a novice, were to remain. It was Catherine McAuley's custom to lend a few Sisters to each new foundation until a sufficient number of candidates entered from the area in which it was established.

The spring morning on which the little colony left for Carlow was damp and dreary, and the carriage jogged along at a slow pace over the bumpy roads of Dublin and Kildare to its inland destination. Reaching Carlow, the mail coach inched its way through market day crowds to the Posting Inn, where the Sisters discovered to their amazement that Bishop Nolan, the clergy, and the laity of the town in large numbers were waiting to welcome them. The whole company then moved in procession to the Cathedral of Carlow for a *Te Deum*.

This beautiful new cathedral had been dedicated only four years earlier under the patronage of the Virgin Mary. It had been begun in 1828 under Bishop James Doyle. A cruciform structure in later English style, surmounted by a lofty tower at the western end of the nave, it is still one of the most magnificent Irish cathedrals. It occupies the site of the old parish church built by Dean Henry Staunton about 1787. The fine stone gateway to this church, bearing the initials H. S. and the date of the dedication of the church, 1792, was later moved to form the entrance to the new Convent of Mercy, begun in 1837. It is still there today.

Next the Sisters were conducted to Carlow College, close by the Cathedral, for a reception by the faculty and students, who had a free day in their honor. Then came an invitation to visit historic Braganza House, Bishop Nolan's residence in the northern suburbs of Carlow beside the Barrow River. This impressive mansion, erected by Sir Dudley Hill, Governor of St. Lucie, who had reaped ducats in the service of the royal family of Portugal, had been purchased by the clergy of Kildare and Leighlin for their beloved "J. K. L." As the home of Bishop Nolan and later of James Maher, it was to have significance in the history of the Carlow Sisters.[6] The Sisters chose rather to visit the Presentation Convent near the Cathedral. That same evening they took possession of their own temporary convent, the old College-Academy Building on the Carlow College grounds.

This abandoned structure turned out to be dingy and dilapidated. The ecclesiastics of Carlow evidently knew little of how to prepare a house for Sisters. Though Bishop Nolan promised the Sisters that a new convent would be built, Catherine McAuley felt dejected. Furnishings were inadequate. There were only a few chairs in the entire house, and the Sisters had to carry them from room to room! The founder offered to take the Sisters back to Baggot Street for a time. But Frances Warde showed her mettle. According to the Carlow *Annals,* she "preferred to cast herself upon Divine Providence and commence the works of the Institute at once." That very day she was appointed Mother Superior for a term of six years and also Mistress of Novices and Bursar by Bishop Nolan. Not only the scanty furniture but all other inconveniences of the convent were turned characteristically to a source of amusement by the new Mother Frances. Bishop Nolan promised financial aid as well as construction of the new convent as soon as possible, and Father Fitzgerald gave the Sisters the old building rent-free. They were happy enough to sleep on mattresses laid on the floor until beds could be secured. Their first act was to choose a small room as a temporary chapel, and there Bishop Nolan offered the Celebration of the Eucharist the following morning. He blessed the convent under the patronage of St. Leo, whose feast day it was. Frances Warde was jubilant. She could not know then that she was to found more than 100 institutions of Mercy before her death, most of them poor in their beginnings but all destined to flourish surprisingly, somewhat miraculously even, under the plan of God.

Within a few days Catherine McAuley was recalled to Dublin with the sad news that two young Sisters had contracted typhoid fever while serving the sick poor. Fortunately they recovered, and she returned to Carlow to help Sister Frances with the new foundation. Visitation of the sick poor and instruction of children and adults in the convent were begun at once. Frances Warde's most successful apostolate, her great charism, was instruction of adults in the Catholic faith. Wherever she went, she brought lapsed Catholics back to the reception of the Sacraments through her religious conferences. Not many years later, in the United States, she was to bring hundreds of non-Catholics to baptism in the Catholic faith. The Carlow people loved the new Sisters, whom they called "Ladies." It was not orthodox, it seemed, to call them "nuns," for they were not cloistered; "Sisters," the townspeople thought, did not convey sufficient respect! And no wonder Frances Warde and her little community were loved. They walked out each day to serve the poorest people of the town, to clothe them, to feed them, to care for their sick. They visited daily the poorest families of all in a dirty little alley called the "Scrags." One appreciative family took their half-door from its hinges to provide an impromptu bridge as a clean pathway for the Sisters. Frances Warde begged them never to do so again. The Sisters of Mercy, she said, wished to move without special privilege among the poor.

Obviously the little convent at first lacked facilities to open even a small school for the Carlow children. Bishop Nolan had allocated the legacy of Michael Nowlan to the service of the poor, not to buildings. Then early in May, 1837, John Nowlan, brother of Michael, offered his life savings of 2000 pounds for the construction of a convent and school. Frances Warde's joy was unbounded. She was to plan the first institute of Sisters of Mercy in the world to be actually built as a convent! Kingstown, Charleville, Tullamore, and even Baggot Street had been founded in buildings which had earlier been intended for other uses. The cornerstone for the new convent was laid May 20, 1837, by Bishop Nolan, attended by the population of the college and the town. Father James Maher contributed 300 pounds to the new project, and Bishop Nolan made the day special by offering fifty pounds and eight silver spoons with the initial "M" engraved on each.

To crown the joy of Mother Frances and the Sisters, three young girls came to enter the Carlow convent. In April came Rebecca Greene, daughter of Major General Joe Greene, a liberal Protestant stationed at Naas Barracks in the British service. In May, a well-to-do widow, Kate Meagher, entered as a postulant. Both were to go on the foundation to Naas with Frances Warde two years later. And Rebecca Greene, later Sister Mary Agnes, was to go on a foundation to Little Rock, Arkansas, in 1850 and to die in New Orleans after the turn of the century. In June, Mary McDarby, a young woman whose spiritual director was Bishop Nolan himself, presented herself as a candidate. She was destined to accompany Frances Warde as one of the "first seven" to found the first Mercy convent in the United States in Pittsburgh. But now Mother Frances thought only of the future of St. Leo's. Her imagination was filled with plans for serving the people of Carlow and developing the spiritual life of her new little Mercy community.

In June, 1837, Catherine McAuley returned to Dublin, to the intense grief of Frances Warde. In leaving Baggot Street, Frances had suffered separation from her loved sister, Sarah, now Sister Josephine. But the joy and excitement of the new foundation had helped her to accept the sorrow of parting. Now, however, separation from Mother Catherine seemed to be more than she could bear. Aside from the necessity of Catherine's presence at the parent house, she returned to Dublin with the special purpose of planning a new foundation in the city of Cork, seaport on the River Lee, early in July. One of the four Sisters assigned to the new convent was Sister Josephine Warde. St. Maries[7] of the Isle in Cork, as we shall see later, became very dear to Frances Warde because Sarah was to be Superior there for almost half a century. She was to be loved universally in Cork for her service to the sick poor, the orphans, and the prisoners in jail, as well as to the school children. And Frances was to commemorate her love for Cork by calling one of her best loved American convents, in Newport, Rhode Island, St. Maries of the Isle. Missions from Cork were to spread as far as the Philippine Islands and Kenya in East Africa. Now Frances was only painfully aware that her sister's future would be divided from her own, even though their lives as Sisters of Mercy would be united in spirit. But somehow the parting with Catherine McAuley was the greatest personal sorrow of her life.

Forty-four years later, the Mercy annalist was to record that Frances Warde could never allude to her separation from Mother Catherine without tears.[8] As a golden jubilarian in Manchester, New Hampshire, in the year 1883, Frances was to announce sadly, "I don't know how I ever survived the parting from Mother Catherine." And speaking of death in her seventies, she would sometimes say, "I often think of the heaven which death will open to us, but to me it would be heaven in itself to see dearest Mother Catherine once more." Frances' dedication to Catherine McAuley on the beautiful summer day of their parting in Carlow in 1837 remained unchanged until death. Mother Catherine was loved by all her Sisters. There is no record of one of them who did not venerate her. But no one ever loved her as Frances Warde did.

The Sisters' August retreat of 1837, conducted by Bishop Nolan himself, was consoling to Mother Frances and all her Sisters. Years afterward, they spoke of these special days as a rare gift of the Holy Spirit, "as an awakening love for their religious vocation and daily gratitude to God."[9] Perhaps without realizing it, Frances Warde transferred to the saintly Bishop Nolan something of the love and veneration she felt for Catherine McAuley. The younger woman's religious consecration was growing in strength and grace. Not only the distinctive works of the Institute of Mercy, but good works of every type seemed to find warm cooperation among the Carlow Sisters. For six months St. Leo's flourished almost too smoothly, for it was Catherine McAuley's belief that "without the cross real progress cannot come." In August, Catherine wrote to Frances, "Thanks be to God you are all so well and happy and doing so much for the afflicted poor. . . . You are truly fortunate in all the circumstances of your little foundation—*nothing* that I know of like it."[10] The relief given to the poor, the large number of townspeople instructed in their religion, gave Mother Catherine and Frances Warde unique joy.

And now came the blow. Catherine McAuley indeed seemed to be right about the necessity of the cross for real spiritual progress. The trial that came to Frances Warde in 1837 had been predicted two years earlier in a legend with the mystical overtones so characteristic of the Irish people. In 1835 Frances' cousin, the saintly Father James Maher, had been present in Braganza House at the death by typhoid fever of a young priest named Duggan. Before dying, the young man had taken Maher's hand and said, "I am going. The others will soon follow. You alone shall remain, and may God preserve you."[11] Before two years had passed, two young curates named Byrne and Kelly died at Braganza. Father Maher was to fulfill the prediction of the dying man by living to be an octogenarian. By 1837 only Bishop Edward Nolan, now aged forty-four, still challenged the truth of the strange prophecy that all at Braganza except Maher would soon die.

In October, 1837, Bishop Nolan set out to visit the parishes of his diocese. In Maryborough, he suddenly became so ill with fever that he was scarcely able to return to Braganza House. The physician who first attended him unfortunately prescribed the obsolete remedy of bleeding. A more experienced doctor was called and pronounced Nolan's case hopeless. Mother Frances nursed him during his last days. Shortly before he died, Bishop Nolan looked in the direction of Father Maher and another clergyman who was present and, pointing to Mother Frances and other Sisters in the room, said, "Take care of them." The priest who was with Father Maher asked, "Is it I?" Bishop Nolan answered "No" and, looking directly at Maher, placed his own hand on the head of Frances Warde, who knelt at his bedside. When Father Maher, suspecting that the Bishop's mind was wandering, gently replaced the dying man's hand, Edward Nolan caught Maher's hand and placed it on Mother Frances' head. Now he could no longer speak but all present knew the meaning of the saintly man's last ritual. Father Maher remained faithful to his charge of the Sisters of Mercy in Carlow until his own death in 1877. Almost fifty years after Nolan's bequest of his care of the Sisters of Mercy to Maher, Frances Warde recounted the death-bed incident with deepest emotion.

Perhaps Mother Frances' recent parting with Catherine McAuley and with Sarah Warde had brought her sorrow to its peak; perhaps she had learned to depend almost too much on the kind and fatherly Edward Nolan; perhaps she knew with the intuition of holiness that in Nolan's death Carlow had lost a saint. In any case, she now gave way to grief so poignant that she became physically ill. In her great sorrow, she asked of Catherine McAuley the fulfillment of a promise made to her by the older woman at their parting during the previous summer. "What shall I do if we are misunderstood, or persecuted, or have troubles which I cannot endure?" she had asked the founder as the latter departed from

Carlow. Catherine had answered, "I will come to you, my darling." And all Frances' fears had vanished.

Now, however, Catherine McAuley recognized the need to encourage her young friend to grow in independence and maturity, to develop the endurance that comes only through personal acceptance of suffering. As soon as Catherine heard of Frances' excessive grief, she wrote from Cork to Sister Teresa White in Carlow[12] who had informed her of Frances' suffering:

. . . My ever dear, affectionate Sister Mary Frances will soon, I trust, give great edification to you all by her . . . composure and entire resignation. . . .

When I promised to go to my dear Sister Frances in time of need, you may be sure, my dear child, I did not mean the trial which death occasions with which I am so familiarized that the tomb seems never closed in my regard. I alluded to those difficulties which her new state exposed her to, such as incurring the displeasure of her spiritual superiors without intention; or experiencing marks of disapprobation and not knowing why. These are some of the bitter-sweets incident to our state and most of all requiring support and counsel.

The sorrow in which she now so deeply shares is extensively divided and equally the affliction of many . . . To regard it as an individual sorrow would not be right . . . Yet I can account for my dear Sister Mary Frances' feeling so much on this distressing occasion. The good Bishop afforded her the first and chief comfort she experienced on parting from me . . . But I know she will not continue unmindful of the . . . obligations of our holy state and I will confide in the generous bounty and never ceasing kindness of our beloved Saviour, to which we must put no impediment, that He will pour down on you all, my dear Sisters, His . . . abundant consolation, and that I will find you in a few days . . . tranquil and reasonably cheerful.

With most fervent prayers and fondest affection for my tender, ardent, beloved Sister Mary Frances and for you all, I remain . . .
Your attached Mother in Christ,
Mary C. McAuley

While Catherine McAuley strengthened her young friend by refusing to encourage immoderate grief, she nevertheless subtly offered the mature support that Frances needed. She herself had lost loved ones over and over again, "so that the tomb seemed never closed in her regard." During the year 1837 alone, three of her promising young Sisters had died of typhoid fever and two of tuberculosis. Her most recent sorrow had been the death of her younger niece, Catherine Macauley (Sister Ann Agnes), at Baggot Street. Personal illness and exhaustive labor both in Dublin and in her new foundations, moreover, not only taught her the purgative value of suffering but convinced her that Frances, too, must accept the suffering in Christ made imperative by the future apostolate that seemed more and more to be in God's plan for her. Six days after her letter to Sister Teresa White, Mother Catherine wrote encouragingly to Frances herself from Cork:

. . . Whatever the case is, I will return by Carlow to see you, if only for a few hours . . .
May God bless and animate you with His own divine spirit, that you may prove it is Jesus Christ you love and serve with your whole heart.[13]

Catherine did visit Carlow on her way back to Dublin to console and advise her friend. Soon after she wrote to Sarah Warde, "We found Sister M. Frances much more reconciled to her great affliction than I expected. . . ." And the "tender, ardent, affectionate Sister Mary Frances" indeed took the older woman's counsel to heart. Somehow, her response to the death of Edward Nolan marked a crisis, a dividing line in her life. Before this experience, she still retained some of the emotional qualities of very young womanhood. She emerged from it a mature, independent woman. The essentially passionate nature of her personality she now centered not so much in purely personal relationships but in the fulfillment of the spiritual commitment which animated the core of her being. From now on, she was lovingly available to all. She sacrificed herself for all. She was to be called "a woman of steel" in her uncompromising pursuit of her commitment to Christ and His people. The quality of "steel" in her personality was tried by fire. Only with such personal purgation could she be prepared for the dynamic apostolate awaiting her in the pioneering American country of the mid-century.

On November 14, 1837, Frances Warde presided at her first ceremony of profession in which she received the vows of Sister Josephine Trenor who had come to Carlow with her from Baggot Street. Rebecca Greene and the widow, Catherine Meagher, received the habit the same day. Two weeks later, Frances' cousin, Mary Maher of Killeany, daughter of her Uncle William and Catherine Maher, entered the community at Carlow. Mother Catherine was delighted with her young friend's success. Writing to her shortly after Christmas, 1837, she commended Frances on her excellent religious instructions: "Show them in your actions as much as you can, my dearest child, and your Institution will outdo us all."[14]

Frances' happiness at the increase of her little community of service was darkened by tragedy the following February. Kate Coffey of Carlow, who had entered the convent in December, died on St. Valentine's day, 1838. She had fallen in the snow while visiting the sick and had died from hemorrhage which followed the accident. With unerring insight, Catherine McAuley again made virtue of necessity, adapting sorrow to the strong spiritual formation of Frances.[15] The founder wrote from Dublin:

. . . You have given all to God without any reserve. Nothing can happen to you which He does not appoint. You desire nothing but the accomplishment of His Holy Will . . . You must be cheerful and happy, animating all around you. This is quite unnecessary, for I know you do not want counsel or comfort, yet I cannot entirely give up my poor old child . . .

You will soon have an increase. The comfort comes soon after a well-received trial. May God preserve and bless you, my own dearly loved child. . . .

Your ever faithful and fondly attached,

M. C. McAuley

It is interesting to note that Mother Catherine's attitude toward her young friend has changed since Edward Nolan's death. "I know you do not need counsel or comfort," she declares. She now addresses Frances as the mature woman she is.

As usual, Catherine McAuley was right in her prediction of an "increase" after a well-accepted trial. Maria Kelly of Castletown, Queen's County, entered the Carlow convent nine days after the death of Kate Coffey, the first Sister to die at St. Leo's. Mother Frances was later to take Maria to Wexford as the first Superior of the Mercy foundation there. Before the close of the year, six more young women entered at St. Leo's. Two of them, Eliza and Ellen Maher, half-sisters, of Freshford, County Kilkenny, were first cousins of Frances Warde. Eliza was later to go on the foundation to Tuam, and Ellen, one of the Carlow Sisters dearest to Frances Warde, was to send foundations to Galway and to Cheadle, England, and then lead the first Mercy colony to Auckland, New Zealand, in 1849. Her work flowered so magnificently that by 1950 nineteen Mercy communities prospered in New Zealand with their mother house in Ponsonby. The third girl who entered in Carlow with Ellen and Eliza Maher was Rosina Strange, of Aylwardstown, Kilkenny, a cousin of Nicholas Cardinal Wiseman, who was to become Superior of the Carlow community in 1850.

The Carlow foundation was indeed successful. In fact, the sleeping quarters of the Sisters, including two garrets, became quite inadequate. Mother Frances playfully called herself "the old woman who lived in a shoe." Providence came to the rescue of this "old woman" of twenty-seven when Mrs. Catherine Nolan, widowed sister of Michael and John Nowlan, benefactors of the Sisters, came to live in a small house adjoining the temporary convent. She was paralyzed and therefore unable to use the second story of her house. Mother Frances asked for the use of the two upstairs bedrooms, and with her characteristic good humor dispatched five young Sisters "to take furnished lodgings next door." Dr. Fitzgerald, meanwhile, had donated a sofa and chairs for the Sisters' living room, and Father Maher provided a piano so that they could offer music lessons. Though Maher never owned a penny, money always seemed to come into his possession, which he disposed of promptly. One day in the winter of 1838, he heard that a girl without financial support wished to enter the Carlow convent, and he immediately offered Mother Frances the interest of 400 pounds annually to support the young lady. Once the initial difficulties of the Carlow foundation were surmounted, no convent progressed so rapidly. To Catherine McAuley, it was best loved of all her foundations.

As Mother Catherine's most intimate associate, Frances Warde received by far the greatest number of her extant letters. The two women wrote fulsome accounts to each other of all that happened in Dublin, Carlow, and all the new foundations of the Institute. Unfortunately, Frances' letters to Catherine were not preserved.[16] In her letters to Mother Frances, Catherine expresses over and over again her joy in the apostolate at Carlow, her happiness that the poor are cared for and instructed. Nothing about Mother Catherine was more striking than her genuine, practical, unsentimental love for the poor, which was her sincere expression of love for Christ. Frances Warde learned from her not a merely vocal or sterile love for God's people, but an active concern which motivated her to work unceasingly for them. "God knows I would rather be cold and hungry than that His poor should be deprived of any consolation in our power to afford,"[17] wrote Catherine. The Carlow Sisters of Mercy have never lost that spirit bequeathed to Frances Warde.

Throughout the year 1838, Mother Catherine shared her joys and sorrows with Frances Warde in numerous letters from Baggot Street to St. Leo's. She wrote in July of the opening of a branch house, St. Anne's Convent at Booterstown on Dublin Bay. Sister Ursula Frayne, who had lived with Mother Frances in Carlow, was first Superior at this convent, which gradually established a nursing home, a national school, an orphanage, and an industrial school. Catherine wrote in September of the new foundation of St. Mary's on the ancient holy ground called St. Peter's Cell, in Ireland's oldest city, Limerick. This convent was to be one of Ireland's finest, sending new foundations within ten years to Kinsale, Killarney, Mallow, Newcastle West, Rathkeale, Adare, and Ennis—and to Glasgow and Edinburgh in Scotland. And Kinsale was to establish religious houses in Newry,

Clonakilty, and Doone, as well as in Derby, England, and in San Francisco and Cincinnati in the fifties. Not only the joys of new foundations for the poor, but the sufferings of Catherine McAuley's life were shared with Frances Warde: the endless and burdensome financial difficulties in Kingstown; the bitter chaplaincy problem at Baggot Street; the intense pain of estrangement from her nephews, James and Robert; the unnamed conflict with ecclesiastics in Dublin which caused her to cry out to Mother Frances alone: "Pray God to take all bitterness from me. I can scarcely think of what has been done to me without resentment."[18] If Frances Warde's letter to Mother Catherine were extant, we would know more of the Carlow Superior's own inner struggles during the late thirties.

Catherine McAuley's encouragement of her "spiritual child," Frances Warde, is constant.[19] She writes that Sister Teresa White "never tired of speaking of the instruction and advantages" she received at Carlow from Mother Frances. She "looks forward with delight to the time of your Chapel being blessed, as I trust I shall meet you then." She reports that rumor makes the new convent at Carlow "quite irresistible. You would wonder how much it is spoken of; it is said to be beautiful . . . How I should rejoice to find your Institute excel in every way the poor old Mother House." Writing from Booterstown in June, Catherine strikes a personal note: "I went in to town. I forgot this letter. I am so confused, and *never* dressed so neat and nice as *my dear darling Fanny* used to dress her *old* Mother. . . ." In August, the founder laments that the Limerick foundation may prevent her attendance at the blessing of the new Carlow convent: "You may be sure this is sorrowful news for me if I am to forfeit the happiness of going to Carlow. . . ." October brings to Frances a letter from Limerick in which Mother

Catherine expresses disappointment that several Sisters could not attend the consecration of the new convent at St. Leo's and plans to take five Sisters to visit Carlow. In November, Catherine writes: "Carlow is keeping pace with Baggot Street as to progress. I suppose it will be spreading through the country in less time." Report has it, moreover, that "the progress of the House in Carlow is like a miracle." In all of these letters, the older woman's farewell to the younger is the warmest found in all her correspondence: "May God bless and preserve you, my ever dearest Child, is the constant prayer of your ever fond, M. C. McAuley."

Nor could Mother McAuley quite conceal from her friends outside the Congregation her joy in the Carlow foundation. Writing to Dr. Andrew Fitzgerald in July, 1838, she says: "The delightful description I get of the Carlow Convent makes me very anxious to see it. My innocent Sister M. Frances says she has the poplars in full bloom with evergreens and roses blowing on the mound . . ."[20] It would seem that Catherine and Frances were not alone in their enthusiasm for the new St. Leo's. Even the passengers on the stage coaches constantly brought descriptions of "the handsomest convent in Ireland" to Dublin. The new Carlow convent, a modest but elegant building, was not unworthy to stand near beautiful Carlow Cathedral. Both structures seemed like miracles to the poor people of the town, who remembered the thatched huts, the bleak hillsides, and the lonely groves in which the secret celebration of the Eucharist had taken place for centuries for fear of punishment under penal laws. The splendid St. Leo's Convent and School was set in a garden that was Mother Frances' special joy, the work of her own tireless hands at recreation. All her life, she was to plant beautiful flowers wherever she went. She had loved gardens as a child at Bellbrook House. As a religious, a garden was for her a source of contemplation, a retreat for prayer and recreation for her Sisters after their long hours in the apostolate. Mother Austin Carroll, annalist of the Sisters of Mercy, wrote warmly of the spiritual meaning of the convent and garden at Carlow at least forty years after Mother Catherine's first visit there:

The neat, handsome Carlow convent now boasts a blessing which many cathedrals of Ireland with their soaring Gothic arches never had. Its corridors and pleasant rooms were once walked by Catherine McAuley and sanctified by her presence; and in its sweet old-fashioned garden are the soaring poplars and the glossy evergreens which she loved; the mound crowned with roses, which gave her such delight; the splendid stock gilly-flowers, in flaunting colors, which brightened the whole garden; and the trim walks which she paced with her "darling Fanny Warde" and the cherished children of her "first flock."[21]

The hallowed room that Catherine McAuley occupied on her visits to Frances Warde in Carlow is now an oratory in which the celebration of the Eucharist frequently takes place.

A visit at St. Leo's was a delight to all the early Irish Sisters of Mercy. The Carlow climate was mild, and Sisters whose health was delicate, or who were exhausted from work, were sent there to recuperate strength. Mother Frances was the ideal hostess to all. In reply to an invitation she once extended to all the sick of the Congregation, Catherine McAuley replied facetiously: "All the Sisters must live between Baggot Street, Booterstown, and Kingstown, as no Sister can go to Carlow who is not to remain; they all get too fond of it."[22]

In the matter of attracting postulants, too, Carlow Convent and its Superior were voted "quite irresistible." In 1839, eight more young girls begged to become Sisters of Mercy at

St. Leo's. Not only the poor girls of Carlow applied; ladies of high social position and excellent education crowded the new novitiate. Three first cousins of Nicholas Cardinal Wiseman and numerous relatives of Paul Cardinal Cullen presented themselves as candidates. On July 2, 1839, Frances Warde and her Sisters moved into their new convent with great jubilation. It was blessed by Bishop Francis Haly, successor to Bishop Nolan, by Dr. Fitzgerald, and by Father Maher. Lovely as it was, the new convent required economy. The food was plain. The Sisters lived simply. Beds were purchased, however, and they no longer slept on mattresses laid on the floor. They confessed to one another that they had been just as happy in the old convent. But they loved the new St. Leo's.

Besides instructing poor children of the town in their religion, Frances Warde had opened a "pension school" for middle-class girls on May 1, 1839.[23] Mother Catherine gave her full approval, as she believed the school would be welcomed by parents who could not afford the more expensive boarding schools. While the chief apostolate of the Sisters of Mercy was with the poor, Catherine made a prediction concerning the pension schools—and she was right, as always—on one of her visits to Carlow: "From schools like these we shall get our best novices." Frances Warde had another motive: tuition schools would give the Sisters the opportunity to educate the families of their students to their obligations to the poor. Adult education was always Frances Warde's forte. Catherine McAuley herself presided at the opening of a pension school in Charleville and sanctioned similar schools in Tullamore and in Cork. In her own brief religious life, in fact, she founded more tuition schools than Houses of Mercy for working girls. She was always guided by the needs of the Church in the particular locality in which the Sisters served and disliked rigid conformity in matters of the apostolate. Frances Warde was later to encounter opposition from some Mercy convents in putting the founder's principles concerning pension schools into effect. The Carlow tuition school, meanwhile, attracted students who later became leaders in the foundations of Sisters of Mercy throughout the world. And the pension schools, later called academies, were established wherever the Sisters of Mercy went.

The summer of 1839 found Frances Warde in the midst of plans for her first foundation from Carlow. The town of Naas, midway between Dublin and Carlow, was to be the scene of her first venture as a founder. Toward the end of August, Catherine McAuley visited Carlow on her way back from Cork, where she had assisted at the profession of Sister Clare Agnew, a prominent British fiction writer whose novel, *Geraldine,* was a best seller and who was soon to go on the first foundation to London. The main reason for Catherine's visit to Carlow, however, was to plan the Naas foundation with Frances Warde. The Sisters in Carlow even today point out the community room at St. Leo's where the two friends projected the future St. Mary's Convent, Naas, to be opened on the Feast of Our Lady of Mercy, 1839—and not only Naas, but many of the convents that Catherine McAuley founded herself, for Frances Warde was her trusted confidante. The Bermondsey convent was to be opened in London in November, and Galway, Wexford, Birr, and Birmingham, England were in the offing. Together the two founders now dreamed, planned, and executed the expansion of the Congregation of Mercy.

5

Surprising Zeal: Carlow, Naas, Wexford

DURING the lifetime of Catherine McAuley, Frances Warde was the only other Sister of Mercy to establish new foundations. Eventually, she was to found more convents than the founder herself. As the first Sister professed at Baggot Street and the closest friend and religious associate of Mother Catherine, she was now well prepared for her apostolate. On the Feast of Our Lady of Mercy, September 24, 1839, Mother Frances opened her first foundation in the town of Naas, ancient seat of the Kings of Leinster, situated on the Grand Canal near the River Liffey.

Naas had once been famous for both the spirituality and the number of its religious houses. But its finest monastic spoils had been granted to high-ranking British families in the seventeenth century—to the Luttrells under Henry VIII and the Aylmers under Elizabeth I. When Father Gerald Doyle was appointed pastor of Naas in 1814, he fell heir to religious turmoil. The population numbered approximately 100 Catholics to every non-Catholic. The town was military, with a regimental school connected with its army barracks. The students, mostly Catholic, were taught the religion of the Church of England by their non-Catholic teachers and forced to attend Anglican church services. Proselytism flourished everywhere in Naas, even in the jail. As early as 1824—even before the Catholic Emancipation Act—Bishop James Doyle of Kildare and Leighlin urged Father Doyle to secure affidavits concerning the proselytism and threatened to lay the whole affair before the British parliament. Sensational demonstrations often reached an explosive stage in Naas, too, when the natives rose in rebellion against the payment of unjust tithes. Because of its location almost midway between Dublin and Carlow, moreover, and because of its intersection by the Grand Canal, Naas was socially and economically a vibrant little town in the first half of the nineteenth century. And Father Gerald Doyle was a dynamic "patriot-priest." He was not the man to sit quietly by and watch his parishioners being spirited away from their ancient faith. He was also an enthusiastic friend of Catherine McAuley, who sympathized with him in his conflicts with local authorities, whether civil, military, or religious.

In 1827 Father Doyle built the parish "Church of Mary and St. David," so-called to distinguish it from the Protestant St. David's, and as early as 1829 he petitioned Bishop Doyle to allow him to construct a convent and school. A Catholic free school, he believed, was the answer to the flagrant proselytism carried on in Naas. The Bishop cautioned against further building until the debt on the new church was paid. So Father Doyle had to content himself with sending girls from Naas to the Mercy novitiate in Dublin until a convent could be established in the town.

Still hoping for the establishment of an Institute of Mercy in 1836, Father Doyle wrote to Catherine McAuley asking her what qualities were requisite for a "Sister of Mercy." His request elicited one of Mother Catherine's best known letters.[1] In it she stated in simplest terms the meaning of a vocation of Mercy. The young woman desiring to be a Sister of Mercy should have "an ardent desire to be united to God and to serve the poor." She should "feel a particular interest for the sick and the dying." She should possess sympathy and patience as well as good health, and she ought to be capable of prudence and recollection. If she is young, she will be more open to spiritual development. But, with characteristic good sense, the founder added that there are always exceptions.

Neither Catherine McAuley nor Frances Warde was surprised when in 1838 Father Doyle declared to Bishop Francis Haly of Kildare and Leighlin, successor to Edward Nolan, that he could wait no longer for the Sisters of Mercy to come to Naas. And when Haly referred the request to Sister Frances, Mother Catherine was delighted to have Carlow send the new foundation. She had established convents in Booterstown and in Limerick in 1838, and the proposed London foundation at Bermondsey was now demanding much of her time and energy. Though the total number of Sisters of Mercy was now over 100,[2] the Baggot Street parent house was temporarily almost depleted because of new foundations. "We are very near to a stop—I should say a full stop,"[3] Catherine wrote to Frances Warde in August, 1838. "Feet and hands are numerous," she added, "but the *heads* are nearly gone." When Sister Frances first wrote to her in February, 1839, that she contemplated a foundation in Naas, Catherine was jubilant:

> I cannot attempt to describe the joy your letter afforded me. I fear I am in danger of getting a little jealous. Poor Baggot Street is outdone if you make a foundation already . . . I may retire from business . . . and certainly without making a fortune! Dr. Fitzgerald is delighted . . . The school [Carlow] exceeds all he hoped for: "I knew when I first cast my eye on her [Frances Warde], she was the girl that would do all." He is really gratified, which is a great comfort to me. . . .[4]

Catherine continued, expressing enthusiasm for Frances' coming foundation and attempting to prepare her for the

pain of parting with the Sisters she would have to send to
Naas:

> We hear the Convent in Naas is beautiful . . . the garden laid
> out in neatest style, and Father Doyle will have none but the
> Sisters of Mercy. I long to hear it is determined, and who are to
> go . . . This is a trial you have to pass through. Remember your
> venerated Dr. Nolan's words, "It is my lot." To reflect that it is
> . . . the lot which God has marked out will be sufficient, and in
> the cheerful performance of every part of it our sanctification
> rests. . . . May God continue his blessings to you, and render you
> every day still more deserving of them. . . .

Mother Catherine visited Carlow in August, 1839, when the
two founders completed plans for the Naas foundation. As
soon as she returned to Dublin, she wrote to Frances from
Baggot Street: "While the stage horses were changing at
Naas, we looked in at the sweet little convent from the windows. It is a nice spot. The walks and shrubs so neatly arranged."[5] This lovely "geometric" garden, with its Pugin-
style entrance, may be seen at Naas even today. Obviously,
Father Doyle was preparing for his Sisters. But they were
soon to discover that convent appearances can be deceiving!

On the afternoon of September 23, 1839, Frances Warde
left Carlow for Naas with Sister Josephine Trenor, the future
Superior, who had come with her from Baggot Street as a
novice; Sister Mary Agnes Greene, the first candidate to
enter at Carlow; and Sister Catherine Meagher, the second.
These three were to remain at Naas. Sister Angela Johnson
was to help temporarily and then return to Carlow with
Mother Frances. Dr. Andrew Fitzgerald and Father Maher
accompanied them in Bishop Haly's own carriage.

In a Mercy tradition then being established rapidly, the
first convent prepared for the Sisters was poor indeed. It was

a converted school building, with a small parlor, a reception room, and several bedrooms without windows.[6] The next morning, the Feast of Our Lady of Mercy, Father Doyle celebrated Mass and blessed the convent with the name "St. Mary's." An old chapel nearby was given to the Sisters for a school building, and Frances Warde began its renovation at once.[7] In October she was able to open a small pension school for middle-class girls, with eighteen students attending. By mid-October, Catherine McAuley was writing enthusiastically to Sister Josephine Warde in Cork, urging her to follow her sister's example in Carlow and Naas and open a tuition school for girls at the Mercy Convent in Cork.[8]

Frances Warde remained in Naas until the difficulties of the beginnings were overcome and returned to Carlow in November. Before she left St. Mary's, the Sisters were engaged in teaching both poor and middle class children, in instructing adults, and in caring for the sick poor and prisoners. The convent at Naas, like that at Charleville, had obstacles of many types to overcome in order to develop the Mercy apostolate. The presence of military barracks there, for example, created many problems with teen-age girls. The growth of the Mercy foundation was slow. "Poor Naas," wrote Catherine McAuley to Frances Warde, "is like the little chicken that belongs to the clutch called *creepy-crawly*— I wish it would take a start . . . It has been a little martyrdom to Sister Josephine—so much to be done and so few to help her."[9] Gradually, the Naas foundation did more than "take a start"—it expanded. The Sisters were to take charge of two government hospitals in the area in the seventies. But as early as 1850 they followed their parent house, Carlow, and their founder, Frances Warde, in sending a colony to the United States, to Little Rock, Arkansas. Aside from Dublin and Carlow, the only houses to send Mercy foundations to

America in the nineteenth century were Kinsale, Ennis, and Naas. In 1969 an amalgamation took place between Carlow with its branch houses and the Mercy convents of Naas and Rathangan. Thus Naas returned to its origins.

When Frances Warde returned to Carlow from Naas in November 1839, Catherine McAuley was about to depart from Dublin for the first London foundation in Bermondsey, opened November 21, 1839. The same month, the founder prepared a petition to the Holy See for confirmation of the Rule of the Sisters of Mercy, to be signed by the Superiors of the foundations in Dublin, Tullamore, Charleville, Carlow, Cork, Limerick, Naas, and Bermondsey. The Bishops in whose dioceses the foundations were made also wrote letters supporting the petition. Mother Catherine carried these precious documents with her to England, to be presented in Rome by the Bishop of London, Thomas Griffiths. The previous January, Catherine McAuley had teased Sister Frances about the possibility of her going on the London foundation.[10] Whether or not Mother Catherine was probing the younger woman's response to the hinted proposal, Frances Warde seems not to have indicated any particular desire to go on the Bermondsey mission. In any case, Sister Clare Moore was appointed as first Superior of the London convent. Providence had other plans for Frances.

The Bermondsey Mercy foundation, the first religious house opened in London since the closing of convents and monasteries under Henry VIII, established eight branch houses and eleven foundations throughout England by the turn of the century, as well as convents in Grafton, New South Wales, Australia, and Kingston, Jamaica, British West Indies. The Mercy convent at Bermondsey, erected by the famous convert-architect, Augustus Welby Pugin, was bombed in March, 1945, and the Sisters then moved to Chislehurst, Kent.

During the winter of 1839–40, the energetic Frances Warde found much to demand her administration and counsel at Carlow. The *Annals* of St. Leo's for these months record many events which are subtle revelations of her character. The warmth of her personality illuminates a special entry for Christmas, 1839.[11] The Sisters were awakened for morning Mass by the singing of the traditional "Adeste Fidelis" rather than by the usual calling bell. After breakfast, Mother Frances asked the seven postulants then in the novitiate how they liked their first Christmas in the convent. When they admitted that they felt "a little lonely," she encouraged them cheerfully with the words of Scripture, "Forget thy people and thy father's house, and the King shall be enamored with thy beauty." Then she suggested that each postulant write a Christmas letter to her own family. Ordinarily only necessary or business letters were written by the Sisters because of the high rate of postage. The young women were delighted. To add to their joy, Mother Frances ordered a special plum pudding for Christmas dinner.

Another entry in the Carlow Annals at about the same time is an amusing illustration of the practical administrative skill of Frances Warde. Two Sisters at Carlow received gifts of fifty and thirty pounds. They decided at once that they would like to purchase an organ for the convent chapel. Sister Frances, however, saw the need for plastering the exterior of the convent to secure the gable walls against the weather—and also the need for a sewer! She convinced the Sisters that practical measures are at times more immediately necessary than aesthetic joys.

One of the most revealing accounts in the Carlow *Annals,* however, is a quaint little human interest story which the convent archivist recorded early in 1840.[12] Father James Maher had spoken to Frances Warde about a town character,

Mary Staunton, commonly called "Poll." A true romantic embodiment of "the prostitute with a heart of gold," Poll had been for years "the first in every good work and unfortunately in every evil one too." In the famous year of rebellion, 1798, when the British army slaughtered the native insurgents in Carlow, the military set up two pieces of cannon at the gateway to Carlow College to blow up the building. Poll ran from one to the other mounted missile, standing at the very mouth of each cannon and shouting, "You cowardly dogs, sure you wouldn't shoot a woman!" The soldiers, somehow impressed, drew off the cannon and left the college unharmed. When typhoid fever ravaged Carlow, Poll tenderly nursed the sick and the dying. And during the cholera of 1832, she attended the victims when others in the town would not dare to go near them. For two years before she died, Poll was blind. Frances Warde appreciated her unselfish charity and sent the Sisters from St. Leo's to care for her regularly before her death. Need the ironic commentary be added that not all religious women in Ireland of 1840 would have had the human understanding of Frances Warde in her sympathy for Poll Staunton?

Frances and Catherine McAuley continued to share their private sorrows as well as community problems during the second decade of the existence of the Congregation of Mercy —and both experienced deep personal sorrows in the early 1840's. Mother Catherine's nephew, Robert, who had been estranged from her because of conduct she could not condone, died repentant on January 4, 1840, at the age of twenty-one, while she was in England on the London foundation. The fact that an actual reconciliation had not taken place was most painful to her. As the year progressed, her nephew, James, aged twenty-four, also developed serious symptoms of tuberculosis. He, too, had been estranged from Catherine, but they were happily reunited before his death on May 1, 1841. Add to these sorrows the voluntary exile of her youngest nephew, Willie, who had shipped to Australia and who was thought to be dead for years before the death of Catherine herself. Frances Warde, who had known all three boys since they were children, shared Catherine McAuley's grief during the trying days of 1840.

Personal sorrow came to Frances, too, with the death of her brother, William, who had moved to Wakefield, England, and who died there late in 1839. Frances' first generous impulse was to do all that she could for William's widow and her niece and nephew, Mary and James. In May, 1840, she wrote to Mother Catherine suggesting that she would like to bring young Mary to Carlow. Surprisingly, Catherine did not sanction the project:

. . . I feel very much for your poor sister-in-law, but I would fear very much your taking the child. These engagements never were designed for our state, and whatever is contrary, or not actually belonging to it will ever create agitation of mind . . . God will assist such a good mother; not one of her children will want. The English Catholics are wealthy and truly zealous . . . It is in this country that danger exists.[13]

The fact that Catherine McAuley had taken her own two nieces as well as her cousin's children to Baggot Street makes it difficult to understand why she disapproved of Frances' desire to bring her niece to Carlow. The pension school there would seem to have been ideal for training a young girl close to the wholesome influence of her aunt. In the case of little Mary Warde, Frances did not follow Mother Catherine's advice. She was Superior of the Carlow community in her own right, and she felt that she must follow her own conscience in the decision to be made. In the summer of

1840, she wrote a beautiful letter to her sister-in-law, telling her that she had secured the approval of Bishop Haly for Mary to come to Carlow, and urging her to send the little girl as soon as possible. She had also invited the widow to come to Ireland for a fortnight of needed rest, and now she suggested that perhaps Mrs. Warde might be able to settle more comfortably in Ireland than in England. Finally, she revealed that she was seeking the aid of her faithful cousin, Father Maher, to enroll her "dear little nephew," James, in an Irish boarding school. The warmth of Frances' invitation is unmistakable: her heart embraces all of her brother's family, and she desires to help each member individually. Since Frances Warde's letter to her sister-in-law is her earliest extant writing, it should be quoted in full as an example of the rich warmth of her style. As Sister Austin Carroll, Mercy annalist, frequently pointed out, Mother Frances was a delightful correspondent as well as conversationalist, and those who received letters from her during her amazingly busy days were indeed fortunate. The letter to her sister-in-law[14] in Wakefield, dated July 30, 1840, is as follows:

> Convent of Mercy
> Carlow

My Dear Sister,

   I fear you will be surprised at my not answering sooner your last letter. I would not now answer it but that I fear it looks like a seeming inattention to your sorrows just now. I have been anxiously expecting the arrival of a clergyman here to whom I hope to make a successful appeal in your little James's regard. This gentleman has been expected here since the 20th Inst., and from what I have heard of him I feel assured that if in his power he will do something for my dear little nephew. Our respected Revd. friend, Mr. Maher, will speak about *James* in the most interesting way. All these Irish colleges are indeed so poor that they could not afford to take a boy who has no means. I am sure that he would be admitted into our colleges for a much less sum than into any in England. I cannot tell you how sincerely disappointed I was to learn that you could not come over even for a week or fortnight, which I think would be of great use to you. Yet if your truly good Uncle thought it imprudent, I am satisfied (although reluctantly so). I cannot indeed express how truly grateful I feel to Mr. Lester for the affectionate solicitude he has evinced in your regard during this time of severe trial, and I pray that heaven's choicest blessings may descend upon him who has been a real father to the bereaved widow of my beloved brother.

You did not say what your beloved Uncle allows you. If I knew, I could enquire whether you could live in Ireland comfortably for so much. I regret exceedingly your not being able to send Mary to me immediately on my getting our good Bishop's permission to take her. He may think that the necessity is not so great, so long a time has elapsed since I got his permission, which I was so pressing in soliciting. Do, if possible, send her soon. I will write the day I see and speak with the clergyman about James, for whom as well as for you and each of the dear children I feel the most anxious interest. Sr. Josephine desires her affectionate love, with kindest regards to Mr. and Mrs. Lester. Assure yourself, my dear Sister, of the unalterable affection of your faithful Sister,

Mary Frances Warde

Present my kindest regards to Rev. Mr. Morris.

In haste. Let me hear from you (if possible) by return of Post—even a few lines.

Little Mary Warde did come to Ireland. She entered the Convent of Mercy at Cork under her aunt, Mother Josephine Warde, and received the name Sister Mary Stanislaus in June, 1843, six months before Frances Warde left Carlow for the United States. As a novice, Mary went on an English foundation to Sunderland, returned to Cork after two years, and in 1858 went to Passage West for the opening of a branch house from St. Maries of the Isle.[15] Her mother, Mrs. William Warde, also came to Ireland.[16] The future of little James is now unknown. No mention of him can be found in any records concerning the Warde family. If it was in the power of the two great-hearted people who desired so much to help him—Frances Warde and James Maher—it is certain that the boy received plentiful guidance and loving care.

In January, 1840, Mother Frances presided at a ceremony of profession and of reception for five young women at St. Leo's. One of the guests was Father James Lacy of Wexford. He spoke with Frances Warde about his desire for a Mercy foundation in the town of Wexford, and when he returned home he secured the approval of his pastor, Father Miles Murphy, and of Bishop James Keating of the Diocese of Ferns, to open correspondence with Mother Frances concerning the proposal. Julia Redmond, a postulant at Carlow who had entered from Wexford, also urged that a convent of Mercy be opened in her home town. She herself wished to go on the mission. Indeed, as far back as October, 1838, there had been rumors of a Mercy convent in Wexford, and Catherine McAuley had joked about the beginning of a foundation that she knew nothing about! Now, during the spring of 1840, discussion commenced in earnest on a mission to Wexford.

As in the case of the Naas foundation, Mother Catherine was delighted to have the work of the new convent assumed by Frances Warde. The founder had contracted to send a colony of Mercy Sisters to Galway in May, 1840; a foundation was also to be sent from Baggot Street to Birr in County Offaly in December; and a promise was already made for a second English foundation in Birmingham. Catherine was also involved in negotiations for the reopening of the Kingstown branch house, which had been closed because of misunderstanding and financial conflict. Illness of the Sisters at Bermondsey, moreover, was causing her great concern. Add to all these demands upon her energies her grief over her nephews, and her quiet joy at Frances' offer to lead a mission to Wexford assumes deeper meaning. December was chosen by the two friends as the month for Carlow to send out its second foundation.

In November Catherine McAuley visited Carlow and made plans with Frances Warde for the new convent in Wexford. The Sisters at St. Leo's noted that the founder's health was declining. They felt that she was not taking the necessary care of herself. Perhaps she had a premonition that this visit to her loved Carlow was her last. She remained several days, taking time out to give religious instruction in the pension school and to remark to Mother Frances that "the education of the middle class was of utmost importance."[17] She admired the curriculum set up by Mother Frances. English and French were the core subjects. Music, art, and other courses were added later. A dancing master came regularly to train the young women in social graces. The new House of Mercy for needy young women, opened two months earlier in "Mrs. Nolan's House" on the Carlow grounds, pleased Mother Catherine almost as much as the pension school. The founder's joy in the accomplishments of her protegé, Frances, at Carlow and her confidence in the younger woman's capability for the Wexford mission found enthusiastic expression[18] as soon as she returned to Baggot Street:

My own Dear Sister Mary Frances,
   The very first prayer of praise I offered on my arrival was to return most grateful thanks to God for the sweet and heavenly consolation I received in my visit to Carlow, and to implore His

blessing and gracious protection for those who have been so instrumental in bringing this branch of the Institute to its present flourishing and happy state. My anxiety about your opening in Wexford weakens every hour, and you must not think me tiresome if I repeat again what experience has imprinted on my mind—commence the visitation (of the sick poor) as soon as possible. . . . While we place all our confidence in God, we must act as if all depended on our own exertion . . .

Six days later, Catherine was suggesting jocosely to Frances[19] that she hoped Father Lacy would not furnish the convent at Wexford "in a worldly style." She did not fear such an event, for she had heard rumors that the Wexford convent would be "in the fashion of Naas"—a poor beginning indeed and already typical of new Mercy convents!

Frances Warde and the Sisters she assigned to the new mission left Carlow for Wexford December 7, 1840, so that the foundation date of the new convent would be the feast of the Immaculate Conception. Wexford was then, and still is, one of Ireland's most historic towns because of the famous Wexford rebellion of '98. The fierce and bloody struggle between the Irish patriots and the British army raged for four months in 1798—now with victory for the insurgents at Gorey, Oulart Hill, and Enniscorthy, now with success for the English, Welsh, Scotch, and Hessian troops at Ross, Naas, Carlow, and finally at the memorable encounter of Vinegar Hill. With a promise of pardon, the rebels surrendered their arms at last, only to be almost decimated at the "Butcheries of Wexford" by the British cavalry. To have bled with the Wexford martyrs was forever after a patent of nobility to the people of the town. Among those who died gloriously in Wexford were the antecedents of President John F. Kennedy, who visited the Convent of Mercy in Wexford in the early nineteen-sixties and there declared his favorite ballad to be the well-known "Boys of Wexford":

We are the boys of Wexford, who fought with heart and hand,
To burst in twain the galling chain and free our native land . . .

I want no gold to nerve my arm to do a true man's part—
To free my land I'll gladly give the red drops of my heart . . .

They came into the country, our blood to waste and spill;
But let them weep for Wexford, and think of Oulart Hill. . . .

Among the inducements to Frances Warde and the Carlow Sisters to come to Wexford in 1840 was the certainty of being able to help the children and grandchildren of the men who died in the fruitless strife of '98.

The seaport of Wexford, at the mouth of the Slaney River within sight of St. George's Channel, is one of the most picturesque towns in Ireland. Founded by Viking sea rovers, its narrow, winding streets and colorful waterfront carry the excitement of a medieval town. For Frances Warde, it had personal as well as historical associations. To Wexford County Bishop James Doyle, the famous predecessor of her beloved Bishop Nolan of Kildare and Leighlin traced his origins, and so did the great Irish poet, Thomas Moore, who had dined with her father, John Warde, on the night of his fatal illness at Monasterevan. Indeed, Wexford was famous for far more than bloody strife; the cultural atmosphere of the town was rich. The great satirist Jonathan Swift had found haven there for his fascinating Stella in the eighteenth century. And the Wexford Opera Festival has been one of the finest European cultural events for generations.

Frances Warde was accompanied to Wexford by Sister Teresa Kelly, whom she chose to be the first Superior of the foundation; Sister Gertrude Kinsella, a novice who was a native of County Carlow and a cousin of Cardinal Paul Cullen; and Sister Aloysius Redmond, also a novice, who had urged the opening of a Mercy foundation in her home town. A lay Sister, Brigid Hackett, was also a member of the group. Sister Teresa Kelly came from Castletown, in Frances Warde's native county, Laois. In the Irish annals, much was made of the fact that she became first Superior of Wexford at the age of only twenty-seven. An amusing circumstance arose because of this emphasis. After Mother Teresa Kelly's death, a young woman named Kathleen O'Meara wrote a short biography of Teresa called *One of God's Heroines*. Evidently unaware that Frances Warde was the founder of Wexford, the author stated in anonymous fashion that "two elderly Sisters" from Carlow accompanied Sister Teresa and the pioneers to help them during the first days of their new establishment. The truth was that Frances Warde, the founder, was herself only twenty-nine! In experience, of course, she was far older than Sister Teresa, who had been professed little more than a year. The second "elderly Sister" was Sister Cecilia Maher, who became the Mercy founder in New Zealand in 1850. The faithful Father James Maher also accompanied his cousin and friend, Sister Frances, to Wexford.

The little party left Carlow under a cloudy, threatening sky for Enniscorthy, where they planned to spend the night at the residence of Bishop James Keating and go on to Wexford the next day. As they traveled along in their "covered cars," the rain poured down in torrents. The storm gradually became more and more violent. Just as they reached Enniscorthy, the horses backed one of the coaches into a ditch, where the Sisters were stranded for two hours. They could not seek shelter because of fierce winds and deluged roads.

A driver went on foot to the town to seek a fresh horse. The Sisters arrived late at the Bishop's residence, where they doubly appreciated his hospitality. In later years, Frances Warde used to comment about her "stormy" life—both literally and figuratively. Wexford, she said, was the earliest of her "stormy" foundations.

The next morning, the Sisters set out for their new convent in Wexford. Situated on the Quay, it was no more than "a roof and four walls." The cold was intense, and a curate in the town went out to beg some blankets and kitchen utensils for them. Their tiny kitchen was also their refectory. The dormitory was a kind of shed across the yard from the house. Every morning when the Sisters awakened, the water in their pitchers was frozen. As in the early days at Carlow, they had only a few chairs, which they moved about at need. Their food was frugal. Surprisingly, the new convent produced one lovely brass candlestick, quite out of keeping with its surroundings and preserved for years as a memento of happy hard times. It goes without saying that Frances Warde was intrepid and undismayed. She immediately set about the establishment of the foundation with the unflagging energy she had displayed at Carlow and at Naas.

At first the people of Wexford were not hostile but indifferent to the Mercy Sisters, whom of course they did not know. In fact, the Wexford newspaper announced the arrival of the "Sisters of Charity" in the town, an error which Catherine McAuley hastened to correct.[20] Benefactors appeared, however, in the persons of Richard Devereux, a prosperous merchant, Father James Lacy, who initiated the Sisters' coming to the town, and Daniel O'Connell, the great liberator and friend of all Sisters of Mercy. Thus the little colony was enabled to move after a short time to a much more convenient home on High Street called Clarence House.

This new convent boasted quaintly enclosed grounds through which a section of the old fortifications of the town of Wexford passed. The shaded walls of the ancient ramparts may still be seen there. The street door to the enclosed garden still bears the old brass plaque inscribed "Clarence House." The Georgian style entrance to the house itself must have reminded Frances Warde of the sweep of stone steps and the double doorway to Coolock House, which she had visited so often with Catherine McAuley. Now the Wexford Sisters were able to live in at least comparative comfort. They remained at Clarence House until September 29, 1842, when they moved to Summer Hill to take charge of the Redmond Orphanage there. The convent at Summer Hill was blessed as St. Michael's, still its name today. The orphanage still remains, together with the expanded convent, the House of Mercy, and the industrial school added later. Within two months after their arrival, the Sisters were visiting the sick and prisoners, caring for the poor, and instructing children and adults. It was not long until they were loved in Wexford as in Carlow.

Frances Warde remained in Wexford for more than two months, encouraged by Catherine McAuley to stay as long as possible to consolidate the new establishment.[21] Four candidates entered the convent within a few weeks. Mother McAuley wrote jubilantly to a native Wexford Sister in London, "Most dashing accounts from your old Town. Sister Frances attracting all around her!"[22] In January Mother Frances presided at the profession of the two novices she brought with her from Carlow. Catherine McAuley, who was at the time establishing the new Mercy foundation in Birr, was so pleased with Frances' success in Wexford that she declared, "If we should not get a postulant for a month [in Birr], it would not cast me down."[23] To emphasize her point, she jocosely compared Tullamore unfavorably with Carlow. The Birr foundation was made from Baggot Street, she said, but it should have been made from Tullamore which was only twenty miles distant. When Catherine passed Tullamore on her way to Birr, she declared, she would "give a bitter scolding and three cheers for Carlow"![24] And to the Baggot Street Sisters she wrote from Birr, "We have great accounts from Wexford, our old dear Sister Frances dashing away."[25] Though Catherine McAuley was unaware of it, in praising her friend she was unwittingly antagonizing some of her Sisters against Frances Warde. And the Sisters who developed resentment toward Mother Frances were probably just as unaware of the real reasons for certain attitudes they felt concerning the founder of Naas and of Wexford. There seems to be little doubt that Frances was the most attractive and most capable of the early followers of Catherine McAuley. The seed of envy had been planted in the early days in Baggot Street. Its unfortunate flowering was not to occur until Catherine McAuley's death almost a year following the Wexford foundation.

An outbreak of severe typhus in Wexford in February, 1841, and illness among the Sisters detained Frances in the convent at Clarence House perhaps longer than she intended to remain. By late February, she was back in Carlow, leaving Wexford in the capable hands of Mother Teresa Kelly. The foundation prospered under the direction of this holy woman. The work at Summer Hill expanded and the Sisters opened a national school within a few years. In 1850 Mother Teresa led a foundation to Cappoquin, on the Blackwater, close to the famous Trappist Abbey, Melleray, in County Waterford. Four years later she established a convent at New Ross, where a poor school and a pension school were opened. A branch house was founded at Enniscorthy in 1858 through the patronage of the Earl of Portsmouth. Through Teresa Kelly's exertion, moreover, a chapel for the poor was built beside the convent at Enniscorthy. Also in 1858, a request came to Wexford from Moorsfield, London, under the patronage of Cardinal Nicholas Wiseman, for Sisters to teach in a poor school at Finsbury Square. Children of all religions soon attended this London school taught by the Wexford Sisters. In 1860, a Night Refuge, "the first absolutely unsectarian charity in London," was established in an old stable in the rear of this London Mercy convent. And eight years later, the new and now famous Night Refuge was opened on Crispin Street, London, dedicated to Benedict Joseph Labre, and providing lodging for 200 men and women. While a bed remains, night lodging is still offered on Crispin Street, Providence Row, with no questions asked.

On Christmas Eve, 1866, Mother Teresa Kelly contracted malignant cholera in Enniscorthy while caring for the plague-stricken poor of the town. She died on Christmas Day, blessed by the Abbot of Mount Melleray. In the seventies, the Wexford community sent a foundation to beautiful Carrick-on-Suir, and in 1890 a foreign mission to Yarrawonga, Victoria, Australia. In our own century, branch houses were established in Lake City and De Land, Florida. The expansion of the Wexford community was the most far-reaching of Frances Warde's foundations from Carlow in Ireland.

When Frances returned from Carlow to Wexford, she did not forget her new foundation. Like Catherine McAuley, she continued to guide and counsel the Sisters in the convents she founded. Mother Catherine expressed her approval of Frances Warde's return to Wexford in a letter she addressed to her at the Clarence House convent on Easter Saturday, 1841.[26] This statement is significant, for it defined a policy established by both founders. Catherine was to live only seven months after she wrote it. Frances was to follow its counsel whenever possible until her death in 1884:

My Dearest Sister Mary Frances,

. . . I am rejoiced to hear you are going to Wexford . . . I have found the second visit to a new branch exceedingly useful. Not for what we can say or do, for our experience in religious life has been so short that a good faithful Sister to whom God has imparted grace may be said to know as much of spiritual life as we do; yet it is certainly most useful to give assistance for some time.

. . . It bespeaks a warm interest in the success of the new branch. . . . It was not thought we would succeed in Galway where there were five old established nunneries. Dr. Browne, on our second visit, said from the altar: "It is impossible that the Order of Sisters of Mercy should fail where there is such unity, and where such affectionate interest is maintained as brings them one hundred miles to encourage and aid one another; and this is their established practice—to look after what has been newly commenced. . . .

The very day that Frances Warde left Carlow to open the Wexford foundation, Catherine McAuley had written to the Sisters in Bermondsey, London: "They are beginning to press us now for Westport."[27] She was never to see the Convent of Mercy in Westport, County Mayo. It was to be Frances Warde's third Irish foundation, the first to be established following the death of Catherine McAuley. Before its accomplishment, Frances had to endure the profound grief of the death of the woman dearest to her in all the world.

6

Frances Warde as Spiritual Director

WHEN Frances Warde founded convents in Naas in 1839 and in Wexford in 1840, she had already served a ten-year apprenticeship in the religious life. Catherine McAuley contributed most to her spiritual development. Frances participated also in annual retreats guided by priest-directors. Even before she left Baggot Street, and particularly in Carlow, her personal spirituality tended to reveal individual emphases without in any way negating the characteristic Mercy spirit she had learned from the founder. At St. Leo's, Frances herself was the spiritual director of the young women who presented themselves as candidates for consecrated religious life. Possessing an unusual talent for writing, she soon began to inscribe notebooks with spiritual counsels to be used in the novitiate at Carlow. Quite naturally, the Sisters assigned to the new foundations at Naas and Wexford carried with them copies of these precious instructions as guides for the formation of young religious in the new convents. The Sisters also prepared handwritten copies of the *Rule* of the Sisters of Mercy (that part of it already approved by ecclesiastical authorities) and of the Mercy ceremonials for profession and reception to be taken to Naas and Wexford.

The handwritten spiritual notebooks compiled by early Sisters of Mercy and still extant in many Mercy convents sometimes present problems to today's reader because it was not customary to indicate sources in such manuscripts. It is often difficult to ascertain how much of the material is the work of the Sister whose name may be attached, how much is derived from traditional spiritual books, how much from retreat notes.

Two notebooks preserved at Naas and one at Wexford, however, can definitely be attributed to Frances Warde and, as such, are priceless guides to her spirituality.[1] One manuscript found at Naas is a well-worn book of private prayers used by Frances Warde[2] and inscribed in her own handwriting: "To the use of Sister Mary Frances Warde, Convent of the Sisters of Mercy, Carlow, June 16, 1837." She had used the book for two years at St. Leo's, and it was probably a parting gift to her friend, Sister Josephine Trenor, first Superior at Naas. It contains Frances' private devotions: an Act of Oblation to God the Father, a prayer for spiritual detachment, a prayer to the Virgin Mary, Litanies on the Love of God (in French), a prayer to be offered before a crucifix, a prayer to the Holy Spirit before meditation, a prayer to be offered before the Eucharist, and subjects for consideration during retreat. Characteristic of all these prayers is the fact that they are singularly untainted with the sentimentality common to so many private devotions of the mid-nineteenth century. Also characteristic is a strong feeling of hope which pervades many of the prayers. For example:

O God, into Your hands I commend my spirit. To You I abandon my hopes and fears, my desires and repugnances, my temporal and eternal prospects. To You I commit the wants of my body; to You I commit the more precious interests of my immortal spirit . . . Though my faults are many, my miseries great, my spiritual poverty extreme, my hope in You surpasses all. It is superior to my weakness, greater than my difficulties, stronger than death. Though temptation should assail me, I will hope in You. Though I should sink beneath my weakness, I will hope in You still. Though I should break my resolutions, I will look to You confidently for grace to keep them at last . . . I trust in You for You are my Father, my God . . . I am Your loving child who put my trust in You, and so trusting shall not be confounded.

The hope characteristic of Frances Warde's prayer was a part of her life. Her own profound trust in the Father manifested itself in a profound trust in her Sisters, the children of God. Everyone who lived with her testified that, no matter what a Sister's offense, a simple word of regret brought immediate and complete forgiveness from Frances. Her hope and confidence seemed to be almost limitless. In her later life, as will be seen, she sometimes pushed her trust to limits which others thought to be foolhardy. But she never expressed the slightest regret for confidence that backfired. If her trust brought grace to others, she thanked God; if her hope was betrayed, she did not deplore the risk she had taken for Christ.

Much more significant than Frances Warde's book of private devotions, however, is the manuscript preserved at Naas and inscribed, *Spiritual Maxims of Mary Frances Warde*, Carlow, February 2, 1839, Convent of Mercy. This completely filled notebook contains the instructions that Frances Warde used for the formation of the young Sisters at St. Leo's. Evidently Sister Josephine Trenor took it to Naas as a basis for her instruction of the novices at St. Mary's. A similar manuscript, also with the title *Maxims,* is preserved at the Convent of Mercy in Wexford. The latter notebook, however, contains additional materials in the same handwriting as the Naas book, indicating that their source is also Frances Warde in Carlow. Finally, a notebook is extant in the archives of St. Maries of the Isle, Cork (convent presided over by Sister Josephine Warde for almost fifty years), with the title, *The Guide* or *Advice to a Superior*. The latter repeats in part the materials of the Wexford manuscript brought from Carlow, with different arrangement of materials and certain changes and omissions. Since the Naas and Wexford manuscripts claim Frances Warde as a direct source, the variations between these and the Cork notebook provide an excellent guide to the particular spiritual counsels which she considered to be significant in her spiritual instructions.

Frances Warde introduces her *Spiritual Maxims* by describing the book as a guide for novices in the spiritual life and "a continual incitement to unite all our actions with those of Jesus Christ." Every religious must be willing at all times "to do and suffer all for the glory of God." Frances Warde believed this principle quite simply. Those who knew her personally affirmed that her simple faith made a strong, sometimes unique, impression on all with whom she was associated. Religious Sisters can learn to do all things for God, she believed, by living in God's presence. Thus a consecrated person can become so penetrated with the love of God that it will appear to others that her actions are performed much less by herself than by the Holy Spirit Who lives in her. The activities of Frances Warde's own life were simply a further development of her spiritual sense of God's presence. To do God's will, to help to bring others to Christ, to witness to Christ by serving the poor and the unfortunate, seemed to Frances to be the only significant thing in life worth doing at all. She never could understand how anyone could fail to find joy in consecration to Christ and in the service of God's people. It sometimes puzzled her when a novice decided to leave the convent. How could the young woman not wish to devote herself completely to Christ under vows? On occasion she even encouraged girls to remain in the convent who doubted that they were positively drawn to the religious life, simply because she found it hard to believe that this life might not be attractive to them!

By the same token, she expected every religious to live the

consecrated life in its fullness. Spiritual mediocrity within a religious community was for her patently unreasonable. A girl offered herself as a candidate for the religious life for one reason: to love and serve God and man completely. There could be no compromise in goals. "We are here for only one reason," she used to tell her Sisters. Thus she sometimes acquired a reputation for severity. The reputation was a misnomer. No one was more lenient or more forgiving than Frances. But, once forgiveness was accepted, complete dedication was immediately expected once again. Those Sisters who were lukewarm in purpose probably found it difficult to maintain their spiritual life on the level that Frances Warde considered to be normal. Her singleness of purpose actually possessed a unique quality. She was far from naive in her expectations of human beings; she was sympathetic toward human weakness; yet she clearly accepted as actuality the Biblical "Follow me" that many Christians verbalize much more than realize. This Christian simplicity and single-mindedness were at the very core of the secret of her influence over others. Her friends were baffled over and over again at her power to change the attitudes and goals of Catholics and non-Catholics, both simple and sophisticated, until they finally realized that her power lay in her simple faith. Unconsciously, she sometimes made her associates aware, too, that they themselves could not move mountains as she did because, ultimately, their faith lacked the pure simplicity of hers. This spiritual simplicity, then, was the experiential meaning of her statement of goals in her *Spiritual Maxims*.

After her communication of purpose is clear, Frances Warde presents in the *Maxims* a prayerful consideration of the everyday actions in the ordinary life of a religious, followed by brief meditations. She discusses participation in the celebration of the Eucharist, prayer, meditation, recitation of the Office, spiritual instruction, visitation of the sick, manual work, spiritual reading, confession, retreat, dinner, recreation, rest. Added to these discussions are counsels on charity, patience, poverty, humility, obedience, and devotion to the Virgin Mary. Perhaps the most surprising characteristic of this part of Frances Warde's instructions is that every section is prefaced by an apt quotation from Holy Scripture, a practice not at all common to books of spiritual guidance for religious in Catholic Ireland of 1840. Frances had learned to love Scripture in her childhood days at Bellbrook. The extant copies of the Bible that belonged to her are worn with constant use. In her last days in New Hampshire, when she was almost blind, she used a Scripture text printed in large lettering. All her life long, the actual Word of God was her continual nourishment.

The appropriateness of the verses from the *New Testament* which Frances Warde chose to introduce the various topics on religious life in her *Spiritual Maxims* reveals not only a knowledge of Scripture but deep spiritual insight. Following are examples of her adaptations of themes from Scripture to the everyday actions of religious women. Each of the Scriptural quotations is followed by a brief meditation.[3]

RISING IN THE MORNING

But he was asleep. So they went to him and woke him saying, "Save us, Lord, we are going down!" And he said to them, "Why are you so frightened, you men of little faith?" And with that he stood up and rebuked the winds and the sea; and all was calm again. Matthew, 8:25–27.

RECITING THE OFFICE OF THE VIRGIN MARY

His mother stored up all these things in her heart. Luke, 2:52.

MEDITATION

Now once he was in a certain place praying, and when he had finished one of his disciples said, "Lord, teach us to pray, just as John taught his disciples." He said to them, "Say this when you pray:

> *'Father, may your name be held holy,*
> *your kingdom come;*
> *give us each our daily bread,*
>
> *and forgive us our sins,*
> *for we ourselves forgive each one who is*
> *in debt to us.*
> *And do not put us to the test.'* " Luke, 11:1–4

REFLECTIONS ON PRAYER

And when you pray, do not imitate the hypocrites: they love to say their prayers standing up in the synagogues and at the street corners for people to see them. I tell you solemnly, they have had their reward. But when you pray, *go to your private room and, when you have shut your door, pray* to your Father who is in the secret place, and your Father who sees all that is done in secret will reward you.

In your prayers do not babble as the pagans do, for they think that by using many words they will make themselves heard. Do not be like them; your Father knows what you need before you ask him. Matthew, 6:5–9.

CELEBRATION OF THE EUCHARIST

Then he took some bread, and when he had given thanks, broke it and gave it to them, saying, "This is my body which will be given for you; do this as a memorial of me." Luke, 22:19.

HOLY COMMUNION

Now while he was with them at the table, he took the bread and said the blessing; then he broke it and handed it to them. And their eyes were opened and they recognized him. Luke, 24:30–31.

SPIRITUAL INSTRUCTION

. . . And when he was in the house he asked them, "What were you arguing about on the road?" They said nothing because they had been arguing which of them was the greatest. So he sat down, called the Twelve to him and said, "If anyone wants to be first, he must make himself last of all and servant of all." Mark, 9:33–35.

MANUAL WORK

This is the carpenter, surely, the son of Mary, the brother of James and Joset and Jude and Simon? Mark, 6:3.

LITANY OF THE SAINTS

Among those who went up to worship at the festival were some Greeks. These approached Philip, who came from Bethsaida in Galilee, and put this request to him, "Sir, we should like to see Jesus." Philip went to tell Andrew, and Andrew and Philip together went to tell Jesus. John, 12:20–22.

COMMUNITY MEALS

Jesus said to them, "Come and have breakfast." None of the disciples was bold enough to ask, "Who are you?"; they knew quite well it was the Lord. John, 21:12.

SPIRITUAL READING

And he went into the synagogue on the sabbath day as he usually did. He stood up to read, and they handed him the scroll of the prophet Isaiah. Unrolling the scroll he found the place where it is written:

> *The spirit of the Lord has been given to me,*
> *for he has anointed me.*
> *He has sent me to bring the good news to the poor,*
> *to proclaim liberty to captives*
> *and to the blind new sight,*
> *to set the downtrodden free,*
> *to proclaim the Lord's year of favour.*

He then rolled up the scroll, gave it back to the assistant and sat down. And all eyes in the synagogue were fixed on him. Then he began to speak to them, "This text is being fulfilled today even as you listen." Luke, 4:16–22.

VISITATION OF THE SICK

That very same day, two of them were on their way to a village called Emmaus, seven miles from Jerusalem, and they were talking together about all that had happened. Now as they talked this over, Jesus himself came up and walked by their side. Luke, 24:13–16.

RECREATION

The apostles rejoined Jesus and told him all they had done and taught. Then he said to them, "You must come away to some lonely place all by yourselves and rest for a while"; for there were so many coming and going that the apostles had no time even to eat. Mark, 6:30–33.

CONFESSION

"Then he came to his senses and said, 'How many of my father's paid servants have more food than they want, and here am I dying of hunger! I will leave this place and go to my father and say: Father, I have sinned against heaven and against you. . . .' " Luke, 15: 17–19.

SPIRITUAL RETREAT

"And now I am sending down to you what the Father has promised. Stay in the city then, until you are clothed with the power from on high." Luke, 24:49.

An excellent example of the type of meditation which follows each of the topics and Scripture quotations listed above is that in which Frances Warde considers spiritual reading. It is also a good illustration of her methodology in instructing her novices. First she quotes from St. Luke's Gospel the passage on Christ reading from the Book of Isaiah the prophet in the synagogue on the Sabbath Day. Then she suggests that each Sister should take up the Scripture daily to read it with the same reverence with which Christ approached the reading of the Word of God, His Father. Just as Christ in the synagogue opened the Scripture to the prophecy of Isaiah which was proper to make him known as the true Messiah, so we should expect that, as we open the pages of Scripture, God will pour the special grace we need upon us as we read His Word. When our Savior closed the Book of Isaiah, moreover, he took care to speak to the people assembled of what he had read. So we too should speak to others of what we have read of the Word of God.

Spiritual reading is a means of receiving and responding to the grace of God poured into our souls. Therefore, says Frances Warde, we should not read the Bible or spiritual books for mere curiosity. A good spiritual book is a letter sent from heaven, a faithful counselor, a mirror in which we see things as they are, a tutor to draw us to do the will of God. We should take up Scripture or spiritual reading with a silent prayer to God to derive grace from this action. In reading the lives of the saints, we see the life of the spirit reduced to practice. This is the vocation of the religious—to live the life of the spirit.

Frances Warde actually lived what she counseled on the reading of Scripture and spiritual books. In the early Mercy convents, reading aloud in community was customary. To hear Frances read "was an experience never to be forgotten. How shall one find words to describe the indescribable? There was nothing dramatic, no conscious striving after effect, but you felt that she saw God before her and that all her thoughts were absorbed in Him."[4] Wherever Frances went, her Sisters loved to hear her read or pray aloud. And they watched her living what she read, making her prayer and life one.

Each topic on the ordinary life of the religious, followed by a Scriptural quotation, is developed in the *Maxims* as a brief meditation in the same manner as that on spiritual reading. Considering the private prayers of the Sisters, Frances Warde suggests the Lord's Prayer, to be said slowly, with a pause at each phrase in response to the Holy Spirit, and with awareness that the prayer is Christ's own prayer to the Father. In the section of the *Maxims* which refers to ordinary actions of the day, Frances proposes that religious women should do nothing through either human respect or custom, but do all with the simple intention of union with God's will. She herself seldom spoke to others of what she herself had accomplished or of the hardships and misunderstandings she had endured. She did not regard her achievements as her own; she was simply God's instrument. As an older woman, she never told even her own grandniece, Sister Paul Xavier Warde, who lived with her in the Convent of Mercy in Manchester, New Hampshire, of the amazing attainments of her life as a religious founder. The girl had to learn the truth about her aunt from her Sister associates.[5] All the good works of a consecrated person, Frances believed, were merely extensions of the work of Christ. The intention of a Sister, therefore, must be pure and single; the work is God's, not her own.

The same simplicity of approach animates the section of the *Maxims* concerned with spiritual instructions. Novices should never hesitate to ask questions, Frances writes, since those who make free inquiry develop more rapidly in the spiritual life than those who do not. The more questions are asked, the more doubts are clarified. Timidity is no excuse for failure to propose problems for discussion. In the ordinary course of Providence, God grants spiritual light in answer to sincere questions. Many persons do not enter upon the road of prayer, moreover, because they are not humble enough to make inquiries. "The conscience that proposes questions," says Frances, "becomes enlightened; one question proposed with simplicity is often the source of many instructions." Again, Frances Warde seems to be far ahead of her time. In an age of spiritual lectures passively accepted by novices, she encourages questioning and discussion as specially blessed by the Holy Spirit.

Naturally, the visitation and care of the sick poor are considered in detail by Frances Warde. Christ, who went about healing the sick and comforting the distressed, is the model of the Sister of Mercy. Visiting the sick has a twofold purpose: bodily care and spiritual instruction and inspiration. Since instruction of adults was Frances' great charisma, she places special emphasis on this aspect of the visitation. She also adds a new dimension: not only do the Sisters bring blessings to the sick poor by nursing care and religious instruction; they themselves are enriched immeasurably by spending their time and energy among God's poor. Until the very end of her life, Frances herself practiced the spiritual and corporal works of mercy. In doing so, she never could bear to have anything like "red tape" interfere with her care for the needy. She counseled her Sisters to meet every emergency among the poor promptly. If investigation proved to be advisable, it could come later. It is far better to err on the side of misplaced charity, she said, than to run the risk of refusing help in case of real need.

In the section of the *Maxims* relating to recreation, Frances Warde regards relaxation of body and mind as a source of new vigor of spirit. Recreation contributes to the spirit of community among religious. Through it, Sisters share their faith, joy, and cheer even after exhausting labor, their love for the poor and for one another, their single goal of doing the will of the Father and serving his people. The simple rite of eating dinner in community is sacramental for religious. The food for the meal is a gift of God. The blessing before the meal gives glory to God the Father. The conversation of the community at dinner is itself a prayer. Gratitude for breaking bread together is the special thanks of those who are free to live in God's house. Cleaning the dining room after the meal is symbolic of collecting the fragments which remained after Christ fed the multitude on the Mount.

Love, the source of all goodness, receives central attention in Frances Warde's instructions. At the core of her doctrine on charity is the following: "Never judge anyone, but endeavor to excuse her faults and have a good opinion of all." This principle Frances Warde lived with such simplicity that her friends found amusement in it. She *always* lived presently in the best convent she had ever lived in, with the best Sisters she had ever known, with the best pastor she had ever worked with, with the best students she had ever taug her Sisters were so outstanding in all good qualities that an associate once remarked, "All Mother Frances' geese are swans!"

Probably the most revealing statement in the entire first part of the *Spiritual Maxims* is the last paragraph, which must be quoted to be appreciated:

As these practices are intended only as helps to enable your soul to acquire solid piety and intimate union with God, it is not necessary that they be strictly adhered to, but only insofar as they tend to facilitate the end.

"In short," Frances Warde seems to say, "I have found all these practices helpful to me in seeking to do God's will. Use them yourself only if they lead you to union with God." Was Frances Warde unaware of the radical quality of this statement in an age of strict conformity and even rigidity in religious communities? She did not believe in too close adherence to ordinary counsels or customs when adjustment to new and different circumstances seemed to be required. She advised her Sisters that customs are not iron-bound regulations which can never be relaxed. God asks only adherence to His will manifested in obedience to the Rule of the Sisters of Mercy in spirit and in truth.

The second part of Frances Warde's *Spiritual Maxims* contains sections on the role of the Superior, on the Director of Novices, and on the "Marks of a True Vocation."[6] Special emphases pointed up by Sister Frances help to clarify a concept of her spirituality.

In discussing the role of the Superior, Frances Warde takes issue with those who prefer "a person who, though with little talent, is nevertheless of an open, sincere, and docile disposition because these qualities suffice for saintliness." There is always hope, says Frances, that an intelligent person may acquire virtue and become both a talented leader and a good religious; on the other hand, a person of little intelligence, should she lose her good dispositions, will be both untalented and disedifying. Persons of small capabilities, moreover, are usually much attached to their own judgments, since they cannot rightly understand the reasons for changing them. Persons of talent, however, if they are not blinded by passion or self-interest, can be reasonable and thus cooperate in a mature way in their own spiritual development. A narrow-minded person frequently takes offense because she does not understand the motives of others; an intelligent person less frequently takes offense without cause. In an age when "docility" was highly admired in religious congregations of women, Frances Warde thus spoke out firmly in favor of female initiative. A certain degree of intelligence and freedom of response, she believed, is essential both to understand the meaning of the consecrated life and to practice it with wholesome human independence. The "docile" but unintelligent person may conform to religious customs for a time, but eventually she will bring unhappiness both to herself and to those with whom she lives. Frances Warde formed her conclusions on the necessity for intelligence and breadth of vision, particularly for Superiors, not through modern psychology but through her own common sense.

Even closer in thought to contemporary times is Sister Frances' discussion of the role of the Director of Novices. The core of her doctrine on the spiritual direction of young Sisters startles with its immediacy:

Above all, novices should be taught to be good Christians, for often professed Sisters as well as novices know their Institute and *Constitutions,* but know little of the Gospel of Jesus Christ. It is

very important to have them study the precepts of Jesus Christ . . .
to show them that a true religious ought not to acknowledge any
Master but Jesus Christ, and Him crucified . . . .

This profoundly simple statement obviously has its source
in Frances Warde's life-long Scriptural orientation. She must
have been aware of the many manuscripts and books on religious life in the eighteen-forties that stressed obedience to
the Rule and the perfection of each religious with little reference to the Christian as defined by the Gospel.

The most effective way that a Director of Novices can
teach, Frances continues, is by her example. Her "exterior"
virtues should be "only an image of her interior." False witness is no witness. It is noteworthy that at this point Sister
Frances' Wexford manuscript significantly lacks a long discussion on the virtues which was added in the Cork notebook. The latter urges the Director of Novices to teach her
young charges "to do all their actions with perfection." Sister
Frances is satisfied to state that charity, sincerity, poverty,
obedience, and patience "cannot be immediately acquired,
but the Sisters should be consoled with the thought that if
they tend with all their strength toward these virtues, they
will acquire them." It is essential, moreover, that the Sisters
practice the Christian virtues from "a motive of charity and
not from worldly civility." In all that she recommends, Frances
never deviates from this singleness of purpose as a spiritual
goal.

It is dangerous, she goes on to say, if human weaknesses in
the young are merely suppressed, for "they will spring up
anew after having been suppressed." With surprising psychological insight, Frances suggests that the Director can combat
suppression of weaknesses by using a positive approach.
Rather than condemn faults, she should "praise the virtues

contrary to the weaknesses evident in the young" and "testify much esteem for those who are of an open, sincere disposition." Thus true virtue "will insensibly make an impression on their minds and self-love, ordered by charity, will introduce the Christian virtues into their hearts on pure principles." How very different from the exhortations of the typical mid-nineteenth-century Director of Novices! How could Frances Warde have been so aware of the psychological principle that true charity must have honest love of self as its basis? Once more, her knowledge of human psychology seems to have its source in the grace of God and her own intelligence and common sense.

"To form a religious is no easy task," Frances Warde declares. Therefore she encourages the Director of Novices to boldly "demand" light from God and to confide in Him as she carries out her task. Moreover, she should use every possible means available to her to direct her young Sisters. She should frequently remind them, for example, "that the children of this world are often wiser than the children of light." And who should be more wise, generous, and grateful to God than Sisters consecrated to Him?

The question of penance and confession, given so much legalistic emphasis in the manuals for novices of Frances Warde's time, is treated by her with typical trust and confidence. The examination of conscience, she says, should be reduced to three simple points: "I have performed an action. How have I performed it? Why have I performed it?" Here again is the characteristic singleness of intentionality proper to the religious person. Frances Warde will have none of the sentimental weeping before the crucifix that was typical of some of her contemporaries. Rather, she strove to influence the Director of Novices with strong, sinewy language: "Let her not encourage the novices in a piety made up of tears and sighs, but endeavor to inspire them with the recollection, the activity, and the charity which can transform a weak woman into a heroine." One of Frances' associates once remarked that she had "the mind of a man and the heart of a woman." Rather, she was far ahead of her time in lacking the weakness associated with the pallid concept of the overly-docile woman. She knew that woman could be highly intelligent without being masculine! She was lucid in her definition of "the transformation of a weak woman into a heroine" as a goal of religious life, and she believed that with the grace of God the transformation could be accomplished. She had seen it accomplished in Convents of Mercy. Perhaps the source of her clear spiritual insight into the difference between sentimentality and realistic Christian love and penance can be traced back to her early days in Baggot Street when, at the age of nineteen, she witnessed with amazement such aberrations as the use of the discipline and the hair shirt and the abuse of all-night prayer vigils. She did not condemn the sincere young women who practiced such exaggerated penances, but she learned the never-to-be-forgotten truths that man is neither beast nor angel, that holiness is a life-time search, that God himself is the source of grace.

The next section of the Wexford manuscript of *Spiritual Maxims* treats of the "Marks of a Good Vocation." In a Frances Warde style already familiar, it begins, "The first mark is to have a sincere and efficacious desire of leading a Christian life because a true religious is no other than a true Christian, a true member of Jesus Christ." The false notion that, historically, sometimes separated the religious woman in an artificial manner from other lay Christians is nowhere to be found in Frances Warde's teaching. The religious woman is consecrated to God, but first she is a Christian. The second mark of the good vocation "is that, knowing the facility which the religious life gives (by the practice of the Evangelical

Counsels) to observe the essential duties of Christianity, the candidate desires sincerely to engage in it by her vows." Significantly lacking here is a passage added in the Cork manuscript to the effect that the religious "must be resolved to receive the treatment which will be given for her cure." This suggestion of discipline might have been offensive to Sister Frances. At times she was accused of too much leniency with novices. She was even known to change the time of the profession ceremony to an earlier date in the hope that the grace of God and complete acceptance into the Mercy community might help to solve the difficulties of some of the candidates for vows! The discussion of vocation continues with Frances' comment on a "mark of a vocation" found in some spiritual books which she accepts only with certain limitations. This mark is "a certain fear of the dangers and corruptions of the world." Frances does not regard the latter as an "essential" mark of a religious vocation: "it is sufficient that the candidate love the religious life." The Director should be less concerned about "fear of the corruption of the world" and more concerned about certain requisite qualities for a good religious: simplicity, openness, sincerity, freedom from party spirit, a mind free from caprice or whim, a willingness to change one's judgment. Frances had learned from experience that certain personalities find religious life extremely difficult. She had also learned that many of these same personalities find Christian life outside the convent difficult!

The final section of the *Spiritual Maxims* deals with the government of religious women. A note in the manuscript indicates that some of the principles are taken from the works of Teresa of Avila, the saint whom Frances Warde as a child at Bellbrook had learned to love, and whose name she had adopted in Confirmation. The opening paragraph on government suggests that "to conduct religious women in peace and to promote their advancement in virtue requires a science quite different from that of the most learned and pious men." This theme remains undeveloped in the Wexford manuscript. An addition at this point in the Cork notebook, however, provides another amazing clue to the modernity of Frances Warde's thought. The Cork manuscript expands the above statement by explaining that "there are particularities in the female character which must be entered into, and to which men can never descend"! Far be it from Frances to make such an admission. In honesty, she could not. Yet the condescension of male ecclesiastics and religious of the period in dealing with religious women reveals over and over again that the statement found in the Cork notebook was much more the norm than the approach of Frances Warde.

To govern a soul, she continues, is to govern a world. What then is to be said of the hardships of a Superior who governs many souls and therefore many worlds, in times of both peace and war, when the goal is an eternal kingdom? It is extremely difficult to find even an accomplished Superior. How, then, find a "perfect" one? There is a note of real humor here. No religious except the ignorant, says Frances, desires to be a Superior. Only the singleness of purpose of the religious woman—the will of God—should lead her to accept the office of Superior.

A knowledge of Frances Warde's life almost predicts the qualities she would expect to find in a good Superior. And the Wexford manuscript is not disappointing. Once again, the Cork notebook contains a significant addition to the Wexford text. In both manuscripts, a series of questions and answers concerning the good Superior is found. Here is a quotation from the Cork notebook:

Is the Superior who pardons nothing a good Superior? No. Is she who pardons all good? No. Is she to be esteemed good who wishes to see nothing and make little account of small faults and defects? No. Or one whose manner is always austere? No. Is she a good Superior who appears weak and irresolute? Certainly not.

Frances Warde's Wexford manuscript lacks completely the second and third of the above questions. The omission is important. One of her own "faults" was that she pardoned all, immediately and without reservation. Another of her "faults" was that she often "made little account of small defects." This great-hearted woman was Christ-like in her forgiveness of others. And, like Catherine McAuley, she could not be concerned about peccadilloes. In one of her letters to Frances, Catherine once added a P.S. concerning another Superior: "She wrote to me in the greatest alarm about a most trifling matter. If you and I were to write on such subjects, we would never be done."[7] The good Superior, according to Frances, must not be extreme in her methods of governing; she must possess a "happy blend" of gentleness and determination, of simplicity and wisdom. Discretion is essential so that she will not wound when she should be gentle or be indulgent when she should correct.

Discussing regular customs and observances in religious life, Frances Warde recognizes that the direction of individual Sisters requires diversity of interpretation. At this point, the Cork manuscript includes a section on "penitential exercises" which is lacking in Frances' Wexford notebook. Obviously, Frances thought it best to omit "penitential practices" completely in her instructions for Superiors, leaving the matter totally to individual spiritual direction. Still later in the text, a section on "extraordinary penance" in the Cork book is again completely lacking. Of "extraordinary penance," Frances deliberately had nothing to say. What she does stress is this: in all things, a good Superior must distrust her own judgments. And Frances adds the spiritual principle that Catherine McAuley had learned from Father Edward Armstrong even before the Congregation of Mercy was founded: the good Superior must place all her confidence in God and not in men.

If a Superior fails to govern well, says Frances, "no matter how attentive she may be to make the Sisters observe their rules," there is great reason to fear for the spiritual life of both Superior and Sisters. In practical, everyday affairs, the Superior must be guided by both love and reason. If a Superior does not love her Sisters, but is content with commanding and reproving, "she is not a Superior but a Mistress of Slaves"! Frances Warde's words are strong. If the Superior is loving, on the other hand, "she will help her Sisters to be united, conduct them in peace, promote their advancement in virtue, and render the yoke of religious observances sweet and easy." There follows a discussion of the dangers of the type of reproof which castigates the person rather than her fault, producing greater evil rather than the desired cure. Beyond condemning hazardous punishments, Frances did not write of punishment at all. The role of the Superior is to love, to reason, to serve.

Above all, the Superior must take care that the precepts of Christ and his Church are observed. These are essential; idiosyncratic religious practices that may distract Sisters from their essential Christian commitment are not. Matters of obligation should be enforced; matters merely of counsel should not be enforced. Exhortation should be given in terms of friendship. "It would be cruel for a Superior not to listen to her Sisters," writes Frances, "when they come to excuse themselves." Christ is the model of "the patient listener." He "did not make His disciples perfect at once," but allowed their spiritual development to be gradual. "Should it then be a matter of surprise that we do not instantaneously learn every-thing, although we have come into religion to lead an evan-gelical life?" The *Spiritual Maxims* end abruptly with an unfinished statement that "the souls of the Sisters are trees of which the Superior is the gardener . . ."

The testimony to Frances Warde's spirituality in her *Spiritual Maxims* is so true to the witness she gave in actual life that the likeness between theory and practice is startling. She lived her *Christian* vocation; her love of the World of God in prayer, contemplation, and spiritual reading; her simple and single goal of love and service to God and man; her faith, hope, and forgiveness divinely humorous in their simplicity; her response to both grace and common sense in her roles of Superior and Director of Novices; her sacramental understanding of recreation; her abhorrence of both sickly sentimentality and unwholesome penance or punishment; her service of the poor and the needy in the corporal and spiritual works of mercy; her understanding of religious vocation in its aspect of the human dignity of each individual Sister as a Christian. Frances Warde *was* all these things in her daily life with her Sisters and the people she served. Her openness to reality in a psychological sense, her singleness of purpose in a spiritual sense, somehow closed the gap between belief and actual witness that for many Christians seems unfortu-nately to be average if not normal.

7

Sorrow and Joy: Westport

WHEN Frances Warde returned to Carlow from Wexford in February, 1841, she entered wholeheartedly into the Carlow apostolate while continuing to keep in touch with her new foundations in Naas and Wexford. Six of her Carlow novices were professed in 1841, and several young women also entered and received the religious habit at St. Leo's. Two incidents of this year point up Frances Warde's deep personal concern for each girl who desired to be a candidate for the religious life in Carlow.

As far back as the spring of 1840, a Carlow girl named Anna Maria Maher had presented herself as a postulant at St. Leo's, but for an unstated reason she was not admitted by the ecclesiastical authorities. Perhaps Bishop Francis Haly rejected her application for financial reasons. Unfortunately, Anna Maria's family could not provide the usual dowry. Frances Warde wrote to Catherine McAuley, requesting that the girl be received as a candidate at Baggot Street. Catherine, who was on the Galway foundation at the time, answered that the Dublin house could not then afford to receive the girl, adding that there was "no chance" in Galway either: a high dowry as well as "education in the modern style" was required by Bishop George Browne as well as by Father Peter Daly, the parish priest. Five months later, Frances was still trying to help Anna Maria. She asked that the girl be admitted in Charleville, but the parish priest objected to her insufficient funds. Catherine McAuley, evidently forgetting that she had discouraged possible admission in Galway, now suggested an application there. When the second Galway attempt produced no results, Frances suggested Birr, where Catherine was establishing a new foundation in the early months of 1841. Again, Catherine wrote that there was "no chance" in Birr. The big problem was insufficient dowry. It is significant that Frances Warde continued unceasingly for ten months to try to place "little Miss Maher" in a Mercy convent. The incident also points up the power of the clergy in the ordinary transactions of Mercy convents in the eighteen-forties. Even a cursory reading of Catherine McAuley's letters reveals that ecclesiastics and spiritual directors dictated not only on questions of admission but even in such personal matters as health and travel. The rejected young woman, Anna Maria Maher, was finally accepted in 1845 in the convent at Kinsale, founded from Limerick. As Mother Teresa Maher, she founded in 1858 the large and successful Congregation of Mercy in Cincinnati, Ohio!

Frances Warde was not always so wise in her judgments of character as she was in the case of Anna Maria Maher. Rather, she simply did not judge. Her concern for the individual person was just as intense in the case of candidates who did not possess the remarkable qualities later revealed by Teresa Maher. In November, 1840, Frances received into the Carlow community a young woman named Ellen Lanigan. She had entered the Baggot Street convent, had left there and joined the Presentation Sisters in Kilkenny, had left there and joined the Presentation convent in Castlebar, had left there and presented herself at Carlow! Mother Frances, the Carlow *Annals* state, "gave her another chance." In 1841, Ellen Lanigan left St. Leo's Convent, too, as might have been predicted. Frances Warde was commended for her insight in

121

the case of Anna Maria Maher; she was criticized for her judgment of Ellen Lanigan and others to whom she appeared to be overly indulgent in a rather rigid era in which a "second chance" in the convent was not common. But Frances had no regrets for her seemingly unsuccessful attempts to help others. In America, too, she was to give "another chance" to many girls, some of whom were less than grateful for her kindness.

In April, 1841, Frances visited Wexford to help and advise the young Sisters in her new foundation, and in May she went back to Naas to offer encouragement to the Sisters at the new convent of St. Mary's. Catherine McAuley wrote in June that "all I hear from chance visitors to Wexford is delightful." And in early fall she spoke of glowing accounts she had received concerning Naas. Like the founder, Frances continued to offer counsel and assistance to her own new foundations. And her efforts seemed to be blessed.

The early months of 1841 would have been thus an especially happy time for Frances Warde had it not been that the health of her loved Catherine McAuley was gradually declining. From the time of Catherine's last visit to Carlow in November, 1840, Frances was daily more concerned about her friend. Catherine's letters to her between March and September, 1841, almost always have some reference to Frances' anxiety about the health of the founder, who attempts to treat her illness lightly so as not to disquiet the younger woman. The cloud of Catherine's illness is always just beyond the surface of their correspondence. Frances urges Catherine to come to Carlow to rest, and the older woman, though desiring to see her friend and St. Leo's again, protests that the demanding work of the apostolate forbids her to do so: "Think of all that must be left behind," she writes. "It is quite impossible for anyone in my situation to think of pleasing herself."[1] Besides her concern for the Baggot Street convent, the two branch houses in Kingstown and Booterstown, and her eight other foundations, Catherine McAuley was planning her tenth and last foundation to Birmingham, England. The prospect was almost more than she could physically bear. And Frances Warde suffered with her friend.

In the summer of 1841 Frances entertained at Carlow two visitors who meant much to her. The first was the great Irish Liberator, Daniel O'Connell, her old friend of her early Dublin days. He came to Carlow to solicit votes of freeholders for his younger son John in a county election.[2] He remained for a month, giving political speeches to crowded audiences from a raised platform in front of the town hotel. After speaking, he went to St. Leo's to pray, to participate in the celebration of the Eucharist, to talk with his friends. Frances was happy to entertain the man who had carved for the orphans at Baggot Street on Christmas Day in 1828, even before the official foundation of the Congregation of Mercy.

An even more welcome guest was Sister Clare Moore, who had been professed among the first Sisters in Dublin with Frances Warde in 1833. Clare Moore had been appointed first Superior on the London foundation to Bermondsey in 1839, with the stipulation that she should return to Cork after the new convent was well established. Bishop Thomas Griffiths of London had hesitated to release her, but now finally she had returned to Ireland to resume her place as Superior in Cork. Before going back to her own convent, she seized the opportunity to visit her friend Frances in Carlow. Sarah Warde, Sister Josephine, was acting as Superior in Cork in Clare Moore's absence, so that the latter could now take home with her a personal report from Frances to her sister. Traveling expenses in the eighteen-forties precluded visiting among the Mercy Sisters except in cases of necessity, and there is no record of a personal visit of Frances and Sarah

Warde between the time of their separation in 1837 and
Clare Moore's visit to Carlow in 1841. Catherine McAuley,
as founder, traveled extensively among the Mercy convents
and was Frances' only personal contact with her sister. Perhaps no two Sisters—with the possible exception of Sister
Elizabeth Moore, Superior in Limerick—knew more about
the joys and sorrows of the young Congregation in 1841 than
Frances Warde and Clare Moore. They were much more in
the main stream of the work of the Sisters of Mercy than
their early companions at Baggot Street. With the exception
of Frances Warde, probably none of "the first seven" Sisters
of Mercy (four of whom were now professed Sisters) was so
capable or so attractive as Clare Moore. Her London convent
in Bermondsey was to be the most prolific of all the English
foundations, and she herself was to lead the first Sisters of
Mercy to nursing service in the Crimean War in 1854.
Florence Nightingale was to write to her on her return to
London: "You were far above me in fitness for the general
superintendency in worldly talent of administration, and
far more in the spiritual qualities which God values in a
Superior; my being placed over you was my misfortune, not
my fault. What you have done for the work no one can ever
say." But the greatest of their accomplishments were still in
the future for both Frances Warde and Clare Moore in
1841. Meeting in Carlow, the two friends had much to communicate to each other. Only the absence of Catherine Mc-
Auley made their visit less than perfect.

Clare Moore did not know then that she would return to
London before the year was out. She told Frances, however,
of the problematic situation at Holy Trinity Convent in
London which she had just left. The British woman ap-
pointed Superior on the departure of Clare Moore from
Bermondsey was Sister Clare Agnew, the former popular

novelist and author of *Geraldine,* who soon proved to be a deluded personality of a destructive type. Scarcely had Clare Moore left London, when Clare Agnew announced that the Sisters could choose between a life of action and a life of contemplation, demanded the establishment of Perpetual Adoration in the convent based on a personal private revelation, and introduced eccentric customs into the life of the Sisters— such as the total community's facing the wall at meals and the construction of special kneelers in the chapel to make all the Sisters appear to be of equal height! Two Sisters at once left the convent in anger, and Miss Agnew was soon "inspired" to join the Trappistines in Dorsetshire. After several months she left LaTrappe and applied for admission to Baggot Street, where she was rejected. She then attempted to secure a foundation from Bermondsey of which she would be Superior, but Clare Moore, then back in London, blocked her plan. Next, Clare Agnew set out for Rome to attempt to secure changes in the *Rule* of the Sisters of Mercy. Failing this, she founded a new community (with the support of Cardinal Charles Acton) which quickly disintegrated. Returning to London, she founded another community which soon disbanded. After this, she applied for admission to St. Edward's Convent, London, founded from Baggot Street in 1844. Rejected again, she appealed to Cardinal Nicholas Wiseman, who unsuccessfully petitioned the London house to accept her. She died writing novels in Rome.

Clare Moore's return to London on the defection of Clare Agnew was personally significant for Frances Warde because it meant that Josephine Warde, her sister, would serve as Superior in Cork nearly the whole of the remaining forty-two years of her life. St. Maries of the Isle in Cork was to become very dear to Frances Warde because of her sister. Josephine Warde was to send Irish girls as postulants to Frances' foundations in the United States for a period of almost thirty years. She even projected a plan to aid her sister's American convents which she did not live to realize: the establishment of a College for Women, somewhat on the order of the Missionary College, All Hallows, Dublin, where young ladies might be aducated and trained for convents in the United States. Surely the idea was initiated by the more creative Frances! Josephine Warde was also to establish foundations or branch houses in Templemore, Bantry, Kinsale, Queenstown (Cobh), Passage West, Cahir, Tipperary, and Sunderland in Yorkshire. Moreover, she was to send to Frances in Pittsburgh and in New England some of the most talented Sisters of Mercy of the late nineteenth and early twentieth centuries in America.

Among them was the historian of the Congregation, Sister Teresa Austin Carroll, author of the four-volume *Annals of the Sisters of Mercy* and of the first comprehensive biography of Catherine McAuley. Sister Teresa Austin went from Cork to Providence, Rhode Island; Hartford, Connecticut; Rochester and Buffalo, New York; Manchester, New Hampshire; Omaha; St. Louis; New Orleans and Mobile; and Belize, Honduras. She settled in New Orleans, from which she established branch houses throughout Mississippi, Alabama, Louisiana, and Florida. When she died in Mobile in 1909, she had in her possession "hundreds of letters of Mother Warde which will, no doubt, yet illustrate the life of that remarkable woman . . . These letters, covering the period from her early days in Baggot Street to her death, nearly sixty years later, abound in . . . zeal, friendship, and generosity, and unlike the letters of other remarkable personages . . . are highly favorable to the character of the writer."[3] All of these letters were burned after the death of Teresa Austin Carroll, together with her total collection of manuscripts. Whether deliberate or inadvertent,[4] the loss of these letters was probably the greatest single loss to the history of the Sisters of Mercy in the United States. For the biographer of Frances Warde, the loss is uniquely irreparable. Sister Austin Carroll was only one of Josephine Warde's gifts to the Sisters of Mercy in the United States. And all of her gifts were given through her sister, Frances. The two Warde sisters became a kind of two-woman, two-continent collaboration in the expansion of the Sisters of Mercy in the West between 1843 and 1880.

Following close upon Mother Clare Moore's visit to Carlow in June, 1841, came the magnificent news that the *Rule* of the Congregation of the Sisters of Mercy was approved by the Holy See. The approval of the petition for confirmation of the *Rule*, drawn up by Catherine McAuley late in 1839, was unbelievably swift—for Rome. The question had been presented at the meeting of the Sacred Congregation of Propaganda Fide in Rome in July, 1840. The vote of all the Cardinals had been affirmative, while certain corrections to the *Rule* offered by the ecclesiastical consultor were accepted.[5] When no word of action by the Sacred Congregation had been received in Ireland by October, 1840, Catherine McAuley addressed a letter to the Sacred Congregation, stating that, although approval had been more or less promised, no decree of confirmation had yet been forthcoming.[6] The Decree was finally signed in Rome by Giacomo Filippo Fransoni, Cardinal Prefect, Propaganda Fide, July 5, 1841.[7] Paul Cullen, then Rector of the Irish College in Rome, at once communicated the information to his uncle, James Maher, in Carlow, who personally brought the gladsome news to Frances Warde at St. Leo's. She was thus the first Sister of Mercy to know of the confirmation of the *Holy Rule,* and she sent the joyful tidings at once to Catherine McAuley in Dublin. Archbishop Daniel Murray of Dublin received the official decree from Rome in August, 1841.

Meanwhile, plans for the Birmingham foundations to be

made in August were progressing. Bishop Thomas Walsh, Vicar Apostolic of the Midlands, had sent four English girls to Baggot Street for their novitiate in preparation for the second English Convent of Mercy. Catherine McAuley was to accompany them to the new convent in Handsworth, Birmingham, as the first congregation of active religious women in the British Midlands. The convent was built and endowed by John Hardman, father of Sister Juliana Hardman, its first Superior, and by John, Earl of Shrewsbury; it was designed by the famous architect, Pugin. The new community was indeed wealthier than any of its sister communities in Ireland.

Five months before the Sisters left Dublin for Birmingham, a strange note entered the correspondence of Catherine McAuley and Frances Warde. The fact that only Catherine's side of the correspondence is extant makes interpretation of the situation difficult. In March, 1841, Catherine wrote to her friend that she had been told two or three times that Frances was to make a foundation in Liverpool, and that plans must not be completed or Catherine would surely be told of them. Two months later, in another letter to Frances, Catherine expressed the hope that the younger woman was not ill: evidently Frances had not written so frequently as usual. The founder added that she was grieved that Father Maher had been in Dublin but had not called at Baggot Street as was his custom. The mysterious references are finally explained in July, 1841.

Dr. Thomas Youens, Vicar General of Lancashire, was a very good friend of Father Maher. In July, 1841, he became a beneficiary of a will which granted him about 15,000 pounds. He proposed to use part of the money to build a convent for Sisters of Mercy in Liverpool. As the will was contested for a time, his offer to finance the new foundation could not be made known until the validity of the will was certified.[8] He evidently wished the foundation at Liverpool to be undertaken by James Maher and the Carlow Sisters of Mercy. If Father Maher confided in Frances Warde concerning the uncertain situation, he probably obliged her to secrecy until the project could be made public. Matters were complicated further by the desire of Bishop George Hilary Brown of Liverpool for a foundation of Sisters of Mercy from Dublin. Bishop Brown was well informed by Bishop Thomas Griffiths of London of Sister Clare Agnew's peculiar innovations at the Bermondsey convent. He wrongly attributed the threatened disaster in the London convent to the fact that the Sisters were trained in Cork, and not in Dublin, the parent house. Therefore, he was to refuse a foundation from any convent except Baggot Street, and whatever plans Dr. Youens and Father Maher may have projected were doomed to failure. To complicate matters further, a young lady from Liverpool named Fanny Gibson, later a Superior of the Liverpool foundation sent from Dublin in 1843, was a postulant at Baggot Street in the summer of 1841 and eager to go on a foundation to her home city. Her family were friends of both Bishop Brown and Dr. Youens, and she would gladly have joined a group of Sisters from either Dublin or Carlow to go to Liverpool.

As soon as Dr. Youens knew that he could offer a convent to the Sisters of Mercy, he went directly to Ireland with his plans. The very day he arrived in Dublin, Fanny Gibson received a letter from Bishop Brown expressing his desire for a Liverpool foundation from Dublin. Between Scylla and Charybdis, poor Catherine McAuley wrote at once to Frances Warde, approving of a foundation from Carlow to Liverpool. Perhaps Bishop Brown might change his mind if she emphasized the excellent qualities of the Carlow Sisters.

Catherine suggested that she and Frances might sail together to England, she with the Sisters for Birmingham, Frances with a colony for Liverpool. If Catherine was hurt by the secrecy of the plans of Dr. Youens and Father Maher, she did not indicate it in her letter to Frances. Indeed, she had no Sisters to offer for a second foundation in the summer of 1841, and she would have been happy—as in the cases of Naas and Wexford—to place the burden of the Liverpool house upon Carlow. She was also contemplating a foundation in remote St. John's, Newfoundland, which she hoped would be her next venture after Birmingham. (The Newfoundland convent, founded after her death in 1842, was to be the first Convent of Mercy on the North American continent.) In two subsequent letters to Frances Warde, Catherine therefore spoke warmly of the possibility of the two friends' establishing foundations in Birmingham and Liverpool together. But a communication from Bishop Brown in early August suppressed all such plans. He would have Sisters only from Dublin; the Liverpool foundation would have to be delayed. Providence intended Frances Warde for the United States, not for Liverpool.

The secrecy which surrounded the Liverpool incident is the only evidence of any relationship lacking complete openness between Catherine McAuley and Frances Warde. The warmth of Catherine's letters both before and after Bishop Brown's decision indicates that there was no break whatever in the correspondence of the two women, nor was there ill will. While Frances could not antagonize Father Maher by violating any confidence he may have offered her concerning the plans of himself and Dr. Youens, she was able to explain the entire situation later to Catherine. Father Maher had become a close friend of his cousin Frances in the four years since the saintly Bishop Nolan, on his deathbed, had placed

Maher's hand upon Frances' head and named him the protector of the Carlow Sisters. The situation was therefore a delicate one. The Carlow and the Westport Annals testify to Maher's faithful friendship for Frances Warde long after the death of Catherine McAuley. Maher's failure to visit Baggot Street while the Liverpool plans were afoot seems to have been intentional. Perhaps he feared that if Catherine knew of plans for a foundation from Carlow, she might prevent their execution by revealing them prematurely to Bishop Brown or to Archbishop Murray of Dublin. Catherine was characteristically docile to her ecclesiastical Superiors. James Maher, who twice refused a bishopric, had a mind of his own. He remained a friend and a support to the Carlow Sisters until his death on Holy Thursday, 1874. The Sisters of St. Leo's nursed him for two years before he died.

A note in the Carlow Convent Annals at the time of his death throws some light, perhaps, on his relationship to Catherine McAuley. Almost every biography of Catherine refers to the fact that James Maher, in his last illness, remarked to the Sisters at different times, "Your foundress was a saint." The full statement in the Annals is as follows: "Your foundress was a saint, but not a learned one."[9] If James Maher formed a patriotic triumvirate with Daniel O'Connell and the famous Bishop James Doyle of Kildare and Leighlin, he was likewise a learned man. His biography and letters, edited by his nephew, Archbishop Patrick Francis Moran of Sydney, are evidence of his scholarship. Perhaps he admired the sanctity of Catherine McAuley more than her intellectual acumen. Like Bishop Edward Nolan, he was one of a number of surprisingly holy and learned men with whom Frances Warde established ties of friendship. Catherine McAuley, too, from her early days at Coolock, was the friend of some of the most learned ecclesiastics in Dublin and Carlow.

Frances was now thirty-one. She was revealing in her everyday life a maturing of the spirit of independence that had characterized her even as a very young girl. Her personality was unfolding as more complex in its lights and shadows, overtones and undertones, than Catherine McAuley's. Catherine was almost transparent in her relations with others; Frances was translucent. Catherine was universally loved, easy to understand, open in an almost childlike way. It would never have occurred to her to question the right of ecclesiastical authority to govern the Sisters. Frances, on the other hand, possessed a thoroughly feminine aggressiveness that made her aware of her rights with regard to Church authority. Often in the future she would have to defer to ecclesiastical authority, but she was sure in her own judgments as to whether the deference was justified or merely necessary. Unlike Catherine, she was not naturally docile. Unlike Catherine, she was capable of taking the offensive when she judged it to be warranted. She therefore antagonized others at times. She was aware of her human dignity as a woman and a religious. Because of the force of her personality, she was deeply loved, but she was sometimes disliked too, particularly by those who prized or profited from docility in women. In short, she was a twentieth-century woman living in the nineteenth. If she were living in the present century, she would perhaps find herself in her natural milieu. Because she was loving and sensitive as well as strong willed, she suffered. As her personality gradually matured, she tended more and more to reveal her deepest self only to those who could understand her on her own level of response. This characteristic was certainly not motivated by smugness. She learned from experience that to spread the kingdom of God with the singleness of purpose that was always hers, she must sometimes be silent. In her thirties she was not always so universally open or spontaneously irrepressible as she was at sixteen. The fact that she often reserved the richest of her thoughts and judgments for those who could really understand as well as trust her, sometimes made her appear to the more simple minded as a puzzling—and perhaps an enigmatic—woman. The person who is born before her time is always a riddle to the more pedestrian personality.

The trip to England and the exhausting work of the Birmingham foundation were almost more than Catherine McAuley was physically capable of enduring. Even before she returned to Dublin in September, 1841, she knew that her death was near. She spent the month of October at Baggot Street putting both spiritual and temporal matters in order. The tuberculosis which had caused the deaths of so many members of her family was gaining rapid headway in her body. In her shorter and less frequent letters to the Sisters in the various Mercy foundations, she spoke of her illness but did not express what she knew—that she was close to death. Early in October, Frances Warde invited Catherine to come to Carlow to rest. She answered that the journey of eighty miles would be too much for her, and she closed her letter with a seemingly innocent statement which unconsciously revealed the impending end of her closest friendship: "You will not forget your ever affectionate, M. C. McAuley." Catherine's last extant personal letter was written to Frances Warde on October 12, 1841:

My Dear Sister M. Frances,
  The Very Rev. Dr. Kirby, Vice-President of the Irish College, Rome, called here the day before he sailed. I mentioned to him some evident mistakes in the copy of our Rule. He told me to select them and forward the document to him, with Dr. Murray's signature, and said he would, without any more trouble, obtain permission to rectify the evident mistakes.
  I have felt the last bad change in the weather very much.

Father O'H. brought your affectionate note. I humbly hope I am done with travelling for some time. If ever any poor sinner got a surfeit of it I have.

I forgot to add what will occur to yourself, that I was cautioned not to speak of any mistakes in the Rule.

God almighty bless you.

> Your ever affectionate,
> M. C. McAuley

As Frances Warde had been Catherine's closest and most capable coworker, now before her death she evidently wished to give to Frances the responsibility for completing the final work on the *Holy Rule*. The closing of the letter is a benediction that only she knew to be Frances' best loved blessing: "God almighty bless you." This last letter is surrounded by puzzling circumstances which had their origin, as will be seen, in the early days at Baggot Street.

As Catherine's health grew rapidly worse in late October and early November, Frances was still unaware that her death was so near. Sister di Pazzi Delaney, Assistant Superior at Baggot Street, sent to Limerick for Sister Elizabeth Moore, Superior at St. Mary's Convent there, to come to Dublin to be with the dying founder. Although Catherine welcomed her cordially, she was evidently surprised that Frances Warde was not present. Sister di Pazzi was unfortunately of a jealous temperament,[10] and she had resented not only Catherine's necessary trips to the various foundations, but especially the journeys of any of the Sisters to Carlow. Catherine's biographer records that the founder asked the infirmarian who it was that sent for Sister Elizabeth. When the answer was that Sister di Pazzi had done so, Catherine asked, "Sister, have they sent for my child?" Her "child" was, of course, Frances Warde. Even after this request, Frances was not called to Catherine's bedside.[11] The Carlow Convent *Annals* have a stark and simple entry for November 12, 1841, the day following Catherine's death:

The whole community were in deep affliction, those Sisters especially who had the happiness of seeing and conversing with her when she visited St. Leo's, but for dear Rev. Mother, who shared her joys and sorrows in the early days of the Institute . . . the trial was a very bitter one indeed.

The special "bitterness" of Frances Warde's sorrow lay in the loss of a final farewell to the saintly woman whom she loved best on earth. The sorrow of parting with Catherine McAuley was the deepest sorrow of her whole life. John Henry Newman, Nicholas Wiseman, Paul Cullen, Orestes Brownson, Daniel O'Connell, and all the Bishops of Ireland might pay tribute to the sanctity of Catherine in sounding rhetoric, and all the Sisters of Mercy in the world might lovingly lament her loss, but the deepest agony of grief for her was reserved to Frances Warde.

After Catherine's death, Frances gathered together many of the founder's letters to her. She gave them to Josephine Warde, who edited them as she copied them in a notebook. Then she took the originals to America with her and distributed them at her foundations as precious relics. Many she kept until her death, and some were lost. In the present century, many have been collected and published. In editing the letters for the notebook still extant in Cork, Sarah Warde rearranged the materials of some of the originals, in some cases putting parts of two letters together as one. The last extant letter of Catherine, already quoted above, appears in a slightly altered form in the Cork notebook. Added to it is a brief statement, not in the original letter, but probably borrowed from a letter sent to Frances at about the same time. The addition is as follows:

I received your welcome letter. How grateful I ought to be for all your anxiety. *We shall meet again, please God, but not at present.* I am sorry to hear poor Dr. Fitzgerald is suffering so much. Tell him I will pray with all the fervor I can for his comfort. I wish Rev. Mr. Maher would bring you to see me.

The fact that Catherine McAuley had expressed a desire to see her loved friend for a last time both in her letter and to those at her bedside added a special poignancy to Frances Warde's sorrow.

Catherine's excellent biographer, Roland Burke Savage, expressed an astute judgment in commenting on the fact that she "appears to have destroyed all her personal papers."[12] He added:

Much as we may admire the humility that prompted her to blot out all traces of her personal life, a biographer may be permitted to express regret at this holocaust. Though hundreds of Catherine's own letters were lovingly preserved by their recipients, only a very few of the countless letters she herself must have received have survived destruction.[13]

A new light on the loss of these letters, so significant to the biographer of Frances Warde, is given by Sister Paul Xavier Warde, grandniece of Frances, who implies that the holocaust may have been the work of persons at Baggot Street other than Catherine McAuley herself. Writing in 1941 in answer to a question concerning the letters of her aunt, Sister Paul Xavier, who had the unique advantage of knowing Frances personally, says:

I understand perfectly why none of her letters to our beloved Foundress were preserved, and so will you if you read between the lines of Mother McAuley's letters to her—also if you remember that they did not send for her when Mother McAuley was dying.[14]

In 1949, Sister Paul Xavier addressed another correspondent who had inquired about the sources of the *Annals* written by Mother Teresa Austin Carroll:

She got most of her information about the beginnings of the Order from Mother Warde herself. There are a few things which she seems to have misunderstood about Mother Warde's experiences in the early days. I know she visited Baggot Street and talked with some of those who seemed to resent the devoted friendship between the Holy Foundress and my aunt. Such is life, you know, Sister! If you remember, when they sent for the various Superiors to come to Mother McAuley's death bed, they did not send to Carlow.[15]

It would seem certain, then, that Frances Warde suffered from the actions of certain persons at Baggot Street whose unconscious motivations were screened by a conscious righteousness based on the "virtue" of mortification of wholesome friendship.

During the spring following the death of Catherine McAuley, an incident occurred which revealed the growing independence of Frances Warde as a Superior. Up until then, Frances had served as Superior, Bursar, and Director of Novices at St. Leo's. Now she felt that the community was sufficiently large to have a Sister appointed to direct the novices, and she named Sister Cecilia Maher, later the founder of the Mercy Congregation in New Zealand, to this post. Sister Cecilia was ideal for the position. Speaking of her years later, Frances could say, "She was the sweet saint of our home at Carlow. How often I wished I could imitate her." Bishop Francis Haly, hearing of the appointment, "reminded Rev. Mother that she should have conferred with him on the matter, as he only could make the appointment."[16] Precisely here lay the seed of future difficulties that Frances Warde was to encounter with certain ecclesiastics. To what degree did the clergy have the right to interfere in the internal government of a Congregation of Mercy? To some Bishops, the right seemed to be almost limitless. The Carlow annalist defends Frances Warde, stating that "her fault was one of ignorance . . . Therefore, she very easily obtained Bishop Haly's forgiveness." It is interesting to note, however, that—unlike Bishop Edward Nolan and Father James Maher—Bishop Haly was not fond of Frances Warde.[17] His disapproving attitude toward her was rather common knowledge in Carlow. He would have preferred a more docile Superior at St. Leo's!

Her Sisters, however, were devoted to Frances. An entry in the Carlow *Annals* not long after Bishop Haly's reprimand describes the Sunday recreations at St. Leo's when all would gather around Frances as she told of the early history of the Congregation and the first days in Carlow:

Of a very cheerful disposition herself, Rev. Mother encouraged the Sisters to be so too; she would laugh heartily at little witticisms, and invariably gave recreation . . . a most gracious approval. Like our Holy Foundress, she was particularly fond of music, and often called on the Sisters to contribute to the general amusement by their vocal and instrumental attainments. During her first years of government, her innate goodness of heart led her to outstep the limits of her authority: thus if a Sister looked sad or dejected, she would endeavor to console her by promising to receive or profess her (as the case might be) before the time prescribed by Rule, hoping that . . . the calm of retreat would work wonders. No matter how grave the fault, or how often committed, the transgressor was certain of a prompt and full pardon if she were only sincerely sorry and willing to repair her shortcomings.[18]

Frances Warde's grief over the death of Catherine Mc-Auley was mitigated providentially by a call to a new apostolate in May, 1842, which at once demanded all her energies. As far back as December 7, 1840—the day before the beginning of the Wexford foundation—Catherine McAuley had remarked that a request for a Mercy convent had been received from Westport, County Mayo, in the far West of Ireland. And not long before her death, she had written an encouraging note to Dean Bernard Burke of St. Mary's, Westport. In May, 1842, Dean Burke appeared at the Baggot Street Convent, now St. Catherine's, to press his claim for the first Mercy foundation in the Diocese of Tuam. Mother di Pazzi Delaney referred him to Carlow where, she said, he would find "heads" as well as "hands." (Catherine Mc-Auley had once remarked facetiously at St. Leo's, to which she was partial, "there are hands and feet in Baggot Street, but *heads* in Carlow."[19]) The Westport *Annals* add that Carlow provided not only hands and heads, but hearts as well for Mayo. If the time that Frances Warde spent at Westport is a criterion, this foundation was very dear to her.

No wonder she loved it. The Mercy Convent of Mount St. Mary's is at the foot of Croagh Patrick, Ireland's holy mountain where, according to legend, St. Patrick prayed and fasted forty days and nights that the Irish people might remain true to the faith that he brought them. Here Patrick did violence to the Kingdom of Heaven and bore it away. The event seized the imagination of the Irish people. The cone-shaped mountain, called the Reek, became a place of pilgrimage, venerated for centuries as the high altar of Ireland. Unchanged and unchangeable, the soaring summit became a symbol of triumph. The Norsemen swept the coasts of Ireland in the ninth century and ravaged its churches and abbeys for 200 years. The British armies drove the Irish people into the mountains to celebrate the Eucharist in the sixteenth century and persecuted them for their faith for 300 years. But Christianity remained and Croagh Patrick remained. It is the one spot where the Irish feel that they can stand where Patrick stood and look upon the earth through his eyes. Here beneath the skies, they worship as their fathers did for a hundred generations.

William Makepeace Thackeray toured Ireland at the age of thirty-one during the very months that Frances Warde was establishing the Westport foundation. He describes what he saw (and what Frances saw too) as he approached Westport at sunset:

And presently I caught sight of the most beautiful view, I think, I ever saw in the world, to enjoy which I would travel a hundred miles in that very coach with that very horse and driver.

The sun was just about to set, and the country round about and to the East was almost in twilight. The mountains were tumbled about in fantastic shapes and swarming with people.

Trees and cornfields made the scene indescribably cheerful, woods stretched away toward the sea; between the hills lay the quiet little town of Westport with the blue smoke rising over it in a cloud . . .

But Clew Bay, and the Reek which sweeps down to the sea with its hundred isles dressed in purple and gold, and the whole cloudy West in a flame![20]

The summit of the Reek so magnificently described by Thackeray is 2500 feet above sea level. There in medieval times pilgrims spent the Eve of the Feast of St. Patrick in prayer and fasting. But one wind-swept March, a number of people were swept to their death by wild storms on the mountain, and the spring pilgrimage was abandoned. Today there is an annual pilgrimage in July to the little chapel on the summit. Below, to the north and west, is the turbulent Atlantic. In the center is Clare Island rising from the isles of Clew Bay. In the distance is Achill Island with its peaks and overhanging cliffs defying the waves that break against its rocky sides into fan-like jets of silver. Long after Frances Warde had gone to America, the Westport Sisters of Mercy were to establish a convent and school on wild Achill Island. To the south are the Twelve Bens, where the Alpine region of Connaught and the huge mass of Mulrea form a framework for a panorama of lake and plain and creeks and isle-strewn inlets. There is no record which states that Frances Warde climbed Croagh Patrick. But, like Thackeray, she was an ardent thirty-one, and her faith was profound. There is little doubt that she reached the summit of the Reek!

Croagh Patrick is in the parish of St. Mary's, Westport, on the River Mall, the destination of Frances Warde and her companions on September 6, 1842, when they set out from Carlow with Dean Burke, who had come to guide them to Connaught. Frances took with her Sister Paula Cullen, cousin of Cardinal Paul Cullen, as Superior; Sister Gertrude O'Brien, a novice, who later founded the Convent of Mercy in Ballinrobe; Sister Magdalen O'Brien, also a novice, who later went on a foundation to Sligo, and alone survived its rigors when her first companions could no longer bear starvation and plague during the great famine of 1847–48; and Mary Walsh, a young girl who desired to go to Westport as a postulant. It was a hardy crew that Frances chose to serve in Ireland's poorest country, Mayo. Frances Warde's traveling companion was her young protégé, Fanny Peppard, who had received the habit three months previously and the name

Frances Xavier in honor of her Superior. Since there were as yet no railroads in the West in 1843, the Sisters traveled by hired carriage. They spent the first night of their journey in the Mercy convent in Tullamore and the second night in Tuam. They had planned to arrive in Westport September 8 so that the foundation day would be the Feast of the Virgin Mary, but Bishop John MacHale of Tuam, the famed "Lion of the Fold of Jarlath," insisted that they remain a day as his guest. Like a Celtic prince, he gave Frances Warde the keys to his residence and commanded his servants to obey her orders!

On September 9 the Sisters arrived at about sunset in beautiful Westport, where they were met by the townspeople and led to St. Mary's Church to chant a "Te Deum." They then took up temporary residence in St. Mary's Rectory, vacated by Dean Burke until their convent should be built. He had secured from the Marquis of Sligo and his son, Lord Altamont, three acres of land on Altamont Street, in the loveliest part of the town, on which to build Mount St. Mary's Convent, at six pence a year in perpetuity! Archbishop MacHale and the Dean themselves secured the funds to build the convent, the first in Mayo for three centuries. And Frances Warde arranged that the dowries of the Sisters would be transferred from Carlow for their maintenance— an unusual procedure. Frances had the great joy of planning the convent from the start, and of course she modeled it on her loved St. Leo's. Even today the visitor is aware of the likeness between the two convents, which are among the loveliest in Ireland. Mount St. Mary's is on a beautiful eminence, surrounded by a range wall enclosing seven acres. Lord Sligo added four acres to the original property and sent his gardener to beautify the land.

Frances Warde commenced the visitation of the sick poor

at once. Followed by crowds, the Sisters went first to the home of a cancerous patient, washed and dressed his sores, and then spoke to him of Christ in a language that he could understand. From that moment, the Sisters of Mercy won the love of the people of Westport. Next, Frances Warde visited two badly attended schools for the poor on Castlebar Street. The buildings were in such dilapidated condition that the Sisters, now placed in charge, dismissed the pupils for several weeks so that they might renovate the classrooms. The schools were reopened on November 3, 1842, with a daily attendance of 500 and sometimes 600. Christian Doctrine was taught every Sunday.

The day following Christmas, tragedy came to the new little community with the death of Frances Warde's little friend, Sister Xavier Peppard. Only nineteen, she had been seriously ill for two weeks. She was the first Sister to die in Westport. "Her only anxiety," wrote the annalist at St. Mary's Convent, "was that her dear Mother Frances should be consoled and comforted." After her burial in the parish church, Frances Warde remained in Westport until February. Her young Sisters still needed her to help to consolidate the establishment. On February 2, 1843, Father James Maher, "the kindest friend of our Sisters in Carlow and the adviser and support of Mother Frances," arrived in Westport.[21] The Sisters at St. Leo's had sent him to bring their Mother Frances home. Before leaving Westport, Frances planned the opening of St. Mary's Convent School for middle-class girls. Most of these children had been attending Protestant schools in the town, where they were taught the religion of the Church of England. The first director of this select school was Sister de Sales McDonnell, sister of the Abbot of the famed Mount Mellaray, who came as a young novice from Galway to Westport. An amazing girl, she set

143

out to visit the sick when school was dismissed at four o'clock, and then returned to the church to conduct a class in Christian Doctrine for men at six-thirty. Also a musician of note, she composed the popular "Clew Bay Waltzes." St. Mary's pension school in Westport was to train innumerable young women who later joined Convents of Mercy in Ireland, England, and America. In the spring of 1843, the foundation stone for the new Mount St. Mary's Convent and School was laid. After many months of sorrow, Frances Warde's old joy and irrepressible vivacity were returning to her.

On the Octave of the Ascension, 1843, Frances Warde resigned her office as Superior of St. Leo's, as specified by the new *Rule* of the Sisters of Mercy. It was customary that the first Superior of a new foundation serve a six-year term before an election should take place. When Catherine McAuley had attempted to resign after serving as Superior for six years, Archbishop Murray declared that, as founder, she should be Superior for life. Many of the early founders also served as Superiors for life. Elizabeth Moore was Superior in Limerick from 1838 until 1862. Josephine Warde in Cork, Teresa Kelly in Wexford, and Paula Cullen in Westport, all served twelve years before a different Superior was elected. As the first founder in Ireland after Catherine McAuley, it would have seemed proper for Frances Warde to serve as Superior beyond the first six-year term. However, Bishop Francis Haly, who was not fond of Frances, had other plans. In March, 1843, he wrote to Archbishop Daniel Murray of Dublin, asking whether a Sister under thirty years of age and not five years professed might be elected Superior. Murray replied affirmatively, stating that exception was made for new foundations. A postscript added that if the Sisters of the community did not number at least seven, the appointment was to be made by the Bishop.[22]

Now, the number of professed Sisters at St. Leo's in May, 1843—despite depletion caused by foundations at Naas, Wexford, and Westport—was eleven. In the *Annals of the Sisters of Mercy,* Sister Austin Carroll assumes that an election took place at Carlow in 1843. The Carlow Convent *Annals,* however, reveal a different story:

Octave of Ascension. Mother Frances Warde resigned office. Rt. Rev. Dr. Haly, with a view to learning the opinion of the Community regarding the qualifications of the Sisters eligible to take her place, held a visitation, and on the same day appointed M. Cecilia Maher, Mother Superior; M. Frances Warde, Assistant; M. Angela Johnson, Bursar; M. Cecilia, Novice Mistress.

The Carlow Convent Chapter Book also confirms the fact that an election was not held. Bishop Haly's original intention is problematic. Cecilia Maher was forty-four years old at the time, so that she could not have been his choice as "a Sister under thirty." Perhaps he desired to appoint Angela Johnson as Superior and discovered that she was not acceptable to the Sisters. In 1848 she left religious life entirely.

Freed of the responsibility of Superior, Frances Warde seized the opportunity to return to Westport to help Sister Paula Cullen with the new foundation there. Frances remained until October, when the beautiful new Mount St. Mary's was dedicated. She had watched it in all stages of its growth, and only Carlow was dearer to her. In the evenings, she walked and meditated in the beautiful grounds of St. Mary's. Its flowers and trees and shrubs, in all their October beauty, must have reminded her of Bellbrook and of Coolock.

The Westport foundation was to have a magnificent history. In 1845 a poor school was built on the grounds of

Mount St. Mary's. The same year the Sisters expanded their service to the poor and began the visitation and care of inmates of the workhouse in the town. In 1846 they sent a foundation to Sligo, a convent which prospered in spite of unbelievable poverty and hardship. During the horrible plague and famine of 1847–48, when poverty was at its worst in the West of Ireland, the Sisters of Mount St. Mary's not only suffered hunger themselves but cared for the suffering and dying victims of malignant typhoid when others feared to approach them because of danger of infection. For two years the Sisters served breakfast daily to children of the poor school numbering from 500 to 650. While they devoted all their services and means to relieve the hunger and plague, "the Sisters could not have provided relief were it not for the charity of Pius IX and the people of America, France, England, Poland, and Turkey. America sent flour, meal, and clothing."[23] In 1849, the first House of Mercy was opened in Westport, and in 1851 a foundation was sent to Ballinrobe. The cholera plague of 1854 saw Mother Paula Cullen and her Sisters nursing the sick and "preparing the dead for burial with their own hands, while friends and neighbors fled in terror." In 1859, six Westport Sisters left on a harassing three-month ocean voyage to establish a foundation in Goulborn, New South Wales. By 1950, the latter had thirty-nine branch houses. Westport established branch houses of its own in Newport, Ballyhaunis, Achill Island, and Mulrany.

Perhaps the most fascinating chapter in the Westport annals, however, concerns the famous Irish Shrine of the Virgin Mary at Knock. Bernard A. Cavanagh, whose family had been driven by the British invaders from Carlow "to hell or to Connaught," was a curate at St. Mary's, Westport, during the darkest years of famine and plague. He was spiritual director of the Sisters of Mercy there for seventeen years. He worked side by side with them in the House of Mercy. They regarded him as a man of God who sacrificed all for the poor. Even though he needed his horse for his visitations to the sick poor, during the potato famine he sold everything, including his horse, to buy food for his parishioners. In 1867 he was transferred to Knock-Aghamore, about thirty-five miles from Westport, where he lived in a tiny thatched cottage of three rooms which he opened freely to all mendicants. On August 21, 1879, an apparition of the Virgin Mary at the south wall of the Church of Knock was reported by fifteen persons. In 1880 Cavanagh testified to the authenticity of miracles performed on the site. At his death in 1897, there were numerous testimonies to his own sanctity. The Westport Sisters considered him to be their own saint.

If Frances Warde had been able to see into the future when she said farewell to the Sisters of her third foundation in October, 1843, she would have been profoundly happy and grateful for the apostolate that was to be theirs. Meanwhile, as she was serving joyfully in Westport in the summer of 1843, her destiny was secretly sealed hundreds of miles away in Italy and in the New World of the West. She did not know, when she returned to Carlow in October, that she would never again live in the land of her birth. A new world was calling her at the age of not quite thirty-three. And her apostolic works up to now, a unique accomplishment for a great woman, would be as nothing compared with the apostolate for Christ which lay before her.

8

From Old World to New: Carlow to Pittsburgh

THE cradle of the Congregation of Mercy in the United States was not in Dublin, Cork, or Limerick, but in the small provincial town of Carlow. The first foundation in the United States was not in New York, Chicago, St. Louis, or San Francisco. It was in Pittsburgh, Pennsylvania, population 25,000, year 1843. The fact that by 1943 the Congregation of Mercy had become the second largest congregation of religious women in the world, with a membership of 30,000 and with the number of convents in the United States[1] more than doubling those of all other Mercy convents in the world combined, indicates that the unprecedented expansion of the Institute of Mercy is due to neither temporal nor spatial factors. The elements that contributed to the unexampled growth of the Congregation were spiritual, structural, social, and personal. The mid-nineteenth-century church was ready for an active-contemplative congregation of women; for a comparatively autonomous governmental structure in religious community; for a congregation that left its cloisters daily to minister to the poor, the sick, and the uneducated; for religious leaders capable of combining personal spirituality with a pioneering spirit of initiative and independence. Perhaps the last named element was the most significant in the development of the Congregation of Mercy.

No one embodied these personal qualities more profoundly than the American founder, Frances Warde.

While Frances was in Westport in the summer of 1841, Father James Maher in Carlow received a request from Rome that determined the direction of her life for the future. In 1810, the same year that Frances was born in Bellbrook, a boy had been born in Cork who was destined, together with Frances, to establish the Sisters of Mercy in the United States. Michael O'Connor was sent, at fourteen, to study in France, and then to the College of the Propaganda in Rome. When he was twenty-three, in the same year that Frances Warde was professed in Baggot Street, he was ordained in Rome and granted a doctorate in theology. His defense of his thesis, one of the most brilliant ever presented at the Propaganda, was publicly commended by Nicholas Wiseman, Rector of the English College in Rome and later Cardinal. O'Connor's friends and fellow students were Francis Patrick Kenrick, later Archbishop of Philadelphia, and Martin John Spalding, afterward Archbishop of Baltimore. The young priest was at once appointed Professor of Sacred Scripture at the Propaganda and soon after Vice-Rector of the Irish College in Rome, of which Paul Cullen, later Cardinal, was Rector.

When Michael O'Connor was offered the bishopric of Pittsburgh in 1843, he preferred to be a Jesuit. But Pope Gregory XVI responded, "A bishop first—a Jesuit afterwards."[2] He was consecrated in Rome as first Bishop of Pittsburgh on August 15, 1843. It was predictable that he would seek priests and religious from Ireland to aid him in the near wilderness of his apostolate in Western Pennsylvania. Back in 1835, he had been asked by the Sacred Congregation of Propaganda Fide to translate certain Chapters of the proposed *Rule* of the Congregation of Mercy into

Italian. His knowledge of the goals and works of the Congregation convinced him that it was particularly suited to the apostolic mission of the pioneer country of Pennsylvania. Beginning in 1839, he had already served as President of St. Charles Borromeo Seminary in Philadelphia, Vicar General of Western Pennsylvania, and Pastor of St. Paul's Church in Pittsburgh. He knew precisely what his new diocese would demand of religious women, and he knew that the Sisters of Mercy could meet these demands. It was likewise predictable that O'Connor would seek Sisters of Mercy in Carlow rather than in Dublin. His friend Paul Cullen was the nephew of James Maher, and Cullen had at least seven relatives in the Congregation at St. Leo's. His friend Nicholas Wiseman, moreover, had three first cousins there. Frances Warde was herself a Maher, and so was Mother Cecilia, the new Superior at Carlow. Before Frances Warde returned from Westport, numerous letters concerning the Sisters of Mercy had been exchanged between the newly consecrated Bishop and his ecclesiastical friends,[3] and the decision had already been made that O'Connor would seek Sisters in Carlow to accompany him back to America. Frances Warde heard the news in Westport.[4]

When the Sisters at St. Leo's were informed of the request of the new Bishop of Pittsburgh for a foundation, they were not at first excited. Bishop John England of Charleston, South Carolina, one of the greatest American prelates of the century, had visited Dublin and Carlow in search of Sisters for the United States in 1841 and nothing had come of it. Besides, Dr. Andrew Fitzgerald, President of Carlow College and close friend of the Institute of Mercy since its beginning, was dying. The Sisters visited him daily and cared for him tenderly. Their thoughts were with him. They regarded a Pittsburgh foundation as a possible distant perspective. Fitzgerald died October 2, 1843. When the Sisters participated in the chanting of the Divine Office for his eternal rest in Carlow Cathedral, the eighth lesson of the Office was chanted by a handsome young bishop with a magnificent voice. They were much impressed.

The following day, Michael O'Connor appeared with the beloved James Maher in the community room of the Carlow convent to plead for help in his faraway mission. He knew how to win the Sisters of Mercy. He spoke of the spiritual and physical needs of his people in America—of the want of religious instruction for both children and adults, of the need for care of the sick and the poor, particularly among homesick Irish immigrants in a strange and distant land. He desired only those Sisters to come to America who felt a strong inspiration to spread the Gospel of Christ and to love and serve the poor. The hardships would be severe, the labor overwhelming. When O'Connor had finished speaking, only one answer was inevitable. At once conjectures were made as to which Sisters would be chosen to go to America. Frances Warde, who had been in Westport for several months, was not present for the discussion. The Carlow Convent *Annals* describe the event:

Of those selected to go to America, Sister M. Josephine Cullen was named as Mother Superior, but the Bishops [Haly of Kildare and O'Connor of Pittsburgh] and Father Maher, having given the matter further consideration, thought it wiser to appoint Mother Frances Warde, for whose judgment and experience this arduous mission would afford ample scope. At first, it was proposed that her services were to be lent for two years or thereabouts. On learning of the decision of her Superiors, our late Revd. Mother cheerfully acquiesced, feeling at the same time a bitter pang at the prospect of parting with so many of her first Sisters. But her spirit was generous, and she began her preparations with edifying zeal and energy. The parents and friends of the Sisters who were to accompany her gave much opposition to the foundation, being unwilling to be separated so far from those so dear to them, but Mother M. Frances encouraged and consoled them and succeeded in obtaining their full consent.[5]

It was a singular circumstance that Bishop Francis Haly stipulated that Frances Warde should return to Carlow in two years—a proof that, while he would have preferred a greater submissiveness in her character, he was thoroughly conscious of her worth! The circumstance of Josephine Cullen's name having been suggested as Superior only to be rejected was to have unfortunate reverberations in America six years later. Frances had suffered from the jealousy of others (perhaps unconscious) in Baggot Street in the early days of the Institute. Envy was to pursue her to the United States.

Frances thus became, at the age of thirty-three, the leader of "the first seven" Sisters of Mercy to go to the New World. "Seven" was a kind of mystic number in the Mercy Congregation. Seven Sisters, among them Frances, had been the first received into the community in Dublin in 1832. Over and over again after that, seven would be chosen when possible to initiate foundations. The early Sisters pointed out the Biblical significance of seven: the seven churches in the Apocalypse, the seven golden candlesticks, the seven branches of the lamp of the sanctuary; the seven stars, seven seals, seven angels, seven trumpets, seven plagues, seven heads of the dragon, seven diadems; the seven sacraments, seven penitential Psalms, seven canonical hours of the Divine Office, seven joys and sorrows of Mary. When the seven Sisters chosen to go to America were serious, they prayed for the seven gifts of the Holy Spirit; in a lighter mood, they called themselves the seven deadly sinners who fell seven times a day!

They were, according to their friends, "the picking choice" of the Carlow community.[6] In addition to Frances Warde, there were Sister Josephine Cullen, aged twenty-eight, first cousin to Cardinal Paul Cullen, a cultured woman and able administrator; Sister Elizabeth Strange, twenty-four, first cousin to Cardinal Nicholas Wiseman, a highly educated and witty girl, a fair poet and a prose writer of style; her younger sister, Aloysia Strange, still a novice, the first Sister of Mercy to make her vows in the United States; Sister Philomena Reid, twenty-three, a well educated novice of rare promise; Sister Margaret O'Brien, twenty-one, a postulant, the first young woman to be received as a Sister of Mercy in America, destined to be the first Superior of the Sisters of Mercy in Chicago at twenty-four; and Sister Veronica McDarby, lay Sister and spiritual protégé of the loved Bishop Nolan of Carlow.

None of the seven was destined to return permanently to Ireland. Indeed, all were fully cognizant of the possible finality of their farewell to St. Leo's when they departed on November 4, 1843. For Frances Warde especially, the parting was filled with quiet anguish. St. Leo's was never more beautiful to her than it was that autumn day. What did she feel as she gazed back from the Dublin Road to the convent she had planned with Catherine McAuley—beautiful in the November sunshine against the background of garden and shrubbery she herself had planted—the simple classic style, the green veranda, the staircase leading to the garden, the balcony, the graceful wings, the chapel with its lovely arches? The "flower of Catherine McAuley's foundations" was a unique part of Frances Warde herself. There she came as a young girl on an April day with Catherine, there she wept for Edward Nolan, there she set out on new and uncertain ventures to Naas and Wexford and Westport, there she knew intense and unbearable sorrow, there she endured alone the loss of Catherine McAuley. Today she would leave the Sisters she had received as novices at St. Leo's. What would be the future of her beloved St. Leo's?

Could she have seen into the years ahead, she would have known that Eliza Ryan, whom she had received in the spring of 1843, would lead a foundation to Tuam, County Galway, from which convents would be established in Swinford and in faraway Sandhurst, Victoria, Australia; that in 1849 Sister Rose Strange, whom she had professed in 1841, would establish a convent in Cheadle, Staffordshire, which would expand to Alton, Bilston, and Shrewsbury in England, and finally back to Rathangan in Ireland; that her cousin, Cecilia Maher, now Superior at St. Leo's, would become the founder of the Congregation of Mercy in Auckland in 1850 and that by 1950 the community there would have expanded to nineteen Mercy communities in New Zealand; and that in 1857 Sister Aloysius Doyle, heroine of service in the Crimean War, honored with the Red Cross by Queen Victoria, would establish a foundation in Gort, Galway. Finally, what would Frances Warde have thought had she known that in 1885, the year after her own death, Bishop James O'Connor of Omaha, brother of Michael, would bring back to St. Leo's Convent the moss from her own grave in Manchester, New Hampshire, and standing in the community room in which Catherine McAuley and she had planned so much for the Mercy Institute, would declare, "When I look around this room and think that these holy women [the seven Pittsburgh founders] once occupied it, I feel that I am visiting the shrine of saints."[7]

The missionaries went by carriage from Carlow to Naas,

where they spent the night at Frances Warde's first foundation from St. Leo's, before leaving for Dublin. At eight o'clock on the evening of November 5 they assembled for Benediction in the Chapel at Baggot Street where Frances Warde had made her vows as the first Sister professed by Catherine McAuley. They then left immediately for the seaport of Kingstown (Dunleary). There was only one railway in Ireland in 1843, connecting Dublin with the port of Kingstown. Since rail travel was still considered dangerous, Bishop O'Connor decided, to their disappointment, that they should travel by carriage. Afterward, in the silence and darkness of night, they steamed out of Dublin Bay, leaving forever the land they loved. Following a rough passage across the Irish Sea, they reached Liverpool on the morning of November 6. The Sisters went directly to the Mercy Convent of St. Ethelburga, founded the previous year from Baggot Street. To O'Connor's regret, the sailing vessel *Queen of the West,* which he had chosen for the journey to America, could not depart for several days. Only three steamships then sailed the Atlantic and, like the railroads, they were considered dangerous. At the moment one of them, the *Atlantic,* was reported lost at sea. O'Connor's choice, a great three-master considered to be the finest sailing vessel on the ocean, had to await fair winds, and so the missionaries were compelled to remain in Liverpool for four days. Frances Warde was greatly interested in the Liverpool convent: she had almost been its founder! She spent her time in Liverpool instructing adults in Christian Doctrine. "They came in such crowds that it was necessary to preserve order at the convent gate."[8]

On the morning of Thursday, November 10, favorable winds came to Liverpool at last. Bishop O'Connor hurried to the convent to announce departure of the *Queen of the*

West. At about noon the vessel weighed anchor. Thomas Cullen of Liverpool, brother of the Cardinal, and other relatives of the Cullens and Mahers saw the missionaries off. Then Thomas Cullen hurried home to write to Paul Cullen in Rome:

They sailed from here with a fair wind . . . God send them safe, poor things . . . Lest I should forget it, the gold rosary ring you left me when last here I gave to Ellen Cullen [Sister Josephine] . . . and the silver crucifix that you were so kind as to send little Mary I gave to Mrs. Warde,[9] thinking they were well disposed of, and that you might on some other occasion meet with one for Mary when she will have more sense to set proper value on it.[10]

When Frances Warde died in New Hampshire forty-one years later, the crucifix given to her by Thomas Cullen was still in her possession, a symbol of her sufferings as American founder of the Sisters of Mercy.

Michael O'Connor also wrote to Paul Cullen from the *Queen of the West* at the very last moment as she set sail:

I have just taken leave of your brothers and friends and we are sailing, or rather being tugged, on board the liner "Queen of the West," the same vessel being—at least the Captain says she is— the very best vessel that ever was built . . . I send these few lines ashore, lest you should imagine that I was unmindful or ungrateful for your kindness. I have on board with me Wilson, who persevered like a man, eight students, and seven nuns—in all seventeen persons!! I cannot tell you how much I feel indebted to yourself and to all your friends in Ireland. I have not room or time for many words, but as far as one big word can do it, I assure you that I am most sincerely grateful. Mrs. Warde is head of the nun mission . . . I have to thank your uncle [James Maher] for my success in this matter.[11]

By the Bishop's special desire, the Sisters traveled in secular dress, wearing black cashmere dresses and white tulle caps trimmed with white ribbon. Their hair was folded back in bands from their foreheads. Frances Warde, as Superior, wore a black lace cap trimmed with lilac ribbon. Since there were no other women aboard, the Sisters had the ladies' staterooms to themselves. For the first three days out, they experienced a frightful storm. November is traditionally the worst month of the year for an Atlantic sailing vessel. At the Captain's request, Bishop O'Connor prayed with the passengers and spoke to them on themes from Holy Scripture. On Sunday the storm suddenly ceased. The Sisters now spent much of their time in a familiar occupation: visiting and caring for the sick poor among the second-cabin and steerage passengers. To pass the time, the gentlemen aboard organized the "Atlantic Social and Literary Association of the Good Ship *Queen of the West*." Michael O'Connor was chosen as president. The Sisters joined too and, like the other members, wrote essays and verse for discussion and fun in the evenings.

After four weeks and two days, the *Queen* sighted land on the evening of December 10 in New York harbor. The Sisters stayed on board until the next day. They remained on deck very late, watching with fast-beating hearts the lights of New York City. The following morning, Bishop O'Connor, who had gone ashore the night before, returned with Bishop John J. Hughes of New York and Bishop-Elect William Quarter of Chicago to welcome them to America. When the introductions were over, the newly consecrated Bishop Quarter turned to Frances Warde and said, "As I have been the first to welcome you to the New World, I trust you will grant my first request, and promise to establish in the new diocese of Chicago a house of your Institute."[12] Three years later, Frances was to nearly lose her life in fulfilling Quarter's request. One of her strongest personal characteristics was that she never forgot a friend, never refused a favor possible to grant, never abandoned a trust. In matters of fidelity, time was inconsequential to her.

The Bishops led the Sisters to the Convent of the Madames of the Sacred Heart on Houston Street in New York where they were warmly welcomed by the French Sisters. The next morning, December 12, by a happy coincidence the Foundation Day of the Congregation of Mercy twelve years before in Dublin, the Sisters participated in the Celebration of the Eucharist for the first time in America. At Frances Warde's request, the students at the Convent of the Sacred Heart were given a free day. On December 14 the travelers set out by rail (their first train ride) for Philadelphia, where they remained for four days with the Sisters of Charity. Bishop Francis Patrick Kenrick of Philadelphia, O'Connor's friend, reminded Frances Warde so strongly of her friend Daniel O'Connell, the Irish liberator, that she could not take her eyes from him as he preached in the Cathedral. He too claimed a right to an early foundation of Sisters of Mercy, a request that Frances was to fulfill in 1861. In Philadelphia she met Emily Harper of Baltimore, granddaughter of Charles Carroll of Carrollton, who remained her close friend and a benefactor of the Sisters of Mercy until death.

Since only nine persons could be accommodated in the stage coaches that crossed the Allegheny Mountains to Pittsburgh, the missionary party broke into two groups. On the evening of December 17 the first contingent took the night train from Philadelphia to Chambersburg, where the railroad terminated. In the party were Michael O'Connor, Frances Warde, Sisters Aloysia and Philomena, and the seminarian, Thomas McCullough, later the Sisters' first chaplain at St. Xavier Academy, Latrobe, Pennsylvania. They arrived in Chambersburg before noon on December 18. Transferring to the stage coach, they traveled the northern route to Pittsburgh along the Juniata River from Harrisburg, through Lewistown, Huntington, Hollidaysburg, Summit, Munster, Ebensburg, and Blairstown. It is difficult today to appreciate the dangers of a journey across the Allegheny Mountains by stage coach in the winter of 1843. High above the narrow, twisting mountain roads were huge rocks that threatened to career down upon defenseless travelers; below were steep precipices down which horses and coach might easily slip from the icy roads. Robbers, too, were often hiding in the wilds of the Alleghenies.

When the stage coach reached the town of Loretto, high in the mountains, Michael O'Connor told Frances Warde about the Russian Prince called the "Apostle of the Alleghenies" who had died just three years before. Demetrius Gallitzin, the first priest to receive all the major orders in the United States, had come to Loretto in 1799, dedicated his mountain settlement to the Virgin Mary, and offered his first Eucharistic Celebration in a log cabin on Christmas Eve. The little church was the only house of God from the Susquehanna to the Mississippi, from Lancaster, Pennsylvania, to St. Louis, Missouri. O'Connor pointed out the chapel house of Prince Gallitzin and his grave in the little cemetery close by. He told Frances that when Gallitzin lay dying in his chapel house, he prayed that Sisters would come to the mountains of Loretto to care for and instruct his people. Frances Warde sat erect in the rumbling stage coach.

In her imagination, she was already establishing a foundation in Loretto. She was to make her dream a reality in fewer than five years. The stage coach reached Pittsburgh in the early morning hours of Wednesday, December 20.

Meanwhile, Josephine Cullen, Elizabeth Strange, Margaret O'Brien, and Veronica McDarby took the day train to Chambersburg on December 18. They were accompanied by the newly ordained priest, Robert A. Wilson, and the seminarian, Tobias Mullen, later Bishop of Erie, Pennsylvania. Their stage coach traveled the southern route through Carlisle, Bedford, Stoyestown, Ligonier, and Greensburg, arriving in Pittsburgh the evening of December 20. The Sisters had traveled nearly sixty hours, day and night. Short stops were made at inns only to change horses.

All the Sisters were warmly received by the Sisters of Charity at their convent on Coal Lane (Webster Avenue). The next morning, the seven participated in the Celebration of the Eucharist by Bishop O'Connor at St. Paul's Cathedral, Fifth and Grant Streets. Thus December 21, which was by happy chance Thanksgiving Day in Pittsburgh in 1843, became the Foundation Day of the Sisters of Mercy in the United States.

On the following day, Frances Warde and her Sisters opened the first Convent of Mercy in the United States in a rented, four-story brick building called the Speer House, located at what was formerly 800 Penn Street.[13] The area was then residential. Attractive homes were fronted by lovely gardens which sloped down to the Allegheny River. The sweet smell of boxwood edging the gardens would be a delight in spring to Frances Warde, who had loved to pray in the quiet peace of the garden at Carlow. Frances set to work at once to furnish the convent, called St. Mary's, and to prepare a chapel for Mass on Christmas Day. A lovely young

Pittsburgh girl sent flowers for the altar for Christmas. She was Eliza Tiernan, the first American postulant of the Sisters of Mercy.

To be sure, the city to which the Sisters had come was quite unlike the Irish towns familiar to them. "Our sense of loneliness was keen," wrote one of the seven, "but we did not allow our feelings to get the better of us." The very immensity of America filled them with awe. The whole of Ireland could be placed in the state of Pennsylvania alone with hundreds of miles to spare! Pittsburgh was the "Gateway to the West," the "Golden Triangle" at the confluence of the Allegheny and the Monongahela Rivers where the Ohio River, itself a tributary of the great Mississippi, had its source. The very Indian names had a strange ring to the ears of the young missionaries.

They soon learned the fascinating history of "The Point" at which the three rivers met. In 1753 Major George Washington, later the first President of the United States, had been sent by Robert Dinwiddie, Lieutenant-Governor of Virginia, with despatches to the French forces in Western Pennsylvania. Washington arrived at "The Forks," as the site of Pittsburgh was then called, on November 24, 1753. He immediately decided that this site, with its absolute command of three rivers, was ideal for a fort. On his recommendation, Captain William Trent was despatched in January, 1754 to construct a fort at the now famous "Point." He arrived there in February with the celebrated pioneer, Christopher Gist, the first resident white man in the area that was destined to be the greatest iron and steel manufacturing city in the world. But the French arrived at "The Forks" in April, 1754, and routed the British. They themselves built a fort, to which they first gave the name "Assumption of the Blessed Virgin" but afterwards changed to "Fort Duquesne," in honor of the

Marquis Duquesne de Meneval, Governor-General of Canada. In 1755, General Edward Braddock, with the largest expedition that had ever crossed the Alleghenies, was sent to recapture Fort Duquesne. His attempt failed, as did a second expedition of 800 men under Major James Grant. Finally, in 1758, General John "Iron-Gut" Forbes, with 6,000 men, successfully routed the French. He changed the name "Fort Duquesne" to "Fort Pitt" in honor of the British Prime Minister, William Pitt. The name "Pittsburgh" was first used in 1758. The first recorded population was 464 in 1760. Pittsburgh was incorporated as a city only twenty-seven years before the Sisters of Mercy arrived.

The French had established a Chapel at the Point in 1754 under the title of "The Assumption of the Blessed Virgin of the Beautiful River." At the first Synod of the new Diocese of Pittsburgh called by Michael O'Connor, the diocese was placed under the protection of the Virgin of the Assumption. Frances Warde and her Sisters were pleased that Pittsburgh, like their Congregation, had the Mother of God as its patron. They did not know that thirty-three years later, the Church of St. Mary of Mercy would be dedicated at the celebrated Point on the Feast of Our Lady of Mercy, and that the same year the Sisters of Mercy would begin to conduct a school there for the children of the surrounding area.

Pittsburgh in the winter of 1843 was cold and muddy and smoky. Most of its "streets" were neither paved, graded, nor lighted. But it was already the "Iron City," an industrial center of bridges and aqueducts with a population of 25,000. Coal and its by-product, coke, were two important factors in its development. Of the entire population, more people were engaged in manufacturing and mining than in any other occupations. The destiny of the city clearly lay in its industry and commerce. The booming traffic on the wharves of the

Allegheny and the Monongahela Rivers represented manufactured products destined for markets as far west as the Rockies and as far south as the West Indies. Despite the growth in industry, handwork still accomplished much that was later manufactured by machinery. Therefore there was a great demand for labor. Although the great influx of Irish immigrants did not begin in Pittsburgh until the famine of 1847–48, there were 12,000 Irish in the city by 1846. The expansion of Pittsburgh throughout the eighteen-forties was almost unbelievable. Seldom in the history of American cities did so many men raise themselves by their own efforts to positions of comparative affluence. Within nine months in 1845, as many as 2,500 houses were built in the city and its suburbs. The Baltimore and Ohio Railroad was soon to be extended through Virginia and Pennsylvania to the Ohio River. By 1851, the development of Pittsburgh—and of similar industrial cities—was unparalleled in the history of nations.

Sister Elizabeth Strange, in a letter to Ireland, declared that, while there were few millionaires in Pittsburgh, there were few people in *real* poverty. She meant, of course, that the dire poverty of Naas and Wexford and Westport did not exist in America in the mid-forties. Food was cheap. Flour was two dollars a barrel, and wheat was forty-five cents a bushel. Yet side by side with amazing industrial expansion developed ugliness and human misery. Housing facilities for poor immigrants did not expand proportionately with the population, and slums multiplied. The suffering of unskilled laborers and their families was an integral part of the technological development of Pittsburgh even before the rise of the "Money Barons" following the Civil War. The "Steel Metropolis of the World" depended for its growth upon exploited laborers who were just beginning the fight for just wages and humane working conditions. Frances Warde and her Sisters arrived in Pittsburgh precisely when the city was on the verge of unprecedented growth. They became a significant part of its religious, cultural, and social expansion.

The "first seven" began at once the visitation and care of the sick poor and religious instruction of children and adults. Their works of mercy soon became quite extensive in both the city of Pittsburgh and its sister city, Allegheny, across the Allegheny River, as well as in the suburbs of both cities. Each week the Sisters visited the poor-house. Frances Warde herself always visited the inmates of the penitentiary, a fine stone structure just outside the city. The managers of the jail became alarmed, however, when many inmates expressed a desire to become Catholics after meeting Sister Frances. An old statute forbidding visits of "gentle-women who came for religious purposes" was put into effect. For many years the Sisters of Mercy were thus denied admittance to the Pittsburgh penitentiary.

A large section of the population of the city was literally floating. No railroad came within 150 miles of Pittsburgh, but boats and steamers moved continually up and down the three rivers. Catholics who came from small settlements called at St. Mary's Convent to be instructed and prepared to receive the Sacraments. Some of them led lives completely circumscribed by the steamboat on the river and the stage coach on land. They could participate in the Celebration of the Eucharist only when they came to the city between intervals of months or years. A beautiful spirit of charity at St. Mary's seemed to attract all. "The Sisters of Mercy are like the first Christians," said Joseph T. Dean, curate at St. Paul's Cathedral, "for all have but one heart and soul."[14] Father Dean knew the Sisters well: it was he who rented the convent on Penn Street for them before they arrived in America.

The Sisters also took immediate charge of the Cathedral

Sunday School of over 500 girls. The boys were taught by the seminarians on the top floor of St. Paul's School (conducted during the week by the Sisters of Charity) which Bishop O'Connor had erected not long before. The girls occupied the second floor. On the first floor, Frances Warde instructed adults in Christian Doctrine. Her empathy with adults in Ireland was repeated and reinforced in America. She used striking examples in her discussions and always made a deep impression on those who heard her. After attending her instructions, many non-Catholics asked to be baptized. During her entire religious life in the United States, Frances maintained a singular zeal for all adults who did not know of Christ, and she won them to the Gospel she loved with amazing success.

Many young women of Pittsburgh were attracted almost at once to the Convent of Mercy on Penn Street. First came beautiful Eliza Tiernan, daughter of a wealthy and respected merchant. Next came Bessie McCaffrey, daughter of a prominent physician who had moved to Pittsburgh from Cleveland. Bessie and her three sisters had been educated in the pension school for girls in Carlow. Once when Catherine McAuley visited St. Leo's, she had put her arms around the little Mc-Caffrey girls and prophesied that they would become Sisters of Mercy. Their dying mother had begged Frances Warde to care for them. In 1842 Dr. McCaffrey had brought his family to the United States. Frances Warde, through her correspondence with the girls, did the rest. Mary and Alice McCaffrey entered the Pittsburgh convent following their older sister, and the youngest—Anna—was preparing to enter when she became fatally ill. The third to offer herself as a candidate was Elizabeth Wynne, daughter of a United States Army Officer, Major Thomas Wynne. She was destined to be the first Superior of both the Loretto and the Baltimore foundations. Next came Bridget Tobin, the first lay Sister to enter in the United States, and Lucy McGivern. All of these young women entered the first convent on Penn Street during the first year. It is singular that from the very beginning Frances Warde's American foundations attracted American-born postulants. The same was not true of many religious foundations from Europe, which depended upon parent houses abroad for years before they attracted native girls in considerable numbers.

The first Mercy religious reception in the United States took place on February 22, 1844, in the little Chapel on Penn Street when Margaret O'Brien, of the first seven, received the religious habit and the name Sister Agatha. The first ceremony of vows was held in St. Paul's Cathedral on April 11, when Sister Aloysia Strange was professed. Eliza Tiernan received the habit the same day. Mother Frances Warde, from the time of her arrival in America, celebrated public ceremonies of reception and profession with dignity and splendor. She regarded these rites as apostolic opportunities during which the public could be educated in the meaning of religious consecration. Tall and erect, wearing white church cloak and sweeping train and carrying a lighted candle in her white-gloved hand, she herself presented the candidates for religious vows to the Bishop in the sanctuary of the Cathedral. Invariably she requested the Bishop to address the invited congregation on the significance of the religious life. And just as invariably, young ladies present in the church were inspired to come to the convent to present themselves as candidates to the Sisters of Mercy.

In August, 1844, the Sisters participated in their first annual retreat, conducted by the young Redemptorist Rector of St. Philomena's Church, John Nepomucene Neumann, later Bishop of Philadelphia. In October, 1963, he became the first

American bishop to be beatified by the Catholic Church. Years after he left Pittsburgh, he used to joke about being a first spiritual director of the Sisters of Mercy, declaring, "If they went wrong, it was my fault." In these days of their early fervor, the seven often classified playfully the objects of their zeal: Josephine Cullen's missionary fervor was for men; Elizabeth Strange's for the black race; Aloysia Strange's for little boys; Philomena Reid's for women; and Frances Warde's for everyone, postulants in particular![15]

In September Frances Warde opened St. Mary's private school for girls, the first academy conducted by the Sisters of Mercy in America, in the little convent on Penn Street. On the morning of the first day of school, Frances walked out into the convent garden. Next door was the property of the Carron family, and sitting on the fence was little Julia Carron, with her father's arms around her. "Here is your first pupil," said Julia's father, lifting her into the arms of Sister Frances. The little girl and Frances talked together until school convened. The founder was very fond of children, and they were always at ease with her. She would sometimes carry on long conversations and arguments with tiny tots, to the great amusement of any adults who were present.

The temporary convent was not well adapted to educational purposes. Classes were taught in a long basement room. Music was taught in the parlor. But the happy children, aged five to sixteen, received what they needed. They learned to read, write, and speak uncommonly well. Their taste for literature was directed and cultivated. Frances Warde established a circulating library in the school at an early date. Music and mathematics were the provinces of all. Needlework, "plain and ornamental," was taught at the end of each school day. Instruction in Christian Doctrine by the Sisters was reinforced by Bishop O'Connor himself. Increasing numbers soon compelled the Sisters to transform their back parlor into an additional classroom.

It was Frances Warde's custom to give "talks" to the Sisters in the school on methods of teaching and discipline. While obedience and politeness were cultivated as the first in the hierarchy of "virtues" in many private schools of the eighteen-forties, Sister Frances insisted first on honesty and sincerity. She believed that her Sisters taught best by example. She forbade any form of severe punishment on the ground that it destroys truth by degrading the person. Love was the best controlling force in the classroom; fear—except for the wholesome fear of God—she discountenanced. Judicious praise and approval by teachers and parents she saw as a powerful stimulus to study. The most successful teaching method, she believed, was to present the lessons in a manner thoroughly interesting to the students. "To instruct," she used to say, "is an easy matter; but to educate requires ingenuity, energy, and perseverance without limit." No wonder Bishop O'Connor pronounced St. Mary's School "the happiest spot in Pittsburgh"!

Hard work and confined quarters, meanwhile, began to affect the health of the young Sisters. Frances Warde felt that Providence had come to her rescue when Henry Kuhn of Westmoreland County offered his farm of 108 acres, about forty miles from Pittsburgh in the area now called Latrobe, as a site for a boarding academy for girls and a convent for the Sisters of Mercy. Seven hours by stage coach from Pittsburgh, the property was one mile west of St. Vincent's Church in Youngstown (Latrobe). The property deeds were transferred on May 17, 1844, for the payment of one dollar. In April, 1845, Bishop O'Connor, Frances Warde, and Josephine Cullen examined the Kuhn farm and decided to build the new convent and school as soon as possible. Father

Michael Gallagher, pastor of St. Vincent's Church, graciously offered the rectory of the church as a temporary residence for the Sisters. The well-constructed parish residence of brick, built by Father James A. Stillinger of St. Vincent's in the eighteen-thirties, was a real godsend to Frances Warde. On April 28, 1845, she opened Mount St. Vincent's Academy for Young Ladies with seven boarding students, daughters of outstanding Pittsburgh families. Within a month the enrollment reached fifteen. A year and a half later, on October 24, 1846, St. Vincent's was the scene of the foundation of the Benedictine Abbey which became the first Archabbey in the United States. While the Sisters conducted the academy at St. Vincent's, they also taught the children of the parish in a small free day school conducted in the sacristy of the church. St. Vincent's Parish School, founded in 1835, was the first in the diocese outside the city of Pittsburgh.

The curriculum of Mount St. Vincent's Academy was outstanding. According to announcements in the *Pittsburgh Catholic,* diocesan newspaper founded by Bishop O'Connor in 1844, the young women were taught English grammar, rhetoric, and composition; history, ancient and modern; philosophy; French; Italian; astronomy; geography; mathematics; music; and Christian Doctrine. Bishop O'Connor himself conducted annual public examinations preceding graduation and "exhibition." The Academy remained at Mount St. Vincent, Latrobe, until 1847, when the new St. Xavier Academy was ready for occupation on the Kuhn farm property. The latter Academy is still in existence (1972) on the same site.*

At the close of the school year in 1845, the Sisters of Charity, who taught at St. Paul's Parochial School and conducted the diocesan Orphan Asylum, were abruptly with-

---

* St. Xavier Academy, Latrobe, was destroyed by fire on March 16, 1972.

drawn from Pittsburgh. Bishop O'Connor attributed the sudden move to "the jealousy of women."[16] Whatever the cause, the Pittsburgh diocese had an immediate need for teachers and social workers. Frances Warde agreed to close St. Mary's Academy on Penn Street temporarily so that the Sisters of Mercy could take over St. Paul's Parochial School in September, 1845. One hundred twenty-five years later, the Sisters of Mercy still teach in this Cathedral school. Bishop O'Connor gave the Orphan Asylum into the charge of three lay women until the spring of 1846, when Frances Warde was able to provide Sisters to care for the orphans. A beautiful new orphanage, St. Paul's, was built for both boys and girls in Pittsburgh in 1867, and in 1901 the Sisters opened a magnificent complex of buildings in Crafton, near Pittsburgh, where they cared for 1,200 orphans. For over 100 years, the care of the motherless was one of their chief apostolic works in the diocese.

To meet the urgent demand for Sisters in 1845, Frances Warde agreed to go to Ireland to seek for young women to aid in the Pittsburgh apostolate. On July 25, she and Sister Xavier Tiernan left for Ireland accompanied by Michael O'Connor in search of priests for his diocese and Brothers to conduct schools for boys in Pittsburgh.

In December, Frances Warde returned to Pittsburgh with four recruits for the American community. Naturally, she had expected to receive help from her sister, Mother Josephine Warde, in Cork and from Mother Cecilia Maher in Carlow. In Cork the volunteers were Sisters Anastasia McGawley, Assistant to the Superior, and Sister Augusta Goold, a novice. Sister Gertrude Blake, the Superior at Birr, also joined the little band. And Jane O'Gorman of Fermoy asked to come to Pittsburgh with them as a postulant. In Carlow, Frances aroused the enthusiasm that accompanied her wherever she went. Three Sisters were at once eager to go to America with their founder: Cecilia Maher, the Superior; Josephine Cullen, younger sister of Josephine Cullen in Pittsburgh (she had adopted her sister's name after the departure for Pittsburgh in 1843); and Alphonsa Ryan.[17] Their zeal was overruled, however, by Bishop Francis Haly (of old a thorn in the side of Frances Warde), who refused to give the necessary sanction. The Carlow annalist recorded the event with great good sense, adding that other members of the community "were childish enough to be offended with M. M. Frances for encouraging the volunteers. In retrospect, it looks a very unreasonable thing to have got into a humour with her, as she was simply trying to do the best she could for her mission"![18] To be thus rejected in her loved Carlow was painful to Frances. She was not now so communicative as she had been when she first came to Carlow in 1837. How could she impress upon her old friends the fact that the Sisters of Mercy were now well established throughout Ireland? How could she make them understand that countless people of a vast continent from the Atlantic to the Pacific were waiting to be served? Above all, how could she fill their hearts with the fervor of her unspoken promises to send Sisters of Mercy to Chicago, to Loretto, to Philadelphia—to the whole of the United States? They could not understand. Sadly, she said farewell once more to her loved St. Leo's.

The happiness of Frances' return to her Pittsburgh home was clouded by the loss of one of the first seven. The hard work and suffering that Michael O'Connor had promised to the pioneers was now an actuality. During the forties, only the strong among the Pittsburgh Sisters of Mercy survived. While Frances Warde was in Ireland, Philomena Reid, aged twenty-five, had died at Mount St. Vincent's Academy, where she had been teaching. When she was buried in St. Vincent's churchyard on a bright October morning in 1845, Frances, who had received her so joyfully in Carlow two years before, was not present.

With the accession of new Sisters from Ireland, Frances was now able to reopen St. Mary's Academy. The little convent on Penn Street, however, had become too small for the increasing number of Sisters and for rooms for the select school. When the two years' lease on the first convent was completed, the Sisters moved in April, 1846, to "Concert Hall," also on Penn Street—a large building which had once been a hotel, the ballroom of which had been used more recently for concerts and lectures. Charles Dickens, during his famous visit to the United States in 1842, had visited this same Concert Hall, and Jenny Lind had sung there. The Sisters now joyfully converted the old building into a convent, and the ballroom was renovated to become St. Mary's Academy. New recruits also enabled the Sisters to take charge of the diocesan orphanage formerly conducted by the Sisters of Charity.

Frances Warde now had the courage, moreover, to open a second free parochial school in St. Patrick's parish in September, 1846. The school was indeed a poor one. Classes were gathered in one long room, their dividing lines being piles of coal and wood used to build the fires in winter. When spring came, long wooden benches separated one class from another. But the Sisters were young, energetic, and happy, and the children were eager to learn. St. Patrick's gave to Pittsburgh some of its finest leaders of Civil War days.

Frances Warde's zeal for seeking more and more Mercy recruits, however, was built upon a vision that encircled far more than the Diocese of Pittsburgh. She possessed the foresight and discernment of the prophet. Her vision was difficult to communicate even to Michael O'Connor and her own

Sisters. The average good person is intent upon the improvement of the work that she must do. The average religious lives and works within the bounds of her immediate apostolate. The religious genius sees what the good religious cannot see. Frances Warde dreamed of Sisters of Mercy caring for the sick poor and instructing children and adults throughout the thirty-one states of the Union and even the Western Territories. Her first promise on landing in New York had been given to William Quarter, the new Bishop of Chicago. Between 1844 and 1846, he had renewed his request over and over again. In the summer of 1846 he declared that he could wait no longer. Neither could Frances Warde!

9

On to the Midwest: Chicago;
First Mercy Hospital

THE courage of Frances Warde and the five young Sisters
who set out with her on the Mercy foundation to the actual
"wild west" wasteland of Chicago in 1846 was literally
heroic. The Pittsburgh missions were demanding, and
Frances was compelled to choose younger members of the
community who could be spared for the Chicago venture. She
chose the youngest of "the first seven," recently professed, as
Superior. In the leadership of Margaret O'Brien, called Sister
Agatha, Frances had perfect confidence. Margaret was only
twenty-four, and the four other members of the Chicago band
were all under twenty-two. The extreme hardship and exposure they were to suffer on this western mission finds silent
testimony in the deaths of three of the five youthful founders
within six years. Within twelve years Margaret O'Brien herself was to die in caring for the sick of Chicago in the horrible
cholera plague of 1858 during which three young Sisters of
Mercy died within twenty-four hours.

When Frances Warde left Pittsburgh for Chicago on
September 18, 1846, she was only thirty-five, but her wisdom
and experience seemed phenomenal when contrasted with
that of the new young Superior and the two novices and two
postulants who accompanied her. Frances was indeed wise in
her choice of Margaret O'Brien as leader. Margaret had entered in Carlow as a lay postulant, but Michael O'Connor and

Sister Frances were quick to discern her potentialities for leadership. She was therefore accepted as a choir Sister in Pittsburgh, the first to be received in the United States. Courage and backbone seem to have been O'Brien family traits. Margaret's older sister, Ellen, had also entered as a lay sister in Carlow with Frances Warde, who chose her for the Westport foundation. In the summer of 1846, precisely when Margaret was preparing for the Chicago foundation, Ellen too was chosen as a choir Sister for a new mission from Westport to Sligo. Like Chicago, the Sligo foundation was at first so plagued with poverty and suffering that the majority of the Sisters sent there found it unendurable. Only Ellen O'Brien persevered with the founder, Sister de Sales Mc-Donnell. The two novices chosen for Chicago by Frances Warde were Sister Vincent McGirr, later Mother Superior, and Sister Gertrude McGuire, who died as first Superior in Galena, Illinois, at the age of twenty-two. The postulants were Eliza Corbett, who was professed on her deathbed four years after her arrival in Chicago, and Eva Schmidt, who died of typhoid in Galena in her twenties.

September is a month of sunshine in Pittsburgh. When Frances Warde and her happy young companions left there a week before Mercy Day, September 24, in order to arrive in Chicago on the Feast of Our Lady of Mercy, it was well that their future was unknown to them. The Chicago mission was to bring greater personal suffering to Frances than any of her other foundations. Traveling from Pittsburgh to Chicago in 1846 was unpleasantly experimental in nature, as the sequel will warrant. Father Walter Quarter, brother of the Chicago Bishop, was sent to Pittsburgh to accompany the six missionaries. The longest but most convenient journey to Chicago was by way of the Great Lakes, and this route was chosen by the travelers. First they sailed thirty miles up the

Ohio River to Beaver, Pennsylvania. There they chartered a stage coach for the fifty mile trip to Poland, Ohio, where they remained overnight. The next morning they engaged a stage for the long journey to Cleveland, during which a wild storm caused them to fear for their lives. They arrived on Saturday night. On Sunday evening they boarded the S.S. *Oregon* on Lake Erie, a steamer which was to carry them to Detroit, then north through Lake Huron, through the Straits of Mackinaw, then south through Lake Michigan to the little port of Chicago. When they reached Detroit, however, their reservations for the remainder of the journey were disputed and they were forced to disembark. Bishop Peter Paul Lefevre of Detroit offered them hospitality and made their forced delay as pleasant as possible. On Tuesday they left for Kalamazoo, Michigan, by stage coach, arriving Wednesday morning after incredible discomfort and fatigue. Here they chartered a stage for the little town of St. Joseph, Michigan, where they had the great luck of catching a small steamer, the *Sam Ward,* which was starting for Chicago. Ordinarily, the road to St. Joseph from Kalamazoo was threatened by stage robbers, but the Sisters were fortunate in that their stage was preceded by a guarded mail coach. After a stormy night and a bright cool day on Lake Michigan, the *Sam Ward* reached Chicago the evening of September 23. The entire journey from Pittsburgh to Chicago in 1846 is a grotesque comparison to the same trip today—a jet flight of less than an hour.

The steamer docked at the mouth of the sluggish Chicago River, directly opposite Madison Street and a stone's throw from the Bishop's house at the corner of Michigan Avenue and Madison. Bishop Quarter had vacated his residence for the Sisters and rented rooms on State Street for himself. Frances Warde and her companions walked to their new convent—the first permanent foundation of religious women in the state of Illinois. Their house was a one-story, unpainted frame building, sixteen by forty feet, a shanty really, without a single living convenience. Later, they called it humorously "a sieve in summer and a shell in winter." Both rain and snow came through the roof. The house was a part of the little "wooden city," or rather village, called Chicago. Its one redeeming feature was that it faced the only beautiful view in sight: the waters of Lake Michigan stretching away to a distant sky.

On the Sisters' first night in Chicago, William Quarter was unable to sleep. He was tortured with doubts and misgivings at having brought five young women to labor in so bleak a wilderness. The next morning, the Feast of Our Lady of Mercy, while he was talking with Frances Warde, he heard the laughter of the five Sisters ringing through the house. They were putting their convent in order. Soon the little cottage would grow with the fruits of their womanly skill and imagination. "I am contented," he said to Mother Frances. "That laughter could never come from the dissatisfied."[1]

There was reason, however, for Bishop Quarter's concern. It has been said that in 1840 the United States was culturally a simple country, but in 1850 it was a complex nation. Chicago in 1840 was a mere trading post with a cluster of families around Fort Dearborn. By 1854 its population was 65,000; in 1857, it was 95,000. When the Sisters of Mercy arrived in 1846, the great expansion had not yet begun. There was not a single railroad out of Chicago. Up until 1852 its lakes and wagon roads were its traffic lines to west, north, and south, and to the commerce of the East. Chicago had no vital connection with the ends of the continent; it was not yet one of the nerves of the nation. Not until 1852 was the most magnificent system of railroads ever established in America begun, and then Chicago became the focus of East-West communication by magic steel. By 1855 the immediate rail connections to Chicago covered 4,000 miles. Underground sewerage was begun the same year, and limestone quarries along the canals initiated a great era of stone buildings.

When Frances Warde arrived with her Sisters, however, life in Chicago was far more primitive than life in Pittsburgh. Only recently the area had been primeval plains occupied by Indian tribes. On the departure of the Sisters from Pittsburgh a city newspaper had stated quite seriously:

Like most of the western cities, Chicago is of recent origin; but, though built in a day, it is a good day's work, and is likely to grow for years. If from the past and present we can judge the future, few places promise better than Chicago.[2]

The population of this new city was made up of trappers, traders, sailors, adventurers, farmers, Indians, and immigrant laborers. Houses were built of logs, cut and laid crosswise upon each other, the spaces between filled with earth and plastered with clay. The unpaved streets were often impassable in bad weather. Sidewalks were of wood: one of the Sisters called them "highways of mud." Traveling and hauling were done by wagon with teams of horses or oxen. Water was carried by bucket. Logs were burned for fire. Wolves appeared now and then at the doors of the log cabins. The frontiers of Chicago were a morass of swampland. Beyond the prairies—perfectly level, immense meadows—were uncharted areas of Illinois still covered with impenetrable forests. Winters were long. There were no libraries, lectures, or theater as in Pittsburgh. Newspapers arrived weekly.

With the spirit of a pioneer, Frances Warde set to work at once to do what had to be done. The thought of failure never entered her mind. William Quarter told her the facts of the religious situation. The Diocese of Chicago comprised the entire state of Illinois. When Quarter arrived in Chicago in 1844, he had found one church and two priests. Hundreds of Catholic immigrants were without spiritual ministry. The first year, the Bishop, traveling 2,000 miles, had made a complete visitation of his diocese. The trails leading out of Chicago, often flooded for weeks, were those made by Indians for hunting, trading, and war and later taken up by trappers and settlers. Over the wild prairies, there were often no roads at all. Quarter sometimes had to go for days without food, depending on farmers for bread, wading knee-deep in mud and water, crossing rivers on horseback, sinking in quagmires, exposed to rain and frost, often spending nights outside on the prairies or sleeping on the floors of poverty-stricken huts. An ordinary sick call sometimes required 100 miles of travel on horseback. Such was the life of the Bishop of the West in the eighteen-forties.[3]

There is indubitable testimony that William Quarter was universally loved, not only by his people but by his priests as well. His suffering made him loving and therefore lovable. When he died suddenly in 1848 at the age of forty-two, he had achieved the unbelievable in four years: he had administered the Sacraments to hundreds, ordained twenty-nine priests and established a seminary, built thirty churches and paid for them, founded schools and the nucleus of a university.[4] Like Edward Nolan and James Maher, he was one of the many saintly priests who became close friends of Frances Warde during her long pioneering apostolate.

Bishop Quarter offered Frances Warde an old frame building in the rear of the convent for the first parochial free school in the state of Illinois. This building had been the first Catholic chapel erected in Chicago. Since his arrival two years before, Quarter had already erected a new church, the

"Cathedral." Between September 24 and October 12, the Sisters succeeded in transforming the old building into "the prettiest and best equipped school on the shores of Lake Michigan." Fifty girls were enrolled at St. Mary's School on October 12. On the same day, the Sisters opened to day students and to ten boarders the first private Catholic academy for young ladies in Chicago, the cradle of "St. Xavier Female Academy of Chicago," officially chartered on February 27, 1847. The power to award baccalaureate degrees was granted with the charter, but St. Xavier College was not opened until 1912. Within only seven years, the Sisters opened a second select school, St. Agatha's Academy. Frances Warde modeled the curriculum of St. Xavier's Academy, Chicago, almost precisely on that of St. Xavier's in Pittsburgh. And Sister Agatha O'Brien named the Chicago institution, like the Pittsburgh one, in honor of Sister Frances.

It was fortunate that the early Chicago Sisters possessed ingenuity, energy, and artistic taste. Because they possessed almost nothing in supplies for their new school, they invented a great deal. Years later, Frances Warde loved to tell how they used parchment sent from Ireland to make geographical maps and finished them with water colors; fashioned globes with sphere-frames of willow branches, over which they neatly fashioned parchment; made blackboards of planed timber formed in squares, fastened to the wall and then painted in the old-fashioned way of producing blackboard surfaces; and constructed numeral-frames on squares of delicate elm framework, with strings of wire stretched horizontally, on which were strung small thread spools painted in bright colors. Near Lake Michigan they collected minerals, sponges, and specimens of vegetation for object lessons.

The children in the first parochial school of Chicago came from families of trappers, sailors, and hardy settlers. Frances

Warde loved the spontaneity of these bright, matter-of-fact youngsters. She often laughed until the tears rolled down her cheeks as she told stories of their unique responses in class and at prayer. On one occasion a little Indian girl appeared at the convent and, clutching the skirt of Sister Frances, "the pale face mother," begged to see "the blackrobe chief." Her father was very ill, and she wished the priest to show him "the kingdom of the Great Spirit."[5]

Frances Warde was busy, meanwhile, in planning the spiritual and corporal works of mercy with her Sisters. She initiated visitation of the sick poor in their homes, visitation of the jail and the almshouse, evening classes for adults, and instruction in Christian Doctrine. On October 9, 1846, she presided at the first public religious ceremony of reception, and on November 21 at the first public religious profession west of the Ohio River. The two Pittsburgh postulants, Eliza Corbett and Eva Schmidt, received the habit. Frances Warde herself conducted a retreat for them and for Sister Gertrude McGuire, who was professed at the Cathedral with all the pomp and ceremony that Frances always used to explain the meaning of religious consecration in the cities and towns of her new foundations. Bishop Quarter addressed all the people of Chicago who cared to attend, Catholic and non-Catholic alike.

Before she left Chicago on November 27, 1846, Frances Warde had already laid plans for an orphan asylum and a hospital.[6] The orphanage for boys, St. Joseph's, and the orphanage for girls, St. Mary's, were opened in the wake of the great cholera epidemic of the summer of 1849 in Chicago. And in 1851 the Sisters took charge of the General Hospital of the Lake, the first permanent hospital in Chicago and the nucleus of Mercy Hospital opened in 1853. In the latter year the Sisters nursed 335 patients, establishing a Mercy tradition in accepting more than half of these as charity patients. The great potato famine in Ireland brought hundreds of Irish laborers to Chicago beginning in 1847, but Mercy Hospital was open to all nationalities and creeds. Between 1840 and 1870 Chicago suffered frequent epidemics of cholera, typhoid fever, malaria, and diphtheria. The Sisters served the city heroically during all of these, especially in 1854 when deaths from cholera numbered sixty a day and 1430 for the year. Besides serving in Mercy Hospital, the Sisters nursed cholera patients at the United States Naval Hospital near the site of old Fort Dearborn. This was the year of Sister Agatha O'Brien's death as a result of contracting cholera from a patient she visited—the same year that three Chicago Sisters died of the plague within one day and four within a week.

As in the case of her previous foundations, Frances Warde would have been happy could she have looked into the future of the Chicago venture of 1846. By 1851 Sister Agatha could write home to Pittsburgh:

Although everything here is plain, it is incredible the good that is being done . . . You can scarcely imagine the amount of labor which our dear Sisters go through; yet all is peace and unity. We have now charge of three Sunday schools . . . We have two free schools well filled, two asylums containing eighty-six orphans, the hospital, and the select school . . . We have to struggle to make ends meet, but yet have all that is necessary, and what more should religious desire?[7]

When Sister Agatha died in 1854, the Sisters conducted nine free parish schools. A branch house had been opened in Galena, Illinois, in 1848, the same year that the Galena and Chicago Union Railroad, the germ of the great Northwestern System, was built. In 1852 another branch house was established in Bourbonnais Grove, Illinois. From then on, the

Chicago congregation developed so rapidly that it became one of the largest of Frances Warde's foundations. It later united with another Mercy congregation that traced its origin to Sister Frances. In 1883 a Mercy foundation came to the West Side of Chicago from Nashville. And the Nashville Sisters had come to Tennessee in 1866 from Providence, Rhode Island, where the Sisters of Mercy were established by Frances Warde in 1851. The South Side and West Side communities in Chicago were united in 1929 with the formation of the Sisters of Mercy of the Union.

There was great sorrow at St. Mary's in Chicago the day that Frances Warde left to return to Pittsburgh. She gathered together her five young friends and talked intimately with them. They seemed like children to her: all were so young to carry on the incredibly hard labor that faced them. But she trusted them completely. She told them that if they possessed poverty of spirit they would be truly loving, for Sisters who are poor in spirit have no ambitions, no personal interests, no opposing wills to clash. They use all their talents for the glory of God, but use them without self-centeredness. Sister Frances recalled to her Sisters the story of St. Francis de Sales, appointed to a sumptuous palace with luxurious apartments, but reserving for himself a narrow, comfortless room in which he studied, wrote, and meditated. She recalled St. Charles Borromeo, assigned to a magnificent castle as Cardinal Borromeo, keeping for himself a wretched attic room with a bed of straw where he prayed and contemplated the goodness of God. The Chicago Sisters had no choice: God had given them poverty of living as a gift. The Sisters treasured for years the words of Frances Warde:

The cup of cold water, the kind word, the gentle look of sympathy, the patient bearing of annoyances from others, forbearance

183

with defects of character; the silent suffering of some trifling insult, some humiliation, some slight injustice; ceding one's rights complacently to others; a soft reply to a harsh word, receiving gracefully and goodnaturedly a refusal or rebuke; an acknowledgment of small favors, a disregard of any want of due appreciation, looking for *no return from anyone* except God alone: such unostentatious practices require holiness. Persons who do not practice these seemingly small responses may repel others by their ungraciousness or put them to inconvenience by their obtrusiveness.[8]

On a cold winter morning with snow and sleet beating down, Frances Warde left Chicago alone for the long journey to Pittsburgh.[9] The rivers and lakes were frozen, so that she was obliged to take a cumbersome Conestoga wagon, full of rough trappers and frontiersmen, over the wagon trails of the prairie wilderness. Since the eighteen-forties were times of "Know-Nothing" attacks, she wore secular dress. In her hands she carried a small muff, in which she held her New Testament and her Office Book. The boat-shaped wagon had one corner set aside for mail bags. Here she contrived to sit for two days and two nights without food or drink. The Sisters, in their grief at her departure, had forgotten to give her the basket of food they had prepared for her. The covered wagon was drawn by horses at a snail's pace through mud often up to the hubs. In the deeper wilderness, the travelers changed from wagon to ox-cart, in which they were bespattered with thick brown mud and often sunk in quagmire. The cart jolted and bounced until all the bones in Frances Warde's body ached. At cheap wayside taverns, only whiskey, black coffee, and black bread were available. When the party stopped, Frances remained in the wagon while rough bordermen stared at her and exclaimed, "Look at the lady!" It was unusual to see a woman traveling alone in such circumstances.

Twenty years later, Frances recalled the sea of snow on the barren prairies, the sullen sky overhead. The boundless West of which she had dreamed seemed awesome in the mysterious solitude of night as she listened to the snoring of passengers and the screeching of prairie chickens.

On the third day, the travelers reached Toledo, then a village of 2,000 people with no streets, only footpaths and wagon trails. It had a number of large houses, a bank, and one hotel, to which Frances hurried. The chambermaid was the first woman she had seen since she left Chicago. The next morning she left the hotel early in fierce winds and drifting snow to search for the only hired coach in town to take her to Mass at the only Catholic church in Toledo. The coachman drove a certain distance and suddenly refused to go farther. No amount of coaxing—and no woman could coax better than Frances—could change his unalterable determination. So she made her way through blinding snow until she reached the church. She participated in the Celebration of the Eucharist, she said later, "getting from the good God more consolation than I deserved." The priest who offered the sacrifice was Louis de Goesbriand, Vicar General of the Diocese of Cleveland. Something in the joyous intrepidity of the plucky woman kneeling before the altar, something in the zeal that sent her to battle a western blizzard to receive the Eucharist in a strange town, aroused the admiration of young Father de Goesbriand. Despite Frances' secular clothes, he knew at once that she was a religious. The two talked together and found in each other the same spirit of the pioneer American apostle. Both had suffered much to spread the Gospel of Christ; both would suffer more. Louis de Goesbriand joined Edward Nolan, James Maher, and William Quarter as members of the increasing band of self-sacrificing priests who found in Frances Warde the religious woman leader gifted with the courage to work side by side with them in preaching Christ. More than twenty-five years later, de Goesbriand, as first Bishop of Burlington, was to ask Sister Frances in Manchester, New Hampshire, to found the first convent of Mercy in the State of Vermont. The two remained friends for life. He stood beside her body when she was buried in 1884.

The morning after Frances met her new friend, she left Toledo in a rickety stage coach. When it had covered only ten miles of rough trails through Ohio, the coach broke down. The male travelers were forced to plow through snow, slough, and mud to drag logs from the woods to raise the wheels of the coach which had sunk into a deep rut. Alone in the coach for two hours, Frances lived in fear of the wild animals of the surrounding country. Then followed hours of cold, weary jogging until the party at last reached Sandusky, Ohio. Frances' tired eyes had never seen a more bleak, desolate spot. Before her was a wretched, straggling hamlet with seeming pasteboard shanties for houses. A huge, swinging billboard marked the "American Hotel," a hostelry not at all inviting. No woman was in sight among the rough trappers with their feet on the bar. Frances hurriedly washed her face and hands in a basin for general use that hung behind a watering trough for horses. Several generations later, a Sister of Mercy in Sandusky erected a small plaque to mark the spot.

In the evening the coach moved eastward again with new passengers. At about ten o'clock that night, the stage again fell into a rut and the horses would not budge. The men passengers went to a farmhouse to borrow two yoke of oxen to draw the coach out of the hole. Continuing on, the stage approached, toward morning, a very hilly region. The men were obliged to get out and hold back the coach as it descended a steep hill, since there was danger of the horses' tumbling into a deep ravine below. The coachman declared that, had not the animals been trained to go up and down almost perpendicular hills, the lives of all would be threatened. As the coach descended, an iron bar from the roof of the wagon fell upon Frances Warde's head. She was almost stunned senseless, but the driver made nothing of the incident. Toward evening the travelers reached Brownsville, a small town with a neat hotel at the foot of a hillside. A good supper was served, but Frances was now too ill and too hungry to eat.

A boat was announced to start at midnight for Pittsburgh. The night was dark and sleety, and rain poured down as Frances crossed the narrow, unsteady plank that led from the river bank to the steamer. In agony from her head injury, she sat quietly among the rough rivermen until half-past three o'clock the next morning when the boat docked in Pittsburgh. No coach of any kind was at the wharf, and the landing area was unfamiliar to Frances. She asked an old man the way to the convent, and he told her it was on Penn Street! Through the blackness of the cold, rainy morning she searched alone through the muddy streets and found St. Mary's before daybreak. Opening the outer gate of the convent with great effort, she knocked on the door. A half hour passed before the Sisters heard her. Then all at once they were with her, removing her clothes saturated with water and mud. From hunger, exhaustion, and the blow she had received on her head, Frances was in a state of utter collapse. Double pneumonia had developed. For ten days she hovered between life and death.

The Chicago foundation, which nearly cost Frances Warde her life, continued to grow under the shadow of suffering. In its early days, "the grass was always green" on the graves of its Sisters. The heroism of its founder was the seed that brought it rapidly to the maturity of an old foundation. Even the great Chicago fire of 1871 was no obstacle. Poverty, plague, fire, war, perils by land and sea produced the fruit of the spirit. Never was it more true that, "unless the seed die, it remains alone."

Frances returned to Pittsburgh with one thought foremost in her mind. Even before she went to Chicago—in fact, back in Carlow when the Pittsburgh foundation had been first planned—a hospital to care for the sick in the City of the Three Rivers had been projected. To be sure, there was no public health nursing service in the eighteen-forties. When the Sisters visited the sick poor in Pittsburgh they bathed their patients, fed them, made their beds, cleaned their homes, and carried out all doctors' directions. Often they carried food and simple remedies with them on their rounds. Meanwhile, the need for a hospital and for nursing care on a more professional level became more apparent. Inventions were revolutionizing medicine. In October, 1846, ether was discovered and demonstrated. Soon after, the microscope was examined with amazement in Pittsburgh. Hospitals existed only in the large Eastern cities like New York and Philadelphia. But civic-minded Pittsburghers were beginning to be critical of the way the city handled its sick, particularly during recurrent epidemics of cholera, smallpox, and typhoid.

In 1845 the city fathers had instructed that an old coal shed of the first water works on Cecil Alley be fitted up for the segregation of smallpox victims. A doctor and a practical nurse were appointed to serve there. Smallpox was a yearly visitant somewhat taken for granted by all urban dwellers in the forties. Vaccination had been introduced back in 1828, but it was not enforced. The "coal shed hospital" rather than the smallpox roused Pittsburgh citizens in 1845. Their civic pride was stung. A group of Pittsburghers organized themselves with the purpose of establishing a hospital, but a year passed without concrete action. In the late summer of 1846 smallpox appeared in the city, and the coal shed hospital again became a municipal issue. Many Pittsburghers believed, however, that hospitals reeked with infection, that the poor preferred the almshouse, that aggregation of the sick only contaminated the atmosphere. So again the idea of a hospital was pigeon-holed. In the fall of 1846, Pittsburgh newspapers condemned the citizenry for lack of concern for the sick.

In this controversial setting, Bishop Michael O'Connor decided in November, 1846, that the Diocese of Pittsburgh and the Sisters of Mercy must take the initiative in providing a hospital. Frances Warde hurried home from Chicago to implement plans. The large ballroom of the former Concert Hall, now St. Mary's Convent, on Penn Street was transformed into a general ward for men, a smaller room into a ward for women, and several adjacent rooms into quarters for private patients. The Bishop appealed for contributions throughout the city. He then established a society called the Brotherhood of St. Joseph to plan and secure funds for a permanent new hospital building. On December 1, 1846, notice was given in the *Pittsburgh Commercial Journal* that a hospital would soon be opened under the auspices of the Sisters of Mercy to "persons of every class, condition, and religious persuasion," and that assistance would be offered "to the poor and destitute to the utmost limit of the means of the institution." The reaction to this announcement was predictable. In 1846 bigotry and "Know-Nothingism" were rampant. A non-Catholic organization immediately announced plans for a rival establishment. But the latter did not materialize. On January 1, 1847, the first permanent hospital west of the Allegheny Mountains and the first Mercy Hospital in the world was opened by Frances Warde in St. Mary's Convent building on Penn Street. The first patient was a sick marine who had just landed at the Pittsburgh wharf in a river boat. By an odd turn of fortune, he was a bigot who had recently taken part in the burning of the Catholic Cathedral in Philadelphia. For fourteen months, the hospital flourished in old Concert Hall. Over 250 patients received care during this time. Sick soldiers returning broken down in health from the battlefronts of the Mexican War made up a large number of the early patients.

Then came the crucial year of test for the heroic charity and mercy of Frances Warde and her Sisters in their first hospital. Toward the end of 1847 and early in 1848 numerous typhoid cases were reported in New York, Maryland, and Eastern Pennsylvania. One day in January a sick seaman was admitted to Mercy Hospital in Pittsburgh. Dr. William Addison, one of the early city's great names in medicine, diagnosed the illness as typhus fever. Frances Warde was called to the council table to share in the necessary immediate decision. Her thoughts went back to the cholera and typhoid plagues in Ireland in 1832 and 1840: she had been through it all. She knew that her Sisters were ready to sacrifice themselves. She decided at once to use the men's ward as isolation quarters for typhus patients. Soon eighteen more cases were admitted from the river boats. From January until April the available doctors and the Sisters struggled with the disease. When spring came, fifteen of the nineteen patients were restored to health.

The Sisters, who exhausted themselves in caring for the sick, did not fare so well. Sister Anne Rigney, a novice, died February 11, 1848. Sister Catherine Lawler, still a postulant, died March 3 and Sister Magdalen Reinbolt, another novice, died March 5. As a crowning sorrow, Sister Xavier Tiernan, Director of Novices and first American Sister of Mercy, died March 9. The letter did not die of typhoid but of erysipelas complicated by extreme exhaustion. All of the small hospital staff of Sisters, with the exception of Sister Isidore Fisher, the administrator, were wiped out. The sad story of sacrifice spread not only in Pittsburgh but throughout the country and beyond the seas. The response of the public was reverential admiration. The holocaust killed all bigotry against the nursing Sisters of Mercy among Pittsburgh residents. The four Sisters were buried in a new little cemetery on the grounds of the new Mercy Hospital not yet completed. Other Sisters took their places. They not only cared for the sick; they buried the dead. The hospital daybook indicates that funerals took place directly from Mercy Hospital. Frances Warde's grief for her young Sisters cannot be described. Her trust in God did not waver. Years later the Sisters in Pittsburgh, remembering their great tragedy of 1848, recalled her words from the Book of Job which she loved: "The Lord gave and the Lord has taken away. Blessed be the will of God."[10]

Frances Warde's own health was now shattered. Following her almost fatal journey from Chicago, the deaths of so many of her Sisters, the labor and anguish of the typhoid epidemic crushed her. Tuberculosis, moreover, had made its inroads among the young Sisters. Aloysia Strange, the second of "the first seven" to die, had succumbed to the white plague in July, 1847, and Sister Anastasia McGawley, who had returned to America with Frances as a recruit from Cork, had died in December, 1847. Death seemed to be a continual visitor at the convent in old Concert Hall. When the last of the typhus patients was discharged, no new patients were admitted to the hospital. Doctor William Addison confided to Bishop O'Connor that he believed Frances Warde would die if she were not removed immediately from this "house of death."[11] The concerned Bishop gave over his own residence near St. Paul's Cathedral to the Sisters in April, 1848, and found a residence for himself on Grant Street.

Despite her illness, Frances Warde now acted with her usual decisiveness. In the spring of 1848 she had the Congregation of Mercy incorporated by the State Legislature as "Sisters of Mercy of Allegheny County." She purchased property on Webster Avenue with the dowries of the Sisters and initiated the building of St. Mary's Convent which was to serve the Congregation as a motherhouse for more than half a century. The Sisters lived in the Episcopal Residence for two years until the new St. Mary's was opened December 26, 1850. St. Mary's Academy had been moved in January, 1847, to a rented house attached to the convent in Concert Hall, then to rooms in the Episcopal Residence which served as a convent, and again to quarters on Webster Avenue formerly used by the orphan asylum. Frances Warde planned the new St. Mary's convent to provide one of the finest private schools in Western Pennsylvania. St. Mary's Academy flourished there until it was moved to Mount Mercy, Pittsburgh, the present site of Carlow College. Our Lady of Mercy Academy, one of the oldest private Catholic schools west of the Alleghenies, is now located in Monroeville near Pittsburgh.

If events in the city of Pittsburgh brought great sorrow to Frances Warde in 1847–48, the academy conducted by the Sisters outside the city in Latrobe brought her quiet joy. The new school on the Kuhn property was opened with great rejoicing in 1847. The graduation exercises of Mount St. Vincent's Academy for the class of 1847 were held on the lawn of the new school, though the building was not quite completed. The class of 1848 was the first to actually attend classes at the new academy. The name "Mount St. Vincent's" was changed to "St. Xavier's" in honor of Mother Frances. She had shown uncanny foresight in her choice of the site for St. Xavier Academy. The school stood on a tree-covered eminence close to the Pittsburgh-Philadelphia turnpike. The building itself was beautiful, nestled in a natural grove of ancient trees, flanked in time by velvet lawns, lovely walks, and colorful landscape gardens with newly planted orchards beyond. Farther away were broad fields edged with greater woods. And beyond all, the magnificent panorama of the Chestnut Ridge. This "select" school soon ranked among the foremost educational institutions in the United States. Its faculty were the best educated Sisters in the community. Bishop Michael O'Connor himself and his gifted brother, James O'Connor, second chaplain at St. Xavier's and later Bishop of Omaha, contributed to the curriculum, the actual teaching, and the public examinations. Many of the courses offered, especially in theology, philosophy, and languages, were actually on a college level. Year after year, the *Pittsburgh Catholic* published regular academic accounts of this superb academy for young women. Of all the institutions in the Diocese of Pittsburgh, it was the apple of Michael O'Connor's eye. Within a few years, some of its outstanding students were novices with the Sisters of Mercy.

But a special joy in St. Xavier's was reserved for Frances Warde. Her own two nieces, Jane and Fanny Warde, were enrolled in the first class at Mt. St. Vincent's Academy and completed their studies at St. Xavier Academy.[12] Like their aunt, they were brilliant young women and received outstanding scholarly awards every year between 1846 and 1852. Their brother John later married one of their classmates, Margaret Keogh, who became a popular fiction writer of the day and established her own private school in Pittsburgh. Chevalier Jackson, who received thirty honors from twelve countries for developing the surgical science of bronchoscopy, was a boy student in "Mrs. Warde's School." Margaret Warde was the author of a best-selling novel of the period called *Going Home* and of a poem, "Casket and Key," declared by Henry Wadsworth Longfellow to be one of the finest poems of the century. Deeply involved as Frances Warde was in the sufferings of the young Congregation of Mercy, St. Xavier's Academy offered her joy. She lived to see it develop and expand beyond her dreams for it.

On May 9, 1848, the Sisters of Mercy under Frances Warde opened the new Mercy Hospital on Stevenson Street to the great rejoicing of the people of Pittsburgh. It was actually a simple establishment of forty rooms—wards, private rooms, maintenance units, and residence for the Sister staff. In 1848 the revolution in medicine which brought medical technology, radiology, and cardiology had not yet begun. The new Mercy Hospital had two goals: to provide the best medical and nursing care known to the age, and to minister spiritually to all Catholic patients. The administrator, Sister Josephine Cullen of "the first seven," filled multiple offices. In the first year, 1848, hospital reports to the public were initiated. The six staff physicians were the finest in the city. Over the years, the Pittsburgh Mercy Hospital was to develop into one of the finest medical institutions in the United States. Modern surgical methods were introduced as rapidly as they appeared. New departments, specialized laboratories, diagnostic clinics followed one another in rapid succession. The Sisters served courageously during the cholera outbreaks of 1848–51, 1854–55, 1866–67, and 1873–77. During the Civil War they administered and nursed at both the Western Pennsylvania Military Hospital and Stanton Military Hospital in Washington, D. C. Training of nurses actually began in the hospital the first day of its existence, January 1, 1847. Officially, the Pittsburgh Mercy School of Nursing dates from 1893. Physical expansion in the hospital kept pace with that of departments until it covered more than a large city block. Frances Warde could never have imagined the future of the tiny hospital she opened in St. Mary's Convent on Penn Street in 1847.

When the new Mercy Hospital was opened in the spring of 1848, Frances Warde was already planning a further extension of the Mercy apostolate. Incredible as it seems—despite the loss of Sisters to the Chicago foundation, despite the tragic loss of the Sister nurses in Mercy Hospital, despite intense personal suffering, illness, and exhaustion—she was now projecting a new foundation for May, 1848, to Loretto, the mountain settlement of Prince Demetrius Gallitzin, which had so stirred her zeal and imagination on her journey across the Allegheny Mountains to Pittsburgh in 1843.

10

Unique Mission: Loretto; Trouble in Chicago and Pittsburgh

OF all the romantic stories of the early days of the Catholic Church in the United States, perhaps none is more fascinating than that of Prince Demetrius Gallitzin and the founding of the town of Loretto in the Allegheny Mountains. Idealist as Frances Warde was, it is no wonder that the odyssey of the Russian prince aroused her missionary zeal for the people of Loretto.

Prince Gallitzin, born at The Hague, Holland, in 1770, was the son of Prince Dimitri Alexeievitch Gallitzin, Envoy Extraordinary of Catherine the Great to the Hague, and Countess Amalia von Schmettau, daughter of a famous Prussian Field Marshall. His father was a friend of Voltaire and Diderot. His mother was the center of a literary group that entertained Goethe. While still a boy, young Dimitri received a commission in the Russian army. His mother took him to Muenster for his university education, and there at the age of seventeen he became a Roman Catholic. Soon he was appointed an aide-de-camp to the Austrian High Command at Brabant. Since he was destined for a military or diplomatic career, travel was considered essential to perfect his education. But political disturbances in Europe rendered a grand tour of the continent dangerous; so he was sent to the New World in 1792 to study the Constitution of the

United States and the character of the American political system. So as not to be recognized as a Prince, he set sail from Rotterdam under the name of Augustine Schmett, carrying with him letters of introduction to outstanding American leaders like George Washington and John Adams.

In Baltimore he met Bishop John Carroll, who two years previously had been consecrated in England for the See of Baltimore, marking the beginning of the hierarchy of the Catholic Church in America. In effect, Carroll was Bishop of the entire United States. Through him, the young Dimitri became acquainted with the Sulpician Fathers at St. Mary's Seminary in Baltimore and, to the chagrin of his own father, decided to become a priest. According to Russian law, he could no longer inherit the estates that were his as the only son of a prince of a Russian family of older blood than that of the Romanoffs. He was ordained in 1795, the first man to receive all the orders from tonsure to priesthood in the Catholic Church in the United States.[1] He was assigned first to Port Tobacco, near Washington, and then to Conewago near Gettysburg, an extensive mission in the wilderness which included parts of both Maryland and Pennsylvania. In July, 1799, he was appointed pastor of a tract of land in the Allegheny Mountains which included all the present Diocese of Altoona and parts of the present Pittsburgh and Erie Dioceses as well. The call for help which brought him this assignment, destined to be his life's work, came from a village called McGuire's Settlement high in the Allegheny Mountains. It was named for Captain Michael McGuire, whose odyssey was almost as romantic as Gallitzin's own.

In 1788 Captain McGuire, a hero of the Revolutionary War, came with his family from Maryland to a spot high up in the Alleghenies where the town of Loretto now stands. He established the first permanent settlement in the area later called Cambria County. Previously, he had explored the territory between Conewago and his chosen tract of land, undertaking a dangerous and daring journey through unbroken forests on horseback, through brushwood so thick that his party had to cut it as they advanced. In these forests were still lingering Indian tribes and wild animals in the dense thickets. An expert trapper and hunter, McGuire decided to establish his own family in "Captain McGuire's Settlement" in the wilderness. Soon other families joined them. Concerned about the spiritual needs of his little colony, McGuire made over to Bishop John Carroll 400 acres of his own land "for the establishment of religion and the maintenance of resident clergy." The challenge of the frontier apostolate appealed to young Gallitzin, who petitioned to serve the Christian people of the Alleghenies. In a little log cabin which he built himself on the mountain-top, he celebrated the Eucharist for the first time at McGuire's Settlement on Christmas Eve in 1799.

Gallitzin called the town Loretto in honor of the Virgin Mary. He laid out a plan for the town himself, naming the main thoroughfare St. Mary's Street, crossed by St. John, St. Peter, and St. Paul Streets. He bought more land, cleared it, and allotted farms to immigrants. He then erected saw mills and grist mills. Soon he had more than forty families in Loretto and extended his labors to other small settlements in the mountains. Gallitzin was everything to his people. With his slight medical knowledge, he was doctor to their ills. He was magistrate to their quarrels. His own log cabin was open in charity to all. Here he lived simply, slept on a mattress on the floor, ate coarse food, and wore coarser clothing. A scholar, he lacked intellectual companionship but found time to publish apologetic works, such as his "Defence of Catholic Principles." Reared a prince, he tramped over

Indian mountain trails or journeyed on horseback to isolated settlements to minister to his people. Accustomed in early years to luxury, he fasted and prayed in a log cabin church never heated by fire even in the depths of winter. When he died in 1840, there were 6,000 Catholics in the town of Loretto alone. Gallitzin had hoped to convert Loretto into a replica of a European city. Hoping that Loretto would be the center of a diocese in Western Pennsylvania, he refused bishoprics in Louisville, Cincinnati, and Detroit. Though his hopes for Loretto were not realized, his apostolate was. And he himself developed at last a reputation as a saint.

The desire of the dying Demetrius Gallitzin in 1840 that Sisters would come to the Allegheny Mountains to serve his people could not be ignored by Frances Warde. Her own spirit was too much like that of the prince priest to leave his dream unfulfilled. Had he lived until 1848, he would have joined the priest-apostles James Maher, Michael O'Connor, William Quarter, and Louis de Goesbriand as associates of Frances Warde in extending the frontier of the Word of God throughout the United States. His spirit was alive in Frances Warde when she decided to establish the Sisters of Mercy in Loretto.

Unfortunately, Frances was still too ill, after the exhaustion of the typhoid epidemic of the early months of 1848, to accompany the Sisters personally from Pittsburgh on the journey to Loretto. She decided that the poverty of the mission required that it should be a branch house for a time rather than a foundation. She chose the Sisters for the new convent prudently: they would have to be able to bear extreme hardship. The pastor of Loretto who invited them to his mission in 1848 was Father Hugh Gallagher, who later provided a link between Frances Warde and the Sisters of Mercy of faraway San Francisco, founded from Kinsale, Ireland, in 1854. Four years after the Mercy Sisters were established in Loretto, Father Gallagher joined Bishop J. S. Alemany in San Francisco. He desired to bring a foundation of Pittsburgh Sisters to the Far West, but Sisters from Pittsburgh were not available at the time.[2] Gallagher therefore went back to Ireland to bring a colony of Sisters from Kinsale to establish the San Francisco foundation, which now has its center in Burlingame, California. In 1848, Gallagher had joyfully welcomed the Pittsburgh Sisters to Gallitzin's mountain settlement.

The Superior chosen by Frances Warde for Loretto was Sister Catherine Wynne. The daughter of Major Thomas Wynne of Pittsburgh, Eliza Wynne was the third postulant to enter in Pittsburgh and had been professed for just a year. She had already acted as Assistant to Sister Josephine Cullen, Superior and Director at St. Xavier's Academy in Latrobe. Later she was to serve in St. Paul's Orphanage, Pittsburgh, and then become the fourth administrator of Mercy Hospital in Pittsburgh. In 1855 she was to become founder of the Sisters of Mercy in Baltimore, Maryland, from which she would also establish a foundation in Vicksburg, Mississippi, in 1860. Frances Warde knew that, with Catherine Wynne as leader, the mission to Loretto would succeed. Accompanying Sister Catherine were Sister Rose Hostetter, daughter of an Ohio judge, who later became Mother Superior of the Pittsburgh Sisters of Mercy; Sister Christine Newman, a novice and a musician, who later became local Superior in Loretto; and Sister Lucy McGivern, a lay Sister who was to cheerfully accomplish the manual work of at least four persons on the new mission.

On a sunny day in May, 1848, Frances Warde said farewell to the four as they left Pittsburgh by stage coach for the journey to Loretto in the Alleghenies. The seventy-five mile trip could not be made in one day; so the Sisters spent the night in Ebensburg, a Welsh settlement. The next morning they continued their journey in the carriage of their host in Ebensburg, whose daughter was one of the first students at St. Xavier's Academy. As they traveled down the plank road to Loretto, all the people of the town came out to meet them. Among the townspeople were six young Franciscans from Ireland who had arrived in Loretto the year before and had already converted an old brewery there into a fine monastery, the nucleus of the present magnificent St. Francis College. The town itself was much the same as Demetrius Gallitzin had left it eight years earlier. Recollections of the holy man were still very much alive among the mountaineers.

The Sisters' convent was a small frame house situated on a few acres of Gallitzin property on St. Mary's Street in the heart of the village. It was a dilapidated little convent, and the Sisters suffered severe hardships during their first winter in Loretto. They were often cold and exhausted. Sometimes they endured real hunger. Fuel as well as food was scarce. Wood was the only fuel, and open fireplaces the only means of heating and cooking. If the fire went out, the Sisters had to run to a neighbor for a burning piece of wood. Bread was baked in a twenty-pound iron pot covered with embers. Water came from an outside pump. In winter, snow drifts piled as high as second story windows.

But the works of mercy were initiated immediately in true Frances Warde fashion. The Sisters had learned well from her how to serve the poor. They started the visitation and care of the sick at once. Since all the children in the settlement were Catholic, the Sisters assumed the administration and teaching of the public school. Classes in Christian Doctrine were begun on their first Sunday in Loretto. These were conducted first in a tinner's shop next to the convent and later in the district school. The simplicity of the children of the mountains made their work exceptionally fruitful. Later, St. Aloysius Academy, a boarding school for girls, was erected on property adjoining the new St. Michael's Church and opened by the Sisters in 1853. It was built largely by the men of the parish, with the understanding that the Sisters would maintain a free day school for their children as long as they remained in Loretto.[3]

The winter of 1848–49, the first for the four Pittsburgh Sisters in Loretto, was a period of anxiety for Frances Warde. She understood the full impact of the privations suffered by her Sisters in the mountains. She did not wish to repeat the holocaust of the typhoid plague in Pittsburgh. She was willing to suffer personally—she had unquestionably demonstrated this willingness—but she was unhappy when her Sisters experienced extreme suffering. At times she almost doubted the wisdom of the foundation. When spring came, she went to Loretto herself, half intending to recall the Sisters to Pittsburgh. But each time she offered them the option of closing the mission, they desired "to stay a little longer." Soon everyone concerned knew that the convent would be a permanent one.

In 1851 the first parish mission in the Diocese of Pittsburgh was held in the old frame church in Loretto. The new St. Michael's Church was not yet completed. The mission was conducted by the Redemptorist Isaac T. Hecker, later founder of the Congregation of Paulists. Neither he nor Frances Warde knew in 1851 that their paths would cross a decade later in the interest of Kent Stone, Father Fidelis of the Cross, one of the greatest of the Paulist Fathers. In 1852, the Sisters at last moved to their own new convent in Loretto. Frances Warde was not present for its opening. She had already moved on to new foundations in New England.

The Sisters of Mercy prospered in Loretto, as they did in all of Frances Warde's early foundations. St. Aloysius Academy moved to a new and beautiful location in Cresson, Pennsylvania, in 1897. The new academy was situated on a commanding hillside near the famous "Mountain House," built in 1860 in Mountain House Park, Cresson. The latter was visited by President Benjamin Harrison and was the site of a summer home built by Andrew Carnegie. On a neighboring hillside was the estate of industrialist Charles M. Schwab, who was taught by the Sisters of Mercy in Loretto as a boy and who later became their benefactor. Directly opposite Mt. Aloysius is Peary Memorial Park, dedicated to Admiral Robert Edwin Peary, son of a Cresson stave maker, who conquered the North Pole on his eighth expedition to the Arctic. When Mt. Aloysius Academy opened in Cresson, the old academy in Loretto became an orphanage. More than twenty-five branch houses were established from Loretto and from the later motherhouse in Cresson. In 1879 the Cresson community became a Congregation independent from the Pittsburgh Sisters. The Cresson Sisters established Mercy Hospital in Johnstown in 1911. They founded the first Junior College in Pennsylvania, Mount Aloysius, in 1939. For years, it was the only junior college between Philadelphia and the midwestern States. The Cresson Sisters joined the Sisters of Mercy of the Union in 1929 and are now affiliated with the Province of Scranton.

Frances Warde's concern for her Sisters in Loretto was not the only anxiety she experienced in 1848–49. The sudden death of her good friend, Bishop Quarter of Chicago, on April 10, 1848, precipitated a crisis among the Chicago Sisters of Mercy which required unusual wisdom in order to restore harmony. Before the Sisters had left for Chicago in 1846, William Quarter had made an agreement with Bishop Michael O'Connor to "provide amply" for them. In 1847 Quarter built the new St. Xavier's Convent and Academy for the Sisters of Mercy. It should be added, however, that Mother Agatha O'Brien herself wrote to the Propagation of the Faith in Lyons, France, in 1847, requesting funds for the Mercy apostolate and that the Society responded with a contribution of $4000 to the Bishop, who was also strongly supported by the French Society.[4] Bishop Quarter and Mother Agatha cooperated beautifully in the Chicago apostolate. There was an understanding between them that the Sisters were to receive seventeen acres on the shores of Lake Michigan between the lake and the old Catholic cemetery. The lake receded and the seventeen acres became twenty. The property also became in time a part of the most valuable lake shore property in the city of Chicago. When William Quarter died suddenly in 1848, his brother, Father Walter Quarter, was appointed Administrator of the Diocese of Chicago. Indicating that fate had prevented the *legal* transference of the lakeshore property intended for the Sisters of Mercy, he gave the deeds for this property to Mother Agatha.

After a lapse of months, Bishop James Oliver Van de Velde was appointed second Bishop of Chicago. He challenged the right of the Sisters to hold property in common and demanded that Mother Agatha return the deeds of the lake shore acres to him. Walter Quarter pointed out that by an Act of the Legislature of the State of Illinois, the Bishop of Chicago held in trust all ecclesiastical property with two exceptions—the University of St. Mary of the Lake and the Convent of the Sisters of Mercy.[5] In true Spartan fashion, twenty-six year old Sister Agatha O'Brien refused to give Bishop Van de Velde the deeds to the property of the Sisters. She wrote to Pittsburgh and secured the support of Michael O'Connor and Frances Warde. On April 23, 1849, she left Chicago for Pittsburgh, adamant in her decision to withdraw the Sisters of Mercy from Chicago if their property rights were not safeguarded. Bishop Van de Velde also went to Pittsburgh to argue his case. But proof was offered that the Archbishop of Baltimore, under whose jurisdiction was the See of Chicago, had approved the Sisters' rights to their property even before Van de Velde's appointment. The Chicago prelate could do nothing. Mother Agatha returned to Chicago August 7, 1849, with a promise that in the future her Sisters would own their own property as a Corporation sanctioned by the Legislature of Illinois. Frances Warde was proud of her young protégée.

The sequel of the above confrontation—truly amazing in the lives of Sisters of the midwest Catholic Church of 1849 —was less happy. Dissensions among clergy and laity became so violent during the administration of Van de Velde that he resigned the Chicago See in 1853. His successor, Bishop Anthony O'Regan, was scarcely more fortunate in his management of diocesan affairs. Eventually, he too was forced to resign the Chicago mitre in the midst of great discord. During the early years of his administration, Sister Vincent McGirr, always docile toward the hierarchy, was elected third Superior of the Chicago Sisters. Frances Warde, then in Providence, Rhode Island, but always watchful of the convents she had founded, was wisely fearful for the Chicago Sisters. Early in 1856, she wrote to Father James O'Connor in Pittsburgh: "I have had a long letter from Sister M. Vincent McGirr. By it I perceive with regret that she is the Mother Superior. I trust in God that my fears may not be realized in her regard."[6] Frances' fears were indeed well grounded. O'Regan at once took advantage of his opportunity. He demanded the deeds to the North Shore property of the Sisters for which Agatha O'Brien had struggled so successfully. On March 20, 1856, he met with the General Council of the Chicago Sisters. Mother Vincent McGirr agreed to give over the property deeds to O'Regan. But Sister Genevieve Granger, the Assistant Superior, refused to sign the agreement. Whereupon Sister Vincent deposed her and appointed Sister de Chantal Maxwell as Assistant Superior.[7] The latter consented to O'Regan's terms, and the deeds to the extremely valuable North Shore acres were exchanged for those of the convent and lot of the Sisters on Wabash Avenue. In addition to their valuable property, the Sisters were also obliged to give to the Bishop a note for $4000 to be paid at six per cent interest. When O'Regan, no longer Bishop of Chicago, died in London in 1866, he "bequeathed" $3000 to the Sisters, so that the $4000 note was reduced to $1000. But their invaluable lakeshore property was lost forever. The ironic conclusion to the Chicago story is that the deposed Sister Genevieve Granger was elected Mother Superior within some years and became perhaps the greatest leader the Chicago Congregation ever had.

Not only was Frances Warde delighted with the firmness and fortitude of young Sister Agatha O'Brien in Chicago in 1849; she experienced great joy in the apostolic ventures of the Sisters in all the convents she founded. The Sisters grew accustomed to calling her "the Reverend Mother" in their letters to one another. This term of address, when used without a Christian name, applied only to Frances Warde. Though the early foundations in Ireland and America were completely independent congregations, all the convents founded by Mother Frances looked to her for counsel and support. She was their source and their head.

One of the Sisters dearest of all to Frances was her cousin, Sister Cecilia Maher, Superior at St. Leo's, Carlow. Since entering St. Leo's in 1839, she had never failed to keep in close touch with Frances. When the latter returned to Ireland in 1845, only Bishop Francis Haly's refusal of permission had prevented Sister Cecilia's returning to Pittsburgh with Frances. When Cecilia received news from Frances Warde in Pittsburgh, she invariably hastened to inform all the Irish convents. Early in 1847, she had written in a letter to Dublin:

. . . I had a long letter from dearest Revd. Mother [Frances Warde]. All going on, thank God, well as possible. I send herewith the account of their hospital, the first in the Order! ! ! The account is from the *Pittsburgh Commercial Journal,* a Protestant paper, which makes one value the eulogies more.[8]

One can imagine Frances Warde's joy, then, when she received a letter in August, 1849, from her dear friend, Cecilia, announcing that she was about to lead the first Mercy foundation to New Zealand from St. Leo's, Carlow.[9] Frances might well have wondered why Bishop Haly would allow Mother Cecilia and several Carlow Sisters to go all the way to the Antipodes but not to Pittsburgh! The same contrariness that once made him resent Frances Warde's independence and yet demand that she return to Carlow after two years in America seemed to be at work again. Now he decided to allow Sister Cecilia to go to New Zealand because of the great good accomplished by Frances Warde in *Pittsburgh!* Cecilia Maher described his response in her letter to Frances. First he had refused to let her go. Then, after he consulted James Maher, he changed his mind. Sister Cecilia wrote:

The Bishop offered the Holy Sacrifice to learn the Divine Will and at three o'clock came into the college [Carlow] parlour, said he had been praying, thinking, and consulting much, and finally came to the conclusion that it was God Who called, that the immense good which had been effected *in Pittsburgh* induced him to come to this conclusion, and finally that he consented! ! !

No one was more apt than Frances Warde to appreciate the droll humor of Francis Haly's decision.

The Sisters left Carlow for their long journey to New Zealand on August 8, 1849. After eight full months of travel, they arrived in Auckland April 9, 1850! Cecilia wrote to Frances Warde again from the Cape of Good Hope. In her letter she told Frances of the unique apostolate of Bishop Jean Baptiste Pompallier of Auckland who accompanied the Sisters to New Zealand. As a Marist at Lyons, France, he had directed 300 novices. But his zeal for the foreign missions had persuaded Pope Gregory XVI to summon him to Rome and to consecrate him Bishop to preach the Gospel in the archipelagoes of Oceania. Pompallier traveled throughout the South Seas, converting and baptizing 10,000 people. In a short time, five bishops were appointed to the vast regions entrusted to his apostolic care. "Fancy us seated around Dr. Pompallier," Cecilia wrote to Frances, "a tropical sky spangled with stars above, the dark sea rolling beneath. He tells us of his wonderful escapes; sometimes he speaks of the secrets of heaven."[10]

What did Frances Warde think as she read, more and more frequently, of Mercy foundations expanding throughout the world—north, south, east, and west? Her dream of spreading the Mercy apostolate, since the time of her visionary days in Dublin with Catherine McAuley, had always embraced the whole world. Now she watched the dream become a reality before her eyes, without Catherine McAuley beside her to see. A few years later, when Frances was in Providence, Rhode Island, Cecilia Maher reminded her of how little the future

was known to the early Sisters in Carlow. Cecilia had written
to their mutual cousin and dear friend, James Maher:

Tell me, dear Father Maher, are not promises delusive? Do you
recollect that you said, "We shall always keep the first twelve
Sisters that entered St. Leo's to live and die here; the young we
shall send forth"? And how these twelve are now scattered over
the face of the earth—in many parts of Ireland, England, Pennsylvania, Illinois, Rhode Island, New Zealand! Well, the last
trumpet will bring us all and our friends together, and we shall,
please God, have a joyful meeting, all, *all*, on the right side.[11]

When Frances Warde read Cecilia Maher's letters in 1849,
she might have felt justly that she had already fulfilled more
than a life's work. In point of fact, she was not yet forty
years of age. In her own eyes, her work had just begun. Whatever the future might bring, it was certain that the Mercy
apostolate would soon call her to new beginnings. Her next
venture, her foundation to Providence, the beginning of her
expansion of the Mercy apostolate into Rhode Island, Connecticut, New Hampshire, Maine, and Vermont, was initiated
by Providence without actual impetus from Frances herself.
The Chicago and Loretto foundations had been fulfillments
of human promises. The Providence foundation was a gift
from God.

Notwithstanding the sufferings that were an inherent part
of Frances' apostolic mission—the dreadful typhoid plague
and the deaths of her Sisters, the almost fatal hardships of the
Chicago foundation, the desperate anxiety concerning the
Loretto establishment—Frances was happy during her early
years in Pittsburgh, her first American foundation. In a letter
to Carlow some time after the first seven arrived in the United
States, Sister Aloysia Strange had expressed well the reason

for Frances' personal fulfillment in her Pittsburgh apostolate: "Dear Rev. Mother has here an ample field for her unbounded zeal; the number of converts she has instructed is almost beyond counting."[12] Frances' sense of mission, of universal mission, was at the core of her religious vocation. Because this was so, her whole being sang with joy as she participated in the spread of the Kingdom. An insight into her happy spirit as well as her rare sense of humor is found in a letter she wrote to Father James O'Connor, brother of Bishop O'Connor, early in 1850. James had gone south for his health during the winter of 1849–50. Evidently he had written Frances a note reproving her for not keeping him informed concerning the Mercy convent in Pittsburgh. She answered with a warm and newsy letter[13] about the Pittsburgh apostolate which is also an example of her writing style. Since so few of her letters are extant, this one will be quoted in full:

> Convent of Our Lady of Mercy
> St. Mary's, Pittsburgh

Dear Rvd. Sir

I received from Washington City your note which conveyed to us the pleasing intelligence that so far your health was improved by your journey southward. And since that time, the Bishop has informed us often of its progress as you advanced toward the Sunny South. We heard with regret of the attack on your chest on your arrival at Charleston, but as a few weeks have passed away since we heard this unpleasant news, we are willing to hope and trust in God that your location for the winter in a Southern clime will finally restore your wonted strength. And I assure you our prayers for that purpose have not nor shall they be wanting to you. Well now, it may be that you expected a letter from me, but as you did not express any wish to that effect, I did not intend to obtrude a letter unsought for. And you know that if I only attended to my duties as I should do, I should not have a moment unoccupied. But yet if I thought it would afford you any gratification to hear from me, I should willingly give an hour from that time appointed for rest to write to one so much interested in our spiritual advancement. And again I was pleased with the reflection that you would hear from a better source and in happier style than I can command, all that would interest you about your Northern home.

I will tell you as briefly as I can all our conventual news lest you may not have heard it. We had two Sisters received soon after you left, and on the Feast of the Purification four more, so that now we have twenty-eight fervent Novices, four Postulants, and twenty-six Professed. Sisters M. Camillus, De Pazzi, and Johanna hope to make their solemn engagements the sixteenth of next month. Sister M. Isidore has not been well for some two or three weeks. She is now recovering from an attack of erysipelas similar to that she had two years since. All the rest, thank God, [are] well or nearly so.

We had all the Professed who could conveniently come to the Convent for the three days' retreat. The Bishop, with wonted kindness, gave us many holy and animating instructions so that we have since here to "walk in the newness of life." I tell you this that you may be consoled in the hope that we are trying to advance in the way we should go.

Sister Isidore received your very kind letter or note. The pupils there now number forty, and we are about to send them five more very soon. The week after next three purpose going out, and two more in the following month. We expect soon a new Postulant from Baltimore, a Miss O'Neill sent us by our former Confessor, the Revd. Father Neumann. And to arouse you, I will tell you of her accomplishments which she describes herself with all possible candor and humility. She has just completed her eighteenth year. Besides a good English education, she has a good knowledge of *French*. She has some of Italian, Spanish, German. She sings, plays the harp, guitar, and piano—but as there must be some drawback to all such fine things, she has some defect in her sight. And now if I should be very good-naturedly asked to write again, I promise you a true description of the postulant when she comes.

The good Bishop and priests are well, I believe, and they all seem animated with holy zeal for conversion of souls during the holy season that is now just at hand, and many holy and salutary regulations have been announced conducive thereto. Your good prayers will no doubt assist them very much in carrying out their pious intentions. I heard lately from Father O'Mealy. He is well and now occupies the place that his holy brother so worthily filled. I had a letter lately from our friend, Mrs. Brent. It breathed throughout a very Catholic spirit, but yet she has done nothing towards embracing the faith. She waits Captain Brent's return to make her final choice in the religious way. I intend answering her letter soon. In a letter I had some weeks since from Madame Calderon, she seems to regret your not going to Cuba. No doubt she had written to her friends to bid you welcome to Havana.

I must not forget to tell you of my successful work in the poor slave's regard for whom you were so benevolently interested. On receipt of your letter, I believe I exerted myself as much as I could. Almighty God seemed to bless the work for I got two hundred dollars in time for her ransom and sent it to the Revd. J. A. Dowlan. He wrote a kind and interesting letter to me on the subject and said that with that sum and what he could himself procure, poor Mary would be free on the first of February. Some good persons sent me since forty dollars, and I have just got an order for that amount and I will send it on this evening to Washington. So I expect this poor afflicted creature will pray much for you and for us. It is consoling to think that we have assisted in redeeming one soul from the slavery of sin.

The gentlemen managers of the Orphan Asylum are just now giving the Bishop much trouble, but he is well acquainted with "the way of the cross." I forgot to say that the Orphan Asylum numbers 71 now. The Hospital is quite full of patients. Mr. O'Neil, the student, is still there, and if report speaks truth, he is near the confines of the "better land." The Seminary is in a flourishing condition. The expected students have some weeks since arrived. Mr. Duffy seems much pleased. The children continue to attend the Sunday School very well indeed. All our schools in town are much better attended than they were wont to be. The converts who entered the Church under your guidance are still progressing in faith and piety. I am taking care until you return of the Griffin family.

Well now, though I am writing at recreation amidst singing, etc., I think I have told all that I think might interest you. Now please write soon but not in a *stiff cold style* like your last or I will not promise that I will be so *humble* again. Pray for me and for us all and believe how truly I am

Your grateful Sister in Ct
Sr. Mary Frances Xavier

Feast of St. Valentine

It is interesting to speculate concerning Frances Warde's activities in ransoming slaves in the years preceding the Civil War. So far as records are concerned, the above letter is the only evidence available of her work in this particular apostolate. Yet the casual way in which she speaks of securing freedom for the slave "Mary" suggests that the ransom of captive or runaway slaves may have been a more or less frequent activity of Sister Frances.

Frances' happiness in Pittsburgh was soon to be challenged. The year preceding the Providence foundation in 1851 precipitated events in her life which brought to her suffering of a different kind than that inseparable from her apostolic mission. A second letter which she wrote to James O'Connor in the early spring of 1850 offers a first hint of a type of frustration she was to experience often in her American missions. After James O'Connor's return from his winter in the South, his brother appointed him Chaplain at St. Xavier's Academy. Shortly before this assignment, he seems to have hinted to

Mother Frances that her responsibility for her Congregation was limited, for she wrote to him as follows:

I am rejoiced to find that you are pleased with your visit to St. Xavier's, for so far it *all* promises fairly, and you must pray that we may get and keep such a spirit as may make it a lasting good. I view it all in the light that you do. Yet I cannot feel myself at all as free from responsibility in all matters there as you seem to think I should, but it may be that I do not understand you clearly. However, I will explain myself more fully when I shall have the pleasure of a tête-à-tête conversation with you.[14]

The implications of the above statement must be understood against the background of the relationships of the early Sisters of Mercy with their ecclesiastical Superiors. There is an oral tradition handed down in Pittsburgh that Frances Warde was strongly aware of her responsibilities as head of her Congregation and therefore thought to be insufficiently docile by Bishop Michael O'Connor.[15] Evidently she did not interpret the role of ecclesiastical Superiors in precisely the manner in which they themselves interpreted it.

Some interesting statements on the role of clergymen as Superiors of religious congregations for women are found in the biennial reports of James O'Connor to the Propaganda Fide in Rome. In 1852, for example, he wrote that "in every diocese the Sisters of Mercy have as *major superior* their own Bishop." In 1854 he wrote that "for four years . . . I was chaplain of the Sisters of Mercy here in Latrobe and, for one year, their Superior in this Diocese." His 1856 report indicates that he has been chaplain for six years and "Superior" for two, and in 1858 he is "Superior" but no longer chaplain.[16] Correspondence of both the O'Connor brothers and the Sisters during the eighteen-fifties evidences that the Bishop and the ecclesiastical "Superior"[17] tended to play dominating roles in both the external and the internal administration of the Pittsburgh Sisters of Mercy.

The tradition that Frances Warde did not accept the role of the ecclesiastical Superior with complete equanimity is perhaps corroborated in the first "election" that was held in the Pittsburgh Congregation in May, 1850. In a new Mercy foundation, the first Sister Superior always served a six-year term. When an election was held, if no Sister received an absolute majority of votes on the third ballot, the Bishop appointed the Superior. In a first election, the first Superior was always eligible for reappointment. It was commonly the custom that a founder be reappointed. Archbishop Daniel Murray of Dublin had declared Catherine McAuley, as founder, to be Superior for life. In Cork, Mother Josephine Warde held the office of Superior for almost fifty years. In Philadelphia, Mother Patricia Waldron, the first Superior, headed her Congregation for life, dispensations being secured for her re-elections.

When the first election was held in Pittsburgh in 1850, no majority was reached after the third ballot. It would have seemed right and proper that Frances Warde, as American founder, regarded as "Reverend Mother" not only by the Pittsburgh Sisters but by all the Congregations she had founded to date, should have been reappointed. Her Sisters did not declare a preference for another by majority vote. Yet Bishop Michael O'Connor appointed Sister Josephine Cullen as Mother Superior on May 16, 1850. Elizabeth Blake, who had returned from Ireland with Sister Frances in 1845, was named Mother Assistant, and Frances Warde, Bursar. Tradition in Pittsburgh suggests that O'Connor preferred Josephine Cullen as Superior because she was more submissive to his ideas.

A careful perusal of the Chapter Book of the Pittsburgh Sisters of Mercy for the eighteen-fifties reveals some amazing statutes regarding the power of the Bishop in the affairs of the Congregation. In January, 1852, the Corporation of the Sisters, with Josephine Cullen as President, granted the following powers[18] to the Bishop:

1. If no absolute majority is secured on the third balloting for election of Mother Superior, the Bishop appoints the Superior.
2. A Superior may be re-elected only with the consent of the Bishop.
3. If the Mother Superior suggests members for the Council three times without a majority vote being secured, the Bishop appoints the members of the Council.
4. The Bishop has the right to depose the Mother Superior or the members of the Council.
5. The Bishop can override a majority decision of the Council.
6. The consent of the Bishop is necessary to enact or change the By-Laws of the Corporation of the Sisters of Mercy.

If these statutes place absolute power in the hands of the Bishop, a statute passed in 1855 is even more absolute in its implications.[19] The Bishop was actually given the right to veto the election of any Mother Superior or to depose any Mother Superior "if he consider it necessary for the welfare of the community"!

It cannot be said that Michael O'Connor did not have the welfare of the Sisters of Mercy at heart. He did all in his power to help the Congregation and to expand its apostolic works. He was indeed a special friend of the Congregation. Yet he did not encourage personal initiative among the Sisters.

He held the reigns of power. It could be argued that his absolute power in governing the Sisters, codified in approved Acts of the Corporation, was a direct source of profound misunderstanding, controversy, and suffering during the administration of O'Connor's episcopal successor. Bishop Michael Domenec's assumption of the powers granted to Bishop Michael O'Connor almost spelled disaster for the Mercy Congregation.[20] This long chapter in the history of the Pittsburgh Sisters of Mercy occurred more than twenty years after Frances Warde left Pittsburgh. The evidence seems to be that she did not subscribe to such absolute episcopal power over her Sisters as Bishop O'Connor demanded. Nor were Bishop O'Connor and Bishop Haly of Carlow the only prelates who found her to be insufficiently "docile," as her later life will reveal.

Personal suffering came to Frances Warde as a result of Josephine Cullen's appointment as Mother Superior in Pittsburgh in 1850. It will be recalled that when the Pittsburgh foundation was contemplated in Carlow, there was talk of Sister Josephine's being appointed as founder. The selection of Frances Warde as American founder may have been a cause for Josephine Cullen's rejection of her when she was no longer Superior in Pittsburgh. Shortly after Sister Josephine's appointment, the latter wrote from St. Mary's, Pittsburgh, to Father James O'Connor, then Chaplain at St. Xavier's in Latrobe:

Since I returned from St. Xavier's, I have been *teasing* your *goodly brother* [Bishop O'Connor] to send Mother Xavier[21] out, but in vain! At length I concluded on doing it myself. You cannot imagine the pain it gave me, to desire her to leave [the convent] where she labored so long. Was it not cruel to ask her to do so? Indeed I felt it dreadfully. And then it made her so unhappy. The idea of being the cause of it. I could scarcely reconcile myself to it. She will never forgive me. The only consolation I have is that I have acted from motives of duty. And the direction of those God has given us for our guides.[22]

It is understandable that a past Superior living in a mother house with a new Superior could create awkward situations, but Sister Josephine's stress on the founder's unhappiness raises a question as to the charity of Josephine's action. Any unhappiness of Frances because of her assignment to St. Xavier's certainly did not arise from an unwillingness to live at the Academy in Latrobe. Indeed, St. Xavier's was probably dearer to her than St. Mary's in Pittsburgh. As Mother Superior, she had sometimes quietly sought a place on the stage coach in order to spend a day or two in the serene and beautiful countryside. Her visits to St. Xavier's were a delight to the Sisters and the students. They loved to walk to the Philadelphia-Pittsburgh turnpike to meet her, and then sit in the grove beside the Academy with her as she told them stories of Catherine McAuley and the Mercy foundations everywhere. The pain suffered by Sister Frances on being sent to St. Xavier's in 1850 could have arisen only from the rebuff it implied.

A second letter of Sister Josephine to James suggests a feeling of guilt on her part concerning her assignment of Frances. Josephine had visited St. Xavier's and evidently had engaged in a slight quarrel with O'Connor. On returning to Pittsburgh, she wrote to him:

Might I ask which of us was wanting in *etiquette* the morning of our departure from St. Xavier's? It seems to me there was a little on both sides. It occurred to me you were not satisfied regarding Mother X. but indeed I do not regret what I have done. At the same time I should be sorry to give you any cause of displeasure. Though I feel anything but cheered at the prospects as to the peace and happiness of the Sisters, still I have great confidence God will bring things to right in his own time.[23]

The third extant letter of Josephine Cullen to James O'Connor is openly condemnatory of Frances Warde. The founder had requested permission from Mother Josephine to allow a young lady, her cousin and evidently an immigrant, to spend a few months at St. Xavier's until she found a position for herself. Josephine disapproved completely of the request as an injustice to the community on the grounds that Frances Warde would discuss the affairs of the Congregation with the "secular lady." Sister Elizabeth Strange had also appealed in favor of the young woman. On this point, Sister Josephine added with some pettiness, "I suppose Mother Xavier asked her to do so." Sister Elizabeth loved and reverenced Frances Warde. Back in Carlow in 1842, she had once written an unusual letter to Frances who was then establishing a foundation in Westport, telling her all the news of St. Leo's. The talented Elizabeth had written her letter (still preserved in Pittsburgh) in quatrains, closing with the memorable lines:

> *Though many dear Sisters are here*
> *Whose love for you never will change,*
> *Dear Mother, there's none more sincere*
> *Than Sister Elizabeth Strange.*

The remainder of Sister Josephine's letter to O'Connor carries with it a special irony for the reader one hundred and twenty years later:

The Bishop wished me to speak to you on all these things. Indeed it pains me to be so troublesome. He is going this evening to the Summit. He will be away for some time. I hate to see him going. We have not a creature to speak a word to in his absence should anything unpleasant occur. As to Mother Xavier's teaching, I do not think she could. It will be harassing to every feeling of her nature. And besides I do not think she is capable. She told me so. I do not well know what she could be engaged at.

To be sure, the unique irony of the above letter lies in the fact that Frances Warde, then forty years of age, had already founded twenty-five convents and schools in Ireland and the United States and was yet to found innumerable more before her death. As a teacher she had already converted hundreds and would yet convert hundreds more to Christianity. Josephine Cullen, on the other hand, was to die in less than two years. She was loved in Pittsburgh as a good, religious person and was deeply mourned at her death. A certain jealousy of her authority, however, seems to have been her fault. On March 30, 1852, Michael O'Connor wrote to his brother[24] that the appointment of a Sister as Superior at St. Xavier's would have to be delayed "until Sister Josephine dies" because the latter would not consent to it! At the time, Josephine was on her death bed, and it was believed "she could not well live another day." She died April 21, 1852. Of six extant letters of Josephine Cullen found in the correspondence of James O'Connor, five are uncharitable in their comments on Frances Warde. In twenty-two extant letters of Frances, there is not one uncharitable word spoken of anyone.

This is not to say that Frances Warde was a perfect human being. Some of her associates loved her deeply; some did not. Some found her difficult to live with. A woman with the force and vitality to spread the Congregation of Mercy throughout the United States in the mid-nineteenth century was by definition a woman who would arouse resentment, some of it strong. Frances Warde dared to take risks. She was lukewarm neither in her personality nor in her ventures for the Kingdom of Christ. She knew that she would make enemies in following her mission. She knew that both her personality and her actions would sometimes rouse indignation. But she was indomitable. She accepted herself humbly for what she was and pursued her apostolate without fear. If there is small testimony to disapproval of her, the testimony of her contemporaries to love and reverence for her is great. With almost incredible consistency, all those who were closely united with her in the apostolate—from Catherine McAuley and Edward Nolan in her youth to William McDonald in New England and the Sisters of her last foundations in her old age—not only loved her deeply but inspired love in their own associates. They formed a community of holiness in the spirit.

At about the same time that Frances Warde was sent to St. Xavier Academy by Josephine Cullen, an incident occurred[25] which demonstrated again a quality in Frances' character that some persons found difficult to tolerate: Frances' trust of others was so great that at times it amounted to folly. Her confidence in others, however, was in no sense naive. She simply continued all her life long to trust others completely unless they proved themselves unworthy of her trust. This attitude sometimes made her appear to be lacking in the wisdom of the serpent. In the early spring of 1850, a young woman student at St. Xavier's Academy left the school suddenly one evening without a word to anyone. Previously she had applied unsuccessfully for admission to the Congregation of Mercy, but had shown no resentment at her rejection. When she left the academy, she sent back a letter of apology without stating reasons for her departure. Toward the end of June, a strange story appeared in the *Philadelphia Sun* under the headline, "A Tale of Romance and Crime." It began with the account of a Presbyterian minister who, in the month of

March with snow on the ground, found himself a fellow-passenger on a stage coach between Pittsburgh and Bedford, Pennsylvania, of an interesting young woman, scantily clad and under great agitation. She told the gentleman that she had escaped from a Roman Catholic convent in Pittsburgh which "she had entered with the purest motives as a refuge from sorrows too sacred to tell," but that she had found "the discipline and the goings on" in the convent unendurable. She had scaled a wall at night, she said, anxious to baffle pursuit, without knowing where she was going. The gentleman gave her a note to a Protestant minister in Bedford, who believed her, pitied her, and eventually adopted her. She was "modest, sincere, and intelligent." Called to be a pastor of a church in Philadelphia, the Bedford minister found his adopted daughter a position as governess in the home of a Philadelphia broker. After about six weeks, during which she was received by the family of the broker with utmost confidence, the young woman departed suddenly one night with all the rich clothing, diamonds, and jewels of the broker's wife. She was never heard from again. Among the possessions she left behind were: the title page of a Catholic catechism; a small book intended as a "particular examen," marked "Academy of Mt. Xavier, February 17, 1850"; and a leaf from a Catholic book with the inscription, "To Mary Frances Wright, from her affectionate friend, M. M. Frances Xavier, Convent of Sisters of Mercy, Pittsburgh—Feast of St. Elizabeth, 1849." The Pittsburgh Sisters were publicly disgraced! Once again Frances Warde had committed the unpardonable sin of trust.

On December 26, 1850, the Mercy Sisters in Pittsburgh moved to their new mother house, St. Mary's on Webster Avenue, from the episcopal residence where they had lived since the typhus epidemic of 1848 when they had moved hurriedly from their old convent in Concert Hall. The threat on Christmas Day of an attack on the episcopal residence by members of the Know Nothing Party precipitated their sudden departure to the new convent, a building which was not quite completed. This beautiful new mother house had been planned by Frances Warde and Bishop O'Connor. But Frances, now at St. Xavier's in Latrobe, was never to live in it. The Christmas holidays must have brought her loneliness, for the magnificent new home of the Sisters in Pittsburgh was her own project, just as St. Leo's in Carlow had been. In later years, many new convents were founded from it. It was the home in which Sister Katherine Drexel, founder of the Sisters of the Blessed Sacrament, was to make her novitiate in preparation for the establishment of her new religious congregation. It was to be visited by Sister Francis Xavier Cabrini, later the first American canonized woman saint. Frances Warde was to return to it briefly once in the sixties and once in the seventies. But she was never to live in the convent she planned—the new mother house which was to be the center for the Pittsburgh Sisters of Mercy for almost three-quarters of a century. On Christmas, 1850, as the Sisters joyfully moved to their new convent, Frances Warde did not know that within a few months she would leave her first American foundation, never to return. Her Providence foundation, in the early spring of 1851, was only the beginning of her establishment of Mercy convents throughout the whole of New England.

The Pittsburgh congregation was to remain the largest of Frances' foundations for many years. During the hundred years after she left Pittsburgh, the expansion of the community gave living testimony to the apostolic spirit of its founder. The spirit of St. Mary's was well expressed in a comment concerning the Pittsburgh congregation made to Bishop James

O'Connor of Omaha, early chaplain of the Sisters, as late as 1885: "The *root* must have been planted deep and firm!"[26] Mercy foundations were sent from Pittsburgh to Baltimore, 1855; Buffalo, 1861; Titusville (Erie), 1870; and Wilkes-Barre (Dallas), 1875. Between 1851 and 1970, more than fifty branch houses were founded—convents, parochial primary and secondary schools, commercial high school, industrial schools, academies, liberal arts college, diocesan house of studies, home for working girls, Mercy House for homeless girls, house of refuge, and hospitals. During the Civil War, the Pittsburgh Sisters nursed both Union and Confederate soldiers at Stanton Military Hospital in Washington and at the Western Pennsylvania Military Hospital in Pittsburgh. Numerous catechetical schools, summer schools, and mission schools were conducted by the Sisters. Foreign missions were established in Puerto Rico and Peru. Frances Warde's name came to be deeply revered in Pittsburgh. In March, 1966, when Pittsburgh celebrated the one hundred and fiftieth anniversary of its charter as a city, Frances Warde was named one of the ten outstanding women in its history. And in 1969 Mount Mercy College, a four-year liberal arts college founded by the Sisters of Mercy in 1929, changed its name to Carlow College to honor Frances Warde and the origins of the Mercy apostolate in the United States. Today Frances Warde is even closer in spirit to the Pittsburgh Sisters than she was a hundred years ago.

11

On to New England: Providence and Newport, Hartford and New Haven; External and Internal Conflict

THE foundation that Frances Warde made in Providence, Rhode Island, in the spring of 1851 was the first permanent convent in New England. There were reasons why the New England states were not the first to shelter Catholic convents. The growth of Catholicity in New England, stronghold in early days of hostility to Pope and bishops, has been compared to the spread of Christianity in the first stages of its establishment in the Roman world. Happenings in many of the American colonies, especially in Massachusetts and Connecticut, had been grimly reminiscent of persecutions of ages before. Irish emigrants, fleeing from penal laws, were not welcome. French Canadians, who carried their faith across the northern borders of the colonies, were scarcely more desired. Irish and French missionaries followed them.

With the increase of the Catholic body after the Revolutionary War, John Carroll, cousin of Charles Carroll, signer of the Declaration of Independence, was consecrated as Catholic Bishop of the United States in 1790. Baltimore, the episcopal seat, became the metropolitan center for a half-century. In 1808, the Dioceses of New York, Boston, Philadelphia, and Bardstown were created, all subject to the primatial See of Baltimore. Not until 1844, Frances Warde's first year in America, was the first Bishop of Hartford consecrated. The new Diocese included the entire states of Connecticut and Rhode Island. Bishop William Tyler established Providence rather than Hartford as the episcopal center. Providence had a large number of Catholics and two comparatively large churches.

As early as 1825, Providence had been recognized as a coming center of cotton and wood manufactures. Samuel Slater, English emigrant, had established in Pawtucket the first cotton mill in America. The industrial boom had attracted hundreds of workers from Ireland, England, and Canada. And Bishop Tyler, mindful of the needs of Catholic immigrants, had set up a Catholic free school in Providence taught by ladies of the city until he should be able to bring Sisters to his diocese. But as in the case of Bishop Quarter of Chicago, the hardships of administering the young diocese soon drained Tyler physically, and he died within five years of his appointment as bishop. It remained for Bernard O'Reilly, second Bishop of Hartford, to bring religious Sisters to Providence.

The spirit of Know-Nothingism was so rabid in New England, especially in the Hartford Diocese, that O'Reilly was judged to be extremely daring in inviting Sisters to come to Providence in 1850. Fifteen years before, the Convent of the Ursuline Sisters in Charlestown had been destroyed by a mob of fanatics who had driven out the Sisters and sixty young girls in the middle of the night. The Sisters, forced to disperse, had not been reconstituted as a community. The blackened ruins of the convent near Boston were a warning to any clergyman who hoped to establish another convent school in New England. Native Americans were determined to allow no "emissaries of Rome" to set up schools within their borders. Bishop O'Reilly's determination to establish Catholic education in the Diocese of Hartford therefore required

had plunged herself into the work and chal-
[...]w foundation with all her characteristic energy
[...]. How much the effort cost her, no one would

[...]d her companions arrived in Providence the
[...]arch 11. They were literally smuggled into the
[...]ation of townspeople came to meet them as in
[...]ces' early foundations. Had the Sisters been
[...]e crime, they could not have been more cautious.
[...]nown to their little cottage on High Street, now
[...]nd the following morning they participated in
[...]ion of the Eucharist, marking March 12 as the
[...]Day of the Sisters of Mercy in New England.
[...]ay was a Feast of St. Francis Xavier, Mother
[...]ron, the Sisters were especially joyful. The first
[...]e those in Latrobe and Chicago, was named St.
[...]honor of Mother Frances. Poverty, the common
[...]r foundations, awaited the Sisters in Providence.
[...]er was happy: obstacles always impelled her to
[...]rt. Christ was with her in her poverty. The visita-
[...]sick poor was begun at once. The people welcomed
[...]because they shared their own poverty. In the
[...]ney was slipped into the Sisters' hands with the
[...]message, "For the poor."
[...]n space was inadequate in the tiny convent, Frances
[...]once opened St. Xavier's Academy for girls, the
[...]tholic secondary school in the state of Rhode Island.
[...]h years, Mother Frances was both Superior and
[...]of the Academy. In the beginning, twenty students
[...]ic and non-Catholic—attended school in two rooms,
[...]after school to enlarge the small chapel and the other
[...]ic lessons. The small tuition received from these
[...]students provided food for the Sisters. Within the

courage based on a realistic fear of repetition of the Charlestown horrors. And where would he find Sisters willing to
withstand the persecution which would be absolutely inevitable upon their introduction of Catholic education to
Providence? He turned for counsel to his friend, Bishop
Michael O'Connor, who invited him to visit Pittsburgh.
O'Reilly was amazed at what the Sisters of Mercy under
Frances Warde had accomplished in seven years: free poor
schools, academies and boarding schools, orphan home, house
of mercy, hospital. He begged O'Connor for a few Sisters of
Mercy to enter into the hard core of Puritanism. He emphasized over and over again that the leader of such a foundation would have to be a woman of exceptional prudence,
tact, and judgment. She would be forced to deal daily with
townspeople who had vowed that never again would religious
Sisters be tolerated on the "free" soil of New England.

O'Connor knew that there was only one woman in Pittsburgh equal to the mission. Frances Warde's full cooperation
could be taken for granted. The most profound apostolic
challenge always inspired her most intense response. No
longer Mother Superior, freed through the "election" of
Josephine Cullen, she answered the call to Providence with
characteristic enthusiasm. The quiet serenity of St. Xavier's
Academy was shattered when Mother Frances volunteered to
found the new mission. The Sisters and students who loved
her dreaded her departure. And just as she had done on leaving Carlow, Frances now found it necessary to conceal her
own grief at parting in order to console those she left in
Pittsburgh. There were also a few who aggravated Frances'
loneliness on departing from her first American foundation
by criticizing her for abandoning them. Though they "had
been so long with her," they were still unable to see that her
Mercy apostolate was not Pittsburgh alone but the entire

United States. The Pittsburgh foundation, she well knew, could now carry out the works of mercy on its own momentum. She herself was called to move on to the poor, sick, and needy in areas where they were completely without care. Four devoted professed Sisters volunteered to undertake the new mission with her: Sister Josephine Lombard, who was to succeed Frances as Superior in Providence in 1858; her younger sister, Paula Lombard, third administrator of Mercy Hospital, whom Mother Frances later chose as first Superior of the Hartford Convent of Mercy and then sent to aid the foundation in Little Rock, Arkansas, established from Naas in 1851; Sister Camillus O'Neill, a young protégée of Frances who had been educated at Villa Marie Convent, Montreal, with the Congregation of Notre Dame; and Sister Joanna Forgarty, faithful friend of Frances, who was to accompany her on the Manchester foundation in 1858.

On Ash Wednesday, March 5, 1851, Mother Frances and her four missionaries, accompanied by Father James O'Connor and Josephine Cullen, left St. Xavier's Chapel in the gathering twilight, walked in procession through the beautiful grove which Frances loved, and then over the forest path to the old turnpike road to await the stage coach for Philadelphia. The Sisters wore secular dress so that they would not arouse hostility on their arrival in Providence. They were accompanied by sorrowful Sisters and students who grieved to part with them. Many times before, these young people had walked with Frances to and from the old Philadelphia road when she had visited St. Xavier's. Years later, Sister Elizabeth Strange was to recall the last sad parting: "Mother Frances was in good spirits. She took an affectionate leave of all. The shades of evening were gathering as we walked sadly home . . ."[1]

The Sisters traveled by way of Harrisburg, through Lancaster to Philadelphia, then on to New York. Arriving in New

York City on Marc[...]
with the Sisters of [...]
Houston Street. On[...]
Byrne, godchild of C[...]
Warde since her ch[...]
Doyle in Ireland a v[...]
Here is her impressic[...]
journey to Providence:[...]

Mother Frances Warde, [...]
has just begun for the fou[...]
the establishment of a C[...]
Dr. O'Reilly, Bishop of P[...]
ing a community of Siste[...]
Mother Superior. They all[...]
It gave us all great pleasure[...]
I did not know Mother Fi[...]
greatly changed in appearai[...]
almost as quiet as yourself.[...]
said that "it was time for her[...]
charge in Pittsburgh had be[...]
many trials". . . .[2]

To compare Frances War[...]
strange indeed—with Mary A[...]
go to the parlor" back in the c[...]
and subdued" were the last w[...]
Frances' personality. Perhaps th[...]
with all its associations of love,[...]
heroic effort of parting with go[...]
for her. Perhaps Josephine Cu[...]
caused her suffering that she cc[...]
was not yet forty-one, she had i[...]
thing was certain: her response v[...]

year, when the Sisters had space in their new convent to accommodate boarding students, young ladies came from the surrounding areas—from Massachusetts, Connecticut, Maine, and Montreal, as well as Rhode Island—and gradually St. Xavier's Academy in Providence, like that in Pittsburgh, became one of the outstanding select schools in the East. Sunday school classes in Christian Doctrine were also initiated as soon as the Sisters arrived in Providence. Because of the large numbers attending, the monitorial system was used. Classes were opened in the Cathedral parochial school, actually the basement of the church, and also in St. Patrick's parish, Providence, in September. The Sisters walked each morning from St. Xavier's to St. Patrick's and returned in the evening.

Meanwhile, the expected harassment had begun. Time and again, the little convent was smashed with stones. Mysterious noises and shouts disturbed the Sisters at night. One bright midnight, all the windows were shattered with rocks. When the Sisters walked to school or to visit the sick, angry insults were hurled at them. One Sister was raised bodily in the street and dashed to the ground by a young man, to the uproarious applause of his companions. Children threw mud at the Sisters and marked their clothing with chalk crosses. But the Sisters carried on. And the numbers of those who loved them, Catholic and non-Catholic, increased.

In the summer of 1851 Bishop O'Reilly purchased the Stead home on the corner of Broad and Claverick Streets for St. Xavier's Convent and Academy. At the same time, a frame building on an adjoining lot was renovated as a home for orphans, and the Sisters were able to care for the homeless poor children of Providence. This one and one-half story asylum was soon to be crowded with children from Connecticut as well as Rhode Island. Without the Sisters to care for them, the happy little girls who lived there would have been quite friendless.

Before the Sisters moved to their new convent in October, Frances Warde displayed special daring by holding the first public religious ceremony for reception into the Congregation of Mercy in the Cathedral of Providence. As in all of Frances' foundations, young women had been immediately attracted to the Sisters, and already the little community had increased from five to twenty. The young, the fair, and the gifted flocked to St. Xavier's from New York, New Haven, Rochester, Hartford, and other surrounding cities. Crowds of friends, as well as large numbers of the curious, assembled for the impressive first ceremony at the Cathedral. Bishop O'Reilly explained the meaning of religious life. New friends were gained, and additional young girls were inspired to seek admission at St. Xavier's. On the other hand, hostility and incredulity were increased among non-believers, some of whom stirred up a false sympathy for the lovely young women "immured behind convent walls." Letters to the *Providence Sentinel* questioned the celibacy of the clergy, the secrecy of the confessional, the morality of the Sisters. It was proposed that civil authorities should hold regular inspection of the convents.

The new home to which the Sisters moved in October was a solid stone house with a fine garden. It was no mansion. The novitiate room was so small that "a tall man standing in the center could reach out and almost touch the walls." But the building was spacious by comparison with the original convent, and a large attic offered sleeping quarters for new members of the community. The garden was Frances Warde's joy. Long narrow walks crossed one another, dividing it into squares bordered with dwarf box. In autumn, a grape vine arbor in the center was heavily laden with fruit. The Sisters enjoyed the cool shade of the garden, and a variety of birds loved it too. There were simple, beautiful compensations for hard work, poverty, and insults!

In the fall of 1851 Sister Agatha O'Brien in Chicago could write to Sister Elizabeth Strange in Pittsburgh: "In Providence they seem to be going ahead. They have twenty-two Sisters already. May Almighty God guide them!"[3] The amazing success of the Providence mission within six months had its ominous side, too. It was threatening to the Know-Nothings. As more and more candidates presented themselves for admission to St. Xavier's, a crisis in Providence seemed to be inevitable. The question was how long the threat of the Catholic convent could be sustained without violence. Frances Warde, meanwhile, serenely continued her apostolate of mercy. She visited New York City to investigate teaching methods and returned with "many useful books for our schools."[4] She expressed fears in a letter to Sister Elizabeth Strange that "all is going on too well and happily." Intuitively, she knew that she had not seen the end of the Sisters' persecution in New England.

At St. Xavier's, Frances continued her custom of giving "talks" to the school Sisters to inspire them in their apostolate of education. She insisted that nothing was so God-like as the development of loving hearts. Like Catherine McAuley, she placed value in example rather than in exhortation. "If the religious teacher is not imbued with a burning love of God," she would ask, "how can she cultivate it in children?" The Sister of Mercy must serve the Lord with joy. "Since God loves a cheerful giver," she would repeat, "let us try to be cheerful *workers,* taking nothing from the glory of His blessed service by half-heartedness . . . We must be steeped in holy joy and eagerness to imitate Christ in labor, prayer, teaching, and instructing . . ." Frances often reminded her

Sisters that "the poor are the special friends of Jesus Christ and should be the particular charge of the Sisters of Mercy . . . Let us do good to rich and poor, but always prefer the service of the destitute and the suffering, as our Divine Master did while on earth."[5]

Frances Warde encouraged her Sisters in Providence to cultivate ingenuity, just as she had done in the poor schools of Pittsburgh, Chicago, and Loretto. Church basements and vestries with improvised equipment did not offer ideal physical surroundings for teaching, but an ingenious Sister could do much with little. The will was all. Books were of the essence. Everywhere she went, Frances established libraries. Donations provided circulating libraries for her Sunday schools. In the Cathedral Sunday School in Providence, she accumulated 400 books in little over a year. The young men of the parish built shelves for them. The entire collection was in circulation most of the time. Improvements in the parochial schools, the academy, the Sunday schools, and the orphanage continued apace. Always at the center of progress and expansion was Frances Warde.

Within one year of the Sisters' arrival in Providence, an amazing apostolic event took place. Perhaps there was nothing comparable to it in Frances Warde's apostolate from the time she left Baggot Street until 1852. In the lovely spring of the latter year, Frances founded a convent in Hartford on May 11 and went on to New Haven to found a second convent on May 12! So many recruits had appeared in Providence that the attraction of St. Xavier's seemed to be miraculous. It was actually possible to open two new convents in two days. Among the candidates in Providence were many members of prominent eastern families, such as the daughter of the editor of the *Boston Pilot* and the two convert sisters of the editor of the *Philadelphia Catholic Herald*.

Mother Frances was invited to open the convent in Hartford by Father John Brady of St. Patrick's Parish, which covered about one-half of the state of Connecticut. Frances chose Sister Paula Lombard, who had come with her from Pittsburgh, as first Superior of St. Catherine's Convent, Hartford. Companions in the new venture were Sister Baptist Coleman, later appointed first Superior of the Rochester, New York, foundation; Sister Teresa Murray; and Sister Lucy Lyons. Their first convent was "a cradle of poverty," a small brick cottage on Franklin Court, now Allyn Street, long since demolished. On May 17, 1852, the Sisters opened the first Catholic school in Conecticut in the basement of St. Patrick's Church. Here was the nucleus of the immense Connecticut diocesan parochial school system. At once nearly 200 girls were enrolled at St. Patrick's. From the beginning, the Sisters also cared for five or six orphan girls in their little convent, which was so crowded that in the spring of 1853 Father Brady purchased a larger building on Trumbull Street for the Sisters. Here they opened St. Catherine's Academy for girls, named in honor of Catherine McAuley. Not until 1855 was the first new Convent of Mercy in Connecticut built in Hartford. The new St. Catherine's provided space for a day and boarding academy and also rooms to care for orphan girls. The latter eventually found a new home in St. James Orphanage, a building next to the convent, and finally in St. Francis Orphan Home in New Haven. In 1866 a new parochial school was built for St. Patrick's parish. St. Catherine's Convent, Hartford, remained a branch house of St. Xavier's in Providence until 1872.

As the Mercy apostolate expanded in Hartford, Frances Warde continued to send Sisters from Providence to teach in the schools, to care for the orphans, and to serve the sick poor until St. Catherine's was able to secure a sufficient number of recruits to carry on the work of the Hartford mission. Within seventy-five years, the Hartford Congregation of Mercy became the largest in the United States, with fifty branch houses. It expanded its works to include secondary schools, liberal arts college, infant home, home for the aged, catechetical schools, summer vacation schools, and retreat house. Mercy Convents established in Middletown and Meriden, Connecticut, from Ennis, Ireland, in 1872, were amalgamated with the Hartford Congregation in 1911. As in the case of Pittsburgh, the seed planted by Frances Warde in Hartford proved to be fruitful indeed.

The New Haven convent founded by Frances in that lovely May of 1852, the day after she established the Hartford community, had its own story to tell. So long as she remained in Providence, Frances continued to care for this branch house, too, and to send Sisters from St. Xavier's to carry on its apostolate. New Haven, the second city and "other capitol" of Connecticut, had long petitioned Mother Frances for a Mercy Convent through its pastor, Edward O'Brien, who was in "holy competition" with John Brady of Hartford to establish the first Sisters of Mercy in Connecticut. Brady won by one day.

As Superior of the four Sisters she led to New Haven in 1852, Frances Warde chose the godchild of Catherine McAuley, Sister Camillus Byrne. The latter, who had come to the United States on the New York foundation in 1846, had joined Mother Frances in Providence in 1851. The first St. Mary's Convent in New Haven was a rented private residence on George Street. The Sisters took over the administration and teaching of St. Mary's parochial school for girls, which had been established with lay teachers in 1834. This "subterranean school," like many of the early Catholic schools in Connecticut, was conducted in the basement of

St. Mary's Church. In the convent, the Sisters established St. Mary's Academy, a private day school. St. Mary's Orphanage was opened the very day Frances Warde and her Sisters arrived in New Haven and found two little wide-eyed, homeless girls among the townspeople who came to welcome them. These little girls, who lived with the Sisters in St. Mary's Convent, formed the nucleus of St. Francis Orphanage, New Haven, which cared for at least 12,000 homeless children during its first century of existence. Years after Frances Warde's death, when the Russell Sage Foundation investigated charitable institutions in the United States, St. Francis Orphan Home ranked fourth in the country.

Two years after their arrival in New Haven, the Sisters of St. Mary's moved to their new convent and academy on Church Street. They conducted classes in Christian Doctrine at St. Mary's, visited the sick poor and the prisoners at the State Hospital, and in the summer of 1855, when cholera struck New Haven, they carried on the Mercy tradition of nursing the plague-stricken. In 1854 they took over the instructional program of St. Patrick's parish school in New Haven.

As in the Hartford mission, Frances Warde never lost interest in the apostolate of the New Haven Sisters. At St. Patrick's School they had the distinction of serving under the New Haven Board of Education with the same status as public school teachers, an unusual procedure for teaching Sisters in New England of the nineteenth century. When Connecticut and Rhode Island became separate dioceses in 1872 and the Hartford Congregation of Mercy became independent of Providence, the New Haven Convent became a branch house of Hartford. All her life, Frances Warde continued to visit the Sisters of Hartford and New Haven, sometimes alone in her carriage and dressed in a plain blue suit and bonnet to avoid being conspicuous. A visit from her was an event in Connecticut. She never failed to talk to the Sisters of the spirit of Catherine McAuley. And she never lost the freshness of enthusiasm which the astonishing growth of the Connecticut convents inspired in her. Once in 1856, after visiting the Hartford and New Haven Sisters in the fourth year of their establishment, she wrote in her journal:

My ardent desire to see Christ's little ones trained under the guidance of religious teachers is coming to pass to an extent far beyond what I ever dared to hope or wish. How true is the old proverb: "The first step is the only difficulty . . . ."[6]

While the Connecticut convents flourished, Mother Frances continued to expand her works of Mercy in Providence. In January, 1854, the Sisters began to teach in St. Joseph's parish in the city. The beginning was a classroom in the small vestry of the Church, where the Sisters taught about thirty pupils while, close by, a school was being built. In May of the same year, Frances founded a convent which became very dear to her for personal reasons.

When Mother Frances passed through Philadelphia on her way to Pittsburgh back in 1843, she had met Emily Harper, the beautiful young granddaughter of the patriot Charles Carroll. Her father was General Goodloe Harper, distinguished jurist and statesman. She was a close friend of Catherine Seton, daughter of Mother Elizabeth Seton, founder of the Sisters of Charity. Catherine entered the Convent of Mercy in New York in 1846. Emily Harper and Frances Warde became friends immediately and remained so for the rest of their lives. Emily and her wealthy mother,

Mrs. Goodloe Harper, became benefactors of the Sisters of Mercy and helped Frances Warde in her many charities. Indeed, Emily Harper supported numerous poor families in New England without the knowledge of anyone except Frances Warde and perhaps Catherine Seton.[7]

The Harpers, who had a summer residence in Newport, Rhode Island, desired to have a Convent of Mercy established there. Mrs. Harper purchased land and a small cottage which had been used as a chapel while St. Mary's Church, Newport, was being built. This cottage became the first Convent of Mercy in Newport. A wing was added to each side of the cottage so that the building could also serve as a parochial school.

Since Frances' friend was the benefactor of the new convent, she felt a warm personal interest in it. Less than two years before, a new Convent of Mercy in Cork, Ireland, had been built under the direction of Frances' sister, Mother Josephine Warde. Frances had become enthusiastic about the new St. Maries of the Isle, a magnificent convent situated between the two branches of the famous River Lee and designed by Pugin. Josephine Warde had written to Frances of the majestic central stairway, the wide, bright corridors, the lead glass windows, the arches mounted by scrolls in community room and chapel. The convent was called St. Maries of the Isle because it was located on one of the five islands of Cork, on the exact spot where once stood an Abbey of the Dominican Friars built in 1229 by Philip De Barry, Welsh knight and progenitor of the noble family of Barrymores of Cork. The River Lee, as it approached the Abbey, St. Maries of the Isle, divided into two streams which by their confluence formed an enclosure ideal for a convent. De Barry had built the famous Shandon Castle for his own residence. In 1690 William of Orange drove the

Dominicans from St. Maries of the Isle, never to return. Frances Warde was fascinated by the thought that a Convent of Mercy dedicated to the Virgin Mary now arose, over 600 years later, on the precise spot on the River Lee once occupied by the ancient Abbey of St. Mary. She decided to call the Newport Convent, on Narragansett Bay, St. Mary's of the Isle.

Frances chose Sister Gertrude Bradley, beautiful young daughter of a Rochester physician recently professed in Providence, as the Superior of the new convent. With three other Sisters, Mother Frances and Sister Gertrude sailed on the steamboat *Canonicus* from Providence to Newport on the afternoon of May 3, 1854. They entered Newport, then called the "Eden of America," in a downpour of rain. An old "hundred and two" coach conveyed them to the cottage that was to be their new home. On May 8, they opened St. Mary's parochial school to sixty scholars. St. Mary's School was to educate many of the daughters of Officers of the Naval Academy during the Civil War when the naval schoolships were located at Newport. When a second parish, St. Joseph's, was opened in Newport, the Sisters taught Christian Doctrine there. In 1867 they established a select academy at St. Mary's of the Isle. Meanwhile, donations from wealthy summer residents of Newport helped the Sisters in their care of the poor and the sick of the city. Frances Warde loved to visit Newport, and Emily Harper loved to visit her old friend there.

The "No Popery" crusade in Providence, meantime, had not abated. Since the great Irish Famine of 1847–48, immigration of Irish Catholics had not subsided. By 1854, Providence counted 41,513 in its census, of whom 8,333 adults were Irish-born Catholics. The Know-Nothings of the eighteen-fifties continued to reinforce the prejudices of the "Native Americans" of the thirties and forties. "Popery" was a false religion which taught the worship of saints, relics, images, and the Virgin Mary; the Mass rivaled heathen idolatry; pardon for sins was purchased in the confessional; Catholic schools were hotbeds of vice; priests and nuns were corrupt. The Church was a political machine, and Catholic foreigners were minions of the Pope. Street fights, mob riots, and church-burning plagued the Eastern States. A long catalogue of outrages upon Catholics might be cited, from the tarring and feathering of Father John Bapst in Ellsworth, Maine, to the attack on the Louisville Cathedral. In a Pastoral Letter of 1854, Bishop Bernard O'Reilly of Providence urged his people to charity and non-violence. Continued immigration of Catholics, however, put the "older American stock" on the defensive. The Know-Nothings took a solemn oath to oppose any but American-born Protestants for office. In the fall elections of 1854, they carried Rhode Island, Connecticut, Massachusetts, New Hampshire, and even Kentucky and California.

Insults to the Sisters at St. Xavier's in Providence came to a crisis in the spring of 1855. A prejudiced gentleman, lecturing in Boston on the dangers of Catholic educational institutions to native Americans, described St. Xavier's Convent and Academy minutely. He suggested that the Convent was within one-and-a-half hour's ride from Boston, and added that a keg of gunpowder placed under the library window opening upon the garden would quickly and effectively dispose of the entire institution.[8]

A "case" upon which to base an attack upon the convent suddenly came to light at about the same time. Rebecca Newell, a woman in her late thirties and a member of one of the most prominent Protestant families in Providence, had heard through a teacher in the local high school of the remarkable gifts of "Mother Frances Warde, Superior at St. Xavier's." The instructor had spoken of her remarkable speech, her conversational powers, her fascinating personality.[9] Intrigued, Miss Newell sought an introduction to Frances. The consequences could easily be imagined. The Puritan lady immediately felt that she was in the presence of a superior woman who would lead her to a spiritual life of grace. She begged to be instructed in the Catholic faith and in due time was baptized a Catholic. Despite the fact that she was no young girl, her infuriated mother drove her from home. Returning to Providence some months later on the death of her brother, she begged Mother Frances to admit her as a Sister of Mercy. Fearing that she was motivated only by the first fervor of her conversion and her brother's death, Frances explained to her all the difficulties of the life of a Sister of Mercy. But Rebecca Newell insisted on giving the religious life a trial.

At once her entrance into the convent was noised abroad. She was pictured as a guileless young American girl (actually she was close to forty), enticed by "the fascinating Madame Warde" (actually forty-four), and detained in the "nunnery" against her will. Had Frances Warde appeared in New England in the days of Cotton Mather, she would surely have been burned as a witch. Crowds outside the convent shouted, "Unlock your prison and free the beautiful Yankee girl!" One morning in March, the residents of Providence were astonished to see posted on walls and fences small handbills printed as follows:

AMERICANS!
TO WHOM THESE PRESENTS MAY COME
GREETING

Whereas, certain rumors are afloat of a certain transaction of a certain ANTI-SAM party in the vicinity of the corner of Claverick and Broad streets, every true Native American Born citizen is requested, one and all, to assemble there, Thursday Evening, March 22, 1855, at 8 o'clock precisely. There with true regard to Law, and consulting the feelings and sympathies of SAM, proceedings of the most solemn and unquestionable nature will be transacted.

One and All to the Rescue! ! ! The Password is "SHOW YOURSELF."

Broad and Claverick Streets meant only one thing: the Convent of Mercy. News spread like wildfire that St. Xavier's Convent was to be attacked. Now Frances Warde was called upon to manifest a blend of aggressive independence, prudence, and diplomacy. The postulant Rebecca Newell offered to talk with her friends and all interested persons. She asked an interview with the Mayor of Providence and the Editor of the *Providence Journal,* declaring her perfect freedom to leave the convent at will. On March 20 she wrote an open letter to the Editor of the *Journal,* explaining her personal decision to become a Sister and expressing her desire to follow peaceably the dictates of her own conscience in a land of boasted liberty and equality of rights. On March 21, the *Journal* published an editorial sustaining Miss Newell in seeking her rights:

However unpleasant it may be to see a young lady of high intelligence and character forsake the religion of her fathers and devote herself to a conventual life, instead of remaining in the society which she is so well qualified to adorn, there is certainly no law against it in the land of Roger Williams, and she must judge for herself.

The next day, the day planned for the attack upon the convent, a second editorial in the *Journal* asserted that "the authorities of the city lack neither the disposition nor the means to preserve the peace of the city . . . Providence is not a city where mobs flourish."

Frances Warde, meanwhile, opened the convent to visitors. Among them was the Mayor of Providence, who advised Mother Frances to send Rebecca Newell home. "Not unless she wishes to go," replied Frances. "What then shall I do to preserve peace?" asked the Mayor. "Is it possible," countered Frances, "that Your Honor cannot assist in saving life and property in the event of a riot?" Then the Mayor begged Mother Frances to leave quietly with her community. She refused.

At the same time, Bishop O'Reilly was insisting on protection from city and state authorities. Uncertain of their response, he thought it wise to call upon parishioners and friends to protect his Sisters if necessary. On the evening of March 22, several hundred men arrived at the convent, armed with whatever crude weapons they could secure. From every man Frances Warde exacted a promise to refrain from violence except in case of absolute necessity. The men took their places at strategic points in the convent and on the grounds. Outside, in the clear moonlight, a large mob gathered, reinforced by Know-Nothings from Boston, Salem, and Taunton. From the convent windows, the Sisters could see, as far as their eyes could penetrate, a dense mass of human faces, glaring wildly at the convent. "The multitude of faces waved to and fro," said one Sister, "like a vast forest stirred by the wind."

The mob demanded the release of Rebecca Newell. Reviling the name of "Mother Xavier Warde," they jeered. As the demands increased, Bishop O'Reilly stepped forward and declared, "The Sisters shall not leave their home . . . I will protect them with my life if necessary." At this point, the owner of the convent property, a Protestant, stood beside the Bishop and said to the mob: "There are four hundred strong men here, armed with weapons. At the least attempt at violence, they will defend the convent." Then the Bishop demanded that the Mayor read the Riot Act. He did. The crowd slowly changed its mood. They had come to attack women: four hundred men and the law were beyond their calculations. Perhaps they had no strong leader. After a while, they slowly began to disperse. There was some stone throwing, hissing, and jeering. That was all.

The Know-Nothings of Providence never again interfered with Catholic education there. The attack upon the Convent of Mercy became a unique part of local myth. Years afterward, it was referred to as the "Siege of the Malakoff Tower." In the Archives of St. Xavier's Convent is a bamboo walking stick with a hollow top which conceals a short sword with a wooden handle. On it is the inscription:

This weapon was used by Philip De Crogan in defending St. Xavier's Convent against the Know-Nothings. It was given to his daughter, Annie Forbes, who in turn gave it to the family of Sister Matthias Brogan. In 1957, following the death of Annie Forbes, it was given to St. Xavier's.

Michael O'Connor was proved to be right. Frances Warde was the woman to enter into the hard core of New England prejudice.

The steady growth of both St. Xavier's Academy and the orphanage in Providence now necessitated further accommodations. A new building, called "Saint Mary's of the Ascension," was begun in 1855 and completed in 1856. Frances Warde's plans called for expenses difficult to meet. With her usual initiative, she raised funds in various ways, including two lectures by the popular Irish-Canadian author and lecturer, Thomas D'Arcy McGee. An "anonymous" friend who knew of Frances' love for gardens—probably Emily Harper —presented the Sisters with a sum of money to beautify the grounds at St. Xavier's. Thus Frances had her heart's desire without scruple concerning funds. The entire garden was transformed: the ground was spaded, and cartloads of rich soil were spread over it; trees were transplanted, new shrubberies introduced, walks laid out to wind through the grounds; the trumpet vine on the house was carefully trimmed and trained; a rustic arbor was built in the center of the garden and covered with rose vines. In June this arbor was a perfect bower. For a time, peace reigned in Providence.

In order to meet the increasing need for schools and orphanages in his diocese, Bishop O'Reilly sailed for Europe in December, 1855, to seek priests, religious, and Christian Brothers. His mission accomplished, he wrote the following letter from Liverpool to the President of the Irish College in Rome on January 22, 1856:

I will sail tomorrow for America so that, no accidents occurring, I will get home in something less than two months . . .

Our sufferings have been great the past year. Governors and people in the States composed of Know-Nothings are our persecutors. The power of this wicked organization is fast culminating: they attempted to destroy the Convent of Mercy at Providence, but failed. God in the conclusion gave us a great, and a bloodless, victory.[10]

These were the last words Bishop O'Reilly wrote. On January 23, he sailed from Liverpool on the ill-fated *Pacific*. The loss of the *Pacific* ranks with the tragedies of the *Lusitania* and the *Titanic* of the twentieth century. But from the latter two some lives were saved. The fate of the *Pacific* was somehow weird and mysterious: not a fragment of wreckage was ever found, not a word came back.

Bernard O'Reilly had been a good man and a faithful friend of Frances Warde. More than once he had proved himself to be heroically selfless. As a young priest during the Asiatic cholera plague in New York City in 1832, he had served the sufferers ceaselessly. He had twice contracted the disease, to recover amazingly and return to the care of the plague-stricken. Less than a year before his death, he had offered to defend the Sisters of Mercy with his life. Frances Warde and her Sisters mourned the loss of their spiritual father. For two years, the Diocese of Hartford was without a bishop. William O'Reilly, brother of the lost bishop, was administrator. With his sanction, Frances Warde continued the expansion of her apostolate.

In 1857, she sent Sisters from Providence to Little Rock, Arkansas, to help the Mercy foundation there. Vocations were plentiful in the East, but recruits were rare in the West. Arkansas was still a Slave State. Imagine the chagrin of Sister Paula Lombard when, a few weeks after she arrived in Little Rock, she answered the door of the convent, only to find a tall black man who offered to sell himself to her! He preferred to work for the Sisters, and his master was agreeable to the sale. When Mother Frances received such news from the West, she was fired with indignation against the abomination of slavery. But no obstacle, no tragedy, it seemed, could hinder her mission to spread the mercy of Christ everywhere in America.

Obstacles there were, within the Congregation of Mercy and without. During the eighteen-fifties and sixties, dissension among the Sisters of Mercy concerning the apostolic works proper to their Institute came to a crisis. As American founder, Frances Warde was called to devote time and energy to the achievement of a peaceful solution to the problem in the United States. While reason would have suggested that Frances, more than any other woman, was best qualified by knowledge and experience to interpret the spirit of Catherine McAuley, this faculty was not granted to her by a minority of Sisters of Mercy in Ireland and America. A spirit of rigidity, a "letter-of-the-law" attitude foreign to the spirit of both Catherine McAuley and Frances Warde, inserted itself into the customs of some Congregations of Mercy in both Ireland and the United States.

If Catherine McAuley had not died within ten years of the foundation of her Congregation, certain customs and attitudes she cherished would have gained greater common ascendancy among her Sisters, or perhaps she herself would have put these customs into written form. It was inevitable that some customs would change within the various Mercy Congregations, particularly since the different foundations became independent congregations, not governed from a common parent house. As early as 1847, Mother Cecilia Marmion, Superior at St. Catherine's, Dublin, proposed a Chapter to be held at Baggot Street to prepare a Book of Customs for the Sisters of Mercy. Agreement was then reached to adopt uniform customs concerning certain matters of conventual living.

Evidently diversity of opinion existed even in the early days of the Institute concerning whether or not the Sisters should devote themselves exclusively to the service of the poor. The establishment of "pension" or tuition schools—day or boarding—for middle class girls was the chief element of contention. The *Annals* of St. Leo's Convent, Carlow, had stated back in 1839, even before the death of Catherine McAuley:

Although properly speaking the education of the middle class is not a feature of our Institute, yet our Foundress gave her fullest sanction to its being undertaken by this community.

Catherine McAuley taught that the Sisters of Mercy should meet the needs of the Church in whatever diocese they found themselves. A manuscript notebook, still extant in Dublin, with the title, *Extracts from Instructions of the Venerated Foundress,* and believed to have been compiled by Mother di Pazzi Delaney, second Mother Superior of the Congregation, reads as follows:

Some persons, unacquainted with the spirit of the Institute, imagine that we should confine ourselves to the Works of Mercy named in the *Rule,* but this is a great error and quite contrary to the intention of the Holy Foundress. All the Works of Mercy belong to the Order, but as it seldom happens that one community could take so many duties upon themselves without overburdening the Sisters, *three* are specified as being peculiarly characteristic of the Institute . . .[11]

When the question arose concerning the establishment of St. Xavier Academy in Latrobe by the Pittsburgh Congregation, Bishop Michael O'Connor, who approved of the project, consulted the Sisters as to whether they should teach "upper or middle class" girls. To his surprise, all the Sisters except Mother Frances Warde feared that an academy might subtract from the time they devoted to the service of the poor. Frances pointed out that Catherine McAuley had opened "pension schools" in the majority of convents she had founded in Ireland; that she gave them a special sanction as the schools from which the greater number of vocations to the Congregation would be drawn; that the Congregation of Mercy cannot *in principle* exclude any work of mercy unless it actually interferes with the most characteristic works of the Institute. "I have always regretted," said Frances, "that I did not ask our beloved foundress to put her views on this matter in writing." She added that, where academies were introduced, the Sisters normally taught fifty or more poor children for every middle class girl. Then, with her usual practicality, Frances added that, while dowries were required of candidates to the Congregation in Ireland, they could not be expected from the children of immigrants in America. To put the minds of all at rest, Bishop O'Connor directed a request to the Propaganda Fide in Rome, asking whether the Sisters of Mercy might carry on without scruple "works of charity of which there is no express mention in their Rule," mentioning particularly the type of education carried on in the academies. An affirmative answer was received from Rome under date of December 4, 1852.[12]

It is interesting to note that a similar request from the Congregation of Mercy in Charleville, Ireland, also received an affirmative reply,[13] while a request to abolish tuition schools sent to Rome by an American Superior in the eighteen-seventies was denied.[14] Again, in the eighteen-eighties, Rome supported the Sisters of Mercy of New Orleans when an objection was raised to their tuition school as being not proper to the Institute.[15] Frances Warde's interpretation of Catherine McAuley's *Rule* was thus officially sustained four times by the Church.

The opponents of academies conducted by the Sisters of Mercy were vocal, however, during Frances Warde's years in Providence, and during her later years in New Hampshire. Objections to pension schools had their sources in both Ireland and the United States. St. Mary's Convent, Limerick, and St. Joseph's Convent, Kinsale, led the opposition in Ireland; in America, disapproval came from San Francisco, St.

Louis, and New York. In 1859–60, a movement arose to hold a General Chapter of Sisters of Mercy to establish a uniform Code of Customs for all the Sisters. In 1859, Frances Warde received a letter from the San Francisco Sisters of Mercy urging her to cooperate in the effort to hold a General Chapter in Dublin.[16] Mother Frances' answer is not extant, but a letter from the West Coast in 1861 accuses her of responsibility for establishing boarding schools in the United States and suggests that the poor schools are of secondary importance in the majority of Congregations of Mercy in America. The writer laments, also, that the St. Louis and the New York Sisters of Mercy have joined those Congregations which conduct boarding academies.[17]

Frances Warde's views concerning the pension school problem were reported to Kinsale by the San Francisco Sisters, and Mother Frances Bridgeman of Kinsale replied with not only a denunciation of pension and boarding schools but an attack upon the character of Frances Warde. Evidently a member of the California Congregation (probably Mother M. Baptist Russell) had written in praise of Frances Warde after consulting her, for the reply from Kinsale is in the form of a denial of her virtues as a Superior:

You were not correctly informed with regard to her perfect control over her Community . . . She leaves the Community she forms and governs in extreme difficulties of all sorts, spends the funds, etc. She is good natured, active, zealous, and pious, but incapable of working up a good school or of establishing strict, judicious religious discipline. This is, I believe, the opinion of all who knew her. She left Pittsburgh and Carlow in a sad state . . .[18]

There can be no question of the extreme bias of the above statement. In 1861, when the letter was written, it was common knowledge that Carlow was the most successful of the Irish foundations and Pittsburgh of the American ones. As for the charge that Frances Warde was "incapable of . . . strict, judicious religious discipline" and "perfect control" over her Community, it is likely that she would have considered the statement a compliment!

The hostility toward Frances' view of boarding schools as a legitimate pursuit of the Sisters of Mercy reached a point of absurdity about a year after the above letter was written. As she patiently continued to clarify the judgment of Catherine McAuley, Mother Frances received an astonishing epistle from San Francisco. A California priest was quoted as authority that boarding schools were contrary to the *Rule* of the Sisters of Mercy. The Chicago Sisters were criticized by him for conducting St. Xavier's Academy. And the final statement of the letter was somewhat shocking in its implications:

I merely mention [these examples] to let you see how many agree in pronouncing Boarding Schools *contrary* to our *Rule* whatever may have been the private views of Mother McAuley . . .[19]

It seems incredible that an unknown priest's views should be preferred to those of Catherine McAuley in interpreting the *Rule* she had written for the Congregation she founded!

A General Chapter of Sisters of Mercy was finally held in Limerick in 1864. Invitations were sent to the Mother Superiors of Mercy Convents in Ireland and England. The Chapter had as its goal to prepare a "Book of Customs" or "Guide" for all Mercy Congregations.[20] Mother Frances Bridgeman of Kinsale prepared an extensive "exposition" of Mercy customs for approval by the Sisters attending the Chapter. The Sisters of Mercy of the parent house in Baggot

Street refused to hold the Chapter in Dublin or to attend it in Limerick. In the Archives of the Sisters of Mercy, Carysfort Park, Dublin, is a series of twenty-nine letters addressed to Mother Mary of Mercy Norris, Superior at St. Catherine's, concerning the proposed Chapter of 1864. Mother Mary of Mercy responded that the Dublin Sisters were satisfied with the Customs established by Catherine McAuley and approved by the Dublin Chapter of 1847. She added, in a letter to Limerick:

Of course, external circumstances may and will alter many regulations, but I feel confident the *essentials* are strictly adhered to, and our *Holy Rule* in its wisdom does not bind us to a similarity of practices. We have heard of a few Superiors who acted unwisely, and indeed I do not believe any *Customs* could guard against a temporary want of prudence . . . of individuals . . .[21]

Many of the Irish and English convents, in agreement with the Dublin Sisters, refused to attend the Chapter, held May 8 to 16, 1864, in Limerick. Nineteen Mercy Congregations were represented. In 1866 a *Guide for Religious Called Sisters of Mercy,* approved by the Chapter, was published by the Sisters of Mercy of Kinsale. Mother Frances Bridgeman published "at the same time the large edition which she compiled herself in an extended form . . . embodying the *small* edition for which *alone* the *votes* of the Superiors passed . . ."[22]

The establishment of pension schools—a major point of controversy—received the sanction of the Superiors assembled at Kinsale:

The greater glory of God and the salvation of souls sometimes render the establishment of *detached schools* necessary . . . They require very judicious management that they become not a source of serious evil to the community . . .[23]

Before the death of Frances Warde in 1884, almost every Congregation of Mercy in the world conducted at least one academy for girls. It is probable that if Frances had yielded to the great pressures placed upon her to abolish pension schools in the eighteen-fifties and sixties, the Mercy Sisters in America would have ceased this particular apostolate entirely. Like Catherine McAuley, Frances would have sacrificed much for union and charity if she believed the work of Christ would not suffer. But she could not reject an apostolate which she believed to be fruitful in the teaching of the Word of God. A letter she wrote to Father James O'Connor, in Pittsburgh, from Providence in the spring of 1856 is a beautiful revelation of her spirit throughout the whole controversy concerning pension schools for middle class girls. Frances had visited New York to discuss with Mother Mary Agnes O'Connor some points of controversy concerning Mercy customs. The New York Sisters were critical of the Pittsburgh Sisters on two scores: a change they had made in the sleeves of the Mercy habit, and the fact that they cared for little boys in their orphanage. Some Mercy Congregations believed that the Sisters should accept only girls in their schools and orphanages. Frances Warde had succeeded in convincing Mother Mary Agnes to accept pension schools for boarding students, and now she suggested diplomatically that the Pittsburgh Sisters should compromise by acceding to the wishes of the New York Sisters with regard to the two customs mentioned above. Frances' spirit is one of complete charity:

Now then I regret to say that the result of my conversations for a few days with M. Agnes and M. Austin on the matters you kindly discussed with me were not satisfactory. They continue to feel so very much opposed to the changes made with regard to some duties and our religious dress. Finally, however, they would be satisfied at present if the Community in Pittsburgh would again assume our religious dress, and as soon as convenient to Superiors give over the Boys' Asylum to some good Brothers or "pious women." Now for the accomplishmeent of so great a good as I deem it would be to have *all* happily united . . . some little sacrifices should be made. This union, if properly effected, would, I am persuaded, greatly contribute to peace and prosperity in the Order. I feel that the houses should all mutually sustain each other. This Mother Agnes seems anxious for also. Before I left, they were willing at length to yield to us the right of having pension and even boarding schools in the way that we have them. I told them the very words of our Holy Foundress on that matter, so they assented. They think that I ought to unite with them and adopt more fully their views [that] our houses should unite in maintaining religious discipline according to the approved customs and usages of the Order in Ireland. Much as I prize the affectionate interest that exists between their Community and ours, I feel bound in honor and conscience to uphold the Pittsburgh house to the last. I very much desire that we could happily arrange all these little matters and that nothing but perfect union and charity should exist amongst us . . . I have said perhaps too much on this matter. And everything that I can do and say to protect union and peace I am most anxious to do . . . .[24]

The spirit of union and charity which sustained Frances Warde during the controversies of the eighteen fifties and sixties within the Congregation of Mercy was the same spirit which she had imbibed from Catherine McAuley in Dublin twenty-five years earlier. It was the characteristic spirit of the Sisters of Mercy.

12

New York Foundation; Apostolic Center in New Hampshire

IN the spring of 1857, Bishop John Timon of the Diocese of Buffalo visited the Sisters of Mercy in Pittsburgh to make the last of many appeals for Sisters to come to his diocese. In 1847, Timon had been consecrated Bishop of a diocese which included all the New York State territory west of the Finger Lake district. When he attended the New York Plenary Council in 1854, Catholic education had been strongly urged. "The Sisters of Mercy of Pittsburgh were attracting much attention at the time. Bishops from all Sees were clamoring for the aid of these women." Timon sought teachers among the Pittsburgh Sisters, but they were about to found a new Mercy Congregation in Baltimore. They could not manage two foundations at once.

Bishop Timon was not a man to give up easily. His dynamism was almost incredible. Before his ordination as a Vincentian priest, he had traveled 1200 miles teaching and lecturing on the Catholic faith in lower Mississippi and Kentucky. Bishop Joseph Rosati had declared that Timon had led back more lapsed Catholics and received more converts to the Church than all other priests of the Diocese of St. Louis combined.[2] After his ordination in 1826, Timon had been called the "Apostle of Texas" because of his outstanding apostolate in that prefecture. As Bishop of Buffalo, he traveled unceasingly in cold, labor, and fatigue to administer the Sacraments to his people. Those who knew him best compared him with St. Paul in his journeying, suffering, and preaching the Word of God. It could be taken for granted that if Bishop Timon desired to have Sisters of Mercy in his diocese, he would succeed in doing so.

Between 1854 and 1857, he continued to plead his case in Pittsburgh. Unable to provide a foundation, the Sisters finally suggested to him that he apply to their own founder, Frances Warde, in Providence. Timon recalled that Bernard O'Reilly, the Bishop of Hartford now lost at sea, and his brother, William O'Reilly, now Administrator of the Hartford Diocese, had both served under him as Vicars-General. He felt that he could not be refused in Providence. On May 16, 1857, he went to Rhode Island to have a "long talk" with Mother Frances and to secure the support of William O'Reilly in his project.[3] Frances Warde recognized a kindred missionary spirit in Timon: he was indeed a brother in spirit to that increasing number of apostles who continued to join her in her ardent mission to the Church in America. On May 17, 1857, Timon was able to record in his *Diary:* "Visited Sisters of Mercy . . . Arranged for Sisters to Rochester . . . ."

With her usual amazing magnanimity, Frances was able to prepare a group of five Sisters to depart for the new foundation within three weeks. She also followed her custom of traveling with them and remaining to assist them until they were well established in their new convent. William O'Reilly accompanied the Sisters to Rochester. As first Superior, Frances chose Sister Baptist Coleman, who had entered the Providence convent from Harold Cross, Dublin, in 1851 and who had accompanied Mother Frances as one of the first Sisters to establish the Convent of Mercy in New Haven. The only other professed Sister in the group was Teresa Austin Carroll, later the author of the *Life of Catherine McAuley* and of the four-volume *Annals of the Sisters of Mercy*. Eventually, she was to found Convents of Mercy in Mobile, Alabama, and throughout the South, as well as in Belize, British Honduras. Two novices were among the Rochester founders: Sister de Pazzi Kavanagh and Sister Raymond O'Reilly.

The little group stayed over-night at the Delevan House in Albany. Bishop Timon had invited them to Buffalo to see the beautiful new St. Joseph's Cathedral, then one of the finest in the country. He made reservations for them at the imposing Clarendon Hotel. On June 7 they participated in the Celebration of the Eucharist and in Solemn Vespers at the magnificent Cathedral. There they met John J. Lynch, Vincentian Rector of a new preparatory seminary just established at Niagara Falls. Timon and Lynch offered to take the Sisters to see the seminary and the Falls. The journey was pleasant, since in 1857 a good train service was already established between Buffalo and the Suspension Bridge. A holiday was declared at the seminary, the Bishop and the Rector donned aprons to serve the Sisters, and the boys entertained with songs. Frances Warde promised to send books for the seminary library. After lunch, all went to see the great Falls. The party crossed the Suspension Bridge to the Canadian side to view the mighty cataract and the beauty of the gorge. Timon reminded them that they followed the path once taken by Father Louis Hennepin, explorer of the Mississippi River. Tradition states that Timon suggested to Frances Warde that she establish a Convent of Mercy just above the Canadian Rapids. Father Lynch, who was to become Bishop of Toronto a few years later, approved of the idea. But Frances is quoted as having said that the beautiful spot offered little possibility for the practice of works of mercy among the poor. By a strange providence, the first foundation of Sisters of Mercy was established in Canada precisely one hundred years later in Prince Rupert, Columbia Territory, West Canada, in 1957, by Sisters from Callan, County Kilkenny. And the Callen Congregation had been founded from Athy, County Kildare, by Sister Michael Maher, cousin of Frances Warde and niece of her beloved James Maher of Carlow! The Loretto Sisters from Dublin eventually established an academy on the site above the Canadian Rapids. There also is the Church of Our Lady of Peace, the oldest Church erected in Niagara Falls. Louis Hennepin celebrated Mass near the spot on December 11, 1678. The Church is the oldest shrine dedicated to Mary in Southern Ontario. From the front of the Church can be seen the Niagara Cataracts and often the rainbow, the Biblical symbol of peace.

From the Falls, the party went on to Rochester, the "City of the Pleasant Valley" near the Genesee Falls. They arrived the evening of June 8 and were welcomed by Thomas McEvoy, pastor of St. Mary's Church. Their new home was a small convent next to the Church and formerly occupied by Bridgetine Sisters. Colloquially, it was called "15 South Street." The next morning, June 9, the Rochester Mercy Foundation Day, Bishop Timon celebrated the Eucharist for the first time in St. Mary's Convent of Mercy. The same day, Catherine McEvoy, sister of the pastor, presented herself as the first Rochester postulant. The little convent was indeed poor in material possessions. Frances Warde set to work at once, arranging conventual matters and laying plans for St. Mary's Parochial School and the Academy of the Immaculate Conception, a convent day and boarding school for girls, both to be opened in September. As was customary, the poor and the sick in the town were visited and cared for at once. Christian Doctrine classes were begun. An industrial school for girls and a day nursery were added later.

Mother Frances held the imposing ceremony of religious profession in St. Mary's Church on June 24, when Sister Raymond O'Reilly pronounced her vows. Catholics and non-Catholics of Rochester attended in large numbers, and Bishop Timon spoke on the meaning of religious consecration and the work of the Sisters of Mercy. Three weeks after Frances Warde left Providence, she felt that the little community was sufficiently well established for her departure. The Sisters were sorrowful to see her go. Bishop Timon promised to be with them in their trials as well as joys, and Frances knew that Timon was a man who would keep his word. She returned by boat to Providence, by way of New York City. Stopping over-night in New York, she secured a promise of a Jesuit Retreat the following August for her Sisters at St. Xavier's. She was not a woman to miss an opportunity!

The foundation in Rochester took strong root. The Congregation was destined to suffer greatly during its hundred-year history because of geographical divisions in the New York Diocese which more than once brought about divisions in the religious communities established from Rochester. The Sisters suffered personally from the formation of the Rochester Diocese in 1868 and the settling of boundary lines of the Buffalo and Rochester Dioceses in 1897. When divisions were made, each of the Sisters had to face the decision of which of two Mercy communities to serve permanently. The first prelate of the new diocese of Rochester, moreover, did not show them the same care and concern as their loved Bishop Timon, who died in 1867. In their days of trial, Mother Frances offered them advice and consolation.

Two Convents of Mercy established by the Rochester Congregation became the nucleus of the Buffalo Congregation of Sisters of Mercy—the foundations at St. Bridget's in Buffalo in 1858 and at St. Joseph's in Batavia in 1862. The Rochester Sisters also founded a convent in 1867 in Auburn, where the Sisters visited the men and women in famous Auburn Prison for over sixty years. From Batavia were established convents in Corning, Owego, Albion, Hornellsville, Wellsville, and Elmira. The hardships in some of these early missions were almost incredible. In Owego the Sisters rode railroad hand-cars to nearby towns to teach Christian Doctrine! From Buffalo was founded the Hazleton Convent of Mercy, the first in the Diocese of Scranton, which later was united with the Wilkes-Barre Convent founded from Pittsburgh. The Buffalo and Batavia Congregations were united permanently in 1896, but the "Southern Tier," four convents founded from Batavia, was annexed to Rochester, the original parent house, in 1901. The Rochester Sisters were also the source of a Congregation of Mercy in Malone, northern New York State, in 1873. It expanded to Hogansburg, New York, where the Sisters worked on the St. Regis Indian Reservation and conducted night classes for lumbermen in the forests of northern New York. This community also established a Convent of Mercy in Gabriels, New York, where they conducted a famous tuberculosis sanitarium. The Gabriels Sisters later joined the New York Province of the Sisters of Mercy of the Union.

The story of the New York Mercy communities which developed from the original St. Mary's in Rochester would require a book to tell. The growth was complex, but the roots were firm. All of the convents founded from Rochester had their source in Frances Warde, and the sisterly relationships of the Buffalo and Hazleton congregations with the Pittsburgh community led back to the more original fountain of Mother Frances' first American foundation.[4] The present Rochester Convent of Mercy, on Blossom Road, is located on the site of the original "bark cabin" which served as the first chapel in Rochester.

When Frances Warde returned from Rochester to Provi-

dence in June, 1857, her six-year term of office as Superior
of the Providence Sisters was completed. Legally, it was time
for an election. But the sorrowing Diocese of Hartford was
waiting, hoping that some word might be received from their
lost Bishop and the ill-fated *Pacific*. The Administrator,
William O'Reilly, delayed the Mercy election until Hartford
should have a Bishop. Two years after the ship was reported
lost, doubt gave way to sad fact, and a new bishop was consecrated on March 15, 1858. He was Francis Patrick Mc-
Farland of New York who, like his predecessor, adopted the
city of Providence as the center for the Diocese of Hartford.
Present at McFarland's consecration was Bishop David William Bacon of the Diocese of Portland, Maine, which had
been established in 1854 to include the entire States of Maine
and New Hampshire. After the ceremony, Bacon drew Mc-
Farland aside and requested him to send Mercy Sisters from
Providence to establish a foundation in Manchester, New
Hampshire. The pastor of that town, Father William Mc-
Donald, was most anxious to have Sisters of Mercy to educate
his people in the Catholic faith, to serve the poor, and to
care for the hundreds of young girls working in factories in
the Manchester area.

Granted that both Bishop Bacon and Frances Warde were
serving the people of God in New England, it was inevitable
that they should be united in their apostolate. When Bacon
became Bishop of the vast territory of Maine and New Hampshire, he had only five priests in his diocese. There were only
twelve churches in Maine, and four in New Hampshire, to
serve 15,000 white Catholics and 2,000 Indians. He wrote in
his *Diary:*

I see before me a vast field to be cultivated; few laborers, only
five, three of whom are unfit for the work; distant journeys to

be made, where the railroad is yet unknown; small means, and this to be gathered with much toil . . .[5]

Bacon's first episcopal act was to lay the cornerstone of a new church in the city of Bangor in June, 1855. Fears for his life surrounded the ceremony, for the pastor of the church was Father John Bapst who had been tarred and feathered by bigots in Ellsworth, Maine, a few months before. Prejudice against Catholics was violent in the new Diocese of Portland, but the young Bishop was strong and zealous. He was without fear. For Frances Warde, to know such a man was to respond to his mission. She could no more have refused his petition for help than she could have refused Catherine McAuley.

The Diocese of Portland was precisely the missionary field to appeal to intrepid pioneers like Bishop Bacon and Mother Frances. Catholics had been the first Christians in the vast area of Maine and New Hampshire. As far back as the tenth century, Christian Northmen had spread the faith along the shores of Maine. Boone Island and Mount Desert possessed ancient altars. Indians whose forefathers had been converted by Jesuits generations before still maintained the Christian faith in the mid-nineteenth century. In Norridgewock, at the junction of the Kennebec and Sandy Rivers, a monument commemorated the martyrdom of French Jesuit Sebastian Rasle and the murder of the members of his flock by British soldiers on August 23, 1724. History records the triumphal procession of these soldiers carrying the scalp of Rasle and those of twenty-six Abenaki Indians through the streets of Boston. As late as 1791, there was only one Catholic priest in the whole of New England.[6] Catholics in the "Granite State" were victims of a Puritanical persecution hardly equaled elsewhere. By a Constitution of 1783, they were denied representation in the law-making body of the State. Though failure of crops in Ireland in the eighteen-forties brought hundreds of Catholic immigrants to America, particularly to manufacturing towns like Manchester, their political status did not improve. In July, 1849, New Hampshire was the only State in the Union in which Catholics could not hold office. A hundred years after the martyrdom of Sebastian Rasle, persecution of Catholics still continued in New England.

On July 3, 1854, a mob had attempted to destroy St. Anne's Church in Manchester. The pastor of this church was Father William McDonald, whose parish was the entire state of New Hampshire, and who now invited the Sisters of Mercy of Providence to settle in his mission. On October 14, 1854, as already stated, Father John Bapst, who served the Abnaki Indians on the Penobscot River, had been tarred and feathered at Ellsworth, Maine. Bapst's tormentors had been arrested, but a grand jury had refused to indict them. After the atrocity, he had set up residence in Bangor. Again, on July 8, 1855, the Catholic Church in Bath, Maine, had been burned by a mob. Such a milieu was particularly challenging to the pioneering spirit of Frances Warde. Before the completion of the eighteen-seventies, she was destined to establish a Mercy apostolate not only throughout the State of New Hampshire but also in Bangor and Portland, and to establish three Indian missions in the State of Maine.

Shortly after the consecration of McFarland for the Diocese of Hartford, Bishop Bacon visited Mother Frances in Providence and begged her to establish a convent in Manchester. He pointed out that the Catholic children of his diocese were taught the Protestant religion, that young girls laboring in the manufacturing town were without religious or moral instruction, that his immense diocese was served only by a handful of priests. Meanwhile, Frances received numerous letters from William McDonald, who protested the great needs of his poor flock and declared that a new convent for the Sisters of Mercy was nearing completion. At the time, Bacon and McDonald were not the only petitioners for Sisters. Frances had on her desk requests from James Roosevelt Bayley, first Bishop of Newark, and also from Worcester, for the establishment of the Mercy Sisters in New Jersey and Massachusetts. But the appeal from Father McDonald touched her heart most deeply. The other areas would have to wait: their time would come. Long before she made it known to her loved Sisters in Providence, Frances Warde had made her decision in favor of Manchester.

In May, 1858, the Providence Congregation of Mercy held its election in Hartford. It is likely that Mother Frances encouraged the Sisters to elect a new Superior. They now knew that her thoughts centered in a New Hampshire apostolate. Though they loved her dearly, they elected Sister Josephine Lombard as their leader in order to free Frances. Before she returned to Providence, an incident occurred which Frances remembered and related with emotion years later. In Hartford there was an old lay Sister named Martha whose reputation for sanctity was already a legend. She was close to death and devoted her time to prayer and meditation. Though confined to bed, her mind was remarkably clear. Frances Warde recorded the event as follows:

I was in a great hurry to return to Providence when Sister Martha sent for me. I sent her word that I did not intend to leave without seeing her. Shortly after, as I was packing a suitcase, what was my surprise to see Sister Martha, like one risen from the dead, standing beside me. She said solemnly, "As I feared I should not see you, Our Lord helped me to come to you.

I hope and pray, dear Mother, that you will not remain in Providence. I am not in the habit of dreaming. Last night, as I was wide awake, I saw you in a newly built convent, with a great number of Sisters around you. The house was large and handsome, with long corridors; it was on a rising ground, and it was built all for God by a holy priest. You are to go there, and you will do more for God than you ever did before. Let nothing prevent your going on this mission."[7]

Frances replied, "I shall go wherever God appoints me to work for His glory." Sister Martha, satisfied with her answer, promised to pray for Frances, went back to her sick bed, and died shortly after. Frances returned to Providence and at once volunteered to lead a band of Sisters to Manchester.

The Sisters at St. Xavier's did not wish to lose the woman who had served them so completely since their eventful arrival in Providence in 1851. She, on her part, felt bitterly the sacrifice of leaving them. She was now forty-eight years old. The parent house in Providence had been the center of her unceasing labor and persevering prayer. She herself had made it a source of friendliness among both Catholics and non-Catholics. She had suffered insult silently. She had shown special kindness toward bigots. She had overcome obstacle after obstacle to her apostolate in Rhode Island and Connecticut. Now all the ill-feeling of the mob riot of 1855 was gone from Providence forever. Non-Catholics respected and loved her Sisters. Frances had formed many friendships, and she was a warm-hearted woman for whom friendship was no ephemeral gesture. Personally she had converted more than sixty townspeople to Catholicism, all of whom were dear to her. Her schools were steadily advancing toward higher standards. Now she might justifiably enjoy her reward. But she left her harvest for others to reap. She sought once again to clear land in less favored regions. Once again she set out as a pioneer. The decision to leave Providence was a wrench to her whole being, probably more agonizing than her departure from Pittsburgh. But she remembered the vision of Catherine McAuley, she reaffirmed her own commitment, she made her choice.

The future was dark and uncertain: the Native Americans of Manchester had sworn that no religious women would ever enter the State of New Hampshire. Bishop Bacon had frankly declared that "only the courage, zeal, and hardihood of a pioneer religious will ever be able to *rough it* in the establishment of Catholic schools in Maine and New Hampshire."[8] Like Bishop O'Reilly, he knew that Frances Warde was the woman to conquer intolerance with loving kindness.

With her usual expedition, Frances required only a few weeks to prepare to depart for Manchester. Four Sisters were chosen to accompany her: Sister Philomena Edwards, whom she named as her Assistant; Sister Gonzaga O'Brien, who was to remain her faithful co-worker until death; Sister Johanna Fogarty, who had accompanied her from Pittsburgh; and Sister Agatha Mulcahy, a novice. The date chosen for the New Hampshire Foundation Day was July 16, the Feast of Our Lady of Mount Carmel. The day before the departure ceremony Bishop McFarland, reluctant yet willing to see Frances Warde leave his diocese, wrote to Bishop Bacon:

Mother Warde has long been accustomed to govern. During her seven years' residence in Providence, I can say, after examining her accounts and the condition of the convent, that her management has been at once prudent and energetic. She gained for herself and her community the highest respect from intelligent Protestants no less than from Catholics.

Her companions are among the most promising subjects of our community. Their Superior parts from them with very great reluctance and only on my representing to them that the new

267

foundation should have able and most exemplary members. They leave with the affectionate respect of the Sisters.[9]

On the morning of July 16, Bishop McFarland offered the Eucharistic Sacrifice in St. Xavier's Chapel. He gave a homily in which he did not minimize the possible sufferings of the pioneers. He spoke of persecution, burning, and stoning. "The prospects are cheerless," he concluded, "but if all fails, or in any case, you will all be sure of a warm welcome in Providence at any time."[10] Yet he knew that Frances Warde had never turned back once she had initiated a mission. "Mother Exodus" was about to set out upon a new life. And like the heroes and heroines of the old Exodus, she never retraced her steps. The carriages were at the door. At nine o'clock, Frances and her companies walked out of the convent named in her honor and the garden she loved as her own, said goodbye to the companions she had received as young girls into the religious life, and left Providence forever.

Frances Warde felt no fear in leaving her Providence Sisters to expand their apostolic works without her. Their history testifies to the strength she gave them and the spirit of mercy they have nurtured down to the present day. Their establishment of orphanages, homes for working girls, homes for the aged, parochial schools, academies, colleges, and other works of mercy throughout Rhode Island, Connecticut, and Massachusetts has continued unceasingly. One year after Frances left Providence, her Sisters sent a Mercy foundation to the oldest Spanish settlement in the United States—the quaint, beautiful town of St. Augustine, Florida. This mission expanded to Columbus, Georgia, in the dark Civil War days of 1862. Personal suffering was intense among the Sisters as they served both the black and the Indian races in the South. In Georgia, the Sisters could not afford shoes and were obliged to cut up pieces of carpet for footgear. Novices were sent back to their homes because the Sisters could not provide food for them. At one point, a company of Union soldiers took up a collection to buy food for the Sisters who nursed their wounded.[11] Two Mercy foundations from Columbus, Georgia, expanded to the West: the first to Macon, Georgia, and to Salt Lake City, Utah, and Pocatello, Idaho; the second to Lacon, Illinois, and eventually to Oklahoma City, Oklahoma. The Providence Convent of Mercy also sent a foundation to Nashville, Tennessee, in 1866, from which developed a Mercy establishment in the West Side of Chicago, which later united with Frances Warde's original Chicago foundation from Pittsburgh in 1846. In the seventies, the Providence Sisters opened a convent and schools in Fall River, Massachusetts. In the nineties, they sent a foundation to West Newfoundland. Like the Hartford Convent of Mercy, Frances Warde's Providence foundation was destined to become at a later date the largest Mercy center in the United States. Today it comprises one of the nine provinces of the Sisters of Mercy of the Union.

The Providence Sisters never forgot their founder. In 1897, when a new St. Xavier Convent and Chapel was dedicated, a stained glass window honored Frances Warde. Thirty years later, a beautiful window in the new Mount St. Rita Chapel was dedicated to Mother Frances, while a window directly opposite honored her beloved Catherine McAuley.

But on that warm summer morning of July 16, 1858, Frances Warde and her Sisters knew nothing of the future of the Providence Congregation. With intense excitement, they boarded the train at Providence for Worcester, where they were delayed for an hour. Then a touching incident occurred. A lad of about fifteen approached Mother Frances and asked her and her Sisters to "please stay in Worcester." Frances

Warde knew then that the time would not be long until Sisters of Mercy would serve in the education of the boys and girls of Massachusetts. At Nashua Junction in New Hampshire, the Sisters were delighted to find Father William McDonald awaiting them at the station. This meeting was one of the most significant in Frances Warde's life. Of all the clergymen with whom she was destined to serve the people of God—Maher, O'Connor, Quarter, de Goesbriand, O'Reilly, McFarland, Bacon, and others still unknown to her—none achieved a richer collaboration in mercy with Frances than William McDonald. Not the bishops, but the simple pastor was to understand best her vision of mercy and to cooperate fully with her for almost a quarter of a century.

Though born in Ireland three years after Frances, William McDonald was in appearance and manner rather the typical Yankee and thus peculiarly suited to his American environment. Above medium height, he was sharp in feature, square of jaw. His habitual expression was one of gravity, of which he had need, for his apostolate was not an easy one. He had studied in Dublin, immigrated to Prince Edward Island, prepared for the priesthood in Three Rivers, Canada, and served in New Brunswick, Maine, and Massachusetts, before his appointment to Manchester. He loved the mountains, streams, and lakes of New Hampshire, the "Switzerland of America," but he loved his people more. For forty-one years he was a light to the grim manufacturing town of Manchester, illuminating its life in a human and Christ-like way. When he first went to Manchester in 1844, however, he found his countrymen and co-religionists far more despised by Yankee and Puritan than the slaves of the South by some of their white neighbors. When he celebrated the Eucharist, he and his flock were hissed and hooted as "blood-hounds of hell."

William McDonald settled among his people in New

Hampshire at the risk of his life. The native Americans at first used every perverse means to intimidate the "dangerous papist." They soon began to admire his daring. In the end they reverenced him. Slowly but surely he won his way among them, and within a year he was able to rent Granite Hall in the center of the town as a temporary chapel. He possessed the virtues his Yankee neighbors admired. He was frugal, industrious, sober, orderly, and civic-minded. His way of life tended to kill bigotry. His Catholic parishioners loved him for other reasons. He knew every member of his flock in Manchester, and he was to each a friend, a father, a refuge. For the exploited mill workers who had no forty-hour week in the eighteen-forties, he remained in the confessional for twelve hours at a time. His charities were boundless. He cared for the sick and the aged. He gave them his last penny and always seemed to have more to give. He found time to read theology, and his sermons were realistic and meaningful to his people. Intolerant of gossip, he considered hospitality a Christian duty. He sent to Boston for altar wine because he knew he would be misunderstood by the Yankees if he purchased it openly in Manchester. Yet if he heard that a young priest had a drinking problem, he would ask his Bishop to send the young man to live with him. Within a year, the young priest would invariably find stability. McDonald's apostolate had no limits. The source of his strength was the Eucharist. His sexton testified that he never opened St. Anne's Church in the morning without finding Father McDonald in prayer. He feared no one, sought the favor of no one, and eventually was loved by all. When he died in 1885, all business in Manchester was suspended, all factories were closed, and the people of the city attended his obsequies in a body. The testimony to his holiness was universal.

It was inevitable that Frances Warde and William Mc-

Donald should become friends. Their goals were unified. They worked together in unusual harmony. Both were strong personalities. They understood each other and knew how to support each other without infringing upon the personal independence so essential for each. The Mercy annalist wrote of their relationship:

Naturally, a woman of Mother Warde's positive character sometimes, during a long life, made enemies or at least excited jealousy of persons less gifted or less successful, and was sometimes misunderstood by the clergy with whom she worked. Troubles arising from such sources were very keenly felt by Mother Warde who, if blessed with a masculine mind, had a most sensitive, womanly heart. Father McDonald . . . made it a duty to keep such unpleasantness from her . . . .[12]

She, in turn, supported him. When the Sisters sometimes complained to her of Father McDonald's abrupt manner, which had its source in shyness and sometimes hid the kindness of his heart, Frances would say, "You must get to *know* Father, and when you need help or guidance, you will be sure of finding it. There is *real worth* in him." In many of her letters, Frances testified to the holiness and zeal of the man who did "all for God."

As early as May, 1848, McDonald had begun the erection of St. Anne's Church in Manchester. Despite the respect the people of the town felt for him, threats against the parish by Know-Nothings continued intermittently. Finally, on July 4, 1854, five hundred armed rioters attacked the Irish Catholics of Manchester, drove them from their homes, destroyed their furniture, and finally shattered the stained glass windows of St. Anne's with rocks. A Protestant neighbor, John Maynard, helped to curb the violence of the attackers. After this incident, parishioners took turns guarding the church from destruction. When McDonald decided to invite Sisters of Mercy to Manchester, his people opposed him, fearing for the lives of the Sisters. He went ahead with plans for the convent, however, and with typical loyalty his people cooperated. School children as well as their parents, all of them poor, joined a campaign to save "a dime for a brick" to build the Convent of Mercy. An attempt to set it afire before its completion led to a nightly guard of the convent by the men of St. Anne's. Finally, a family lived in it to protect it until the arrival of the Sisters.

In July, 1858, all was ready for Frances Warde and her companions. When they reached Manchester, Father McDonald led them to a comfortable residence close to the church. They thought it was their convent. After dinner, one of the Sisters went to the window and exclaimed, "Mother Frances, come and see the grand building at the other side of the church. It must be a Catholic institution—there is a cross on the cupola." Frances looked out at the attractive building and answered, "It looks like a college." Father McDonald said nothing. Later, he offered to take the Sisters to their new home. Mother Frances was startled. "Why, are we not in it?" she said. "This is my house," said McDonald. "I'll take you to yours." He then led them to the attractive building that had excited their admiration. At the door, he told Mother Frances to take possession of her convent. Her eyes filled with tears: the convent was a perfect realization of "Martha's vision." "It is like St. Leo's in Carlow," she said. Then Father McDonald said quietly, "Unless you have another suggestion, I thought we might call it Mount St. Mary's." Frances' joy overflowed. Like her loved Mount St. Mary's in Westport, the convent that she herself had planned to resemble St. Leo's, the Manchester convent was on elevated ground and was dedicated to Mary. In later years, Sisters of Mercy would ask why Frances Warde chose to remain the rest of her life in Manchester when she could have carried on her apostolate from her foundations in large cities like Chicago and Philadelphia. The truth was that in Manchester she had come home—home to Carlow and Westport and Catherine McAuley. She loved Mount St. Mary's and she chose to remain there. Before Father McDonald left her on that memorable day, he blessed the convent and dedicated it to Mary. Then he handed Frances a hundred dollars to begin her works of mercy. The next day she entered the amount into her account book. For twenty years, she kept an exact account of all her expenditures. The books are still extant in the New Hampshire convent archives.

The day after their arrival in Manchester, the Sisters began the visitation and care of the sick poor. On the streets, they were at first a subject of curiosity and alarm to the natives. Only gradually, as the people began to appreciate the relief and comfort the Sisters brought to the neglected of the town, they became friendly. When the Sisters appeared in their garden on the first summer evenings, onlookers peered in at them and asked questions about their life. With typical diplomacy, Frances Warde invited them to visit the convent on Saturday afternoons. After that, many a day was spent conducting visitors through Mount St. Mary's. Suspicious persons looking for trap doors, underground passages, dungeons, and diabolical contrivances were disappointed. Some of the visitors invited the Sisters to effect an escape, promising them any assistance they needed. Meanwhile, the Sisters were accepted more and more among the people. When they offered to give private lessons in music and in French, the wife of the Mayor of Manchester was the first to apply. She was soon followed by many Protestant friends.

Frances Warde initiated her customary instructions in

Christian Doctrine for adults—both Catholics and non-Catholics. Her first converts were a Baptist and a Universalist. She spent long evenings instructing factory hands and other laborers of the town. Almost until her death, she acted as honorary godmother to innumerable converts to the Catholic faith as Father McDonald baptized them in the chapel at Mount St. Mary's. The Manchester *Annals* relate that, of all the works of mercy carried on at the convent, conversion to the faith was the most remarkable. Much of Frances Warde's work with catechumens was little short of miraculous. On one occasion, an enraged husband came to the convent to drag his wife and child from the baptismal font. With her extraordinary persuasive powers, Mother Frances prevailed upon him to witness the ceremony. In a short time, he himself was baptized.[13] Years later, when Frances was scarcely able to walk, her Sisters assisted her to the parlor to instruct her beloved catechumens. Here was the center of her apostolic mission.

Frances also continued in Manchester her now famous "talks" to her Sisters. They preserved her words as precious gifts.[14] The good religious is faithful to prayer and contemplation, she taught them, as well as to the spiritual and corporal works of mercy. Fidelity to the spiritual life results in fidelity to duty. No duty toward others is of small importance when all is done for Christ. Frances reminded her Sisters that they must listen to the voice of the Holy Spirit speaking within them—a voice which is sometimes so low that its sound can be drowned out by carelessness, bustle, and noise. The Spirit speaks in a secret way, unobtrusively, to those given to Christ by the Father. The faithful follower of Christ responds in secret, unmoved by human applause. Frances counseled gentleness and patience toward all those who were suffering, weak, or tempted. The test for response of a Sister of Mercy, she said, should be this: "How would the loving Master deal with the person before Him?"

As usual, young women attracted by Frances and her Sisters presented themselves as candidates for the religious life in Manchester almost from the beginning. Six girls were received within the first year. On July 30, 1858, two weeks after the opening of Mount St. Mary's, Frances received a prophetic letter from her friend, Bishop Bacon, in Portland:

You may be assured that I bless the kind Providence Who has sent you and yours to aid me in my laborious mission, and that I shall spare no pains on my part to protect and assist your Institute in the different works of Mercy which it will undertake. You may have your struggle at the commencement, but patience and perseverance will carry you through; and the day will come when your community will be numerous and prosperous, and when you will have houses in every section of the States of Maine and New Hampshire.

Before the death of Frances Warde, Bacon's prophecy was a reality.

Early in September, 1858, Mother Frances organized a Sunday School of Christian Doctrine at St. Anne's. In November, she initiated a night school at St. Anne's for the instruction of older girls and boys who worked in the factories during the day. Classes were held in both religious and secular subjects. Illiterate, exploited young people were taught to read, write, speak, and think intelligently. Within a year, several hundred were in attendance.

Also in September, 1858, Frances opened a free school for the younger girls of Manchester in the basement of St. Anne's Church. This school marked the beginning of the parochial school system in New Hampshire. The classes were overcrowded. Every Catholic girl in Manchester withdrew from the public school in which she had been enrolled previously and attended St. Anne's. Accommodations were crude in the makeshift classrooms, but the Sisters were knowledgeable, capable, and ingenious. The curriculum was similar to that established by Mother Frances in her schools in Pittsburgh and Providence. Soon St. Anne's Free School enjoyed a fine professional reputation.

In the fall of the same year, Frances founded Mount St. Mary Academy in the northern wing of the convent. She established it precisely when the controversy over "pension schools" was at its height among the Sisters of Mercy in America and Ireland. This school was to become one of the finest select schools in New England, attended by Catholics and non-Catholics alike. The friendships established among the students did much to break down religious prejudices. Mount St. Mary's marked the beginning of Catholic secondary education in New Hampshire. It is still in existence, though now located in Nashua.

In 1861 the Manchester City Council was sufficiently un-prejudiced—because of the influence of Father McDonald and Mother Frances—to allow the Catholics of the city free use of the Park Street Grammar School. The building was vacant because of a classroom upheaval several years before, when the boys of Manchester, most of whom were Catholics, arose en masse and expelled their teachers from the school because of their unsavory remarks about the "popish clergy." Now William McDonald enlisted a layman, Thomas Corcoran, as principal of the reopened school, and the Sisters of Mercy began the instruction of over 300 boys. In 1863, the Park Street School was classified as a public school, and the Sisters teaching there received their salaries from the city government. By 1869, they were teaching in several public schools in the Manchester area under the jurisdiction of the public school system. This fact is an interesting commentary on the interpretation of separation of Church and State in education accepted by the people of New Hampshire in the eighteen-sixties. The graduates of the Park Street school taught by the Sisters were outstanding. They became doctors, lawyers, and clergymen in large numbers. At Holy Cross College in 1876, there was only one Maine boy, but there were eleven New Hampshire natives, eight of whom came from Manchester.

The growth of the work of the Sisters of Mercy in Manchester was indeed "phenomenal."[15] A profound "revolution" was quietly at work in the old New England town. Within a few years, the mark of the Sisters of Mercy was felt throughout the State of New Hampshire in a cluster of educational and charitable institutions. Frances Warde was achieving rapidly in New Hampshire what she had already achieved in Pennsylvania, Illinois, Rhode Island, and Connecticut. "It was a rare blessing for the Catholic Church of New England that Mother Xavier Warde spent so many years of her life in two New England dioceses."[16]

Mother Frances, meanwhile, was happy in Manchester. Besides the extraordinary expansion of her active apostolate, she found time for prayer and contemplation. And she engaged in those characteristic human relationships that made her loved by Sisters, students, and parishioners. The *Manchester Union Leader* reported, for example, her attendance at a May Crowning and a May Day picnic. And the *Manchester Daily Mirror* noted that she led a procession of the Sodality of Mary accompanied by two little four-year-old girls. As in all the convents she founded, Frances Warde planned a delightful garden at Mount St. Mary's. On spring and summer evenings she found recreation in digging and planting flower-beds, training the beautiful woodbine on wall and arbor, and improving walks, shrubbery, and grass plots. In the garden was a beautiful path lined with tall pine trees which the Sisters called "St. Xavier's Walk" in her honor. Later St. Francis Xavier Memorial Library at Mount St. Mary's was named for her.

Indeed, Frances loved the academy she founded in Manchester. Its curriculum equaled in every way the nationally known St. Xavier's Academy she had established in Latrobe. Latin, French, English, geography, singing, drawing, speech, plain sewing and fancy work, physical culture were part of the regular course offerings. "Extras" were German, Italian, piano, organ, harp, oil painting, and china painting. Despite Frances' dislike for publicity, she allowed herself to be persuaded to place an ad in the *Manchester Mirror*. With the flamboyancy that sometimes characterized her, the ad read: "Apply by letter to Mother Superior, Mary Teresa Frances Xavier Warde"![17] The daily newspapers recorded faithfully the annual "exhibitions" held at the graduation exercises each July. The nature of the performance was of a high caliber:

Last evening we had the pleasure of witnessing the annual exhibition given by the pupils of Mt. St. Mary's School, and we can truly say we have never attended an exhibition in this city where so much talent was shown, and where the audience seemed so highly pleased. Although it was twelve o'clock before the exercises were over, no one was weary of seeing or hearing. The historical drama of Elizabeth and Mary Queen of Scots was given, and it seemed as if professional actresses were on the boards rather than mere school girls. The costumes were rich and evidently selected with great care. The music was excellent and reflected much credit on both scholars and teachers. A large number of prizes were awarded to the scholars, and the White Rose conferred on the graduates . . . .[18]

Excellent public reports brought many promising students, Catholic and non-Catholic, to Mount St. Mary's. A typical example was Harriet Stanley Dix, a lovely young New York society girl whose guardian was a United States Army Colonel and who lived with her uncle, a Presbyterian minister. Attracted by an ad for Mount St. Mary's in the *Boston Pilot,* she determined to attend this school and no other. No persuasion from her relatives would deter her. She had never been baptized and had joined no church. She was much admired as a debutante and had been presented to Abraham Lincoln at the White House. Two years after her admission to Mount St. Mary's, she begged Mother Frances to instruct her in the Catholic faith. Frances told her that she must secure the consent of her guardian. His answer, addressed to Harriet through Mother Frances and still preserved in Manchester, reads in part:

I hardly know how I feel about your Roman Catholic convictions, looking at it from a mere worldly and selfish point of view. But when I remember what my heart and hope and prayer for you have always been, I simply say to myself, "Well, this is God's work and it must be right."

. . . I don't know whether it is best for you to join the Catholic Church. I can only pray that God, Who has begun your spiritual schooling, will complete the work, as seems good to Him. I only know this, that nothing on earth would make me as happy as to know that you are tending toward the heaven where I know my mother is. You know you always reminded me of her. She was angelic in character and in love for me. She died divinely happy.

If you really feel deeply in your very soul that the Catholic religion is the only true one, and realize how little this life is, and how unlimited eternity is, then follow the impulses of your lovely nature.

I feel that my own life is passing rapidly away, and the

thought that you are going forward toward Heaven will comfort me in every remaining day of my totally unsatisfied existence.

Observe then, my darling child, that I advise nothing on a subject so awful as religion. I say, follow God's lead wherever it goes . . . .[19]

Harriet Dix was baptized in the Convent Chapel at Mount St. Mary's and later became Sister Madeleine of the Manchester community. She had taken the name "Xavier" in confirmation because of her love for Mother Frances, who always called her by the pet name, "Hattie Xavier." She was only one of hundreds that Frances Warde led to Christ.

The increased attendance at the academy, the large number of recruits for the religious life, the supervision of the works of mercy, the Christian Doctrine courses and night school—all these demanded more and more of Frances Warde's time during her first two years in New Hampshire. She determined to find an excellent Director of Novices to whom she could intrust the formation of the young Sisters. But her visionary mind was also moving toward the future. She was beginning to believe that the various Convents of Mercy she had founded in the Eastern States would benefit from a central novitiate to which the various houses could send novices for training. Thus the Mercy spirit could be better maintained, to say nothing of the saving of time and labor. Frances decided to seek for the Director of Novices she required in Ireland.

She wrote to one whom she knew would not fail her. Sister Gertrude O'Brien had entered the Carlow community under Frances Warde in 1840. Frances had sent her on the foundation to Westport in 1842. Then she had been sent in 1851 as first Superior of a foundation from Westport to Ballinrobe in County Mayo. Mother Gertrude responded to

Frances' appeal by sending her most promising young Sister, Patricia Waldron, with two companions to Manchester. Sister Patricia possessed exceptional qualities of leadership. While still a novice, she had been a director of student teachers. As a young professed Sister, she had managed the household affairs of her convent. When she arrived at Mount St. Mary's, Frances Warde immediately appointed her as Mistress of Novices, with the thought of a later central novitiate in mind. But a strange quirk of providence had destined Patricia Waldron for a future not planned at the moment by Frances Warde.

13

Expansion to Philadelphia; Service in the Civil War

FRANCES Warde never failed to respond to a request for help. A promise from her, explicit or implicit, was equivalent to its fulfillment. When she first arrived in America in 1843, even before she reached Pittsburgh, she received three requests for foundations of Convents of Mercy. The first, a petition for a Chicago establishment, had been accomplished in 1846. The second, a tacit agreement to fulfill the prophecy of Prince Demetrius Gallitzin by founding a convent in the mountains of Loretto, had been realized in 1848. But the third, a request that the Sisters of Mercy be established in Philadelphia, was not yet achieved. Though other Eastern foundations had intervened, Frances Warde had not banished Philadelphia from her mind.

In the summer of 1861, Father Charles I. H. Carter, pastor of the Church of the Assumption in the Quaker City, visited Mount St. Mary's Convent to ask Mother Frances to initiate in his parish a Congregation of Sisters of Mercy. Since a foundation in Philadelphia had long been one of her goals, she assented readily. She visited Philadelphia and agreed with Bishop James Frederic Wood and Father Carter that her Sisters would teach in the parochial school attached to the Church of the Assumption at Twelfth and Spring Garden Streets.[1] Bishop Wood also agreed that the Sisters

283

might carry on the corporal and spiritual works of mercy among the poor of Philadelphia, irrespective of parish limits.[2]

With her usual insight, Frances Warde knew that a foundation of Sisters of Mercy in Philadelphia would possess tremendous possibilities for growth and expansion. She determined to do all that she could to give it strong roots. The Convent of Mercy in Manchester was flourishing, and she decided to give the Philadelphia house a larger contingent of Sisters than she had ever granted to a new mission: six professed Sisters and four novices. And with her characteristic selflessness, she would send to the new convent the best qualified Sisters she could. She had continued, meanwhile, to invite candidates for the religious life to come from Ireland and England to her convents in the United States. At the time of her negotiations for the Philadelphia foundation, she was corresponding with a very capable Sister of Mercy in Wolverhampton, Staffordshire, England, who desired to serve in the United States' missions. Sister Gertrude Ledwith had entered the Mercy Convent in Birmingham, England, in 1847. She was a well-educated and experienced woman, whom Frances Warde considered ideal to serve as first Superior of the promising Philadelphia convent. Sister Gertrude accepted Mother Frances' invitation to assume leadership of the Sisters at the parish of the Assumption. The other nine Sisters destined for the new mission were all younger than Sister Gertrude. Most of them had received their religious formation under Frances herself.

Two of the professed Sisters chosen—Sisters Francis de Sales Geraghty and Philomena Hughes—had come from Ireland with Patricia Waldron, whom Frances had appointed Director of Novices in Manchester. Sister Rose Davis, a talented organist and pianist, had come from Carlow to enter the Providence Congregation in 1851 and had followed Frances Warde to Providence in 1858. Sister Madeleine

Mathey, a linguist, artist, and singer born in Limoges, France, had been professed at Mount St. Mary's in 1860. And Sister Mary Anne Coveney had been sent by Mother Josephine Warde from Cork, Ireland, to enter the convent in Manchester. Four novices trained by Mother Frances—Scholastica Murphy, Gertrude Dowling, Angela Curtin, and Veronica O'Reilly—completed the number of the Philadelphia pioneers.

Mother Frances had promised Father Carter to open the parochial School of the Assumption in September. As the summer progressed, no word was heard of the arrival of Sister Gertrude Ledwith from England. Communication across the Atlantic was not always a simple matter in 1861, and Frances Warde may have concluded that Sister Gertrude either was delayed or had changed her mind about coming to America.[3] In any case, Frances could not delay the departure to Philadelphia. She appointed her Director of Novices, Sister Patricia Waldron, in place of the British Superior. It is difficult to know precisely what Mother Frances' intentions were, but it would seem that Sister Patricia's appointment may have been a temporary measure until the possible arrival of Sister Gertrude. The ten Sisters left for Philadelphia with Frances on August 21 and arrived August 22. A Philadelphia newspaper noted that Mother Frances planned to "remain within the new Institute for about three months."[4] Normally, she remained at her new foundations for one month. It is possible that she had received, meanwhile, some word from Sister Gertrude in England and planned to remain in Philadelphia to install her as Superior after her landing in America.

The eleven pioneers reached the City of Brotherly Love on an intensely hot afternoon. Their comfort was not enhanced by the noise of the lorries and horse-drawn trolleys that lumbered over the cobblestones of Spring Garden Street, where the small convent was located. Manchester was much more quiet than Philadelphia! True to Mercy custom, visitation of the sick and care of the poor were begun at once. And with incredible speed, Frances Warde opened three schools on September 2, 1861, eleven days after her arrival. The Assumption School enrolled ninety pupils. Thirty girls presented themselves for attendance at the academy which was opened in the convent. And a parish night school was initiated for young women. From the start, the Academy of the Sisters of Mercy offered a curriculum of high quality. The course of instruction included "the English, French, Spanish, and Italian languages, Belles-Lettres, Ancient and Modern History, Geography, Arithmetic, Rhetoric, Astronomy, Natural Philosophy, Botany, Chemistry, Mythology, Music, Drawing, Needlework, and all the usual requisites and accomplishments of female education"![5]

Because the convent was small, the select school presented problems which the Sisters solved with rare good humor. The inconvenience of removing the straw mattresses and blankets from the parlor in which the youngest of the eleven slept, in order to convert it into a classroom, and the trouble of rearranging the dining room to serve alternately as infirmary, community room, recreation hall, and refectory were laughingly called "the morning exercises." There was no alternative to these maneuvers. The tuition of the girls attending the academy was essential to provide food for the Sisters.

But perhaps the real problem of the Sisters was the character of the pastor. He demanded literal and complete obedience even in matters beyond his jurisdiction:

Zealous and devout priest though he was, he was also a man of ultra-rigid economies. He held . . . that religious would be spoiled if they handled any money at all . . . and that people pledged to obedience were to be allowed little discretion; they were sure to abuse it.[6]

Frances Warde was quick to comprehend the dangers faced by her Sisters. The new convent was poverty-stricken. There were nine Sisters, all of them young. Patricia Waldron, appointed Superior, was still in her twenties, and she had lived in America only one year. It is uncertain precisely what information Frances had at the time concerning Sister Gertrude Ledwith. Whatever Mother Frances' strategy was, she proposed that the Philadelphia Convent of Mercy become not an independent foundation but a branch house under the governance of the Manchester Congregation of Mercy. She also offered herself as Superior of the proposed Philadelphia branch house. The reason for this move, according to Philadelphia tradition, was Frances' desire to protect her Sisters. "Both Wood and Carter were severe, rigid, and difficult." On the other hand, "the Sisters loved and respected Mother Frances Warde."[7] With her years of experience, she could mitigate severity and manage financially so that the Sisters would not suffer excessive want. Evidence that Frances Warde did not decide to offer herself as Superior until after she evaluated the situation of the Sisters is discovered in her previous announcement that she would remain three months in Philadelphia. Now she was willing to remain permanently as "local Superior" and give up her Superiorship of the entire Manchester Congregation. Bishop Wood, however, under the strong influence of Father Carter, refused to accept Mother Frances' proposal. He wished his complete authority over the Sisters to be unhindered.

On September 16, Frances made known publicly for the first time a proposal that she had formulated when she in-

vited Sister Patricia Waldron to America to head a central
novitiate for Sisters of Mercy of various United States' foundations. Mother Frances now revealed her belief that the
entire Mercy Congregation would benefit by having a General Superior and a central novitiate. She proposed to establish the novitiate in Manchester and to recommend that a
Council of Superiors elect a General Superior. Her own
offer to serve as local Superior in Philadelphia would leave
the candidacy for General Superior open. Thus the Sisters
would feel no pressure to elect her to the highest office. Her
delicate gesture would also help the young Philadelphia
Sisters who needed her. Frances Warde's proposal arose from
no sudden impulse. She had long considered the values of
centralization and had consulted Bishops concerning it, as
her subsequent correspondence revealed.[8]

After presenting her plan in Philadelphia, Frances Warde
went to Pittsburgh to consult with the Sisters of her original
American foundation. During her absence, Sister Patricia
Waldron urged Father Carter to accept the plan. He positively refused. He considered the Philadelphia Sisters to be
completely under the jurisdiction of Bishop Wood and himself. On September 26, Mother Frances returned to Philadelphia and told Sister Patricia Waldron of her disappointment in Pittsburgh regarding the acceptance of her proposal
for the Congregation of Mercy. The Philadelphia *Annals*
do not relate whether the rejection of her plan came from
the Bishop or the Sisters of Mercy in Pittsburgh. Bishop
Michael O'Connor had resigned the See of Pittsburgh one
year earlier to become a Jesuit. His successor, Bishop Michael
Domenec, regarded the Pittsburgh Sisters of Mercy as entirely under his jurisdiction. It is unlikely that either Domenec or the Pittsburgh Sisters in 1861 would have responded
warmly to the idea of general government and central train-

ing for young Sisters. On Frances Warde's return to Philadelphia, Bishop Wood informed her with some severity that
"she had no right to exercise any authority from the moment
she arrived in his diocese."[9]

A strange circumstance concerning Frances Warde's proposal for general government and a central novitiate lies in
the fact that it is recorded nowhere except in the *Annals* of
the Philadelphia Sisters of Mercy. There is no reference to
it in either written records or oral tradition in Pittsburgh.[10]
Moreover, no reference to it exists in either the written or
the oral history of the Manchester Sisters of Mercy. Nor is
it mentioned in the four-volume *Annals* of the Congregation
of Mercy compiled by Sister Teresa Austin Carroll between
1881 and 1895. The omission is unfortunate, since Frances
Warde's judgments and actions relative to so major an issue
concerning the Sisters of Mercy should hold a central position in any history of the Mercy Congregation.

On October 1, 1861, Sister Patricia Waldron was officially
appointed Superior of the Philadelphia Sisters of Mercy by
Bishop Wood. And on October 10, Frances Warde returned
to Manchester. Great rejoicing greeted her arrival at St.
Anne's. A special concert in her honor was presented by the
Sisters and students of Mount St. Mary's, and a triumphal
arch was erected at the entrance to the convent.[11] If the
Manchester Sisters had lost her to Philadelphia, they would
have been inconsolable.

On October 28, 1861, Frances Warde wrote a letter to
James O'Connor, brother of Bishop Michael O'Connor and
later Bishop of Omaha, in which she referred to her efforts
to improve the novitiate training of the Sisters of Mercy.[12]
Since James O'Connor was evidently cognizant of her proposal, she did not elaborate upon it but merely commented
upon the reasons for its rejection. The tone and context of

the letter indicate that Bishop Michael O'Connor shared her views concerning the training of Sisters. There is no reference in the letter to general government for the Congregation of Mercy:

Mount St. Mary
Manchester

Dear Revd. Father:

I thank you very much for your kind note which I received in Philadelphia and had not leisure to acknowledge sooner. I left all in the new establishment giving fair promise of future growth. I tried to arrange matters in a spiritual and temporal way as well as I could, but in truth it was very difficult. I often thought of your advice in the matter. Sometimes I was amused. The Bishop said I must be very particular with Father Carter and arrange everything carefully with him, that he was very peculiar. And when I expressed some fears that Father Carter would be displeased, he said it is better 'to have trouble in the beginning than afterwards. Father Carter told me that the Bishop was very peculiar. And the truth is, between ourselves, I found both exceedingly peculiar.

But, after all, we did arrange everything pretty fairly, and the Academy was quite promising before I left. The free school [is] very small; our poor Irish people do not seem to harmonize very well with Father Carter. All seemed delighted to have our Sisters amongst them. Please God, in due time they will have a fine, useful establishment there.

I fear that we will never be able to get the least change in our Novitiate by any of the Bishops. As to Bishop Wood, I never yet knew any Pastor or Bishop so tenacious of his authority. He must have everything just as he approves in his diocese, so that, it seems to me, all must of necessity rest for the present. This letter, of course, to you who take such an interest in the Order [of Mercy], you will consider as quite confidential. I trust that our truly good Bishop, your brother, continues to improve in

health. How very few in high stations have his large and enlightened views.

Pray for us, I am sure you will, and if you can venture as far
North, you can be sure of a warm welcome from our holy
Pastor as well as from the Sisters of Mercy. And believe me to be
very gratefully

Yours in Christ,
Sister Mary Frances Teresa

It is interesting to note that while Frances Warde does not
challenge the authority of Bishop Wood, she considers his
"tenacity" of authority to be detrimental to needed change
in the Congregation of Mercy. She expresses no anger toward him (amusement rather), but only an implicit judgment on the value of his principles. She herself commends
the "large and enlightened views" of Michael O'Connor, and
while pointing out that Wood "does not care what other
Bishops do or say," comments on "how very few in high
stations" have the vision of the first Bishop of Pittsburgh. It
would seem that Michael and James O'Connor were informed of and approved of the proposal she offered in Philadelphia and in Pittsburgh. Unfortunately, it cannot now be
known with certainty how far the plan related to general
government and how far merely to a felt need for a central
novitiate. Perhaps Frances Warde believed that the only
way to establish a central novitiate was through general government.

Additional complication arises from the fact that Mother
Frances deprecates the absolute authority of Bishop Wood
while praising the enlightened views of Bishop O'Connor,
whose authority in Pittsburgh—according to the Chapter
Decrees of the Pittsburgh Congregation—seems to have been
more or less absolute in legalistic terms. Sister Teresa Austin

Carroll, on the other hand, suggests that Michael O'Connor was consultative rather than directive in dealing with the Sisters of Mercy.[13] Perhaps O'Connor's personal approach to decisions concerning community matters rendered his policies more acceptable to Mother Frances. Also, the Chapter Decrees of the Pittsburgh Sisters which gave more or less absolute authority to the Bishop were approved *after* Frances Warde left Pittsburgh. Tradition in Pittsburgh, on the other hand, suggests that O'Connor preferred the "docility" of Sister Josephine Cullen to the intrepid spirit of Frances Warde. Without more direct evidence, it is impossible to define precisely Frances' response to the authority exercised by O'Connor and by Wood.

Shortly after Mother Frances' return to Manchester, the Philadelphia Sisters received a communication from the Superior of Sister Gertrude Ledwith's Congregation in England.[14] Bishop William Ullathorne of Birmingham required a signed agreement concerning the release of Sister Gertrude to the Diocese of Philadelphia. This Sister spent so much time preparing for the journey and arranging to bring British girls as postulants to America that she did not leave England until November. On arriving in the United States, she was greatly chagrined that she was not to be the Superior in Philadelphia. Eventually, however, Sister Gertrude became an outstanding Sister of Mercy with a varied career of service. She joined the New York Sisters of Mercy; served in the Hammond Military Hospital in Beaufort, North Carolina, in 1862; volunteered for the Albany foundation of Sisters of Mercy in Greenbush in 1863; went with the Mercy foundation to Worcester, Massachusetts, in 1864; served in the House of Mercy and in St. Catherine's School in New York from 1866 until 1871; and went as founder and first Superior of a Mercy foundation to Eureka, California, in 1871.[15]

She died in Sunderland, England, in 1918. If Frances Warde inadvertently diverted Gertrude Ledwith from service as first Superior of the Philadelphia Sisters, she opened up to her a broad apostolate in America. And Patricia Waldron, who took her place in Philadelphia, proved to be an outstanding leader who guided the Philadelphia Sisters toward the apostolic expansion that Frances Warde dreamed of for them.

Mother Patricia and her Sisters suffered as Mother Frances feared that they would. But they were equal in every way to the sacrifices demanded of them. According to their *Annals,* the Pastor of St. Malachy's Church, Philadelphia, applied for the transfer of the Mercy Sisters to his parish on February 2, 1863. And on April 19, "the community left the Assumption parish, under somewhat painful circumstances, which need not be recorded, and repaired to the School House adjoining St. Malachy's Church which Reverend Mother had accepted as a temporary residence until she could find a house suitable for a Convent."[16] Oral tradition relates that Father Carter unceremoniously consigned the Sisters with their few possessions to the street. The kind women of St. Malachy's Parish provided the Sisters with food, bedding, and furniture. Within a week, they were again teaching in St. Malachy's Parochial School, their own private school, and an evening school for older girls! Their poverty was extreme, but under the guidance of the indomitable Mother Patricia, the Sisters survived. In August, 1863, with only five dollars in her possession, Patricia Waldron signed a lease for a house at the corner of Broad Street and Columbia Avenue which remained the center for the Philadelphia Sisters of Mercy until their removal to Merion, Pennsylvania, in 1884.

The apparently ironic manner in which providence dealt

with Frances Warde's Sisters in Philadelphia provides an interesting historical note. Father Charles Carter was a convert from the Episcopalian faith who had come originally from Kentucky. His ancestry was British. Perhaps he would have appreciated Sister Gertrude Ledwith for, in Frances Warde's words, the Irish people "did not harmonize very well" with him. In 1862, the Sisters of the Holy Child Jesus, an English teaching congregation founded by Cornelia Connelly, once a resident of Philadelphia, received a grant of land in Towanda, Bradford County, Pennsylvania. On the arrival of the Sisters in Philadelphia from England, Bishop Wood appointed Father Carter to accompany them to their new convent in Towanda. The house in Towanda proved to be in such deplorable condition that the Sisters could not remain there. On his ejection of the Sisters of Mercy from Assumption Parish in Philadelphia, Father Carter brought the Holy Childhood Sisters from Towanda to serve in their place. A kind of "holy irony" developed in 1877 when the Sisters of Mercy of St. Mary's Convent, Wilkes-Barre, then a branch house of the Pittsburgh Sisters of Mercy, opened St. Agnes Convent in Towanda with a parochial school and academy. Tiny town as it is, Towanda played a dramatic role in events which affected so vitally the future of both the Sisters of Mercy and the Sisters of the Holy Childhood. While the latter Sisters found an opportunity to expand their apostolate from Philadelphia, as perhaps they could not have done from Towanda, the Sisters of Mercy in Philadelphia continued to develop and expand with amazing rapidity despite their removal from Assumption Parish. And as time progressed, Father Carter again became their friend and even contributed largely to the acquisition of their Mother House in 1867 by assuming a mortgage of $10,000 on the property!

Frances Warde must have viewed her growing Philadelphia foundation with joy as she observed how Providence solved problems that seemed to be beyond human solution. The expansion of the Philadelphia congregation paralleled that of the Convents of Mercy in Pittsburgh, Chicago, Providence, Hartford, and Manchester. Within 100 years the small community grew to fifty-three convents with 800 members who conducted forty parochial schools, fifteen secondary schools, and five academies in fourteen dioceses; six hospitals; schools of nursing; faculty houses; home for business women; technical school; and liberal arts college. The Philadelphia Mercy Sisters now teach in Pennsylvania, Florida, Virginia, North Carolina, New Jersey, Georgia, and Oregon. In 1953 they opened the first Mercy foundation in the Orient, a hospital in Jamshedpur, India. It was often said of Frances Warde that the beginnings of her foundations were marked with poverty and suffering, but their apostolates developed miraculously. Never was this statement more true than in Philadelphia.

Several months before Frances Warde set out from Manchester for Philadelphia, the fall of Fort Sumter had caused sounds of ominous civil strife to echo throughout America. The Sisters of Mercy responded at once to the cries for help from the sick, the wounded, and the families of the combatants—just as their predecessors had done in the Crimean War. Sisters of Mercy from Pittsburgh, Chicago, Baltimore, New York, Cincinnati, and Vicksburg volunteered their services. They nursed both Union and Confederate soldiers, and to do so they were given the right to cross over lines without a password. The Pittsburgh Sisters served at Stanton Military Hospital in Washington where they had 450 wounded soldiers under their care. After the Battle of Fredericksburg, the Union and Confederate soldiers were laid side by side in this hospital. The Sisters also cared for the wounded and sick at the Pittsburgh Mercy Hospital and at the Western Pennsylvania Military Hospital, where they nursed 240 wounded men who had been transported by boat to Pittsburgh after the bloody Battle of Shiloh. The Baltimore Sisters of Mercy, whose convent had been founded from Pittsburgh in 1855, served at the Douglas Military Hospital in Washington.

At one point in the struggle, when Sister Otillia Dusch of Pittsburgh was unable to secure suitable nourishment for her fever patients at the Stanton Hospital, she personally visited the Secretary of War, and a proclamation was issued a few days later:

To Whom it may Concern
On application of the Sisters of Mercy in charge of the military hospital in Washington, furnish such provisions as they desire to purchase and charge the same to the War Department.

Signed:
Abraham Lincoln

Lincoln visited the military hospitals unfailingly during the war. The *Annals* of the Sisters of Mercy at Stanton Hospital recall the tall, slender man with drooping shoulders who came at dusk to comfort the sick and suffering during the campaign of the Army of the Potomac in 1864. A famous painting of a Sister of Mercy nursing a wounded soldier in a tent hospital at Vicksburg, Mississippi, was commissioned by Lincoln after he had conferred with General U. S. Grant concerning the services of the Sisters of Mercy. Many copies of the once popular painting are extant, but the whereabouts of the original is unknown.

The Mercy Sisters in Philadelphia also served the sick

and wounded. A Military Hospital of more than 150 beds was opened at Twelfth and Buttonwood Streets, almost at the Mercy Convent door. Another hospital was set up at Broad and Cherry Streets. The New York Sisters of Mercy served at the Military Hospital in Beaufort, North Carolina. The Cincinnati Sisters, under Mother Teresa Maher, friend of Frances Warde, nursed the soldiers of the Ohio regiments in tents at the front battle lines at Pittsburgh Landing in Tennessee. In St. Louis, the Sisters of Mercy served at the Military Hospital set up at the City Fair Grounds, where about 1500 sick and wounded were cared for daily. In Chicago, the Sisters organized a band of volunteer nurses who followed "Mulligan's Brigade" to Lexington, Missouri. The Chicago Sisters also conducted the Military Hospital in Jefferson City, Missouri.

Frances Warde, now in her early fifties, was deeply concerned over the civil strife in her adopted country. She also suffered personal involvement through relatives who fought in the Union Army and Sisters who served in the military hospitals. Her nephew, John S. Warde, brother of Jane and Fanny Warde who had so distinguished themselves at St. Xavier Academy in Latrobe, had volunteered for the Fifth Regiment of the Excelsior Brigade in Philadelphia immediately after the Fall of Fort Sumter. He was honorably discharged in 1862 because he had developed rheumatic fever.[17] A diary of Civil War days written by his wife, Margaret Keogh Warde, popular novelist of the era, is a beautiful tribute to John S. Warde. Sister Xavier Warde, Pittsburgh Sister of Mercy and cousin of Mother Frances Warde, served at the Stanton Military Hospital in Washington. But perhaps the most interesting story concerning the Warde family in the Civil War is that of Frances' cousin, Sister Stephana Warde, also of Pittsburgh.

Stephana Warde was one of the Pittsburgh Sisters of Mercy who took charge of the Washington Infirmary in the District of Columbia in 1852 at the request of a group of doctors who conducted a medical school there. When the Pittsburgh Sisters made a foundation in Baltimore in 1855, the Sisters at the Infirmary naturally joined the Baltimore Congregation. And when the Baltimore Sisters sent a foundation to Vicksburg, Mississippi, in 1859, Sister Stephana volunteered to serve in the southern mission. The Sisters were in Vicksburg only two years when they became involved in the War between the States. The Confederate government ordered that their academy for young ladies be converted into a hospital, and the Sisters were asked to give nursing care to the sick and wounded. Because the opening up of the Mississippi River to cut the Confederacy in two was a major object of the Union Army, Vicksburg—as one of the strongest forts on the River—saw intense action. In 1863 it fell into the hands of the Union Army, and the Convent of the Sisters of Mercy became the headquarters of General Henry Warner Slocum and his federal officers.

The Sisters left Vicksburg with the other evacuees and nursed their patients in camps, barns, abandoned railroad stations, and army tents around Oxford, Mississippi Springs, Jackson, and Shelby Springs. Despite the lack of even necessities—they had to wear shoes made of rabbit skins—they served the wounded of the Confederate Army heroically. Finally, Sister Stephana Warde's contingent was captured by Union forces. A prisoner of war, she now had only one overwhelming desire: to return not to the Baltimore or the Vicksburg Convents of Mercy but to her old convent home in Pittsburgh that she had left more than a decade before. Sick at heart, dressed in tattered clothing, she awaited her release. It came in mid-winter. Wearing an old army coat, she arrived one night at St. Mary's Convent on Webster Avenue in Pittsburgh. No one recognized her. There was now another Sister Stephana in the Pittsburgh Congregation. But the exhausted woman pulled from her pocket the soiled parchment of her vows of religion that she had carried with her since leaving Vicksburg. Tradition relates that after recuperating her strength, Stephana Warde went to Washington to continue serving American soldiers in the Stanton Military Hospital.

Not even the Civil War was an obstacle to Frances Warde in her continual mission to spread the apostolate of Mercy throughout the United States. The fall of Fort Sumter did not delay her foundation in Philadelphia. And the ravages of war, while hindering the establishment of her next foundation, did not prevent it. If any of her friends suspected that Frances, now fifty-four, intended to confine her foundations between New Hampshire and Chicago, they did not understand the breadth of her mission. In 1864, Frances looked again to the West. She responded enthusiastically to a request to send a colony of Sisters of Mercy from Manchester to Omaha in the Nebraska Territory.

14

On to the West: Omaha; Northward to Maine

IF Chicago was a "shanty town" on Lake Michigan when Frances Warde established her Sisters there in 1846, Omaha was still little more than "a ragged cluster of houses springing out of the mud" in 1864. Only fifty years before, with the expedition of Meriwether Lewis and William Clark under President Thomas Jefferson, Americans had secured their first accurate information concerning the future Nebraska Territory which was part of the immense Louisiana Purchase of 1803. Almost throughout the first half of the century Nebraska, labeled the "Great American Desert," was a trackless wilderness. A thin fringe of settlers spread itself along the banks of the Missouri River. And a thin thread of white men ran crosswise through the future State of Nebraska, leading to the Mormon tents of Utah and the gold fields of California. This advance guard of white men was made up of fur traders, prospectors, home-seekers, and a corporal's guard of soldiers. Refugees from justice and soldiers of fortune also came from the East, bringing with them crime and violence.

The second half of the century, however, saw white men pouring in from the East like a tidal wave. In 1854—when Frances Warde was founding schools in Providence, Hartford, New Haven, and Newport—the Omaha Indians, under their celebrated Chief Logan Fontanelle, were ceding their land to the United States government. The same year,

Nebraska was organized as a territory. The process of building the frontier village of Omaha began. Deer, wolves, and buffaloes still roamed the prairies. A hotel, some homes, a sawmill, a grocery, a dry goods store, a saloon: this was Omaha. The first post office was the hat of the postmaster; mail was so scarce that a hat could carry it! In 1855, Governor Mark W. Izard called the first territorial legislature into session at Omaha. The location of the capitol was the burning issue. When Nebraska became a State in 1867, three years after the arrival of the Sisters of Mercy, Lincoln became the capitol. But by that time, Omaha's priority had been definitely determined by the railroads.

When gold was discovered in Colorado in 1858, the year of Frances Warde's Manchester foundation, the commercial life of Omaha quickened. Omaha was "the western outpost of civilization," and there gold-seekers stocked their covered wagons. Supplies were freighted across the great plains by mule or horsepower, for there was no railroad in 1858. Little barges brought their cargoes up the Missouri River to the port of Omaha. Then the cargoes were transported westward by mule train. The Missouri was also used for passenger travel. Not until 1862 did President Lincoln authorize the construction of the Union Pacific Railroad starting westward from the Missouri River. Omaha was fixed as the eastern end of the road, the construction of which brought a population boom. At the same time, the Central Pacific Company was authorized to build eastward from California until the two roads should meet. It is difficult today to realize the significance of the historic moment on May 10, 1879, when the Union Pacific and the Central Pacific joined rails at Promontory Point, Utah, and the East and the West were one. In Chicago and New York bells pealed, flags flew, and orators exulted. The United States were at last united.

But in 1864, when Frances Warde made her decision to establish a Mercy foundation in Omaha, the triumph of Promontory Point was still in the future. The Chicago and Northwestern Railroad, moreover, did not reach the Missouri River until 1867 to end the isolation of Omaha from the East. In time, Omaha was to become the fourth largest railroad center in America. But when Frances Warde chose to move westward for the second time, Omaha was still in comparative isolation from the East. And no one knew better than Frances, who had almost lost her life in establishing her Chicago foundation, the realistic meaning of such geographical isolation. She knew also of the hazardous three-month voyage that the Sisters of Mercy from her Naas foundation in Ireland had endured in order to found a convent in Little Rock, Arkansas, in 1851. They had sailed from Dublin in November, 1850, crossed a stormy Atlantic, labored through the Gulf of Mexico to New Orleans, and then taken passage on a steamer up the Mississippi, reaching Little Rock in February, 1851. Frances also knew that the Sisters of Kinsale, Ireland, who had established the San Francisco Mercy foundation in 1854, had crossed the Atlantic to New York, sailed southward to pass over the Isthmus of Panama, and then journeyed northward up the Pacific to the Golden Gate. All this sea travel was chosen to avoid the primitive and dangerous overland travel across the great plains of America.

If tortuous and perilous travel had been a deterrent, Frances Warde and her Sisters would never have moved westward. But the pioneering spirit of Mother Frances was not only in spiritual realms: she was a pioneer in all aspects of her existence. She followed the people of God who needed her and her Sisters. The greatest need was always on the frontiers. Omaha was a challenge to Frances. She seemed to have a sixth sense, moreover, concerning the best geo-graphical centers for Mercy foundations. Just as she knew that Chicago, Providence, Hartford, and Philadelphia were nerve centers for expansion, so she seemed to know instinctively that the Mercy apostolate must move westward from Chicago, and that Omaha should be her next move across the great central plains. In 1864 there was no Catholic parochial school between Chicago and California. In later years, the Mercy apostolate would spread to North Dakota, Kansas, Alabama, and Texas; to Montana, Colorado, and New Mexico; to Oregon, Idaho, and Arizona. But in 1864 the Mercy movement westward was in its infancy. Frances Warde's path was clear.

The Bishop who invited Mother Frances to establish a Mercy foundation in Omaha adds one more name to the roll call of holy men closely associated with her in her American apostolate. James Myles O'Gorman, born six years before Frances, spent his boyhood in Tipperary, Ireland, as a member of the Anglican Church. His mother, Mary Myles, was a Roman Catholic convert. His uncle, Major General Sir Edward Myles, financed his education at Trinity College, Dublin. After his graduation, he became a Roman Catholic and in 1839 joined the Irish Trappists. Ordained in 1843, the year of Frances Warde's American foundation, he was sent in 1849 as first Superior of the original band that founded the Trappist Monastery of New Melleray in Iowa. In 1859, after having served as Prior of New Melleray, O'Gorman was appointed Vicar Apostolic of Nebraska. He desired to remain a Trappist, but Rome thought otherwise. His immense Vicariate covered 580,000 square miles—the present States of Nebraska, Wyoming, Montana, and the western parts of North and South Dakota! One of his Trappist brothers wrote, "O'Gorman has a new diocese to form, and he is poor as poverty itself." He had no See. He was free to choose his own. "I have traveled 1300 miles and have not yet found a home," he wrote to his brothers in New Melleray. Finally, he chose Omaha as his See. When he established his new Vicariate, O'Gorman found three churches and four priests in his huge territory. One of the priests was in distant Montana working with the Indians. Gradually, O'Gorman increased the numbers of his ministers. Tradition says that his method of appointing pastors was unique. He would walk arm in arm with the prospective appointee to the back door of his poor bishop's house on Eighth Street in Omaha. The two would scan the western horizon, and then the Bishop would point in a certain direction. "Father," he would say "you go that way."[1] Bishop O'Gorman was gentle, kind, generous, benevolent; he suffered incredible hardships, privations, and disappointments. Obviously, he was the type of apostle Frances Warde could not refuse.

In the summer of 1864, Mother Frances completed her plans for the Omaha Mercy foundation. A "mystic seven" made up the candidates for the new convent in the West: Sister Ignatius Lynch, Superior, who had come to Manchester from Ballinrobe, Ireland, in 1861; Sister Teresa Austin Carroll, Assistant Superior, who had gone back to Rochester after her failure to persevere as Superior in Buffalo and then returned to Manchester, and who was to leave Omaha for St. Louis within six months; Sister Joseph Jennings, destined to serve as Superior in Omaha from 1876 until 1888; Sister Frances O'Hanlon, who died of pneumonia within two years; Sister Augustine Meagher, who died of tuberculosis within three years; and two novices, Sisters Regina Crane and Anne Fahey. Of all of Frances Warde's foundations in America, perhaps the Omaha Sisters were destined for the most intense personal suffering.

In July, Mother Frances wrote to Bishop O'Gorman in Omaha, concluding with some nostalgia:

Now that our affairs are finally arranged or nearly so, may I beg as a great favor that you will try to come to meet us, either in Chicago or as near that city as possible. Many years ago I went from Pittsburgh with six Sisters to establish that Convent for the saintly Bishop Quarter. I remained three months, but now I shall be quite a stranger there except with a few of the Sisters. The fine Sister whom I left as Superior [Agatha O'Brien] has long since slept in the Lord. I humbly trust that, after all your toils and trials, our good Sisters will be a source of much consolation to you . . . .[2]

The missionaries left Manchester July 27 on their journey of more than 1,500 miles to the West. Stops were made in Albany, Syracuse, Rochester, Batavia, and Buffalo. Some of the little band made their August spiritual retreat in Buffalo, others in Rochester. On August 12, Frances Warde wrote an altogether unexpected letter to Bishop O'Gorman from Rochester.[3] She had just received word from Manchester that her Assistant, Sister Philomena Edwards, was dangerously ill with typhoid fever. She was requested to return home at once. Her sorrow was profound. "I regret exceedingly not being able to accompany the Sisters to Chicago," she wrote, "but as it is, I have only again and again to commend them to your fatherly care and protection . . . I shall be quite uneasy until I hear from you of the safe arrival of our dear Sisters . . . ."

Without their leader, the seven Sisters went on from New York to Chicago. On the way, they spent a night at South Bend, Indiana, where they were warmly welcomed by Father Edward Sorin, founder of the Congregation of the Holy Cross in the United States in 1841 and of the University of Notre Dame in 1844. Mother Angela Gillespie of the Holy

Cross Sisters offered them hospitality. In Chicago, they remained with the Sisters of Mercy for several weeks. Unable to go to Chicago himself, Bishop O'Gorman sent Father James M. Ryan, pastor of St. John's Parish, Columbus, Nebraska, to meet them and escort them for the rest of their journey. They made plans to board a steamer, which was en route from St. Louis to Omaha, at St. Joseph, Missouri. The Illinois and Missouri country, through which their trip from Chicago to St. Joseph lay, was in a greatly disturbed condition. Guerrillas carried on irregular warfare throughout both States. Railroad bridges had been burned, tracks torn up, trains delayed for weeks, stage coaches attacked, food stolen. Several military companies had been disbanded, and tramps surrounded railway stations and stage coach stops to intimidate travelers. Friends advised the Sisters not to go on, but they left Chicago on October 11, 1864. Tradition states that they secured a military escort for part of the journey through Missouri, which was patrolled by both Union and Confederate forces.

At St. Joseph, Missouri, the party stopped at a wild-looking barn, styled by courtesy the Waverly Hotel. By an extremely economical arrangement, the family and servants of the proprietor, for whom there were just a sufficient number of beds in the "hotel," gave up their beds at any time of night to travelers. The Sisters arrived at midnight. The beds offered to them were still warm and very dirty. They soon chose to lie on the floor, where they attempted to rest until daybreak. In the morning, an immigrant train came in, from which poured out innumerable sick, hungry, and weary families of many nations. The Sisters comforted the sick and suffering and helped to quiet the babies until the pastor, Father John Hennessey, later Bishop of Dubuque, arranged to take the tired travelers to the Convent of the Sacred Heart.

On October 13, the steamer *Montana* arrived in St. Joseph from St. Louis, and the Sisters boarded it gratefully. The landscape as they journeyed up the Missouri River was strange to them. The country was wild and bleak. Along the shore were coarse and scentless prairie flowers. On October 21, the *Montana* anchored at the town of Omaha, the new home of the Manchester Sisters. The first religious congregation in Nebraska, the pioneers of Catholic education in the future State, had arrived! Their first impression was concentrated in one word: mud. Later, they enjoyed much laughter over the native word for the special type of mud peculiar to this western town: "gumbo." A versifier from New York thus described the effect of Omaha on the traveler from the East in the sixties:

> *Have you ever been in Omaha,*
> *Where rolls the dark Missouri down,*
> *And four strong horses scarce can draw*
> *An empty wagon through the town?*
> *Where mud is splashed from every mound*
> *To fill your eyes and ears and throat—*
> *Where all the steamers are aground*
> *And all the shanties are afloat?*
> *If not, take heed to what I say:*
> *You'll find it just as I have found it;*
> *And if it lies upon your way,*
> *For God's sake, go around it!*

Indeed, the seven Sisters had need of humor. Just as the sun was setting, they stepped from a carriage at the foot of a high flight of steps leading to their convent at Twenty-fourth Street and St. Mary's Avenue. There, at the end of the muddy trail, was a three-story brick building severe in its simplicity. Picturesquely situated on a bluff high above

307

the Missouri, the convent stood alone, only the prairie between it and the Capitol far to the east. Exhausted after a journey of three months, the travelers found only a stove and a piano in the entire building! The furniture had not yet arrived; the piano was a happy accident. The Sisters slept on the floor, amusing themselves with such remarks as, "Please hand me the brush from the rosewood table." Yet the house had real possibilities. On the first floor were parlors which could serve as music rooms. The second floor provided classrooms, and the third was a future dormitory. It had small compartments that reminded the Sisters of a stable. They would sleep in the stalls!

With characteristic enterprise, they opened Mount St. Mary's Academy or "select school" in the convent, and a parochial school, Holy Angels, at Eighth and Howard Streets. It was the only parochial school between Chicago and San Francisco. By February, 1865, a new parochial school was being built because of the increase in pupils.[4] The Academy was a splendid private school, comparable in teaching and curriculum to the select schools in Frances Warde's eastern foundations. Boarders came from as far as Council Bluffs and Sioux City. After school each day, the Sisters traveled the muddy roads to care for the sick and carry food to the poor. They also visited the poor house and the jail regularly. Their hardships were extreme; they were often hungry themselves. Too few priests, too few Sisters rendered the service of Catholic immigrants pouring in from the East a seemingly impossible task. Music lessons were offered to secure funds, but there were few pupils able to pay. Indians watched stoically and silently through the convent window as Sister Ignatius played the piano. It was difficult to be optimistic. But the Sisters persevered.

Complete accounts of the new foundation were written

by Bishop O'Gorman and the Sisters to Frances Warde back in Manchester. Except for the establishment of the Sisters of Mercy in Loretto, Pennsylvania, the Omaha Convent of Mercy was the first of her foundations that Mother Frances was unable to direct personally. On her return from Rochester to Manchester at the end of July, 1864, she found her Assistant, Sister Philomena Edwards, still able to recognize her, though fatally ill. She died on August 14. Providence had not destined Frances Warde to go West personally in 1864.

Despite both external obstacles and internal dissension, the Omaha foundation prospered. Parochial schools, academies, college, high schools, hospitals, orphanages, homes for working girls and for the aged—all developed over the years in Omaha and throughout Nebraska. Though Omaha was a rough frontier between civilization and wilderness in 1864, Frances Warde had seen it as a flourishing city of the future. And she was right. Omaha not only became one of the largest railroad centers of the United States; it also became the second largest live stock market in the world. And in Mercy history, Omaha became in 1929 the center for the Western Province of the Sisters of Mercy of the Union, extending from Missouri to California and from New Mexico to North Dakota.

While the Sisters of Mercy in Omaha were struggling in their new foundation, Frances Warde was unusually active in the East. The manner in which she combined the contemplative life of prayer with continuous work in the apostolate seems almost miraculous. Never in her religious life was there a time when she was not either planning or engaging in an apostolic work which turned her vision toward the future. Now, only five months after she had established the Mercy Sisters in Omaha, she suddenly received a letter from Bishop Bacon in Portland, requesting Sisters for Bangor, Maine.[5] Though the Diocese of Portland then included the entire States of Maine and New Hampshire, Bishop Bacon had invited Frances Warde to establish convents in New Hampshire, but never in Maine until now. The reason seems to have been that he hoped to bring about harmony between the Irish and the French Canadian immigrants in Maine by engaging the Canadian Sisters of the Congregation of Notre Dame as teachers in the parochial schools. In 1865, however, he yielded to strong pressure from his pastors to invite Frances Warde to introduce Sisters of Mercy into the State of Maine. He wrote to Mother Frances on March 22, 1865:

My dear Mother Xavier:

Do you think you could divide your little community so as to take the Bangor mission in May? The parish schools number about 400 children; there will also be excellent chances for a paying academy. There is a good house and plenty of land. There is also a mission at Whitefield, where there is a small wooden house, and land—several acres. There I intend an asylum for orphan girls. I am sorry now that I consented to the establishments in Philadelphia and Nebraska. But I could not foresee at the time that I would be so soon prepared [for the Sisters of Mercy] myself.

The house in Manchester is to be the Mother House until I can, as I hope, transfer it to Portland at some future day.

The division of the nuns will weaken the house in Manchester for a while. But a kind Providence will send us good subjects . . .

Please answer me immediately and state your views, and precisely what you can do. The priests in both these places are pressing me to let them know what can be done for them . . . .

Frances Warde must have smiled when she read the above letter from her friend. She had been "dividing her little community" since 1839, and somehow she always had Sisters to send on new missions. Her community was always small but always replenished. The Philadelphia and Omaha foundations had drained the Manchester convent of almost twenty Sisters. Well, she would lead a colony of Sisters to Bangor, but Whitefield would have to wait for a while.

Bangor was not a familiar town to Mother Frances. She soon learned that, despite its location in the backwoods of eastern Maine, Bangor had been incorporated as a town back in 1791 and now boasted a flourishing trade in lumber. She found a note of droll Irish humor in the name "Bangor." Tradition related that the name was given to the town by Reverend Seth Noble, its first resident Protestant clergyman. The natives of the area had intended to call it "Sunbury," but Noble liked "Bangor," the name of his favorite hymn melody, and so inserted it in the Act of Corporation. The melody took its name from Bangor in County Down, Ireland, where after the coming of St. Patrick, a thousand monks sang praises to God in glorious melody day and night for untold years! More familiar to Frances was another town of Bangor in Mayo, not far from the convents of her Westport Sisters.

She chose six Sisters to accompany her to the manufacturing town called rather flamboyantly the "Queen City of the East." Sister Gonzaga O'Brien, her faithful Assistant, she named as Superior until the new convent would be well established. Then she was to return to Manchester. The others were Sisters Agnes Neville, Xavier Byrne, Martha Dillon, Aloysius Kelly, and Gabriel Fahey, a novice who was the first Sister of Mercy professed in Maine.

On August 4, 1865, Frances Warde and the six pioneers "with sore hearts and tearful eyes said goodbye to loved Mount St. Mary's and turned their faces toward their new home in the backwoods of Maine."⁶ They wore the "outdoor dress" of the Sisters of Mercy designed by Catherine Mc-Auley—large black bonnets, thick veils, cloaks falling in ample folds from throat to feet. In Ireland of 1840, this costume was fashionable for elderly ladies. In New England of 1865 it elicited a bizarre response. Some of their fellow travelers, who had never seen Sisters before, inquired in hushed and sympathetic tones, "Is the corpse on board?"

The Sisters arrived in Bangor on August 5, but according to custom they considered the Maine Foundation Day to be August 6, the date of their first participation in the Celebration of the Eucharist in their new mission. The convent was an attractive brick building in a secluded spot on Newbury Street on the right bank of the Penobscot River. As happened so often in Frances' foundations, the convent was not quite ready for the Sisters, who arrived before the furniture. They named the new convent St. Xavier's in honor of Mother Frances.

In a short time, Frances Warde and Sister Gonzaga opened St. Xavier Academy, a select school in the convent, which was the first private school in Bangor; St. John's Parochial School; and a night school for young people who worked during the day. The enrollments were large. Indeed, the parochial school was so well attended—and so small— that it was necessary to expand it to the basement of St. John's Church. The dark rooms under the church were not the most desirable for classrooms, but they were used until 1879. In that year, a residence on State Street was purchased for St. Xavier's Convent and Academy, and the old academy was remodeled as a fine parochial school.

Funds were scarce during the early days of the Sisters in Bangor, and they suffered the usual privations of a new foundation. The convent library boasted only one spiritual book!

The people of St. John's Parish were poor, and it was difficult for the Sisters to secure the food and clothing they were accustomed to distribute on their visitations. The climate in this northern city was remarkably healthful, however, and St. Xavier's Convent in Bangor did not suffer the usual number of deaths by tuberculosis which struck the hardworking Sisters in most of the early American Convents of Mercy. The Bangor establishment prospered, both as a branch house from Manchester and later as a local convent attached to the parent house in Portland and then in Deering, Maine.

After several weeks in Bangor, when the three schools were well established and the works of Mercy among the people well begun, Frances Warde returned to Manchester. But Bangor was only the beginning of Mother Frances' apostolate in Maine. Whitefield, Portland, and the Indian Missions awaited her. Within thirteen years she would return to Bangor to cross the Penobscot River and found a convent and school among the Indians at Old Town, Maine. And the year before her death, all her Maine convents would be united with the Portland convent as their center.

While she expanded the works of mercy to Nebraska and Maine, Frances did not neglect New Hampshire, where she cooperated closely with Father William McDonald. Of all the priests with whom she ever worked in America, no one could compare, in her opinion, with Father McDonald in holiness and zeal. Frances mentioned him frequently in her letters as the man who did "all for God"—a phrase borrowed from Sister Martha of Hartford, the visionary who predicted Frances' apostolate in New England. One day in May, 1865, while Frances was preparing for the Bangor mission, the pastor of St. Anne's appeared at the door of Mount St. Mary's. When Mother Frances answered her bell, she found a smiling Father McDonald with a pink-cheeked little girl of about seven holding his hand. "Have you any room in your house for this little girl?" he wanted to know. The child went straight to Mother Frances' arms. McDonald had found her in the Alms House in Manchester. "I just had to bring her back with me," he said.

Thus began St. Mary's Orphanage in Manchester. Mother Frances renovated a little cottage on the convent grounds as a home for orphans. Sister Liguori Griffin was placed in charge. For the next forty-five years she poured out her love upon the motherless children of New Hampshire. The home was Father McDonald's pet project for the rest of his life. Contrary to nineteenth-century custom, he would not permit his little orphans to wear uniforms: they were not to be pointed out as objects of charity. Within seven years after the opening of St. Mary's Home, McDonald bought an estate in Manchester which Mother Frances remodeled for the orphans. It was dedicated to St. Patrick. Over the years, hundreds of children found a home there.

In the same spring of 1865 that the Orphan Home was opened, Frances Warde received a request from Father Daniel Murphy of Portsmouth, New Hampshire, to establish a parochial school in his parish. Frances sent five Sisters to open St. Patrick's Convent and School. This mission marked her first school in the State of New Hampshire outside of Manchester. Because of economic pressures, Father Murphy's successor was later obliged to close St. Patrick's School. This school would have been the only one of Frances' ventures to terminate, except for a singular circumstance. Twenty-two years later, the Sisters from Manchester returned to Portsmouth and reopened St. Patrick's School!

The number of Catholics in Manchester, meanwhile, had increased to such an extent that Father McDonald initiated a second parish, St. Joseph's, in 1869. Mother Frances opened a school in a public building on Lowell Street in Manchester for the children of this new parish, and within a year her Sisters were teaching boys and girls in a newly purchased St. Joseph's School.

Frances Warde was now in her fifties. If anything, she was more intrepid and courageous than she had been in her thirties and forties. And she attracted others to Christ with continually renewed inspiration. Sister Austin Carroll, Mercy annalist, frequently interrupts her narrative to tell of the amazing results of Mother Frances' instructions in Christian Doctrine in Manchester.[7] A few words from Frances almost invariably opened her listener to eager inquiry concerning the Word of God. With amazing continuity, Frances and her Sisters also attracted girls to the religious life. Only a continuous inflow of young women to Mount St. Mary's Convent permitted Mother Frances' unceasing initiation of the works of mercy in widespread areas throughout the United States. The response of young girls to the Mercy apostolate under Frances was a continual source of conversation among her contemporaries. One unusual example, selected from many, illustrates her inspirational spirit.

Early in 1861, Frances Warde made an appeal to her friends in Westport, Ireland, to send to Manchester any young girls whom they knew to be attracted to the life of a Sister of Mercy. In May of that year, Sister Mary Clare Leeson, a young woman of twenty-four, came to Mount St. Mary's as a postulant. Her older sister had already entered the Convent of Mercy in Galway where she served for fifty years. In September, 1861, two more members of the Leeson family came to Manchester and were received as Sister de Sales and Sister Gertrude. Five years later, a fifth sister, Mary Teresa, crossed the ocean to enter at Mount St. Mary's. She became

Sister Frances Xavier Leeson, one of Frances Warde's dearest friends and namesakes. The relationship between the two women was somewhat like that of Catherine McAuley and Frances Warde. Though Mother Frances was over thirty years older than Frances Leeson, they developed an inspiring friendship. After Frances Warde's death, her young friend was elected Superior of the Manchester Sisters of Mercy. To crown the Leeson story, Mrs. James Leeson, mother of five nuns, came to Manchester from Dublin on the death of her husband at the age of sixty-two, and entered the convent under Frances Warde. She brought with her her youngest daughter, Eleanor, to be enrolled as a student at Mount St. Mary's Academy. At the age of twenty-two, Eleanor became Sister Camilla, the seventh member of the Leeson family to become a Sister of Mercy. The Leeson chronicle is unusual, but placed in context with other events of Frances Warde's life, it somehow loses the quality of unexpectedness. With Mother Frances, the rare became usual.

The warmth of her love and compassion for others led her to an openness and trust of others that was uncommon even among mid-nineteenth-century Christians who had dedicated their lives, as she had, to the spread of the Word of God. She could open her heart to a criminal and suffer recrimination for her pains without regret. Often her trust was rewarded; often it was not. The main point is that, while she was always happy to receive a response to her love and trust, she was never discouraged by a failure of that response. The rare quality of her compassion is revealed in a typical relationship she developed with the young sister of Bishops Michael and James O'Connor.

A few years after Michael O'Connor came to America himself, he arranged for his sister, Mary Anne, to come from Ireland too. In 1843, when Frances Warde first came to

Pittsburgh, Mary Anne was attending Georgetown Academy in Washington. When she visited her brother in Pittsburgh, she always received a warm welcome from Mother Frances. In 1850 she became a postulant in the Ursuline Convent, Brown County, Ohio. Two years later, as Sister Aloysia, she was professed. She was a bright, witty, restless girl, with casual manners and conversation that did not always appeal to her dignified brother, James. Her letters to him reveal her resentment because of the infrequency of his visits and letters to her.[8] James O'Connor was the center of an admiring group of women, many of them Sisters of Mercy, who revered him almost excessively as their spiritual father. Mary Anne was candid with him as a sister can be. Perhaps he did not appreciate her frankness. Yet she was a loving sister who greatly desired her brother's affection. When she offended him, she mended the rift. About nine years after her profession, James expressed his fears of her leaving the convent, which she denied angrily, at the same time accusing him of visiting her only once a year.

Some time later, Mary Anne O'Connor did leave the Ursuline Convent. Soon after, she regretted the loss of religious life and applied to Frances Warde to join the Sisters of Mercy in Manchester. It was not customary in many religious congregations in 1863 to receive a candidate from another community without good reason, but Mother Frances Warde gave Mary Anne a second chance in religious life. She would have done the same for almost any girl. Frances Warde did not care greatly about criticism which might arise from her efforts to help others. After a few years, it became evident that Mary Anne's old restlessness had returned. Again she desired to leave the convent. Mother Frances wrote to James O'Connor, explaining Mary Anne's situation to him, urging him to encourage his sister to use her talents after her release from vows, and promising that "anything I can do for her, I am ever willing to do."[9] Frances then wrote to Bishop Bacon to secure Mary Anne's dispensation from her vows. Within a short time, Mary Anne was back in Manchester, begging Mother Frances to receive her into the convent for a third time. Such a situation in 1867 was completely out of order. Ordinarily, a girl was not accepted in a convent a second time, and a third time was almost unheard of. But Frances Warde's trust could extend to seventy times seven times. "It is sad to think of Mary Anne's wanderings," she wrote to James O'Connor. "Yet I am willing to hope that she will now persevere . . . The Bishop advised me not to consider receiving her into this or any of our convents again. A few days later, she quite unexpectedly arrived almost in despair at what she had done . . . I felt deeply for her . . . So I wrote to the Bishop in her favor . . . ." Because of the understanding warmth of Frances Warde's response to her, Mary Anne O'Connor was now back in the convent for a third trial. Eventually, she again left Mount St. Mary's for good.

The significant point in the entire series of events, however, is that Frances Warde "felt deeply for her" over and over again, as she did for everyone who sought her help. Frances was Christ-like in her concern for others. And Mary Anne, who eventually died all alone in St. Louis, was Frances' friend forever. Who can measure the effect of Mother Frances' trust upon her personality? Years later, in 1875, Mary Anne found herself one day in a situation in which she heard another religious speak negatively of Frances Warde. Commenting upon the uncharitable one, Mary Anne wrote indignantly to her brother:

I met her by accident a short time ago, and she told me that Mother Warde had none of Mother McAuley's *spirit* about her.

318

As much as to say, "I have." I had a great mind to tell her that with all her spirit, she could not succeed in getting up one convent . . . that bore any resemblance to the dozens Mother Warde had established . . . .[10]

Spontaneous and unguarded remarks often reveal truth more precisely than calculated statements. Mary Anne O'Connor in her indignation focused unwittingly upon a significant truth concerning Frances Warde. The "dozens" of fruitful apostolates founded by Mother Frances were a cause of joy to the large majority of her Sisters and associates. To a small number, Frances' accomplishments in Christ appeared as a condemnation of their own failure to achieve, and they defended themselves unconsciously by attacking Frances. Such is the experience of every strong, dynamic apostle of Christ.

In 1870, Frances Warde encountered a person with whom she developed a relationship revealing her Christ-like qualities so superbly that no account of her life could be complete without it. James Kent Stone was thirty in the summer of 1870 when he met sixty-year-old Mother Frances. For him, the encounter was crucial to his life commitment; for her, it was the source of mingled joy and pain.

15

Suffering and Resurrection: Frances Warde and Kent Stone

OF all the saintly men with whom Frances Warde was associated, perhaps the saintliest was James Kent Stone, Father Fidelis of the Cross in the Congregation of the Passion. Certainly none of her friends lived a more extraordinary life than Kent Stone. It was typical of Mother Frances that she trusted him completely when others did not, that she offered him her utmost assistance in his greatest need, and that she stepped quietly out of his life when he no longer needed her.

James Kent Stone, born in Boston in 1840, was the son of John Seely Stone and Mary Kent. The men of the Kent family were Presbyterian ministers of the old school. The Stones were Episcopalian clerics. When Kent was born, his father was Rector of St. Paul's Church in Boston. The early years of the boy's life were spent in Brooklyn where his father became Rector of Christ Church; later, the family moved to Brookline, Massachusetts, when John Seely Stone was called to St. Paul's Church there. The elder Stone eventually became Professor of Theology and Dean of the Faculty of the Episcopal Theological School at Cambridge, as well as a preacher and theological writer of note. Kent Stone's grandfather was the famous jurist, James Kent, Chancellor of New York and author of the epoch-making treatise on American law, *Kent's Commentaries*.

Young Kent Stone prepared for Harvard at Mr. Dixwell's private Latin School in Cambridge. Oliver Wendell Holmes, Jr., later Supreme Court Justice, was his classmate. Stone entered Harvard at sixteen, but soon left to tour Europe. After traveling in England, France, Italy, and Switzerland, he returned to Harvard. He went to Europe again in the summer of 1860, visiting Germany and Switzerland and gaining a reputation as an Alpine climber. In 1861 he returned to Germany to attend the University at Gottingen, and then came back to Cambridge to graduate with the Harvard Class of 1861. At the age of twenty-one, he joined the faculty at Dixwell's School, where one of his pupils was the future Senator Henry Cabot Lodge. At about the same time, Stone was engaged to marry Cornelia Fay, close friend of Emily Daniels, who later became Mrs. Henry Wadsworth Longfellow. The Civil War delayed Stone's marriage. He became a Lieutenant in the Union Army in 1862–63 and fought at Antietam.

In January, 1863, Kent Stone became Assistant Professor of Latin at Kenyon College, Gambier, Ohio, and in the same year was advanced to Professor of Latin and Philosophy. Harvard honored him with the degree of Master of Arts, and Racine with that of Doctor in Theology. After several terms at Kenyon, he was inaugurated as President of the College. Meanwhile, he was ordained a Deacon of the Episcopal Church at Kenyon in 1863, and three years later a Presbyter. In 1868, at the amazing age of twenty-seven, he resigned the presidency of Kenyon College to accept that of Hobart College in Geneva, New York.

In August, 1863, Kent Stone had married Cornelia Fay. Their first child, Cornelia, was born in 1864, and their second, Ethel, in 1866. After the family had moved to Geneva, in 1868, a third child, Fanny, was born. Five months later,

Cornelia Fay Stone died, leaving Kent alone with his three little girls. The loss of his lovely young wife and the care of his babies would have brought suffering and anxiety enough to any young man in his twenties. But Kent Stone was forced to endure, at precisely the same time, a soul-shaking personal experience of a quite different nature.

Kent had left Kenyon College because of religious controversy which alienated him from his colleagues. During the sixties, the Episcopal Church in America as well as in England was embroiled in uncertainty and questioning. In 1864 John Henry Newman had published his *Apologia Pro Vita Sua*. Stone had moved to Hobart College because his High Church sympathies and "primitive Christianity" were more welcome in Geneva than in Gambier. Then suddenly, in the autumn of 1868, Kent Stone's spiritual world crumbled beneath his feet with the impact of an earthquake. Later, he described this crisis of his life most graphically in *The Invitation Heeded*, a book sometimes called the American *Apologia*, just as Stone was named by his contemporaries the American Newman:

I was not conscious of the smallest change in my theological opinions and sympathies; when all at once the ground upon which I had stood, with such careless confidence, gave way. Like a treacherous island, it sank without warning beneath my feet, and left me struggling in the wide waters . . . How it came about—by what intellectual process my position had been undermined—by what unconscious steps my feet had been led to an unseen brink, I did not know. I was only aware of the sudden terror with which I found myself slipping, and the darkness which succeeded the swift plunge . . . And then the Hand of God drew back the veil . . . and I saw for the first time, and all at once, how utterly steeped I had been in prejudice, how from the beginning I had, without question or suspicion, assumed the very point about which I ought reverently to have enquired with an impartial and a docile mind . . . Had there ever been a time when it was an *open question* in my mind whether the claims of the Roman Church were valid? Had it ever crossed my thoughts that the Church in communion with the See of Peter might be indeed the only one Catholic Church of our Lord Jesus Christ? . . . This is the "plunge" I spoke of. I used the word because it expressed . . . the terrifying rapidity which marked the steps of my intellectual crisis. Upon some men the discovery of a life-long error may break gradually; truth may be said to have its dawning; but to me it came with a shock. The rain descended and the flood came; my house fell; and great was the fall of it . . . And I found the Kingdom of Heaven as in the parable, like a treasure hidden in a field . . . And when I had found it, I hid it, scarce daring to gaze at its splendor . . . And then, for joy thereof, I went and sold all that I had, and bought that field.[1]

In June, 1869, Kent Stone resigned his presidency of Hobart College; in October, he resigned his ministry in the Protestant Episcopal Church. And on December 8, 1869, he was received into the Roman Catholic Church. Almost at once, members of his wife's family prepared papers to commit him to a mental institution. His heart-broken father refused to sign the papers. His grief-stricken mother, remaining true to him in love and trust, nevertheless believed that some form of insanity must have struck her son. Kent Stone's crucifixion had begun. He wrote long letters to his family, especially to his mother whom he loved deeply, explaining that he was not "under a delusion": "I am as sure that the Roman Catholic Church is the true Church of our Lord Jesus Christ as I am that there is a God in heaven, or that I have a soul to be saved."[2] Catholic sympathizers offered him a position on the faculty of Georgetown College, but he refused it. He had determined to become a priest. His mother begged him not to do so. If God had not spoken, he told her, he would cheer-fully do as she wished, cost what it might. But he had been ordained in the Episcopal Church, and he had believed him-self to be truly and validly a consecrated priest. Already dedi-cated to Christ, he must now become a Roman Catholic priest. It was the will of God.

Over and over again, Kent Stone found it necessary to assure his anxious mother that his little girls were his dearest love and first concern, that he would gladly die for them. But now he must remove them from the care of their maternal grandmother, Mrs. Harrison Fay, whose family threatened him so that he feared to lose the children. Above all, he must provide for the Catholic training of his small daughters. He found it bitter to do what he had to do. In the Church of Rome there was no human attraction for him, "there was *absolutely nothing*—unless, indeed, it might be some attrac-tion lurking in the very completeness of the immolation."[3] To be true to himself, he felt that he had to sacrifice everything dear to him.

On July 22, 1870, Kent Stone went with his three little girls to see Mother Frances Warde at Mount St. Mary's Academy in Manchester. The older woman and the zealous young convert responded to each other immediately. Kent knew within a few minutes that Mother Frances understood and trusted him. He asked her to assume complete responsi-bility for training his little girls. Cornelia was six, Ethel four, and Mary Frances not quite two. The young man explained his situation freely. He wished to be a member of a religious congregation, he desired to become a Passionist, but he was not accepted as a member because of his responsibilities to his children. The Paulist Fathers, founded twelve years before by Isaac Hecker and his associates, seemed to offer a practical solution to Stone's problem. Their religious structure was less strict than that of the Passionists. They did not take evangelical vows. They were all American converts like himself, and their particular objective was to preach to the non-Catholics of America. Such a congregation should be congenial to the ardent young ex-President of two Episcopal colleges. Yet Stone's inward yearning was for the more austere life of a Passionist. He told Frances Warde that he now eagerly awaited acceptance by the Paulists as an entrance to the religious priesthood.

In order to understand the implications of Mother Frances' complete assent to Kent Stone's plans, it is necessary to view his life situation against the background of the American Catholic Church of the sixties. The four founders of the Paulists, all converts, had been members of the Congregation of Redemptorists. In 1857, because of difficulties within their community, they had been dispensed from their vows. Forming an independent band of missionaries, they had secured approval of their Rule through Archbishop John Joseph Hughes of New York. Naturally, a certain element of the Catholic hierarchy at first disapproved of them. In August 1858, for example, Archbishop Francis Patrick Kenrick of Baltimore had written to Bishop Michael O'Connor of Pittsburgh:

> The action of the ex-Redemptorists appears to me irregular . . . They have taken the form of a Congregation of missionary priests, and a corporate name, and purpose building a Church and convent, and receiving Novices, although they take no vows whatever . . . Four converts—ex-Religious—are not well suited to found a new Institute . . . .[4]

Michael O'Connor, after a conversation with Isaac Hecker, responded to Kenrick, stating that he was satisfied that the

Pope had approved the new venture of Hecker and his associates, and that he thought "the new group should have a fair trial."[5] Certain hard-headed Catholics doubted that the Paulists would succeed in their apostolate. The Paulists were off the beaten track of religious congregations. They were "different."

"Realistic" critics might consider Frances Warde imprudent to become the patron of the romantic young convert, Kent Stone, who now desired to be a Paulist. But Frances had suffered similar criticism in the past. She was always ready to take a risk on the side of trust in others. Besides, she had no doubt whatever concerning Kent Stone's complete dedication to Christ. She helped him gladly. She must have smiled quietly to herself when one of her Pittsburgh Sisters later objected to her admiration for Stone. This Sister was to write to Bishop James O'Connor in Omaha:

Mother Frances writes occasionally. She is quite taken with Dr. K. Stone's piety. In my last letter to her I expressed a hope he might persevere, and I do not expect to hear from her soon . . . .[6]

This sardonic comment, read one hundred years after it was written, conveys the same sharp irony as certain other critical remarks written long ago concerning Frances Warde. Formerly, General Chapters were held among the Sisters of Mercy and other congregations to determine whether or not candidates might be received into religious communities. A stock phrase used to express non-committal approval was, "I hope she may persevere." The writer of the above letter, with its caustic implications of doubt concerning the spirituality of Kent Stone, was proved to be totally in error. Frances Warde's trust, on the other hand, proved to be well founded. Kent

Stone became one of the most heroic religious figures in American Catholic history.

In July, 1870, then, Mother Frances accepted "entire charge" of training the Stone children. In August of the same year, a beautiful correspondence[7] originated between her and Kent Stone. Frances preserved his letters carefully. She had the insight to realize their value. Ironically, just as in the case of Frances' friendship with Catherine McAuley, her own letters to Stone were destroyed. Long after Mother Frances had died, when Kent Stone was asked for the letters of a well-known friend, he did not have them. "The only explanation I can give," he wrote, "is that I have not kept anything whatsoever from anybody." It is an irony of fate that Frances Warde possessed the sensitivity to recognize greatness in her associates, while they somehow lacked—despite their eminence—that special responsiveness which treasures the words of rare personalities.

A month after Kent Stone placed his little girls under Frances Warde's care, he wrote to her that he still awaited the decision of Archbishop Hughes of New York, to whom Father Hecker had referred his application to join the Paulists. Kent's closing words revealed his suffering at the separation from his children:

Will you please, dear Reverend Mother, drop me a line . . . telling me how my babies are. And don't scold me, however much I deserve it. Notwithstanding my silence, my thoughts have been half the time at Manchester. Indeed, I have passed a divided existence.

Five days later, Kent wrote that the Archbishop of new York had approved of his becoming a Paulist and also "expressed warm approbation of my course in putting the children where

I have. He said I could not have done more wisely." Then the young man added: "Thank you much for your comforting letter. Little Cornelia in her note says: 'I love all the Sisters very, very much; but I love Reverend Mother best of all because she is a dear kind Mama to us.'" Frances indeed loved the children deeply, so much so that the inevitable parting from them was to be for her a cause of intense suffering.

A note of pathos soon entered the correspondence of Frances Warde and Kent Stone. On October 14, 1870, Mother Frances received a letter from Father Isaac Hecker, founder and Superior of the Paulists. In it he suggested a course of action to Frances that she evidently had not anticipated. Assuming, with her usual warmth of heart, that Kent would deeply desire all possible news of his small girls (as he did), Frances had been writing to him graphic descriptions of all the little events of their lives at Mount St. Mary's. Now Father Hecker wrote to her:

For one to devote himself to the great work of the priesthood, and that in a religious community and being the father of children, is a delicate and unusual enterprise. His duty as a priest, and a missionary priest especially, requires of him to subordinate his affection for his children to the great work of the priesthood . . .

Before [his] entering into our Community, my own advice to him was to remain a couple of years in the world—and as he was so decidedly averse to this, after you had engaged to take the entire charge of his children, I left the decision of his entering with the Archbishop of New York.

I confess to some apprehension of its success. Mr. Stone for his part, and disposition, leaves nothing desirable. But will he in the future be able to do the work of his vocation undisturbed by his affection for his children? This is the delicate point and the difficulty.

It is here where your cooperation becomes most important. With my views, I would advise your writing to him seldom and then in [the words "in such a way as not to awaken" are crossed out] speaking of his daughters use a large dose of prudence and a small number of words . . .[8]

It is not difficult to imagine Frances Warde's spontaneous reaction to such a letter. In dealing with the members of her own family in Ireland and in America, she had not withheld her affection. Since Kent Stone's little girls were well provided for, it would be difficult for Frances to comprehend how his love for his children could be a real hindrance to so dedicated a man. Would not the mutual love of father and babies be a welcome support for both? Frances respected, nevertheless, the will of the Superior of the Paulists.

Ten days later she received a letter from the unsuspecting Paulist novice. Kent told her that his thoughts turned many times a day to Manchester. He thanked her for telling him "all the little matters" related to his babies. He suspected that "your letters will be to me at the same time a delight and a trial. You will not wonder, I am sure, that my heart should yearn for my little girls. But I know that God will give the grace to turn the pain of absence into a blessing. Your account of Mary Frances and all her ways was touching . . . ." Kent also discussed in his letter the appointment of an official guardian, a New Haven judge, for his children. He added that he was presently engaged in writing a long letter, an account of the principal events of his life thus far, and of his religious experience, to be given to Cornelia at the age of fifteen, in case he should die before that time. He then told Mother Frances of his great joy on receiving a letter from his own mother, Mary Kent Stone, telling him of her visit to Mount St. Mary's, of the obvious happiness of his children, and of

329

the great charm and kindness of Frances Warde herself. Kent Stone's letter was long. He concluded by shyly suggesting that Mother Frances read an article he had written for the *Catholic World,* and then declaring that the happiness he now enjoyed was quite beyond his comprehension. Another time, he promised, he would tell her about his everyday life in the Paulist novitiate.

Obviously, Kent Stone could write warmly and freely to Frances Warde. They were friends. She would be a support to him. But now there rose between them the dark cloud of the letter of Isaac Hecker, the admonition that she "write to him seldom . . . and use a large dose of prudence and a small number of words . . ." Frances did not answer Kent Stone's beautiful long letter. She respected the will of his Superior.

The following month, Kent wrote a pathetic little note to Mother Frances. Between the lines was an implicit appeal for communication. The children had been baptized in July in Mount St. Mary's Chapel. Each had been given the name Mary, prefixed to her own name. And little Ethel had been given the name Xavier in honor of Mother Frances, who called her Ethel Xavier. Now Kent reminded Mother Frances that Ethel's birthday was only two days away, on November 7, and he sent "a little picture of St. Francis Xavier to my baby Ethel." He asked Mother Frances and the children to pray for him on November 10, when he would be thirty years old. And then, with a special delicacy of feeling, he remembered that November 11 was the date of Catherine McAuley's death in 1841. He closed the brief letter with a simple statement:

I hope you received the letter I wrote you some time ago. I have heard nothing since I left you, except your letter of

September 17th. But I trust that God and the Blessed Virgin are taking care of you all.

Kent Stone was longing to hear from his children. All the joyous spontaneity of his long letter to Frances Warde in August was gone. There is no way of knowing whether he found out the reason for Mother Frances' seeming coldness. In the eighteen-seventies, it was not customary to confer with novices concerning the decisions of their Superiors. The tone of Father Hecker's letter to Frances Warde suggested that of a private communication. But Frances knew how to judge precisely when human considerations should override merely legal decisions. She responded warmly to Kent's appeal. And his joy in her response was unbounded. He sat down at once and wrote to Mary Kent Stone:

Dearest Mother:

The enclosed letters came last night [from Mother Frances and little Cornelia]. I send them to you, thinking that you and Father will be glad to know how my babies get along . . . The feast referred to in Cornelia's letter was St. Francis Xavier's, the third of December . . . It does seem indeed, as Reverend Mother says, as if God were giving me "a hundred fold" even *in this* life. Tears of inexpressible happiness have been blinding my eyes since I received this letter. I went down last night into the Church, all silent, and lighted only by the light which burns before the Blessed Sacrament, and I laid the little letter of my darling on the Blessed Virgin's altar and said my rosary for her there, that she might indeed become a saint—and who can tell the joy that seemed to overwhelm me?

I do not know how the little thing knew that the Feast of the Immaculate Conception was the anniversary of my reception into the Church . . . On that day (day before yesterday) I made a pilgrimage of thanksgiving to the Passionist Monastery . . .

O sweetest day of all the year to me—the prelude of the Incarnation![9]

Of course it was Mother Frances who directed little Nellie's six-year-old hand to write the letter which filled her father with joy. It was Mother Frances who was nourishing Kent's new-found faith through his love for little Nellie, Ethel, and Mamie.

The next letter in the series so carefully preserved by Frances Warde is dated December 16, 1870. In less than a week after Kent's great gift of joy, he and Mother Frances were to suffer one of the profoundest sorrows of their lives. They proved to be as capable of sorrow as of joy. Early in December, little Ethel became ill with a severe cold. The Doctor felt certain that she would improve. But as pneumonia seemed to be developing, Mother Frances sent for Kent at once. Shortly before he arrived in Manchester, the crisis came. When he reached Mount St. Mary's, Ethel was dead. Frances led him to the little girl's bed. A silver rosary was in her fingers. He took it from her small hands and, afterwards, always held it while he prayed. The child was buried on December 16 in the little convent cemetery in Manchester. The simple inscription, "Ethel Xavier," was placed on the tiny tombstone.

Kent Stone's living faith was as strong as Frances Warde's. He believed quite simply that Ethel was with her heavenly Father. On the night of the child's burial he wrote to Mother Frances from Cambridge:

My heart is full tonight (ah! *more* than full) of gratitude to Almighty God for the mercies he has showered upon me . . . He has given me more than a hundredfold in this life in showing me how he has raised up in you and your kind Sisters at Manchester so many sweet mothers for my little children. Believe me, I have been most observant, and most profoundly touched by the self-forgetful devotion and the delicate sympathy which have been silently shown during the past two days. Should I live to be a century old, the freshness of these scenes will not grow dim in my memory . . .

I could not but fear, as we stood by the little grave this morning, and the icy wind blew over the wintry hills, that some of you, and perhaps some of the little children, would be chilled, and perhaps made ill. May God prevent it . . .

I do not think that the gracious little life which has been so soon closed on earth has been wholly without its lesson. And now her soul is surely already made radiant by the vision of God . . . As Cornelia said this morning when we left the tiny open grave, "Goodbye, little Ethel, and pray for Papa and me." Yes, and for us all!

Do not be troubled by any painful things that may have happened; and read, when you find a little time, the 47th Chapter of the Third Part of the *Imitation of Christ:* "That All Grievous Things Are to Be Endured for Life Everlasting."

Kent Stone and Frances Warde suffered intensely with the death of Ethel Xavier. Grief they could bear. Their faith was greater than their grief. But trial now came to them from a far different source. The day following the funeral, Kent's brother-in-law, Clement Fay, wrote an extremely harsh letter to Mary Kent Stone. Her son was accused of being "heartless and cruel" in not allowing his daughter to be buried near her mother in the Protestant cemetery in Brookline, Massachusetts. The Fays could not understand Kent's belief that his daughter should be buried in "consecrated ground." Moreover, his refusal to allow Cornelia and Mamie to visit their mother's relatives for a time caused Kent's mother-in-law to regard him with "feelings of horror and aversion."[10] Kent now feared that his wife's relatives would attempt to take the children from him and train them in the Protestant faith. He had reason to believe that his brother-in-law and former friend, John Fay, would do all that he could to control the lives of the children. Kent therefore went to Cambridge directly after Ethel's burial to execute the formality of appointing a legal guardian for Nellie and Mamie in case of his death.

Two days later Kent wrote to Mother Frances again, asking her to have nothing more to do with the Fay family than was necessary. Her response was predictable. She reserved the right to be kind to the Fays. On December 22, Kent wrote once again, informing Frances at length of the reasons why he felt justified in believing he would have to face a lawsuit if the Fays succeeded in their desire for "the small boon of a week's visit" from the two little girls. He foresaw that the Fays would attempt to enlist Mother Frances' sympathies on their side. Yet he apologized for being "too ready with words of counsel" to her. Kent was soon to learn that Frances was capable of guarding his children from all danger and of being kind to their relatives at the same time. In the end, her wisdom was perhaps greater than Kent's. She did nothing to alienate the Fay family.

On December 21, 1870, Kent received the Sacrament of Confirmation and adopted the name of Mary Magdalen. On July 22, 1869, the Feast of St. Mary Magdalen, he had first taken his three little girls to Frances Warde in Manchester, and he considered the day one of the most memorable in his life. Also, on that day he had prayed to a saint for the first time in his life. He began to use the signature "J.M.M.S." for James Mary Magdalen Stone. In January, Frances Warde sent to Mary Kent Stone a little gold locket of Ethel's with a lock of her hair. Mrs. Stone wrote warmly to Kent of her admiration for and gratitude to Mother Frances. She was beginning to learn that Catholics, and especially Frances Warde, were not so peculiar as prejudice pictured them to be. As for Kent, he appreciated Frances more and more. On January 16, 1871, he wrote to her: "Your letter of the 26th of December reached me safely and was a *real treat*. I almost had a scruple over the pleasure which it gave me." The warmth and spontaneity of his early letters—before the warning of Isaac Hecker—were completely restored. Kent was delighted with his mother's positive response to Mother Frances and Mount St. Mary's. He begged Frances for prayers for Mary Kent Stone. And he closed his letter with a question: "How can I thank you for making Cornelia's Christmas—and all her days—so happy?"

Cornelia—little Nellie—was especially dear to Kent Stone. But Mary Frances—little Mamie—was Frances Warde's favorite. Not quite three, she would follow Mother Frances everywhere, even to the chapel at Mount St. Mary's where she would sit smiling on the kneeler at Frances' feet as the Superior led the community in prayer. When Frances wrote letters, Mamie would beg to be lifted up to her desk, where she would sit with her little legs dangling and watch her beloved "Reverend Mother." Often Frances would stop her work to chat with the child. She was the pet of the Convent of Mercy. But Kent Stone had always loved his oldest little girl, Cornelia, with the deepest attachment. One day, when she was not quite three, she had been allowed as a great privilege to sit with the family at the dinner table in her own high chair. After a while she began to bang the table with her spoon, and her Aunt Fanny, who was visiting, said to her, "Nellie, if you don't stop, your father will punish you." Nellie paused, spoon uplifted. Then, without raising her eyes, she said in a cool, nonchalant voice, "Papa would die for me," and gave the table a final bang. There had always been a special feeling between Kent and the child.

Sometime in the summer of 1871, when Nellie was about seven, she wrote one of her frequent little notes to her father. In it she told him in her childish way that she would like to be a nun. Kent was overjoyed. He began to dream of the day when his little girl would be a religious too, and he could share his most sacred thoughts with her. He hoped one day to be his Nellie's spiritual director. His answer to her was cherished by Frances Warde:

My dear little Sister—my little Cornelia of the Infant Jesus,

I had only sent my last letter off a little while, when *your* dear letter came, telling me how you wanted to be a little nun, and that Sister had told you how you could begin to be a true little nun even now; and then you asked me, you remember, "What do you think of *that,* dear Papa?"

So I think I must send you a few little lines to answer your question, because this evening we all go into retreat for a week, and then our Fall term of studies begins.

Well, my sweet little one, I will tell you that nothing in all this world could give me greater happiness than to know that my daughter—you, my Cornelia, were from your heart a true Sister and Spouse of our dear and blessed Lord Jesus Christ. Do you think you can be one? Well, I hope so. It would not be very hard to *play* at being a Sister, that is, to *fancy* for a while, a few weeks or a few months, that you were a grown-up Sister, like the dear nuns at Mt. St. Mary's. But that isn't what I mean at all.

It is *possible to be a real true nun,* even now when you are only seven years old, and that is something very different from *imagining* yourself one. It is not the wearing a habit, and a veil, and a rosary in one's girdle, that makes a nun. But it is giving up all the world beside, and taking our dear Lord Jesus Christ to be your one and only love for all your life, yes, and for all eternity in heaven. It is to love Him with all your little heart; and to be content with His love alone, whatever happens, whether you are alone or with others, whether He sends you sorrow or joy, pain or pleasure. It is to keep your true heart pure and quiet for Him to rest in day and night; and to visit Him when you can in the Blessed Sacrament; and to remember often what He suffered for love for you, and how He *died* for love of you; and to be gentle and loving to everybody, and to your little companions, whether they are kind to you or not, because you wish to be like Him whom you have chosen for your own.

Do you want to try to do all this, my little one? Oh, then you will be a little nun, indeed; and then you will love your poor Papa better than you ever did before, but in a different way— that is, not merely because he is your Father, but because your dear Lord loves even him also.

And I will be your brother, Brother James of the Immaculate Conception, because I have a great love of that beautiful mystery, and our Immaculate Lady has saved me many times over, and I became a Catholic on her Feast Day. And if I live to be a priest, I will be your true Father, your spiritual Father, and you will be my dear spiritual daughter.

And now I must send my letter, for retreat will begin in a few minutes. Will you say a prayer for me, that our dear Lord would make me very humble, and send me many precious crosses and sufferings?

Kiss dear little Mary many times for me, and tell her that her Papa is oh! so happy to hear she has been a good and obedient little girl lately. And tell Reverend Mother that I can never forget her. Goodbye, my sweet little Sister.[11]

Throughout the year 1871 Kent Stone was happy at the Paulist house in New York, while Frances Warde watched carefully over Cornelia and Mary Frances, growing to love them more and more. As was customary in novitiates, Kent did not write letters during Lent, but as soon as Easter arrived he hastened to tell Frances Warde: "Do not think I have forgotten you all. The fact is, my heart runs away only too often to those New Hampshire hills, and I have not always easy work to bring it back. . . ." In June, Kent wrote to Frances concerning efforts of his relatives to win the children away from their father. And he added with utmost trust:

Nor would I have you think that I am ruffled with the smallest anxiety about the little ones; for indeed I have always the most serene and happy confidence concerning them. I am certain that God and our Blessed Lady will guard them with the most sheltering care, and that this will be done *through you* whom God has inspired to be the angel of my little family.

Ah, dear Reverend Mother, how much I owe you, and how little I can ever do in return! I wish our dear Lady would put down *all* my past prayers and satisfactions to your account. Perhaps she does—who knows? I think it would be more than fair . . . .

Kent was planning a visit to Manchester in July, and he added a shy P.S. to Mother Frances: "It seems as if I could talk pretty fast when I see you." In a letter written two weeks later, he teased Frances about her deep attachment for three-year-old Mamie: "Little Mary is quite a marvel. But take care you don't spoil her, or let her spoil you. (This is only pleasantry. I don't think there is really any great danger.)"

December brought sorrow again when little Mamie became ill. Frances' anxiety was great, and she told Kent of her fears concerning the child. But Mamie was soon well again, and all were happy as before at Mount St. Mary's. Kent's friends and ecclesiastical Superiors, however, had been offering him advice for several months which he had not confided to Frances so as not to disturb her. In the seventies, the majority of religious Superiors felt that a widower, in order to become a priest, should break completely with his children and devote himself undividedly to his vocation. Isaac Hecker's letter to Frances Warde had represented a common judgment. Nevertheless, Mother Frances was unprepared for the letter she received from Kent Stone just before Christmas in 1871:

> I am coming to see you about a matter which, I fear, will give you a good deal of pain. But one thing is certain, that any natural sorrow that you may feel will not be half so acute as my own. It is something which is harder to me than the severance of ties when I became a Catholic; it is far harder than the taking of the children away from their grandparents a year and a half ago.
>
> After much prayer and consultation . . . I have decided to give the children to Mr. and Mrs. Michael O'Connor, of San Francisco, who have offered to adopt them. I will speak of my reasons when I see you. Father Hecker and Father Deshon, also Archbishop McCloskey and Archbishop Spalding say they think I am following God's will in the matter . . . And now, dear Reverend Mother, pray for me, as I shall for you, that our dear Lord would give us grace to do His blessed Will in all things, and to make Him a complete and willing sacrifice of ourselves with all our hopes and all our affections . . . .

With their legal adoption of Nellie and Mamie, the O'Connors made one stipulation: Kent Stone was to surrender all his rights as a parent. He was to give up not only legal but also natural relations with his children. It would be better, the O'Connors felt, if there were no further communication between Kent and his little girls at all, so that they might belong entirely to their new parents.

The young father believed, on the advice of his Superiors, that the adoption and the excellent provision for his daughters' future was the will of God for him. He accepted the unbelievable pain of separation. He wrote at once to Hobart College and ordered the furniture he had stored there to be sold at auction. Then he collected all the memories of the past still in his possession—letters, poems, manuscripts. In the back yard of the Paulist monastery in New York he made a bonfire of them. Finally he gathered together his dearest treasures: pictures of his wife Cornelia and his three little girls, Cornelia's ring and small jewels. He put them in a rosewood box which had belonged to his wife and weighted it with a piece of iron. When it was dark, he walked down to the old abandoned pier that ran out from the foot of Fifty-ninth Street, and with an anguished prayer dropped the box into the Hudson River. A week later, he became seriously ill with pneumonia, and for some months his health was in a precarious state. His Paulist brothers feared that he might not live through the year. The sacrifice that Kent Stone demanded of himself seemed too great for human nature to bear.

Frances Warde's pain of separation from the children to whom she had been a real mother for a year and a half was perhaps as intense as that of Kent Stone. Manchester convent tradition states that she suffered so profoundly from the sudden break with little Mary Frances Stone that she resolved never again to allow herself to become deeply attached to a child. Like Kent, Mother Frances too became seriously ill. Between Christmas, 1871, when the O'Connors took the two little Stone girls to New York, and April, 1871, when they left the East permanently for California, Kent and Mother Frances exchanged brief, heartbreaking letters. "Your baby is as well as when she left you," Kent wrote on December 26, 1871. "Though she evidently thinks regretfully of her *dear Reverend Mother*, yet she continues bright and happy . . . Cornelia's cough is rather more severe . . ." And on February 24, 1872, Kent wrote from his sick room to Frances in hers: "I hope our good God has made you as well and strong as I shall probably be in a few days. I am sitting up this afternoon in a big easy-chair, after having been in bed five weeks with pneumonia . . . It will be a pleasure which I do not deserve to see you once more . . . ."

On March 3, Mrs. O'Connor, who had not communicated with Mother Frances since she took the children on Christmas day, finally wrote to her:

I have to apologize, my dear Reverend Mother, for not sooner answering your very kind letters. You know that I am only a visitor in New York, and I have a large circle of relatives and friends who claim any moments that can be spared from my two dear little charges, who of course require most of my time . . . I was glad to hear that you were recovering from your severe illness, and I hope you have before this time fully regained your strength . . . .[12]

Clearly, Mrs. O'Connor meant to make the break between Frances and the children clean and complete. Kent Stone wrote to Mother Frances again on March 19: "I allowed myself a good deal of selfish pleasure when I learned from your note that your expected visit [to New York] would have to be postponed until after Easter. Had you come when you at first anticipated, I should no doubt have lost the great gratification of seeing you. The Doctor and Father Deshon will not let me leave my room . . . I have not seen the children yet . . . ."

Frances Warde did go to New York. But what transpired there remains a mystery. Precisely what Mother Frances thought about the adoption of Cornelia and Mamie is not recorded. One may speculate that, with characteristic human warmth, she questioned the complete separation of Kent Stone and his little girls for whom she cared so tenderly. On July 18, 1872, Kent Stone wrote to her in a tone of gentle reproach:

Your kind letter, which did not reach me till yesterday, recalled many pleasant memories. Indeed I was glad to know that you were alive and well . . . From the time that you . . . left me that afternoon in our Convent parlor I have been in ignorance of your fate. You promised that after you got out to New Jersey you would write and let me know when you would be back in the city, so that I could call upon you at the Convent in Houston Street—but never a letter came. I did not even learn whether you were successful in seeing the children; for I did not see Mr. and Mrs. O'Connor after that.

. . . I am growing quite strong; though whether my lungs will ever be perfectly sound again is somewhat doubtful . . .

. . . Father Hecker was really disappointed at not seeing you in New York, though I think he rather dreaded a scolding . . . .

Reading the above letter after one hundred years, one can only conjecture without evidence why Mother Frances failed to write to Kent Stone between Easter and mid-July, 1870, why she failed to keep her appointment with him in New York, why Isaac Hecker, Superior of the Paulists, expected a "scolding" from her. The warmth of her love for the Stone children, the human understanding she revealed even from her earliest days in Dublin, her unsympathetic attitude toward many of the Jansenistic tendenices of nineteenth-century American Catholicism, lead one to speculate that she perhaps doubted the wisdom of Kent's sacrifice. Did she fail to write to Kent after her probable visit with the O'Connors in New York because she disagreed with them in their demand for complete separation of the children from their father? Did she fail to visit Kent in New York because she did not wish to hurt him by reporting the truth of her interview with the O'Connors? Did Father Hecker fear a "scolding" from her because she disapproved of the plans for the children? Since Frances' letters were not preserved, one can only surmise what happened. But it is quite conceivable that Frances Warde, who had agreed to assume complete responsibility for Kent Stone's children, saw no conflict between their remaining in their happy home at Mount St. Mary's and their father's vocation.

With her womanly feeling, Frances would have been completely cognizant of the relationship between Kent's serious illness and his almost inhuman separation from his little girls. She had demonstrated over and over again a motherly concern for the health of the young Paulist who seemed destined to suffer so bitterly. She had frequently revealed her awareness of the effects of his anxiety upon his health. Shortly before the adoption of the children, he had written to her jocosely:

I must not forget to say that I had a good laugh at your motherly anxiety a few weeks ago. Father Deshon one day, without any apparent cause, gave me a long homily on the duty of taking care of my health. It turned out that you had written to Father Hecker, telling him how anxious my mother was, etc. So I have been leading lately a very luxurious and unmortified life; and you are really to blame for it, Madam . . . .

Perhaps the womanly wisdom of Frances Warde should have been brought to bear upon the decision which affected so strongly the future of Kent Stone and his little girls.

On December 21, 1872, as the Sisters of Mercy celebrated the anniversary of their first American foundation in Pittsburgh, Kent Stone was ordained as a Paulist. He was still not physically strong. Nor did he regain his normal strength for many months. Now that his children were permanently adopted, however, he reconsidered his first desire on becoming a Roman Catholic: to follow his vocation to the monastic state as a member of the Congregation of Passionists. It was a coincidence that Bishop Michael O'Connor had brought the first members of the Congregation of the Most Holy Cross and Passion from Rome to Pittsburgh back in 1852, nine years after he had accompanied Frances Warde and the "first seven"

Sisters of Mercy from Carlow to the Pennsylvania city. In the spring of 1876, Father Kent Stone, now thirty-five years of age, entered the Passionist novitiate at the monastery of St. Paul of the Cross on a high hill in Birmingham, just across the Monongahela River from Mother Frances' first American foundation. Kent received the habit of the Passionists in 1877, and a year later made his profession of vows. Then began a long life of service as missionary and retreat master throughout the western world. From the time of his profession, Kent Stone, now Father Fidelis of the Cross, never called a spot on earth his home. Between 1878 and his death in 1921, he carried the Word of God wherever obedience sent him: Rome, Buenos Aires, Paraguay, Chile, London, the Canal Zone, Mexico City, Sao Paulo, Spain, Cuba, and throughout the entire United States. In 1897, he was Consultor-General of the Passionists in Rome; in 1898, Consultor to the American Provincial; in 1905, United States Provincial; in 1911, South American Provincial.

Father Fidelis' life was one of total and heroic sacrifice. He became a world-famous missionary, the spiritual father of thousands. He continued to keep in touch with Frances Warde. In May, 1873, he wrote to tell her, "you needn't suppose that I forget you . . . I scarcely hear from the children oftener than you do . . . I am getting stronger but not very vigorous yet." A letter of October 1875, refers to the mutual apostolate of Frances Warde and Father Fidelis, with no mention of the children. Three years later, in August, 1878, the young Passionist conducted the annual retreat of the Sisters at Mount St. Mary's on the invitation of Frances. In the spring of 1880, he wrote from Rome to sympathize with Mother Frances on the death of her sister, Josephine Warde, in Cork. To judge from his letters, the children of Kent Stone were not foremost in his thoughts.

The truth was, however, that they were never far from his thoughts. To the uninvolved observer, it would seem that surely here was a tragedy which might have been averted. Try as Kent would to forget, the images of Cornelia and Mary Frances were engraved on his heart. In the long watches of the night, whether on the Pampas of Argentina, in the harbor of Rio, or the ravines of the Andes, in Rome or Spain, Panama or Cuba, recollections of the past came back to him. The knowledge was always with him that those nearest to him in blood, dearest to him in love, were as far from him as though they were strangers.

In 1885 Cornelia reached the age of twenty-one and the official end of her adoption. No longer bound by legal promises of separation, Kent Stone hopefully wrote a letter from Buenos Aires to his daughter in San Francisco. To his grief, it was returned unopened. Probably it never reached Nellie. At about the same time he wrote in a rare tone of near-despair to an intimate friend:

As for me, I must expect nothing, hope for nothing, think of nothing—I must leave all in the hands of God. To cherish a fluttering hope would go nigh to kill me. It has been only by abandoning everything that I have saved myself from utter shipwreck and the loss of reason . . . .[13]

But Father Fidelis' agony was always a dark night of faith, never despair. Late in the eighties, he was appointed to the Chilean mission of the Passionists. There one day, in Miramar on Valparaiso Bay, he composed a poem into which he poured all the sorrow of his heart. Later, he wrote:

When I composed those stanzas I was not looking back, not as Lot's wife looked back, nor with any regret . . . I have never had such a temptation . . . There was sorrow in my heart that afternoon, yes; but no undoing, no wish to undo the past . . . The spell of the place, the witchery of the scene was upon me, and for the first time since I turned my back upon the old life years ago, I gave my memory full play, and let my fancy loose—as you would let a child go play upon the beach, watching it lest it stray too far.[14]

These are the stanzas that Kent Stone composed on the beach at Miramar:

> A name I wrote upon the sand,
>> Where curled the long wave's foamy crest,
>> Drawn from the mystic molten West,
> To break on Chile's loveliest strand.
>
> Deep in the curvings of the bay
>> The city slept in dreamy light,
>> And on the Cordilleras' height
> The splendor of the sunset lay.
>
> The cliff hung o'er the gleaming tide,
>> And at its base, with muffled shocks,
>> Reverberant amid the rocks
> Tumultuous music woke and died.
>
> And, drawn from out the slumbering past,
>> Weird thoughts awoke within my soul,
>> Like echoes of the ocean's roll,
> Or driftwood by the waves upcast.
>
> I wrote; and thrice the encroaching foam
>> Swept seething upward, and erased
>> The furtive lines which I had traced,
> In vain recall of youth and home.

Dear God! In all the empty world,
I seek no home for evermore,
Nor look for rest, till by the shore
Of death my ship her sails hath furled.

'Twas but a brief beguiling spell
That held me by these rushing seas,
And I but played with memories
To which long since I bade farewell.

Once, in a far-off happy day,
As in a dream, I sang and wrote;
But sudden floods arose, and smote,
And swept my paradise away.

And now, throughout the silent years,
The sand-wastes lie, remote and dead,
By loving steps unvisited,
Nor ever dashed by showers of tears.

O Western Sea! O fair, fond Sea!
I stretch my arms to greet thy light.
Uplift me with thy generous might,
And breathe thy greatness into me!

Thy voices whisper peace; the breath
Of heaven is on the summits steep
That guard thy coast; then let me keep
Here by thy waves my tryst with death—

No more to wander, and no more
In all the world to seek for rest—
Only to wait, and by the West
Look wistful toward the unseen shore.

To a close friend Kent sent the above verses with an explanation simple in its pathos: "I need scarcely tell you that the name written on the sand, and which the waves erased, was only that of a little girl, seven years old when I last saw her sixteen years ago, and whom I never expect to see again."[15]

Such moments of indulgence of painful remembrance were rare in Kent Stone's life. He abandoned himself utterly to his apostolate. When he wrote *Valparaiso Bay*, he was almost sixty and Frances Warde was dead. When the Sisters of Mercy at Mount St. Mary's sent him in 1903 a biography of Mother Frances just published, he wrote to Manchester to say: "Of course, I myself have peculiar and personal reasons for cherishing the saintly memory of your dear Mother Xavier. Her generous kindness, her wise and gentle ways, can never fade from my recollection . . . ." And in 1907, twenty-three years after Frances' death, he went back to Manchester to conduct once again the annual August retreat of the Sisters. A month later he wrote to Frances' namesake, now Mother Frances Leeson:

I must confess that the reviving of so many memories that had lain dormant so long proved a harder trial than I had expected. For this reason I did not think it wise to go to the little cemetery. This might seem strange to some—but I think you will understand . . . .

An indirect reference to Frances Warde follows:

I know not whether I shall ever see dear Mount St. Mary's again—it does not seem likely; but there is a better and happier Home, to which so many whom we once knew have already gone, and where we shall join them if we are only faithful for a little while longer; so it does not matter much after all whether we meet at Manchester, New Hampshire.

Father Fidelis' last letter to Mount St. Mary's was penned January 1, 1920, to Mother Frances Leeson. In a reminiscent mood, the eighty-year-old priest wrote:

Those dear old days at Mount St. Mary's seem far away now, but indeed I have not forgotten them. It is fifty years since I joined the Paulist Community in New York, and forty-seven years on the Feast of St. Thomas since I was ordained a priest. Thank you for recalling that the day is also the anniversary of the landing of the first Sisters of Mercy on these Western Shores. How many things have happened since then! For myself, after many journeyings and some trials, I find myself safe and happy again in the monastery, and here I hope to remain . . .

Kent Stone, after a half-century of joy and heroic suffering in the service of Christ, had yet one more soul-shaking experience before him. In December, 1919, he finished writing his apologia, *An Awakening and What Followed*, actually a revision and enlargement of *The Invitation Heeded*. When it was published in 1920, a copy came into the hands of his daughter, Mary Frances. At the age of fifty-three, she came to understand at last the love and sacrifice of the father she had never known. Crushed with grief at his martyrdom, she poured out her feelings in a letter to him. On January 20, 1921, in the eighty-first and last year of his life, Kent Stone sat down and wrote to his child:

Frances, My Daughter—Dearest and Best:
Your letter has overwhelmed me. It carried me away with a rush of conflicting feeling. The fountains of the great deep have been broken. I did not expect it . . .
I am very weak, dear, I can scarcely guide the pencil . . . For the last twenty-four hours, since your letter came, I have been praying in an agony to our Blessed Lady . . . to get me the strength which I need to answer you, my darling . . . To her I gave you so long ago, and whenever during all these weary years I have been tempted to faint, I have gone straight to her . . . I have never asked her to give you back, never asked her to put it into your heart to write to me; I simply told her that she knew it all—she who knows what it is to love her Only One with a love

beyond our comprehension. . . . I told her that I trusted her, and would always trust her; and that I knew she would keep you safe. And lately, when I knew that I was failing fast, I told her that I freely gave up all hope, the last hope, of ever hearing from you, or ever knowing that you cared . . .

In all my life I have had four great loves: my mother; my sister, Bessie; your mother—and your sister, Mary Cornelia. And I think the last was the greatest. Her's was the name which I wrote upon the sand, and which the waves washed out. It was not of her mother I was thinking. And I used to fancy that some day I might publish the verses in a book, and that at last some day, when I should be long gone, and almost forgotten, she might come across the book, and might light upon the verses, and wonder whose the name could have been, and might come to the conclusion that it was probably her mother's—and she would be mistaken . . .

And you, my daughter, how is it that after all these long years . . . you should suddenly without warning take the place in my poor heart which no one had ever really filled? . . . Our dear Lord, through His Blessed Mother, gave you to me, as His best earthly gift, unasked for, undreamed of, a gift that more than makes up for all that ever was, or was ever lost. I desire no more. I die happy . . . .[16]

Joy came at last to Kent Stone. Mary Frances came to Chicago to take her father back to San Mateo, California, for a visit with Cornelia, now Mrs. Charles de Cazotte, Cornelia's son, Michael, and herself. Father Fidelis spent a quiet, happy summer with his children. He was preparing to return to the Passionist monastery in Chicago when he died calmly on October 14, the Eve of the Feast of St. Teresa, whom he loved. He died with the children around him whom he had lost for fifty years. He had dreamed of religious vocations for his children and of years of spiritual communion with them. When he saw the impossibility of all he longed for, he accepted his destiny in the will of God. He suffered heroically; he never wavered.

The life of Kent Stone was both a tragedy and a spiritual triumph. Frances Warde suffered with him, particularly in the years of his youthful conversion. Viewing his life from the vantage point of one hundred years, one feels a sense of tragic waste as well as spiritual fulfillment. The wisdom of the terms of the adoption of Cornelia and Mary Frances Stone was less questionable in 1870 than now. It is idle to speculate concerning the possible lives of little Nellie and Mamie had they remained with Frances Warde at Mount St. Mary's in Manchester. Mother Frances' training might have brought to completion the promise which filled the heart of the young Kent Stone with joy. The name on the sand might never have been washed away at Miramar on Valparaiso Bay.

16

On to the Far West:
California; Maine Once Again and Vermont

In 1870, the year she met Kent Stone, Frances Warde reached the age of sixty. If she had not been so extraordinary a person, the intensity of her apostolic involvement would indeed have lessened. As a matter of fact, it increased. The eighteen-seventies were perhaps the decade of her greatest service to the people of America. With the establishment of her foundation in Bangor, Maine, in 1865, Frances had extended her mission of Mercy to the far eastern shores of the United States. She had sent her Sisters as far west as Omaha in 1864, but not yet to the Pacific Coast. The Sisters of Mercy had been established in San Francisco in 1854, however, by Mother Baptist Russell and a volunteer group of eight Sisters from the Convent of Mercy in Kinsale, Ireland.

Like most American Mercy convents, the foundation in San Francisco was related in its origins to Frances Warde. Father Hugh Gallagher, the priest who welcomed the Pittsburgh Sisters of Mercy to the mountain mission of Loretto, Pennsylvania, in 1848, had gone to California in 1852 at the call of Joseph Alemany, appointed in 1849 as Bishop of the entire state of California. Alemany became the first Archbishop of San Francisco in 1853. He asked Gallagher to go to Dublin to seek Sisters of Mercy to serve in the cities of San Francisco and Sacramento. Knowing the courage of the Pittsburgh Sisters of Mercy during their struggles and hardships in the mountains of Loretto, Father Gallagher thought that to bring the Sisters of Mercy from Pittsburgh would be wiser than to seek Sisters of Mercy in Ireland. But Alemany knew that St. Mary's Convent in Pittsburgh could not spare Sisters at the time,[1] and so he sent Gallagher to the "fountain-head" in Dublin. The Baggot Street Sisters directed him to Kinsale in the County of Cork.

The San Francisco foundation soon became a center of Mercy on the West Coast. During the devastating epidemics of cholera and smallpox in the fifties, sixties, and seventies, the Sisters served the victims day and night. They operated the pioneer City and County Hospital of San Francisco, and in 1855 they established St. Mary's, the first Catholic hospital in the Far West. The Sisters served the people of San Francisco during the terror of the Vigilantes in 1856; visited and instructed prisoners at San Quentin Penitentiary; opened the first home for unwed mothers in the West, the first Catholic home for the aged, and five of the first Catholic schools in the Archdiocese of San Francisco. Mother Baptist Russell, the leader of these pioneer religious, was the sister of Sir Charles Russell of Killowen, the last Attorney-General of British Prime Minister William Gladstone. She was called the "Mother of the Poor" by the slum dwellers of San Francisco.

Frances Warde, however, was to make her personal contribution to the saga of Mercy in California. In 1860, the Vicariate of Marysville was established in Northern California with Eugene O'Connell as its first Vicar Apostolic. Six years later, this Vicariate became the Diocese of Grass Valley, with O'Connell as its first Bishop. Late in 1870, Frances Warde, whose fame had spread as a founder of Convents of Mercy which fulfilled their mission even under the most desperate circumstances, received a letter in Manchester from Bishop Eugene O'Connell in far-off California. He requested that she open a day and boarding school for girls in the town of Yreka, the most northern town in the State, on the Oregon border. Yreka is situated in the Cascade Mountain Range, not far from Mount Shasta. Today it is a charming small town surrounded by hills with valleys beyond. In 1870 it was a once-prosperous, worked-out mining town.

Yreka was a challenge to Frances Warde. There were many reasons why she was not at first eager to send her Sisters there. Although travel across the United States was less hazardous in 1870 than during the fifties and sixties, such a journey was still a dangerous undertaking. The request for Sisters came, moreover, in the depth of winter. Finally, there was a debt of $20,000 on the California property purchased for the Sisters' convent and school. The *Annals* of the Sisters of Mercy reveal Frances' reluctance to found a mission in Yreka. Perhaps Bishop Eugene O'Connell provides the clue as to why she finally agreed to the venture. Like so many of the Christian apostles with whom Frances Warde was associated in works of mercy, O'Connell was undoubtedly a man of God. Frances did not know him personally, but copies of his letters to her are preserved. He was the type of man to arouse the zeal for the people of God which was Frances' deepest motivation:

Someone has left a portrait of Bishop O'Connell as he looked toward the close of his eventful career. It is a masterpiece. To anyone who has closely followed this patriarch's life of trials, labor, and sorrow, the spell is indefinable; and even to those who did not know him, there must appear in that chiseled countenance a reflection of the inner working of a self-sacrificing spirit. His deep-set eyes seem to be appealing to you to tell him whether life is as complicated to you as it has been to him, at the same time that they seem to be endeavoring to pierce the mystery of the future. Lines of wistfulness furrow a determined mouth, as if he would convey a silent message to the priests who are still carrying on in the rugged hill country he loved . . . whispering to them never to depart from the spirit of their predecessors who blazed the trail for the Church of Christ . . . He radiated a graciousness which made everyone feel at home in his presence.[2]

Eugene O'Connell wrote from across a continent to Frances Warde, telling her of the need for the Gospel of Christ among the people of "the rugged hill country he loved." And she answered yes. In a few weeks, her plans were completed. Frances chose four professed Sisters, one novice, and two postulants from among the Sisters who volunteered to go West. Selected as their leader was Sister Camillus McGarr, a remarkable woman whom Frances chose with unerring insight. One of her sisters was Sister Stanislaus McGarr, who had established the Convent of Mercy at Batavia, New York, from the Rochester, New York, Convent founded by Frances Warde. Another of her sisters was Sister Francis de Sales McGarr, who volunteered to assume leadership of a group of Sisters in the rigorous Mercy mission in the town of Malone, upper New York State. Sister Stanislaus later joined Sister Francis de Sales on the Indian mission of the Sisters of Mercy in Hogansburg, New York. Because of the former's long years of work on the St. Regis Indian Reservation, she was called the Apostle of Mercy among the Indians of New York State. All three of the McGarr sisters of Albany were received into the Manchester Community by Frances Warde. Accompanying Sister Camillus McGarr to Yreka were Sister Helena Dickson, who came to Manchester from Canada; Sister Monica Delaney, from Ireland; and Sister Pauline Whelan.

These Sisters were met in Omaha, Nebraska, by their future pastor, Patrick Farley. He accompanied them to Marysville, California, where they were welcomed with joy by Eugene O'Connell on January 30, 1871. The next day, O'Connell wrote to Frances Warde:

Yesterday afternoon, our Sisters arrived in Marysville . . . Thank God! And after God, my best thanks to you, dear Mother. They all seemed to be in good health and spirits, and as far as I can judge, correspond with the high recommendations which you gave each of them. I thought to prevail on them . . . to rest for a few days; but, as they were bent on reaching the Yrekans before the Feast of the Purification, I was obliged to yield to their request and let them go the same day! . . . So far, dear Mother, I hope you are satisfied . . . Again and again may God pour His blessings upon you all that remain; may these whom in your charity you sent us produce abundant fruit, and may their fruit remain . . . .[3]

The California *Annals* of the Sisters of Mercy reveal that the journey from Marysville to Yreka, in far northern California, was the most hazardous part of the trip from Manchester: "We have not the remotest idea of the hardships on that long cold journey made in winter on a lumbering stage coach, the only means of traveling the 170 miles between Tehama, the nearest railroad town, and Yreka, the County seat of mountainous Siskiyou." The annalist continues: "The Sisters set out northward, arriving in Yreka late on the evening of February 2, 1871. Cold, tired, and weary after the long stage coach ride over mountains and valleys, snow and ice, through streams where there were no bridges . . ."[4]

Yreka shared the lot of all California mining towns whose mines were almost completely worked out in the seventies.

Large numbers of its inhabitants had gone in search of new fields of labor and scenes of adventure. The Sisters' convent, a converted residence, was poor as Frances Warde's foundations usually were. The house was almost bare. By degrees, furniture was procured. The school offered a more hopeful future. Built by a committee of businessmen of Yreka, it promised to accommodate seventy boarders and over 100 day students. The citizens were happy to have a first-class academy in their town. Soon student applications were received from Surprise Valley, a hundred miles away, from Redding, and from even more remote points. St. Joseph Academy was opened February 13, 1871. The curriculum was superior. Despite the remote location of Yreka, the school promised to prosper.

Tragedy struck Yreka on July 4, 1871, when a destructive fire broke out, destroying a large part of the town, including St. Joseph Church and Patrick Farley's rectory. The convent and the school were only slightly damaged. Eugene O'Connell hastened to write to Frances Warde:

At the conflagration, the citizens turned out "en masse" and by almost superhuman efforts succeeded in saving the convent. May they all obtain Mercy from God in return for their exertions to save the Sisters of Mercy.[5]

The people of Yreka had scarcely recovered from disaster by fire when, in November of the following year, the Modoc Indian War broke out in Northern California. Yreka, the center of the southern route to the Modoc Lava Beds, was in close and active contact with the war zone. The lives of the townspeople of Yreka were under continual threat from November, 1872 until June, 1873. The young son of a prominent Yrekan family was brutally murdered by the Modocs.

The Sisters went to sleep at night dreading what might happen to their neighbors before morning. Often they wished they had never left New Hampshire. Finally, in the summer of 1873, peace was restored. Young girls now came to offer themselves as Sisters of Mercy, and St. Joseph's Academy flourished.

Mines continued to close, however, in Northern California; the heavy debt on the Sisters' property was difficult to meet; and the cost of living was high in remote Yreka. Attendance at the school eventually began to fall off. Protestant bigotry among a minority of the population, moreover, became strong and troublesome in the town. The Sisters frequently received anonymous letters urging them to leave town or see their convent burned down. By the spring of 1876, Sister Camillus McGarr came to the decision that she would no longer continue to struggle in Yreka. On the invitation of Archbishop Alemany to open a school in Rio Vista, a town halfway between San Francisco and Sacramento, she asked for volunteers to accompany her. Three Sisters agreed to do so, and five remained in Yreka.

On November 15, 1876, the Convent of Mercy in Rio Vista was opened by Sister Camillus McGarr and her companions. A day school for boys and girls was opened at once, and soon after, a boarding school for girls, St. Gertrude's Academy. The latter school was amazingly successful. More than twenty-five years later, a boarding academy for boys was opened by the Sisters in Rio Vista. The demands made upon Sister Camillus McGarr and her community at this time were met by a providential occurrence which was linked, almost uncannily, with the apostolate of Frances Warde.

Back in February, 1871, precisely one month after Frances had sent her Sisters from Manchester to Yreka, the New

York Sisters of Mercy sent a foundation to Eureka, Humboldt County, Northern California. Eureka is on the extreme West Coast of the State, forming a triangle with Yreka to the north and Red Bluff to the southeast. The Sister who led the mission to Eureka was none other than Sister Gertrude Ledwith, the British nun from Staffordshire whom Frances Warde had invited to lead the Mercy foundation from Manchester to Philadelphia ten years earlier, but who arrived in America too late for the venture.[6] St. Joseph's Convent at Eureka did not prosper long, and after about ten years the community disbanded. A small number of the Eureka Sisters, led by Mother Josephine Cummings, opened a school at Ukiah, a town close to the Pacific Coast, about halfway between San Francisco and Eureka, and close to the present Fort Bragg. Precisely when the Rio Vista Sisters from Yreka needed reinforcements for the opening of St. Joseph Academy in 1903, the Mercy Sisters of Ukiah, who had labored long and selflessly with the Indians of Northern California, asked to be incorporated with the Mercy Sisters of Rio Vista. The threads of Frances Warde's apostolic penetration into California were now beginning to unite in miraculous fashion, but the union was not yet complete. During the first half of the present century, St. Gertrude's and St. Joseph's Academies were among the finest elementary and secondary schools on the West Coast. The Rio Vista Sisters also opened another beautiful academy, Mount Carmel, in Sausolito, north of San Francisco. And in 1917 the Sisters of Mercy of Rio Vista were incorporated with the San Francisco Sisters of Mercy, closing a major link which united the Mercy foundations of San Francisco, Yreka, Rio Vista, Eureka, and Ukiah.

The five Sisters who remained at Yreka when Sister Camillus McGarr led her little band to Rio Vista were meanwhile developing their own chapter of Mercy history in California. Young ladies entered the Congregation, and for a time the work of the Sisters was fruitful, but the town continued to decline. Efforts to clear the property of the Sisters of debt were unsuccessful. Finally, in 1881, Patrick Manogue, newly appointed Coadjutor Bishop of Grass Valley, arranged for the Sisters of Mercy remaining in Yreka to move to Red Bluff, a town about 200 miles south of Yreka. Sister Helena Dickson was the leader of the mission to Red Bluff. A Canadian convert to Catholicism, she carried with her to Red Bluff a copy of the Holy Rule of the Sisters of Mercy and a little silver bell that Frances Warde had given to her on leaving Manchester.

"On December 3, 1881," relates the Red Bluff annalist, "when the only train that came to the northern part of the Sacramento Valley rolled into Red Bluff at four o'clock in the morning, four Sisters alighted at the station. By some misunderstanding, the pastor failed to have anyone there to meet them . . . ." The pattern was significant for an establishment of Frances Warde's Sisters. The beginnings were poor. But the Academy of Our Lady of Mercy and St. Elizabeth's Hospital at Red Bluff were destined to flourish for one hundred years. The apostolate of mercy of the Red Bluff Sisters extended throughout Northern California. They were among the first Sisters to teach religious summer schools. Interestingly enough, they returned to Yreka after 1914 to teach Christian Doctrine there. Somehow, Frances Warde's foundations did not die!

In 1930, the Red Bluff Sisters joined the Sisters of Mercy of the Union. They became a part of the far-flung Province of Omaha. Frances Warde's work of mercy in the West had now come full circle: her Omaha, Yreka, and Red Bluff daughters were united. And her Rio Vista Sisters were united with the San Francisco Congregation of Mercy. Meanwhile, the Grass Valley Sisters of Mercy founded from San Francisco had become part of the Omaha Province, and the San Diego, Los Angeles, and Phoenix Sisters of Mercy were incorporated with the San Francisco Congregation. Frances Warde did not live to see the weaving of all the threads of the Mercy foundations in the West. But even in her own lifetime, she was astonished to watch the expansion of the mysterious pattern of Mercy. Often she must have remembered Catherine McAuley's words:

When God institutes a religious Order, He gives at the same time the grace that is necessary for such an Order and for all those that are called to it . . . None can attribute to themselves the success that may attend their exertions, because it is the fruit which God intended to produce when He instituted the Order . . . .[7]

Back in Manchester, Frances Warde followed eagerly the early expansion of her California mission. But she was far from idle in the East. As early as 1865, when Bishop David William Bacon had asked her to establish the Sisters of Mercy in Bangor, Maine, he had also begged for a mission to North Whitefield, Maine, a town three hundred miles from Boston and not far from Gardiner, the "Tilbury Town" made famous by Edwin Arlington Robinson. Bacon wished the Sisters to open a home for orphan girls there. North Whitefield had an interesting historical background.

In 1810 Pope Pius VII had appointed John Cheverus the first Bishop of Boston with jurisdiction over all New England. Seven years later, when Denis Ryan was ordained first priest in the New England diocese, he was made pastor of Whitefield because Whitefield was then the center of Catholicity in New England. In this little town on the

Sheepscot River is the second oldest Catholic Church in New England, St. Denis, dedicated by Bishop Cheverus in 1822.

Early in 1871, James Peterson, then Pastor of St. Denis, was preparing a convent and academy for the Sisters of Mercy in North Whitefield. Winifred Kavanagh of Damariscotta, granddaughter of Andrew Jackson and sister of Edward Kavanagh, first Catholic Governor of Maine and later Ambassador to Portugal, had donated land with a house and orchard and offered financial aid for the establishment of the Sisters of Mercy in North Whitefield. Frances Warde appointed five Sisters for the new venture, including Sister Gertrude McConville, a cousin of the Kavanagh family.

In May, 1871, Mother Frances accompanied her Sisters to Maine to found the Academy that soon earned the reputation of "the best convent school in the State of Maine." A home for orphan girls was also opened on the property given by the Kavanaghs. The local school board, moreover, invited the Sisters to teach at Public School No. 13 under State supervision. New Hampshire had accepted the Sisters of Mercy as public school teachers ten years earlier, and now Maine did the same in Protestant New England! The North Whitefield establishment differed in its origins from the great majority of Frances Warde's works: because of the largesse of Winifred Kavanagh, it did not have its roots in poverty.

During the early part of the following year, 1872, Frances Warde received a letter which suddenly recalled to her mind memories of a quarter of a century earlier. Louis de Goesbriand, Bishop of Burlington, Vermont, requested Sisters of Mercy for his school in the parish of Notre Dame des Victoires in St. Johnsbury, on the northeastern border of Vermont. Frances' imagination was crowded at once with pictures

362

from the past. Back in 1846, when she was making the return trip from her Chicago foundation to Pittsburgh that almost cost her life, she had braved a blinding snow storm to participate in the Celebration of the Eucharist at the only Catholic Church in Toledo. The thirty-year-old priest who offered the Sacrifice had responded immediately to the glad courage of the unknown young woman kneeling before the altar. Though she wore secular dress, he had recognized her as a Sister and invited her to his rectory for breakfast. The two had become friends at once. Now, as Bishop of Burlington, de Goesbriand desired her to establish her Sisters in his Diocese. Frances' answer was immediate and enthusiastic. She would take her Sisters personally to the Diocese of the saintly man who would be her friend until death.

Louis de Goesbriand, now in his fifties, had already merited a reputation for holiness. Born at the de Goesbriand Castle of Lanurven in Saint Urbain, Brittany, he might have been a nobleman, for his father was the Marquis Henri de Goesbriand and his mother Emilie de Bergean. Ordained at Saint Sulpice in Paris, he had gone to America to serve in the Diocese of Cincinnati for seven years and then as Vicar General under his friend, Bishop Amadeus Rappe. When the State of Vermont was separated from the immense Diocese of Boston in 1853, de Goesbriand was consecrated Bishop of Burlington. Like Frances Warde's, his vision of the Church in America was ahead of that of his contemporaries. He sometimes startled the American hierarchy with his penetrating ideas. Once, for example, he wrote the following surprising letter to Archbishop Martin John Spalding:

I should be glad to see someone preach a spiritual retreat to Bishops. I would certainly attend it. I do not know that it is ever done. If the thing were possible, I know it would be productive of much good.

We have had in America such a poor home to prepare ourselves, that lectures upon the episcopal office would prove I am sure very useful—Pardonnez moi, Monseigneur![8]

De Goesbriand's office of Bishop was more than challenging. When he went to Vermont in 1853, Know-Nothingism was rampant there. The people of Burlington gave him a chilling reception. Shortly after his arrival, his effigy was burned at an assembly of citizens. But he did not allow himself to be intimidated. Like Frances Warde, he devoted himself always to the poor and the suffering. As Bishop, he served in the Vermont missions just as his youngest priests did. During the fierce Vermont winters, he wore a buffalo robe to keep from freezing while hearing Confessions. Once, on a distant mission, his face actually became paralyzed from exposure to cold. As a young nobleman, de Goesbriand had owned a private fortune of $1,000,000. He often wrote personal letters to the priests of his Diocese, all of whom were poor, and he usually enclosed a bank note. A Bishop deeply loved by his priests, he died leaving no will. He needed none. He owned only $2.12 which was found in his pocket after he died.

There was a special reason why Bishop de Goesbriand desired to have Frances Warde's Sisters at the parish school of Notre Dame de Victoires in St. Johnsbury. When he was made Bishop, he dedicated his entire episcopate to God under the patronage of the Virgin Mary. His first act in his new Diocese he recorded in his *Diary* in 1853: "Said the Angelus at 12:00 in the railroad cars crossing the Connecticut River at Bellows Falls." He also dedicated the City of Burlington to Christ under the patronage of Mary and later consecrated its new Cathedral of the Immaculate Conception on December 8, 1867. During his first year as Bishop, de Goesbriand visited St. Johnsbury and offered the Holy Sacrifice there. He made a promise that he would complete the Church of Notre Dame des Victoires and appoint a resident pastor for the people of St. Johnsbury. Within four years, the church was finished and Stanislaus Danielou was appointed Pastor. The people of St. Johnsbury were very poor, however, and not until 1872 did Father Danielou even attempt to establish a parochial school. When he finally proposed the idea to de Goesbriand, the Bishop thought immediately of Frances Warde and the Sisters of Mercy who served the Church under the patronage of Mary.

On July 19, 1872, Danielou wrote to Mother Frances: "I am trying to secure a few of your Sisters to take charge of our Catholic school in this growing and beautiful village . . . I am of the opinion that religious communities can answer for our Catholic youth."[9] On August 16, de Goesbriand recorded in his *Diary* that he went to Manchester to see Mother Frances and to arrange for the Sisters of Mercy to come to St. Johnsbury.[10] Four days later, he made a triumphant entry in his journal, stating that Frances and three of her Sisters had arrived in the Green Mountain State. Frances had already established far-flung Convents of Mercy in four New England States—Rhode Island, Connecticut, New Hampshire, and Maine. Now Vermont was added to her apostolate.

She chose as first Superior in Vermont a young woman of twenty-six, Sister Stanislaus O'Malley, who had made her vows only a year earlier. Her uncommon courage and patience qualified her for imminent hardships in northern New England. Father Danielou offered the Sisters his own house for their residence and promised to build a convent.

The parochial school was successful, but the poverty of the people of St. Johnsbury was great. In 1874, Father Danielou was reluctantly forced to close the school. When Bishop de Goesbriand heard that the Sisters of Mercy were returning to Manchester, he at once asked Frances Warde to send them to Burlington instead to teach in his own St. Mary's Cathedral School. The Sisters of Providence, who had conducted both the Cathedral School and the diocesan orphanage under great pressure, were now free to devote themselves to the orphans of the Burlington Diocese. For the expansion of the Mercy apostolate in Vermont, de Goesbriand could not have made a better move.

In 1874, the little city of Burlington, a lake port in a strategic location to tap the richest cities of Canada for the benefit of the Hudson River towns, was becoming a center of trade and transformation. After the construction of the Champlain Canal, Burlington formed a natural link between Canada and southern New York State. All along the lake front in the vicinity of Burlington, lumber which had been floated down from the Canadian forests in great rafts was prepared for market. Fleets of barges carried the lumber to docks in Albany and Troy. All types of manufacturing related to lumber sprang up. The poor, especially immigrants, came to Burlington to seek employment. The "poor farm" of the city was the chief institution that served the most unfortunate. It was a combination hospital, refuge for the aged, orphanage, pest house, and insane asylum. Burlington had private charitable institutions, too, but the workers were voluntary and therefore not always available. After 1874, the Sisters of Mercy were to serve the needy and the sick of the city as well as to educate the children of the poor.

With Sister Stanislaus O'Malley as their leader, four Sisters arrived in Burlington September 13, 1874, to take charge of St. Mary's Cathedral School of four hundred pupils and to care for the sick in their homes.[11] For one week, they lived in a tiny house on North Street which they playfully called "Thimble Castle." Next they lived for a year in a house on Pine Street, and then for another year on the third floor of the school, called "Old St. Mary's Hall." A year after their arrival, they opened a night school at St. Mary's for young people who worked in the factories during the day.

The pecuniary difficulties of these first Sisters in Burlington were comparable to those of the Sisters in Frances Warde's most poverty-stricken foundations. The work was heavy and the winters were harsh and long. Little markers in the Convent Cemetery at Burlington indicate that in Vermont, as in many early American Convents of Mercy, Sisters in their twenties died of tuberculosis because of the hardships they suffered in the service of their neighbors.

In 1876, the new St. Patrick's Convent in Burlington was finally ready for occupation. Frances Warde came from Manchester for the dedication of the new building. She came early to prepare three novices for their profession, which took place on the same day as the blessing of the Convent, Pentecost Sunday, June 4, 1876. At a Pontifical Mass in the Cathedral of Burlington, Bishop de Goesbriand preached on the Congregation of Mercy and its founder, Catherine McAuley. He proudly introduced his friend, Frances Warde, as one of Catherine's first companions. "You should feel honored," he told his parishioners, "to have her in your midst. Her daughters are now the adopted daughters of this Diocese, and they belong to us."[12] On the following day, the Burlington Convent of Mercy, which until then was a branch house of the Manchester Congregation, became an independent Mercy foundation. Sister Stanislaus O'Malley was appointed its first Mother Superior. Frances Warde returned joyfully to Manchester, her apostolic mission accomplished.

As in the case of her other foundations, the Sisters in Vermont continued to seek Mother Frances' counsel. She was always *the* Reverend Mother of the Mercy Sisters throughout America. In September, 1876, the Burlington Sisters opened an academy for day students at St. Patrick's Convent, and within two years they added a boarding school. Five years later, when the convent school became too small for its purpose, a new academy was contemplated. Sister Stanislaus was about to purchase property, and her financial problem was acute. On the verge of a critical decision, she wrote to Frances Warde for advice. Mother Frances' letter to her, dated February 2, 1882, is still preserved in Burlington. She urged Sister Stanislaus to trust Bishop de Goesbriand and to follow the plan suggested by him. Then she added:

Pray to our Divine Lord and our Blessed Mother to bless and direct you. Do not be too anxious. Please God all will yet be well . . . All that we can do at any time to aid you, you may count upon.[13]

Sister Stanislaus found the support she needed in her Manchester Superior. How wise Frances' advice was soon became evident. In February, 1882, the Burlington Sisters purchased property from Bishop de Goesbriand for $5,500. This land was sold at a gain of $7,600, and the Sisters thus were able to purchase property suitable for their new academy, built in 1885. To the joy of Frances Warde's Sisters in New Hampshire, it was called Mount St. Mary's in honor of the Mother House in Manchester. In this fourth Mount St. Mary's, Carlow and Westport and Manchester came to life again in 1885 in Vermont.

The apostolate of the Sisters of Mercy in Vermont developed with the same miraculous fruitfulness that became almost predictable for Frances Warde's foundations. The Sisters opened many parish schools throughout Vermont—in Burlington, Montpelier, Barre, White River Junction, and Middlebury. Vacation and catechetical schools were established throughout the State. Just as the Mercy Sisters in Red Bluff, California, eventually went back to their first home in Yreka to teach the Word of God, so the Burlington Sisters went back to St. Johnsbury to teach Christian Doctrine. The line of life that joined Frances Warde's missions seemed never to be completely broken at any point. When the Vermont Sisters of Mercy opened Trinity College in Burlington in 1925, another chapter was written in the amazing history of Frances' mission to New England.

While the Sisters of Mercy in Vermont were developing their New England apostolate during the seventies, Frances Warde was characteristically turning her eyes to new fields white for the harvest. The State of New Jersey was virgin territory for her. She could not see the people of God in need in any region without turning to them with loving care.

17

Spreading the Good News in New Jersey: Jersey City, Bordentown

THE apostolic work of Frances Warde in the eighteen-seventies was phenomenal. It is probable that at this period in her life a larger number of Bishops and priests applied to her for the services of Sisters than to any other religious leader in the United States. Requests came to her from everywhere in America. The name of "Mother Warde" was synonymous with the fruitful service of the poor and the sick and the education of children and adults. The numbers of adult non-Catholics received into the Catholic Church after participating in Frances Warde's Christian Doctrine classes continued to multiply.

After her California and Vermont ventures, Frances gave her thoughts to a request for a Mercy foundation from Bishop James Roosevelt Bayley of the Diocese of Newark, which then included the entire state of New Jersey. It was difficult for Frances to refuse James Bayley, a convert from the Protestant Episcopal Church, a former President of St. John's College, New York (now Fordham University), and a founder of Seton Hall University. Bayley belonged to the families of the late Franklin Delano Roosevelt and of Elizabeth Seton, founder of the Sisters of Charity. Sister Catherine Joseph Seton of the New York Sisters of Mercy, daughter of Elizabeth Seton, was a friend of Frances Warde. The parish of St. Patrick, South Bergan (now Jersey City), had requested Sisters of Mercy for a parochial school through its pastor, Patrick Hennessy.

By 1872, New York City was already stretching its urban extremities east to Long Island, north to the Bronx, and west across the Hudson River to the Jersey shore. New towns were springing up; old ones were growing. Jersey City was part of the suburban movement. Father Hennessy of St. Patrick's built a new church in his new parish with an eye to the future: its seating capacity was two thousand; its cost was $300,000; its debt was unbelievable. The proposed parish school was the basement of the new church, divided neatly into classrooms. Hennessy intended to build a school within two years. According to her custom, Frances Warde planned to establish an academy for girls in the new Mercy convent to secure a livelihood for the Sisters. She chose a "mystical seven" Sisters for the Jersey City foundation.

With characteristic unselfishness, Frances prepared to part with her most promising Sisters. The leader of the New Jersey mission was a most unusual young woman. Mary Wade had come alone from Galway City in the summer of 1868 to enter the Manchester, New Hampshire, Congregation under Frances Warde. She carried with her an appealing letter from her spiritual director, Patrick Kiernan, a Jesuit. He wrote to Mother Frances,[1] whom he admired from afar, in a manner reminiscent of St. Paul's Epistle to Philemon:

> College House
> Galway City
> June 21, 1868

Dear Reverend Mother:

Miss Mary Wade will present this to you and with it herself, to become your spiritual daughter in the Lord, and if she is as obedient to you as she has been to me, I shall never regret having asked you to adopt her as such. Nor, I hope, will you have cause

371

to regret having granted me the favor. I have known her well and long and have been edified by her virtues and instructed by her example; if in the midst of the world and entangled in its cares, she has given such promise, what may not be hoped for from her when under your guidance in the great Order of Mercy?

To your care then and protection I commend her, hoping that in your home and heart she will never find cause to mourn for the home she has left and for the fond hearts that loved her here. On the contrary, I hope she will rejoice because she was made for the happiness I am sure she will enjoy with you and her future Sisters, a happiness which must be a foretaste of the happiness of heaven. I sincerely hope that she will be a source of joy to you. Do not, I pray you, forget that it will be calm and gladness to my heart to hear that she has realized the hope I have entertained for her for so long.

And amid those cares of which only those in the sacred ministry can tell, what consolation it will be to me to know that one of my spiritual children has merited the approval of you who hold the place of God's representative in her regard.

I send you by Miss Wade a little reliquary, of itself worthless but priceless because of the relics of St. Thomas of Villanova, St. Leonard of Port Maurice, and St. Paul of the Cross. The case is a little tarnished owing to its never being off my person since I got it, and perhaps never would be were it not that I feel I have nothing more valuable of which I could beg your acceptance.

Again commending my dear child to your care and love and begging a remembrance in your prayers,

> I am, dear Reverend Mother,
> Most sincerely yours in Christ,
> P. Kiernan, S.J.

Mary Wade was destined to prove herself worthy of Patrick Kiernan's hopes for her.

Frances Warde accompanied the seven chosen Sisters to

Jersey City. The parochial school and the academy were opened as planned. But Frances was deeply concerned for her young Sisters. They were scantily provided for and poorly housed. Frances returned to Manchester fearful for their future. Her only comfort was that Sister Regis, Mary Wade, would do all in her power to support them.

St. Patrick's Convent in Jersey City was opened as a branch house of Mount St. Mary's in Manchester rather than as an independent foundation. At first, Frances Warde had hoped to establish a mother house in Jersey City. Circumstances prevented the fulfillment of her desire. In 1872, Bishop Bayley was appointed Archbishop of Baltimore, and in 1873 Michael A. Corrigan, later Bishop of New York, became the second Bishop of Newark. Bishop Bayley had introduced the Congregation of the Sisters of Charity of St. Elizabeth into Newark in 1859. When Frances Warde petitioned Bishop Corrigan in 1873 to declare the Convent of Mercy in New Jersey to be an independent foundation, he replied: "I cannot permit the erection of another Novitiate until the Sisters of Charity are solidly established."[2] A similar request from Sister Regis Wade in 1874 received the same negative answer. A mother house of the Sisters of Mercy was finally established in 1877 at Bordentown, New Jersey. For these historical reasons, the Sisters of Mercy teach in the Dioceses of Trenton and Camden today, but not in that of Newark.

Bordentown became the site of Frances Warde's second New Jersey convent in the fall of 1873. While her Sisters were still struggling through their first year at St. Patrick's School and the Academy of Mercy in Jersey City, Bishop Corrigan invited Frances to establish a convent and school in Bordentown. It is fascinating to speculate as to why, with the innumerable requests for Sisters of Mercy that continually reached her in Manchester, Frances chose to extend her apostolate to a second New Jersey mission only a year after she had introduced her Sisters into Jersey City under such difficult circumstances. In 1872, she had responded to appeals from Yreka, California, because of the great needs of the people served by the Christlike Eugene O'Connell; from North Whitefield, Maine, because of her friendship for the saintly Bishop David Bacon of whose Diocese the Manchester convent was a part; and from Jersey City both because the State of New Jersey was virgin territory for her works of mercy and because of the entreaties of James Roosevelt Bayley. But why Bordentown?

In making Mercy foundations in Chicago, Providence, Hartford, Philadelphia, and Omaha, Frances Warde had demonstrated that she had a sharp eye for cities and towns that eventually would become great population centers, and therefore great apostolic centers for the spread of the Gospel of Christ and for the care of His poor. The truth is that quaint little Bordentown, New Jersey, in the third quarter of the nineteenth century, gave promise of spectacular growth and expansion which it did not achieve because of subsequent industrial and economic circumstances. Bordentown's past in 1873 boasted as magnificent a history as any town in the United States. An annalist of the New Jersey Sisters of Mercy wrote with perspicuity:

How could one think of writing anything interesting about Bordentown? This view may be acceptable as far as ordinary opinions go, especially when little more than a lingering sentiment remains of the glowing and passionate picture of bygone days.[3]

Frances Warde had heard of the glory of Bordentown in the early nineteenth century. If the town failed to become the great city it promised to be, Frances was not alone in her speculations concerning it. And with her customary intuitive feeling for the future, she was not wrong in choosing Bordentown as the nucleus for a fruitful Mercy foundation in New Jersey. Perhaps she realized that the Jersey City Convent of Mercy lacked the necessary qualifications for apostolic growth. In any case, Bordentown provided the roots for one of her finest Mercy foundations. Jersey City did not.

When Frances came to Bordentown in 1873, it was a two-hundred-year-old thriving center between New York and Philadelphia, "located just below Trenton where the Delaware crooks its elbow to gather more sunsets." This little Colonial town was founded in 1682 by Thomas Farnsworth, a Quaker, who called his eight hundred acres "Farnsworth's Landing." Thirty-five years later, Joseph Borden came down from New England to acquire this beautiful site. He established a stage line at Bordentown, connecting New York and Philadelphia by packet and stage coach. Soon the town became an inland trading and shipping port to which goods were brought from England and from which products were carried on sloops to Philadelphia and Burlington. In his *Autobiography*, Benjamin Franklin tells of staying overnight at Joseph Brown's Inn in Bordentown during his famous foot journey from Boston to Philadelphia. In 1762, a ferry was established between the town and the opposite shore of the Delaware. Rivermen stopped at the Bordentown taverns on their way to the Quaker City. Hessians were quartered there, and Continental regulars passed through. In the nineteenth century, the town boasted a fine Opera House. *Rip Van Winkle, East Lynne,* and *The Gay New Yorker* were performed there.

Frances Warde knew of the famous personalities who had lived in Bordentown. Thomas Paine once owned a home at

Main Street and Graveyard Alley. He wrote to London: "I had rather see my horse, Button, eating the grass of Bordentown, than see all the pomp and show of Europe." Francis Hopkinson, signer of the Declaration of Independence, and author of *The Battle of the Kegs,* lived in Bordentown. So did Joseph Hopkinson, artist, judge, and author of "Hail Columbia." Thomas Buchanan Reed, poet; Richard Watson Gilder, poet and editor of the *Century* magazine; F. Marion Crawford, popular novelist; and Clara Barton, founder of the American Red Cross and of the Public School System of New Jersey—all lived in this picturesque town. So did politicians and military geniuses. For example, Rear Admiral Charles Stewart, Commander of the famous frigate, *Constitution,* lived in a beautiful home, Montpelier, in Bordentown. His grandson, Charles Stewart Parnell, became the tragic Irish patriot and leader of the Irish Home Rule Party in the British Parliament.

Bordentown was known, too, for great days in steam navigation and rail locomotion. Nineteen years before Robert Fulton's steamboat, *Clermont,* plied the Hudson River, John Fitch guided his own steamboat from Philadelphia to Bordentown. And in 1831, Robert Stevens, founder of the Camden and Amboy Railroad, steered his famous *Engine No. 1,* or *John Bull,* on its first trip from White Hill to Bordentown. Construction of shops along the Delaware River front, beginning in 1832, employed hundreds of men in building locomotives and passenger coaches.

Frances Warde knew the history of Bordentown. She desired to serve its immigrant workers and their families. She was fascinated, too, with the colorful background of Bordentown's most famous personality of all—the man who gave the town the reputation of entertaining more world-famous personalities than any town in America. Joseph Bonaparte, Count

376

de Survilliers, ex-King of Naples and Spain, brother of Napoleon Bonaparte, came to Bordentown to live in 1816. After Waterloo, he knew that his brother's star had set. He purchased one thousand acres in Bordentown, where he built a magnificent mansion called "Point Breeze." Here also lived his son, Prince Charles, and his daughters, Princess Zenaide and Princess Charlotte Julie, who exhibited her paintings at the Pennsylvania Academy of Fine Arts. Among Joseph Bonaparte's guests at Bordentown were Lafayette, Napoleon III, Talleyrand, and Walter Scott. And among the Americans he entertained were Henry Clay, Daniel Webster, and John Quincy Adams. A deputation from Mexico came to Bordentown to offer Joseph Bonaparte the crown of that country after the termination of the power of the Emperor Augustin de Iturbide in 1823. The Count refused the honor. He went to England in 1832, returned to America in 1837, went abroad again in 1839, and died in Florence in 1844, Frances Warde's first year in America. He left his estate in Bordentown to his eldest son, Prince Joseph Lucien. A later owner of the property, "Henry Beckett the Destroyer," tore down the Bonaparte mansion.

In 1842, a lot was purchased on the "Hill Top" overlooking the Delaware River for the first Catholic Church in Bordentown. The new St. Mary's was built at Second and Bank Streets. In 1869 Father Patrick Leonard came to Bordentown as Pastor, and in 1872 he completed a second new church on Crosswicks Street. The following year he invited Frances Warde, through Bishop Corrigan, to bring her Sisters to Bordentown to open a school on the "Hill Top" in the old church building. A new rectory had also been built, and he offered the old pastoral residence as a convent. Not far from this convent-to-be stood "Linden Hall," a once-famous private school in Bordentown. Here Joachim Murat, sometime King of Sicily, had lived with his wife, Caroline Bonaparte, sister of the Emperor Napoleon. When Murat became "Prince Reckless" and lost all his money, Caroline opened "Linden Hall" as a select school where wealthy heiresses from the West Indies were educated. High up on the historic "Hill Top" of Bordentown, with a majestic view of miles of fertile farm land intersected by the waters of the Delaware, was the cradle of Frances Warde's first permanent foundation in New Jersey.

Frances responded to the beauty of the town, she responded to its fascinating history, but above all she responded to the plight of its poor Catholic immigrants who had come during the sixties to secure employment on its railroads and in its river-front shops.

On September 22, 1873, Frances left Manchester with five companions. Sister Joseph O'Donahoe was chosen as Superior of the new Convent of Mercy. The Sisters arrived in Bordentown, as planned, on the night of September 24, the Feast of Our Lady of Mercy. Second Street ran directly from the center of the town to a sudden end at the River Bluff. Miscellaneous pavements and dwellings, a canning factory as an interlude, and an abandoned cemetery ended with the Convent and a sudden breath-taking view of the Delaware. St. Mary's Convent was a small, plain, substantial house. Much humor attended the arrival of the Sisters. Father Leonard remembered suddenly that there was no mirror in the new convent. He sent his sexton to bring one from the rectory. When the latter appeared at the convent, holding the mirror in front of him, Sister Raymond O'Donahoe opened the door and saw herself! No one enjoyed the incident more than Frances Warde, who afterwards always included the story in the repertory that made her so delightful a conversationalist.

Across the lawn from the convent on the riverside was St.

Mary's School, the old Church building. It was converted easily into three main sections for classrooms. On the floor of this old building was a tombstone bearing the name of a scion of the Bonaparte family and the date 1821. By early October, St. Mary's Parochial School was well in progress. An academy, later called St. Joseph's, was opened in the Convent to help provide a livelihood for the Sisters.

Construction of the Amboy Railroad and the Delaware and Raritan Canal, with Bordentown as a terminal for both, brought settlers and traffic to the town. Also, the Pennsylvania Railroad shops along the river front employed hundreds of men. Boat-building, mills, pork-packing plants flourished. There was a need for the schools opened by the Sisters.

Frances Warde remained with her Sisters until the new mission was well established. She returned to Manchester, filled with deep concern for the Sisters in Bordentown as well as those in Jersey City. Despite the employment offered the Bordentown immigrants, wages were poor and so was St. Mary's Parish. The Sisters lacked many of the necessities of life. Frances sent them furniture and household articles from Manchester. She knew that the convent and the school, situated on the bluff of the Delaware, would be hot in summer and bitterly cold in winter. The convent had only a kitchen stove for heating. An outside pump offered the total water supply. The house had one wooden tub for all ablutions. Kerosene lamps and candles provided light. The night Frances Warde arrived in Bordentown, she had asked Father Leonard about the gas light she supposed would be provided. He replied that the gas installation "was coming up the street, but hadn't arrived yet." It did not arrive for thirteen years!

With the spirit of compassion that so marked her life, Frances Warde wrote to her Sisters in Bordentown during their first years: "Return to Manchester if you will." A council was held in the little convent on the "Hill Top." The

Sisters remembered the constant prayer of Frances: "The cross of Christ be always with us." They chose to remain in Bordentown and, like Catherine McAuley, "suffer with God's poor." Their care of the poor and the sick consoled them. In 1875, the carshops in Bordentown closed, and depression came to the little town. Men flocked to other towns to seek employment. Gloom came to St. Mary's and its people. But the Sisters persevered.

Frances Warde visited Bordentown frequently, and the Sisters were delighted with her presence. Her constant good cheer lifted their spirits. She spoke to them of the great things they would accomplish for Christ. She walked and talked with them in the garden beside St. Mary's Convent where she herself planted roses and lilies-of-the-valley. Flowers to make the Sisters happy were not expensive. They laid out garden paths covered with trellises of grapevine and morning glory. And on the charming "Hill Top" there were fruit trees —pear, apple, quince—and current and gooseberry bushes. In this lovely setting, Frances prophesied the future of the Sisters of Mercy in New Jersey, and characteristically her prophecy was to come true!

The Sisters in Jersey City, meanwhile, were not prospering so well. St. Patrick's School there and the Academy of Mercy were undoubtedly successful. But the immense debt on St. Patrick's Church led Father Patrick Hennessy to decide, in June, 1877, that he could no longer maintain the Sisters of Mercy or continue the parochial school. Hennessy met with strong opposition in his parish. Bishop Corrigan recorded in his *Diary:*

In order to retain the Sisters of Mercy, Mr. Hugh McKay made a proposal, through me, that he would donate to me in trust for the Sisters of Mercy five lots which he owns near the

Church, free of all encumbrance, provided a suitable academy and residence for the Sisters were built thereon, and that he would, moreover, advance the funds to erect the building. After much consultation and correspondence . . . it was finally decided that the offer would not be accepted.[4]

A delegation of the most prominent men of St. Patrick's Parish, meanwhile, visited the Convent to urge the Sisters to remain and carry on the work of the parochial school and the academy.

What went on behind the scenes when the Sisters of Mercy left Jersey City can be inferred without difficulty from historical sources. Father Hennessy did not tolerate opposition to his plans, even when his parishioners were as generous as the above statement of Bishop Corrigan intimates. Mercy tradition relates that one fine day the meager possessions of the Sisters of Mercy were put out on the sidewalk, and seven Sisters were left homeless on the street. The rent for the convent was unpaid. The Sisters moved themselves and their furniture to a few rooms offered by a kind parishioner.[5] The intrepid Frances Warde betook herself at once to Jersey City, berated Patrick Hennessy with the utmost frankness, and took her Sisters immediately back to Manchester.[9]

Patrick Hennessy did not fare well at the hands of New Jersey Church historians. Edwin V. Sullivan, in his *Annotated Diary of Bishop James Roosevelt Bayley,* stated:

[Reverend Patrick Hennessy] was loud in his praise of Bishop Bayley's *Pastoral on Education,* and yet in his long term at St. Patrick's, he did not build a school.[7]

Joseph M. Flynn, in *The Catholic Church in New Jersey,* was less kind to Hennessy:

St. Patrick's Parish enjoys the distinction of possessing the most perfect specimen of Gothic architecture in the Diocese of Newark, and another, less honorable, of being the only parish of any considerable size without a parish school.[8]

A parish school was not opened at St. Patrick's until 1924.

At the same time the Sisters of Mercy withdrew from Jersey City to Manchester with Frances Warde, in June, 1877, Bishop Corrigan announced that the Convent of Mercy in Bordentown was established as an independent mother house. Frances' desire for an actual foundation—not merely a branch house—in New Jersey was achieved at last.

Frances had apostolic work aplenty in Manchester for the seven Sisters who returned to Mount St. Mary's. Their life in Jersey City had been so severe that two of the original seven Sisters had died within five years. The returning seven had been completed in number with the addition of two more Sisters.

One year after the closing of the Jersey City convent, in 1878, the indomitable Frances Warde set out upon a third Mercy establishment in the State of New Jersey! This time the request for Sisters came from the college town of Princeton. Frances had several reasons, personal and apostolic, for accepting an invitation to conduct Mercy schools in Princeton.

St. Paul's Catholic Church in Princeton was founded in 1794 during the infancy of the American Republic. It antedated the creation of the Diocese of Newark by sixty years. Catholics from France and Belgium settled in Princeton as early as 1795. Fifty years later, the Irish Famine of 1846–47 brought Catholic immigrants to Princeton to seek employment in building railroads and barge canals. The university town became a cauldron of bitterest antipathy toward Roman Catholicism.

The first native pastor of St. Paul's Church was Alfred Young, a former Princeton student who, in the wake of the Oxford Tractarian Movement, became a Roman Catholic convert and a priest. Bishop James Roosevelt Bayley appointed him Pastor of St. Paul's in 1857, when at the age of twenty-six he asked to be released as Vice-President of Seton Hall University to become a simple parish priest. Father Young dreamed of becoming a missionary, and in 1861 he was released from his Princeton pastorate to join the Paulists. A gifted musician and writer, he became a friend of Father Kent Stone when the latter joined the Paulists in 1870. Through Kent Stone, Father Alfred Young also became a close friend of Frances Warde, and the three remained friends for life. The Sisters of Mercy in Manchester still preserve the beautiful tribute that Father Young wrote to Frances in 1883 on the celebration of her Golden Jubilee as a Sister of Mercy.

By a curious coincidence, the pastorate of St. Paul's in Princeton once held by Alfred Young was given to Thomas R. Moran in 1866. Moran was born in Dublin on the first Feast of Our Lady of Mercy, September 24, 1832. He was ordained in 1861 at St. Vincent's Seminary, Latrobe, the original site of St. Xavier Academy, founded by Frances Warde back in 1845. The Pittsburgh Sisters of Mercy maintained ever after a close relationship with the Benedictines of St. Vincent's Archabbey. Father Moran built a new St. Paul's Church in Princeton in 1869 and a rectory in 1871. He converted the old St. Paul's Church into a parochial school and the old priests' residence into a convent. In 1878 he wrote to Frances Warde, inviting her Sisters to take charge of St. Paul's School for 250 boys and girls and to care for the poor and sick of his parish.

Moran was an ecumenist far ahead of his time. He made friends of the Professors at Princeton and supported President James McCosh in his fight for just tax legislation and in all other matters of public concern and social reform. The *Princeton Press* hailed Moran as a true friend of the University, "always ready to render valuable service." He helped to break down feelings of misunderstanding between Roman Catholics and Protestants in Princeton during the seventies and eighties. Thomas Moran knew that Frances Warde, who had converted innumerable Americans to Roman Catholicism, and who had a widespread reputation for her understanding approach to Protestants that many Catholics of the seventies did not possess, was the ideal person to establish a convent and schools in the university town of Princeton.

Frances was delighted to receive Moran's invitation. The new mission in Princeton would be a strong support to her Sisters in Bordentown who still suffered extreme hardships. They celebrated exultantly the return of "the Reverend Mother" to New Jersey to found still another convent. Best of all, the same five Sisters who had been pioneers in Jersey City volunteered to open the new convent in Princeton with Sister Regis Wade as their Superior once again. Frances added two more Sisters to the little community to make the mystical seven. She set out with them for Princeton in late August, 1878.

The *Princeton Press* was enthusiastic over the arrival of the Sisters:

The Sisters of Mercy are here, not only as educators but as assistants to Father Moran in his parochial labors. They visit the sick and nurse the dying. For both teaching and ministering to the helpless and sorrowing, they have been carefully trained. We do not doubt that their works, besides being acceptable, will yield great benefits to our people.[9]

Within two years of the arrival of the Sisters, Thomas Moran erected a new convent and boarding school for them.

He called it "St. Scholastica's Boarding and Day School for Young Ladies of Princeton." By 1889, the parish school of St. Paul's had an enviable record among the schools of New Jersey. On June 21, 1889, the *Princeton Press* declared, "We are particularly struck with the evidence of refined culture manifested by the pupils of this school . . . ." The Sisters of Mercy are still teaching in Princeton.

In November, 1881, the Diocese of Newark, which had comprised the entire State of New Jersey, was divided. Michael O'Farrell was appointed first Bishop of Trenton. One month later, on December 12, 1881, as the Sisters of Mercy throughout the world celebrated the Golden Jubilee of their foundation in Dublin, O'Farrell proposed to Frances Warde the union of the Bordentown and the Princeton Sisters of Mercy, with St. Mary's in Bordentown as their mother house. And in the spring of 1882, at the first Chapter of the Sisters of Mercy of New Jersey, Mother Regis Wade, former local Superior in both Jersey City and Princeton, was elected the first Mother Superior. All that Patrick Kiernan of Galway City and Frances Warde had hoped for young Mary Wade was fulfilled. Among the New Jersey Sisters, she is still called "the saintly Mother Regis." The union of the New Jersey Mercy Sisters in 1882 was only the beginning of the expansion of innumerable works of mercy by the Bordentown Sisters.

In 1886, these Sisters moved from old St. Mary's Convent on the "Hill Top" to their new St. Joseph's Convent, which became their mother house and novitiate as well as a day and boarding school. The same year, St. Scholastica's Academy in Princeton was incorporated with the new St. Joseph's in Bordentown. In rapid succession, the New Jersey Sisters expanded their apostolic works north, south, east, and west—to Lambertville, Camden, South Amboy, Burlington, Phillipsburg, Cape May, Keyport, Perth Amboy, Raritan, Woodbridge, Bound

Brook, Sayreville, Lakewood, Trenton, Atlantic City, and other cities and towns.

The New Jersey Sisters transferred their mother house and academy in 1908 to Mount St. Mary's, North Plainfield, where they also opened Mount St. Mary College. Frances Warde's favorite name, which delighted her in Westport, Manchester, and Burlington, was now given to the Mercy center in the State of New Jersey. The new convent and school was built at a magnificent site upon the sloping hills of the Watchung Mountains overlooking North Plainfield, New Jersey. This land was once sacred to the Watchung Indians. The word "Watchung" means "High Hill," and the area was also known historically as the "Blue Hills," so named by John Laing, a Quaker, who once owned the valley widening out below Mount St. Mary's.

The Sisters owed their new mother house to the generosity of David T. Kenney, Plainfield engineer, who invented the vacuum cleaner! Kenney had become wealthy through the invention of the flushometer. In 1902, he installed a successful two-ton vacuum cleaner in the basement of the Frick Building in Pittsburgh. The next step was the portable vacuum cleaner for home use. Kenney purchased three hundred acres in Watchung Mountain from an estate originally owned by John Taylor Johnston, a former President of the Central Railroad of New Jersey. He offered land to the Sisters of Mercy for the new Mount St. Mary's—a far cry in its richness from the original Mount St. Mary's built by Frances Warde at Westport and modeled on her beloved Carlow Convent.

So Frances' Sisters moved from their "Hill Top" in Bordentown to their "High Hill" in North Plainfield. When they left St. Joseph's Mother House in Bordentown, the Poor Clare Sisters established a foundation there. In the little cemetery beside the cloister, Mary Wade of Galway City is buried side by side with the Poor Clares of New Jersey.

In 1924, the Plainfield Sisters of Mercy, feeling the need for expansion of Mount St. Mary's, purchased Georgian Court, the famous Gould estate in the pines of Lakewood, New Jersey, for a college. Millionaire George Jay Gould had built a mansion at Georgian Court in 1896 at a then fabulous cost of $1,500,000. He had spent another million to beautify the grounds of the estate. Gould had attempted to reproduce a European baronial existence in late nineteenth-century America. The Georgian style mansion was an architectural masterpiece. The chandelier in the great hall was comprised of fifty thousand distinct pieces of glass. The superb Canterbury frieze on the wall of the main entrance was the work of Robert V. Sewall. The Fountain of Apollo on the grounds was unique. On an impulse, Gould also ordered a Casino to be built on the estate, containing a great hall for exercising polo ponies, as well as guest rooms, swimming pool, and squash courts. The entire estate suggested the luxury of a Roman Emperor, but it was also a witness to tragedy and suicide. This multi-million-dollar estate was purchased by the Sisters of Mercy, by a stroke of sheer luck, for $500,000. One wonders what Frances Warde would have thought at the opening of Georgian Court College in 1924, forty years after her death.

Perhaps Frances would have responded as journalist Arthur Brisbane did in his column titled "A Rich Man's Extravagance" in the *New York Evening Journal:*

Nothing really well done in this world is wasted . . . A girls' school in a palace! It was built for a few, but it is used by many. What is called the luxury of the rich becomes in due time a source of education and great public benefit . . .

The mansion was converted into a dormitory; the stable into an administration building; the casino into an auditorium and basketball court. A small chapel became the center of the college campus. If Frances Warde had been alive in 1924, perhaps she would have recalled the estate of Lord de Vesci at Abbeyleix in County Laois and the ill fortune of her own father, John Warde. Perhaps she would have commented on the strange ways of Providence.

But the Sisters of Mercy of Plainfield still love Bordentown and the memories it recalls of Frances Warde. There is a mysterious spiritual atmosphere about Bordentown and its history which is unforgettable. In 1945, when St. Mary's Church of Bordentown celebrated its centenary, William A. Griffin, Bishop of Trenton, wrote to Francis J. Lyons, then Pastor of St. Mary's:

There must have been something peculiarly attractive and inviting in the Catholic atmosphere of Bordentown on the Delaware, when the heads of several religious communities of men and women laid there the foundation of their apostolic work in this State and beyond. It is no mere accident but rather a direct evidence of the finger of God pointing to spiritually congenial Bordentown, that Reverend Mother Warde made it the cradle of her Sisters in New Jersey and that through the decades her inspiring example was followed by the Vincentian Fathers, by the contemplative Poor Clares, and latterly by the Fathers of the Society of the Divine Word. And all this within the confines of a Catholic parish whose population never exceeded sixteen hundred.[10]

18

A Full Life and a New Foundation in Portland; Controversy with Hierarchy and Successful Petition to Rome

BECAUSE Frances Warde was engaged continually in establishing new convents, schools, and social service centers, there is danger of viewing her as a woman who devoted her energies exclusively to new foundations. Such an approach to her life would be false. A person with less spiritual and organizational genius would indeed have exhausted her personal resources in founding far fewer schools, orphanages, and hospitals than Frances. But the life of the American founder of the Sisters of Mercy reveals unique fulfillment in diverse areas of personal development.

In the early seventies, while she was initiating missionary apostolates in California, Maine, Vermont, and New Jersey, she was experiencing a full personal and apostolic life which extended far beyond the labors of her foundations. She was a busy Mother Superior in Manchester, directing her Congregation with all its branch houses with a personal concern for all her Sisters. She continued to visit the Mercy convents and institutions which were no longer under her jurisdiction, for the Sisters in these convents always sought her advice and regarded her as *the* Reverend Mother. In one of her letters to a friend, she wrote: "I was obliged to go on business to Hartford, and the Sisters in Providence said if I failed to call on them, they would take it as an everlasting slight."[1] Frances was also caring for Kent Stone's children and helping him to live through a severe personal crisis. She found time, moreover, to talk with and write to students and former students and to visit with the little girls in St. Mary's Orphanage, Manchester, and other homes.

Frances was carrying on, meanwhile, a world-wide correspondence with other Mercy Congregations and welcoming to Mount St. Mary's at Manchester new members from faraway towns and cities. With Mother Josephine Warde, her sister at St. Maries of the Isle in Cork, she established a "holy alliance" for fostering Irish vocations to the Sisters of Mercy in America. And she herself continued to replenish with new members the Mercy Convents in the United States and elsewhere that needed assistance. For example, she wrote to Mother Cecilia Maher, her cousin from Carlow Convent who had founded the Mercy Congregation in New Zealand, inviting her to visit Manchester and promising to send two new postulants back to New Zealand with her.[2] Among the Convents of Mercy not founded directly by Frances Warde but to which she sent Sisters to help in their apostolates were those at Baltimore, Maryland; Little Rock, Arkansas; Macon and Columbus, Georgia; and St. Augustine, Florida.

Frances continued to teach Christian Doctrine classes also, and never failed to keep in touch with those in whose conversion to Catholicism she was instrumental. The directness of her approach to those whom she dared to lead to Christ was disarming. To a former student who had become a Catholic through her instruction, she wrote, "You must soon come back to the quiet holy chapel [at Manchester] where you so often prayed and received so many graces and blessings. Plain as it is at present, I see nothing anywhere I love half as well. Mary B. writes that she must come back to us, and, better still, that she is now eighteen and will become a Catholic . . . ."[3] And

Frances once wrote the following at Christmas time to the non-Catholic husband of her niece, Jane Warde:

It would rejoice heaven if you were received into the Church at this blessed time. We pray faithfully for you. My dear, noble, generous friend, our holy pastor [William McDonald] has said that he was sure Our Lord would give you the great gift of Faith. I never knew him to evince such deep interest in any one . . . I do hope that you will have a most blessed Christmas, and that our good God may soon draw you by His Grace.[4]

The gentleman addressed became a Roman Catholic.

The wide correspondence of Frances Warde included letters to Bishops and priests, men and women of many religious congregations, famous people of many countries. She influenced in conversion to the Catholic faith a Russian princess who visited her at Newport, and to whom she often afterward wrote encouraging letters. The charm of Frances' correspondence, on the testimony of her contemporaries, was a gift she used to draw others to Christ. She kept a journal, too, and its loss to the history of the Catholic Church in the United States is comparable to the loss of her letters.

All in all, Frances Warde filled the hours of her days with an almost unbelievable fullness of living. And when all was done, she found time to plant roses and lilies of the valley and to walk and talk and pray with the Sisters she loved in the gardens she loved at Manchester and Providence and Bordentown. How did she accomplish so much, how did she live continually in such amazing fulfillment in Christ? A spiritual lecture she often read to the Sisters at Manchester, quoted later by one of them,[5] gives us at least the hint of an answer:

It is astonishing how much time was at the command of saints, and how little seems to be at the disposal of the generality of Christians!

391

How eminently did the saints fulfill the duties of their life—union with God, devotion to the different offices their life called for—and still they did not fail to find time for the charity for which only *the few* seem to find time today.

Frances Warde was indeed a woman united with God. Through her union with Him, her time assumed a kind of eternal timelessness. Her love and service of others transcended time. She was able to do more than is humanly possible. "Every moment of her life seemed to be filled with her apostolate to such an extent as to appear almost miraculous."[6]

The foundations of Frances Warde in Bangor and in North Whitefield, Maine, were especially dear to her friend, Bishop David Bacon, but he also desired from the time of his appointment as Bishop to have the Sisters of Mercy in Portland, his Episcopal See. After the Sisters' first difficult days in Bangor, they firmly established their parochial school, academy, and night school there. North Whitefield was a bleak region with a very severe climate, far from the few large population centers in Maine of the eighteen-seventies. The Sisters were obliged to walk to school through heavy snowdrifts. Of the first Sisters who settled in North Whitefield, all but one contracted illnesses from exposure that later proved to be fatal.[7] Yet the Sisters prospered in this mission as well as in Bangor, and the Whitefield convent became one of the best-loved of the Manchester Sisters of Mercy. The townspeople possessed a warmth of spirit and a sincere, authentic way of life that endeared them to Frances Warde and her Sisters.

Bishop Bacon's desire to have the Sisters in Portland encountered many obstacles. In an effort to satisfy the French-Canadian immigrants in Maine who resented Irish-American domination of the hierarchy and the schools, he had invited French-speaking Canadian Sisters of Notre Dame rather than Sisters of Mercy to teach at the Cathedral School in

Portland. His efforts to build a Cathedral, moreover, had been hampered not only by the Civil War but by the Great Fire of 1866 in Portland, in which the Cathedral property, including chapel and school, were destroyed. When the new Cathedral was dedicated finally in 1870, a fierce New England storm demolished its steeple on the very day of the dedication. Not long afterward, however, it became known that Winifred Kavanagh, friend of Frances Warde and of the Sisters of Mercy, had given Bishop Bacon $50,000 to build a convent near the Cathedral.

Finally, early in 1873, Bishop Bacon asked Mother Frances to send Sisters of Mercy to care for the little orphan children of the Diocese of Portland. Probably Frances was not surprised. The establishment of the Sisters of Mercy in the city of Portland was inevitable. Frances again chose her Assistant, Mother Gonzaga O'Brien, as first Superior of the new convent. Sister de Sales Tierney and Sister Jane Doyle, a novice in her teens, were also appointed. Sister Jane was to spend the rest of her life in Portland.

Thus on a bright spring day in 1873 the Manchester Sisters set out to establish Frances Warde's third mission in Maine. If Bangor was picturesque, if North Whitefield was loved, Portland was beautiful:

> *Often I think of that beautiful town*
> *That is seated by the sea . . .*

Longfellow's city by the sea, with its broad streets and stately arching elms, its great open harbor with hundreds of islands dotting its shorelines as they reach out toward the ocean, was in 1873 already a center of historic and literary landmarks. The Sisters were happy to go there. The care of orphans, moreover, was an apostolate they loved.

On the last day of May, Bishop Bacon welcomed the

Sisters to his own episcopal residence. A house at 100 Free Street was being renovated and enlarged to become St. Elizabeth's Convent and Orphan Home. Since it was not yet ready for occupation, Bacon offered the Sisters a temporary suite of rooms adjoining the Cathedral Chapel in his own home. Each day for a month they participated in the Celebration of the Eucharist with Bishop Bacon in the Cathedral Chapel and shared meals with him. On the last day of June, the Sisters moved to their new home at St. Elizabeth's. As they arrived, a workman offered them a bouquet of roses which gave a springtime air to the founding of the new community. In a short time, forty little orphans were living with the Sisters at St. Elizabeth's. A real home was created for them. They did not wear a uniform as was customary in orphanages in the seventies. "It is not necessary," said Bishop Bacon, "to keep the fact of their being orphans constantly before their minds."

Apparently Bishop Bacon did not intend to make any change in the routine management of his schools in Portland. The Notre Dame Sisters from Montreal conducted an academy, St. Aloysius School, and St. Dominic School in the city. Now, suddenly, in the summer of 1873, the Notre Dame Sisters notified Bacon that they were withdrawing to Canada. On July 23, 1873, the Bishop wrote to Frances Warde expressing his chagrin. The opening of his letter[8] indicates, however, that he had had some previous hint of the sudden withdrawal of the French-Canadian Sisters from Portland:

My dear Mother Warde:
   When I wrote, asking if you could give me eight or nine Sisters well qualified to teach, I had fears that I might need them; today all suspense is at an end.
   The Lady Superior . . . to whom I had made known that I

would wish her to send me English-speaking nuns instead of [French-speaking] Canadians, has assured me that I need not count any longer on [her nuns] for my schools . . .

Since Mr. M. has sent his daughters to Manchester [to Mount St. Mary's Academy], and especially since the orphan asylum has been opened, they fear their sun is setting, and hence the uncourteous action of a woman too young to be the Superior of a large religious community.

If you cannot help me, I must without delay seek Sisters elsewhere . . . It seems to me that Providence in trying me is opening to your community a noble field . . . .

Yours sincerely,

✠David W., Bishop of Portland

Despite the fact that within two years Frances Warde had sent colonies of Sisters to California, to Vermont, and to three cities in New Jersey, as well as Bangor, North Whitefield, and Portland, she could not refuse a request of David Bacon. Frances knew intuitively that Bacon's invitation was the first step in the establishment of a Mercy mother house in Portland. William Leo Lucey, author of *The Catholic Church in Maine,* declares that Frances Warde saved Bishop Bacon from sending the children of the Catholic schools in Portland to the public schools (which were openly anti-Catholic in the seventies).[9] He adds that the fact that Mother Frances could supply Sisters for the four schools in Portland within five weeks is a clear testimony to the growth of the Congregation of Mercy in Manchester.

The Sisters were established in their new home on Free Street in July. When September arrived, they opened St. Elizabeth's Academy, St. Aloysius School, and St. Dominic School. They taught approximately nine classes in the parochial schools and eighty girls in the Academy, as well as night classes for students who could not attend during the day and private classes for music pupils. In addition, of course, they were caring for the orphans of the Diocese at St. Elizabeth's. Shortly after the opening of the orphan home, a young girl from Calais unfortunately brought diphtheria to the other children. Bishop Bacon himself and the Sisters cared for the victims of the epidemic day and night. For fear of infection, no one else would assist them.

Perhaps David Bacon's care for the orphans of Portland was the crucial event that led to the death of this already tired and weary Bishop. In the spring of 1874 he set out on a necessary visit to Rome. When his party arrived at Brest, he was so ill that he was unable to go farther. His friends went on to Rome without him, leaving him in a hospital in Brittany. Hastening back to him after their business in Italy was completed, they found him in a half-dying condition. David Bacon desired to die in his own country. He feared death at sea. His father, William Bacon, a sea captain, had died with his entire crew on a voyage from Europe to America when David was a child. Bishop Bacon was carried aboard ship and, after the long journey home, was rushed to St. Vincent Hospital in New York. He died a few hours after landing on November 4, 1874. The Sisters of Mercy, and especially Frances Warde, had lost one of their best friends in the United States. And the Catholic Church in America had lost a leader of energy, courage, and simple sanctity.

The last apostolic work undertaken by Frances Warde under the guidance of David Bacon as Bishop was the establishment of a Home for Aged Women in Manchester just six months before Bacon died. Father William McDonald, Pastor of St. Anne's, had purchased the well-known "Harris Estate" in Manchester as an Orphan Home and removed the little children from St. Mary's Orphan Home on the grounds of Mt. St. Mary's to the new property in the heart of the city which became known as St. Patrick's Home. On these grounds was a modest house facing Hanover Street which Father McDonald proposed to Frances Warde to be used as a Home for Aged Women. All that the poor old people of the Diocese needed, he told Frances, was a quiet corner in which to dream or pray, an occasional cup of tea, and a Sister or two to make them feel wanted. Mother Frances at once appointed Sister Aloysius Kelly to the new home, and twelve elderly ladies applied immediately for admission. Sister Aloysius served her clients faithfully for twenty years. And they were always favorites of Father McDonald, who loved old people in need as well as orphans.

It was fitting that such a work of loving kindness should close an era—for the death of David Bacon indeed closed an epoch in the history of the Catholic Church in New England. A profound spiritual and cultural revolution[10] had taken place in the Diocese of Portland, especially in Manchester, chiefly attributable to David Bacon, William McDonald, and Frances Warde. Tributes paid to Father McDonald and Mother Frances give lucid recognition to the nature of that revolution. Yankee prejudices had been broken; educational and charitable institutions devoted to the care of the young and the old had sprung up. When Bacon had come to the Diocese of Portland (Maine and New Hampshire) in 1855, he had found only five priests to serve 15,000 people. When he died in 1874, he left fifty-two priests in the service of 80,000 people. Churches, schools, and homes for the needy had sprung up everywhere in the Diocese.

Father McDonald openly gave much credit for this quiet spiritual and social revolution in New England to Frances Warde and her Sisters. In 1875, Sadlier's *Catholic Dictionary* numbered ninety-four Sisters of Mercy in the Manchester Congregation. If we add to these the Sisters who left

Manchester for foundations in Philadelphia, Omaha, California, New Jersey, and Vermont, we have a total of 150 Sisters in Manchester between 1858 and 1875.[11] Their apostolic work was immeasurable.

There are other reasons, however, for considering the death of David Bacon both the close of an era in Catholic New England and a milestone in Frances Warde's life. For Bishop Bacon's successor indeed initiated a new epoch in the Diocese of Portland.

Bishop-Elect James Augustine Healy received the Papal Bull of his appointment on April 10, 1875, and arrived in Portland five days later. It is difficult to imagine a man more different from the gentle David Bacon than James Healy. He was the first son of Michael Morris Healy, an Irishman from County Roscommon who had run away from the confining atmosphere of his home to join the British Army, taken French leave from garrison duty in Nova Scotia, settled in Georgia where he had clandestinely married a mulatto slave girl named Eliza, fathered eight children, and developed a huge and prosperous plantation on which he worked sixty slaves.[12] Michael Healy sent his sons to the North to be educated. James' attendance at Holy Cross College in Worcester, Massachusetts, was crucial in his life. In the South, the Healy boys had not been baptized because of the caste system and the disorganized condition of pioneer life. Now they became fervent Catholics. Partially through the influence of Bishop John Bernard Fitzpatrick of Boston, James Healy decided to become a priest. He was destined to become the first Chancellor of the Diocese of Boston and the Pastor of its Cathedral Church. When David Bacon died, Healy was appointed, at the age of forty-five, second Bishop of Portland.

James Healy's first years as Bishop were not particularly happy ones. A long and painful dispute with a pastor in his diocese so disturbed him that twice he offered to resign his office.[13] Frances Warde found it difficult to work with him. One historian speaks of a clash of personalities that brought on a coolness between Mother Frances and Bishop Healy.[14] Both of them were strong personalities accustomed to control the administration of their affairs. Bishop Bacon had given Frances Warde a free hand in conducting her Congregation of Mercy; he never interfered with the internal management of her convents. Healy was not inclined to give much freedom of decision to anyone who served within the framework of his authority.

Four days after his arrival in the Diocese of Portland, Bishop Healy visited Mount St. Mary's in Manchester and interviewed Frances Warde. The students of the Academy had prepared an evening entertainment to welcome their new Bishop. He objected strongly to the late hour and to that part of the program which included students dancing.[15] As the Sisters gradually came to know Healy better, they discovered that he did not consider it undue interference in their internal government of the Congregation to regulate even small details of their lives. When novices received their religious names, he approved or disapproved. He outlawed the custom of handshaking among the Sisters. When introduced to strangers, they were told to bow courteously. In Mount St. Mary's Academy, the students were forbidden to wear jewelry. All dancing was prohibited in school socials or plays. At a school performance where guests were present, Bishop Healy was known to stop the program and order off the stage a girl who appeared in an elaborate style of dress or who allowed her lace pantaloons to show.[16] Nor did he hesitate to tell a Sister that the habit she wore required cleaning or mending. A year after his arrival in Portland, when he attended a spring concert offered by the children of the Portland parochial schools, he noted with great relish that for the first time in the history of such performances, the Sisters did not attend! Healy laid down academic regulations too and, to the great chagrin of the Sisters, ordered that every child be promoted whether he deserved it or not. He reserved to himself the right to expel a recalcitrant child from school. And the Bishop saw to it that his own arbitrary laws were obeyed.

Despite the fact that Frances Warde always resisted Jansenistic moral tendencies, she was not unduly irritated by the more or less trivial annoyances caused by many of Bishop Healy's regulations. Unfortunately, the tension between herself and Healy had deeper roots. Mother Frances had reason to believe that "interested parties" prejudiced him against her from the start.[17] Healy's own *Diary,* moreover, is revealing of his attitude toward the Sisters of Mercy. Three months after his arrival in Portland, he visited the Sisters at St. Xavier's Convent in Bangor. He praised them highly in his *Diary,* noting incorrectly, however, that they were independent of the Manchester Convent of Mercy.[18] Actually, the Bangor community was a branch house of Manchester. Four months later, after a visit to the Portland Convent of Mercy, he found there "an excellent, contented, and fervent spirit, but hampered in all by the ridiculous rulings from Manchester."[19] On January 1, 1876, he visited the Bangor convent again and reversed his good judgment completely.[20] He now found the order, the discipline, and the fervor of the Bangor Sisters to be at low ebb. And "the cause" was "the childish attempt to govern it as a mere branch house of Manchester." Quite obviously, Healy wished the Bangor and Portland Sisters to be completely under his own jurisdiction.

The chief cause of friction between Frances Warde and

her Bishop, however, was an even more serious one. Next door to the Bishop's episcopal "palace" on Congress Street in Portland stood the unfinished building destined by Bishop Bacon to be a Convent for the Sisters of Mercy. Winifred Kavanagh had given the former Bishop $50,000 for the construction of the Convent. Bishop Healy, however, had other ideas.[21] He converted the structure into a magnificent school, which he proudly dedicated as the Kavanagh School, undoubtedly the finest school in the State of Maine when it was opened in 1877. The Sisters of Mercy remained in their residence on Free Street which had once been the old home of Bishop Bacon. Frances Warde always showed Bishop Healy the respect due his office, but she did not consider it an unmixed blessing to do business with him. The Sisters of Mercy in Maine and New Hampshire sorely missed David Bacon.

Meanwhile, Frances Warde felt obliged to close the Academy for Young Ladies in North Whitefield in 1875 in order to provide Sisters to teach in the Academy and the parochial schools of Portland. At the same time, the orphan children were moved from St. Elizabeth's in Portland to North Whitefield, so that St. Elizabeth's could serve as a convent home for all the Mercy Sisters in Portland.

Frances never gave indication to outsiders that Bishop Healy was a difficult man to deal with. The year after his consecration as Bishop of Portland, she wrote from Manchester to her old friend, Mother Catherine Maher, in Carlow:

We have five branch houses in this diocese, and two in New Jersey.

Here we have about eleven hundred pupils, and an Orphanage; in Portland, another Orphanage and eight hundred pupils; a third Orphanage at North Whitefield, Maine.

This is the Parent House, surrounded with every blessing.

Our late dear Bishop, and our present Bishop, most kind. Our pastor, Rev. William McDonald, is considered a saint . . .[22]

For Bishop Healy, Mother Frances had only words of kindness.

In 1877, Healy had the duty of presiding at the election of the Mother Superior in Manchester, held every three years according to the *Rule* of the Sisters of Mercy. The circumstances surrounding the election revealed his authoritarianism very clearly. As American founder of the Sisters of Mercy, *the* Reverend Mother of the Mercy Sisters in the United States, it was most fitting that Frances Warde should remain as Mother Superior in Manchester if her Sisters so desired. Catherine McAuley, as founder of the Sisters of Mercy, had been declared Mother Superior for life by Archbishop Murray of Dublin. Mother Patricia Waldron of Philadelphia, first appointed by Frances Warde, was Superior of the Philadelphia Sisters for life. The request for dispensation for re-election in such cases was a routine matter. The Bishop of the Diocese merely wrote to Rome for the proper sanction. Frances Warde had already served as Mother Superior in Manchester for nineteen years.

As the election was to be held in August, 1877, Bishop Healy began to busy himself in the internal affairs of the Mercy Sisters three months before the event. On May 14, he recorded in his *Diary* that he "interviewed the Sisters at Bangor with a view to ensure a peaceable and judicious election." On June 30, he visited Mount St. Mary's in Manchester, "conferring with such as have the right to vote at the election of the Superior." He came to the decision that "none but the Foundress is again eligible." On July 5 he heard gossip from Manchester, "some suspicion of scheming on the part of the Reverend Mother. This pains the Bishop beyond measure and may result in his putting a veto on her election"! Two days later, he noted that the Bangor Sisters *now* desire not to be subject to Manchester.[23]

On July 25, 1877, Healy received a letter from Cardinal John McCloskey advising him that Mother Warde should not be re-elected without permission from Rome. Since the latter information was merely ordinary procedure, it should have presented no difficulty to Bishop Healy. It is probable that he requested the information from Cardinal McCloskey, since it was not ordinary procedure for McCloskey to write such a letter at the time of an ordinary election of a religious congregation. When Frances Warde was elected *unanimously* as Mother Superior of the Manchester Sisters on August 15, 1877, Bishop Healy would not assume the customary responsibility of the Bishop to seek proper sanction from Rome for her re-election.

A letter filed in the Archives of *Propaganda Fide* in Rome[24] should be quoted in full because it reveals so unmistakably the attitude of the Sisters of Mercy toward Mother Frances. As a historical document, it is significant:

PETITION OF THE SISTERS OF MERCY

> Convent of Our Lady of Mercy
> Mount St. Mary's
> Manchester, New Hampshire
> U. S. America, Aug. 15, 1877

To His Eminence Cardinal Franchi:

The undersigned professed Sisters of Mercy, Mount St. Mary's, Diocese of Portland, Manchester, New Hampshire, U. S. America, showeth:

That their Convent was founded twenty years ago, with Sister Mary Frances Xavier Warde as their Rev. Mother;

That it is over forty years since she entered the Novitiate in Dublin, Ireland, under the Foundress, Mother Catherine Mc-Auley;

That owing to her long experience, to her inheriting the spirit of our Foundress, and her uninterrupted successful government of our Community, our late lamented Bishop Bacon continued her in office, to our very great happiness, until his death in 1874;

That our present beloved Bishop Healy, being unwilling to take on himself the responsibility of our having re-elected her, suggests to us to state to your Eminence through him, our wishes in her regard.

We, therefore, most humbly solicit your Eminence to grant us the dispensation approving of our having re-elected our present beloved Rev. Mother, and thus not only gratify our most ardent desire, but contribute to the salvation of many, who—judging from her past religious labors—will be served through her Superior prudence and supernatural wisdom.

The above letter was signed by all the professed Sisters in Manchester, beginning with Frances' old friend and Mother Assistant, Sister Gonzaga O'Brien, and ending with young Jane Doyle, only two years professed. The request for sanction of the election was presented to Pope Pius IX on October 21, 1877, and of course answered affirmatively.[25] The election of the Manchester Sisters of Mercy in 1877 was not the last in which Bishop Healy would involve himself. He considered the Sisters of Mercy to be a Diocesan Congregation, and he desired to act as their Superior, in both important matters and small details of living. His brother, Father Patrick Healy, once advised him "not under any circumstances to interfere in the internal government of any religious order."[26] But Patrick Healy was a Jesuit and therefore understood better than James the government of religious congregations.

For Frances Warde and her Sisters, the big event of 1877, following the election of Mother Frances, was the opening of the Kavanagh School. If the Sisters felt an inward sadness that the site of the most beautiful school in Maine should have been that of their Mother House, if they saw in imagination a Convent of Mercy, they gave no indication of their disappointment. Kavanagh School was the model private school of Portland and the pride of the Diocese. Today the Sisters of Mercy are still teaching in the old Kavanagh School, later called the Cathedral School.

In late October of 1877, Bishop Healy recorded in his *Diary* a visit to Manchester. He did not indicate a conversation with Frances Warde. It is likely that he talked with her, however, for on October 31 he visited Augusta, Maine, to confer with Governor Selden Conner concerning a possible mission of the Manchester Sisters of Mercy to the Indian Reservations of the State of Maine to serve the Penobscot and the Passamaquoddy Indians. In late January, 1878, Healy again visited Manchester to prepare for a trip to Europe on which he persuaded Father William McDonald, the saintly Pastor of St. Anne's and close friend of Frances Warde, to accompany him. Father McDonald's visit to Ireland was his first vacation in forty years, and only his Bishop could have persuaded him to take it.

Father McDonald and Frances Warde had worked so closely together for twenty years in the New England apostolate that their works in education and in the service of the poor, the sick, the orphaned, and the aged were often linked. Both Mother Frances and "Father Mac" were well loved in Manchester. The European journey of Bishop and Pastor precipitated a very amusing incident involving Frances.

A beautiful feature of Father McDonald's character was his loyal support of Frances Warde. He knew that a woman of her strength of character must at times excite the envy and misunderstanding of others. He also knew that she responded with womanly sensitivity to misunderstanding. He protected her when he could. When Bishop Healy and he arrived in Dublin, the Bishop told McDonald that he wished to celebrate the Eucharistic Sacrifice the following morning at St. Catherine's Convent, Baggot Street. Knowing the Bishop's resentment of Mother Frances, Father McDonald slipped away secretly to Baggot Street to prepare the Sisters for any ungracious remark the Bishop might make. The Superior at St. Catherine's defended Frances warmly. "We all love and revere Mother Warde," she said. "Is she not a child of this Convent and the first to be professed in it?"[27] The Mercy annalist does not record the visit of Bishop Healy to Baggot Street. She merely adds: "Next morning the good Mother understood better the purport of Father McDonald's evening visit." But Bishop Healy did not comprehend the full measure of Father McDonald's devotion to Frances Warde.

When the travelers returned to Manchester, it was time for Mother Frances to turn once again to a new mission apostolate. In July of 1878, she was seriously ill with a gastric ailment that troubled her more frequently as she grew older. Yet in August she not only planned the establishment of the Convent of Mercy in Princeton, New Jersey, but negotiated plans for an entirely new type of apostolic work among the Indian tribes of Maine. At the age of sixty-eight, she now approached the foundation of convents, schools, and social service centers on the Indian Reservations of the Northeast with the same enthusiasm that she had set out from Dublin for Carlow in her twenties. Quite clearly, Frances Warde's mission to America would continue with unmitigated zeal for Christ until her very death.

19

On to Indian Missions: Indian Island, Pleasant Point, Peter Dana Point

THE Sisters of Mercy under Frances Warde became the first and only Sisters to do missionary labor among the Indians of the State of Maine. Frances established three missions there—at Indian Island, Old Town, in 1878, among the Penobscot Indians; at Pleasant Point, Perry, in 1879, among the Passamaquoddies; and in 1879 at Peter Dana Point, Princeton, also a Passamaquoddy reservation.

The Indian tribes served by the Sisters of Mercy belonged to the Abnaki Confederacy of the Algonquin Nation, once extremely powerful in the area which is now Northeastern United States.[1] At the start of the French and Indian Wars, they numbered 35,000. They occupied the territory from the shores of the St. Lawrence down to the Atlantic Ocean and from the mouth of the Kennebec River to the Eastern part of present New Hampshire. Though the Abnakis are almost decimated today, their total number in the Maine reservations being little more than 1,000, their names are still alive in every hill and valley, river and brook, lake and pond, every bay and promontory in the State of Maine.[2] A granite monument on the left shore of the Kennebec River near Norridgewock points out the lovely spot of one of the last Abnaki strongholds in Maine.

"Abnaki" refers to all Northeastern Indians, chief among

whom were the Penobscots and the Passamaquoddies. The name "Abnaki" means the "Dawn People," while "Passama-quoddy" means the "White Rock People." These Indians adopted family names from those of water creatures: Mitchell (lobster), Francis (fisher), and Neptune (eel).[3] They counted the months by moons, and the first day of each new moon was the first day of the month. Since in some years there are thirteen moons, the Abnakis skipped the moon between July and August and called it "Let This Moon Go." Each month was named poetically. For example, February was the "Moon in which there is crust on the snow"; July was the "Moon in which the berries are ripe"; and December was the "Long Moon."[4]

Paradoxically, these Aborigines of Acadia were the first native harbingers of Catholicity in the United States. Before George Calvert, Lord Baltimore, in the *Ark and the Dove,* entered Chesapeake Bay and planted the Catholic religion on the shores of the Potomac, the mission of St. Saviour near the present Bar Harbor had been established among the Abnakis by Father Pierre Biard at Mount Desert, and the Catholic faith had acquired the right of entrance to the present Northeastern United States, sealed with blood of the martyr, Brother Gilbert DuThet. Seven years before Samoset from the Rock of Plymouth welcomed the Pilgrims of the Mayflower, the Abnakis of the Indian villages of Mount Desert had begged for the waters of Baptism from Jesuit missionaries. Before George Popham had stepped on an island of the Kennebec River, the shores of the Kennebec and the St. Croix had been dedicated to Christ by Pierre Biard, by missionaries from France, and by French settlers on Boone Island. The promise of Bishop John Carroll of a permanent shepherd to the Indians of Maine, however, was not finally fulfilled until David Bacon was appointed to the

Portland Diocese of Maine and New Hampshire three years before Frances Warde came to Manchester.

The Sisters of Mercy had much to learn concerning the Abnakis they planned to serve in the eighteen-seventies. The right of the Abnakis to the title of the earliest Catholicity in America dates back to the explorations of Samuel de Champlain who, in 1604, moved westward from Nova Scotia accompanied by Catholic missionaries, entered Passamaquoddy Bay, and proceeded to St. Croix Island. In July, 1604, Nicholas Aubry offered the first Celebration of the Eucharist there. Before spring came, he and his fellow missionaries were dead. The colony was left without spiritual assistance until 1608, when Fathers Pierre Biard and Ennemond Masse arrived. Biard and his followers went as far West as the Kennebec River. On the island they named St. Saviour, they planted the Cross in 1611. Thus the Abnaki Indians, predominantly Catholic since 1608, formed a bridge of Christianity to the New World.

In the mid-seventeenth century, a delegation of Abnaki Indian Chiefs journeyed from the banks of the Kennebec to Quebec to ask for Jesuit missionaries "to live among them" in Maine. A mission was established among them near Norridgewock, south of the present Madison, by Father Gabriel Drouilettes. In 1669, many Abnakis, most of whom were Penobscots, were forced to flee to the banks of the Penobscot River. Their main settlement was on Indian Island, in the middle of the Penobscot, opposite Old Town, Maine. Here Frances Warde was destined to make her first foundation among the Maine Indians one hundred years later. And here the Penobscots erected a small Chapel and kept their Catholic faith alive, even during long years without benefit of clergy.

The Chief of their Tribe was called Sagamore; their

Council were called Sachems. The first great Chief was Madocawando, whose daughter married the famous Baron Jean Vincent de Castine in the sixteen-sixties. The French de Castine was for years the real leader of the Penobscot tribal organization, which has maintained autonomous self-government ever since. The sceptre of the Tribe was the tomahawk; the chariot was the birch bark canoe. Because the Penobscots had always believed in the Great Spirit, the Evil Spirit, and the Spirit Land, the doctrines of Catholicism were very congenial to them.[5] In 1688, Louis Pierre Thury of the Foreign Missions established the first regular Catholic mission on Indian Island and dedicated its Church of St. Ann. This foundation became the oldest Catholic settlement in New England and the second oldest on the Eastern Seaboard. In 1703, Jesuits assumed care of the mission. And in 1724, it received recruits as the result of a tragedy.

Father Sebastian Rasle, who served the Indians at Norridgewock after Father Drouilettes, saw his Church and Mission destroyed in 1722 by a detachment of the British Army. His famous *Abnaki Dictionary* was stolen by the British and is now in the Harvard University Library. In 1724 Rasle himself was martyred at Norridgewock. His Indian disciples abandoned their settlement on the Kennebec and fled to Indian Island. They took with them the iron cross that marked Rasle's grave and preserved it for over 200 years. In 1931 it was incorporated into a beautiful monument at St. Ann's Church on Indian Island.

The Sisters of Mercy also learned about Father Virgil Barbour, who came to Indian Island more than fifty years before their own arrival. Like Kent Stone, Barbour was a convert from the Episcopalian ministry. He and his son became Jesuits, and his wife and four daughters became Sisters. While Barbour served the Penobscots on Indian Island, an invading band of Massachusetts Puritans, in 1828, burned down St. Ann's Church. Barbour rebuilt it in 1830. He himself taught the Indians to read and write. A famous successor of Barbour was Father John Bapst, later President of Boston College, who came in 1848 to serve the Penobscots on Indian Island. In 1854 Bapst was tarred and feathered by Know-Nothings at Ellsworth, Maine. Until his death in 1887, he suffered intensely as a consequence of this abuse.

Such is the background, in brief, of the Indian missions in Maine to which, in 1878 and 1879, Frances Warde decided to send her Sisters to serve. Indian Island, Pleasant Point, and Peter Dana Point became legal possessions of the Penobscots and the Passamaquoddies. The reservations were held by the Indians and recognized by the State to the extent that they were permitted formal representation in the State Legislature. Indian Island continued to manage its own government, complete with local officers from Governor down to Constable. In short, the Indians had autonomy under the sovereignty of the State.

Tradition states that when Bishop James Healy visited Pope Leo XIII in Rome in 1878, the Pope suggested to Healy that religious Sisters should establish schools for the Indians of Maine. To be sure, the initiation of the idea in Rome came from Healy himself. Before leaving for Italy, he had already consulted in Maine concerning the possibility of sending Sisters of Mercy to the Indian Reservations.[6] With the approval of Leo XIII, Healy returned to Maine and asked Frances Warde to send Sisters to serve at Indian Island in Old Town. She consented gladly.

In the summer of 1878, Frances had to make a decision as to where she could best serve personally. In August, she planned to establish two new Convents of Mercy, the one at St. Paul's Parish in Princeton, New Jersey, and the other at Indian Island. Added to the exhausting work of preparing for two new missions was a serious illness which she herself suffered in July. Although she was now nearing seventy, she recovered with her usual resilience. Her energy never flagged. In August, she decided that her own presence was needed at the Princeton foundation more than in Old Town. At Princeton, she would have to negotiate plans for her Sisters with a more sophisticated people. The Indians were simple people. She would let the Sisters assigned to Indian Island establish their mission without her. Later, she would visit them. Frances was right in her assumption concerning the Penobscots.

On August 25, 1878, four Sisters, with Sister Borgia Toomey as leader, left Manchester for Portland, where they remained until September 11, when they set out for Old Town, accompanied by Michael O'Brien, visiting Pastor of St. Ann's Church, Indian Island. They passed through forests of pine, oak, maple, and swaying birch, until they finally reached Old Town and the Penobscot River on September 14. A delegation of Indians awaited them. The church bells of St. Ann's announced their arrival at Indian Island in the canoes of the Indian leaders.[7]

The Sisters were led to the wigwam of the Chief of the Penobscots, Stockvesin Swassin, who gladly vacated his home for them. Small huts had not yet replaced the Indians' wigwams. In two years, the Indians would build, with the help of private donations, a small Convent of Mercy. It would rise on the site of a one-time fort used for protection against the Mohawks. Sacrifice, hardship, and suffering awaited the Sisters at Indian Island. The life style of the Penobscots in 1878 was quite unlike that of the Sisters of Mercy at Manchester! The Sisters not only took over the management of the Indian school founded by Virgil Barbour; they performed all of the corporal and spiritual works of mercy.

They immediately set about learning the Abnaki language. The school curriculum was the same as that of the schools in Old Town across the Penobscot River. The ramshackle, cold school house, heated by one wood stove during the freezing Maine winters, was not replaced with a more serviceable building for twelve years. Soon, however, the grateful Indian women were selling baskets to provide necessities for the little school. The Sisters also opened an evening school for young men who worked at Old Town during the day, and for young women to learn to read and to sew. In after-school hours, before dinner, they taught Christian Doctrine. They visited and cared for the sick. They helped to bury the dead. When they found that the Indians slept on their floors on skins of deer, moose, and bear during the freezing winter, the Sisters taught the Penobscots the use of beds. When they found the Indian women washing their clothes by beating them with sticks at the river bank, the Sisters taught them the mysteries of laundering. They visited the wigwams and taught the women to clean, to cook, to sew, to care for their families. The Indians were grateful. On Saturday evenings, they visited the Sisters with gifts of canned goods, rice, sugar, and tea. On Sundays, the Sisters taught the Indians singing and Church music, in which they excelled. They loved ceremony. On Good Friday, for example, they walked in procession for a mile to drink the waters of the Penobscot River as a symbol of drinking from the Brook Cedron.[8]

The Sisters maintained their joyful spirit despite extreme hardships. One of them, writing in winter to Frances Warde, spoke gratefully to her of all those who "owe their all to you and for which I hope a bright future is waiting." Then she added that December was the hunting season and the Braves would be gone until after the New Year. Deer, caribou, antlers would be brought back as gifts for the Sisters. Frances was promised a "real Indian room" for her proposed visit to Indian Island. The letter was rich with the joy experienced in a demanding apostolate.[9] The Sisters had to wait for thirty years until a serviceable convent was built for them in 1910 through an appropriation from the State Legislature of Maine requested by the Indian representatives in Augusta. Their old convent—built by the Indians in 1880—was then converted, also through a State appropriation, into a home for young girls, where the Sisters taught them home economics and other fundamental subjects. Government funds and donations also helped to build St. Ann's School.

In the Church of St. Ann at Indian Island is a two-hundred-year-old canvas painting of the Crucifixion.[10] The artist, Joe Paul Orson, never studied art. He was an unusual young Indian boy, known to be a contemplative. He prayed, fasted, and accompanied the visiting Pastor on his missionary journeys. To paint the Crucifixion, he used the juices of fruits and berries and the tail of an animal as a brush. Museums of three large cities have tried in vain for many years to buy the painting from the Penobscots. It has two figures, the dying Christ and Magdalen. She kneels at the right of the cross, one arm clasped around the body of Christ, the other staunching the wound of His right foot. The faces of Christ and Magdalen are Indian. The tension of the body of Christ, the drawn features, the swollen eyes, the wounds are realistic, while the uplifted eyes of Christ are fixed as if upon the Father. Frances Warde loved the painting, which has a wood and gilt frame which she sent as a gift to the Penobscots.

Also at Indian Island is a relic of quite another type. In the little cemetery close to St. Ann's Church are a marble tombstone and a plaque marking the burial place of the great athlete, Louis Sockalexis, who gave the Cleveland "Indians" their name. The plaque is decorated with two crossed baseball bats. "Sock" was born in 1873 and taught by the Mercy Sisters at Indian Island. He probably met Frances Warde during her visits to the Island in the early eighties. His career ended, he went home to Indian Island, where he died in 1913. His cousin, Andy Sockalexis, was a great marathon runner in the early nineties.

When the Mercy Sisters first opened their mission on the Penobscot in 1878, Frances Warde in Princeton, New Jersey, joyfully received the news of her first Mercy foundation among the Indians. St. Ann's on Indian Island began to thrive immediately. On February 16, 1879, Bishop Healy recorded in his *Diary* that "attention most favorable has been called to the Indian School directed by the Sisters of Mercy at Indian Oldtown. Attendance at school [has] quadrupled . . . Evening school for young men. Sewing and reading school for young women." In June, 1879, Healy went to Indian Island to dedicate the new Church of St. Ann. He saw a "wonderful improvement" in the Indians. They were "all that could be desired."[11]

Frances Warde, meanwhile, was already planning her second mission among the Maine Indians. In June, 1879, she sent another band of Sisters to the Indian Reservation at Pleasant Point, near Perry, on Passamaquoddy Bay opposite Deer Island and not far from Eastport. Pleasant Point, high on a Maine promontory overlooking the Bay where it joins Canadian waters, is the easternmost Indian reservation of the United States, granted to the Passamaquoddy Tribe by the General Court of Massachusetts in 1794. Frances sent three Sisters: Clare Leeson, as Superior; Sister de Chantal, Clare's mother; and Martha O'Brien. Unable to accompany the Sisters herself, Frances promised to visit them within a month. The three Sisters traveled from Eastport across Passamaquoddy Bay to Pleasant Point by canoe in torrential rains.[12] The tide was heavy and the waters were exceptionally rough. Weary and drenched, they found no fire awaiting them in the dreary, damp hut that was to be their Convent of Mercy. A few musty crackers were all the food they could find. There was one dirty bed in the hut. Sisters Clare and Martha gave it to Sister de Chantal, aged seventy-four, and they themselves slept on the floor. It was covered with filthy animal skins, and the wind blew through the cracks in the wood. Obviously, there was no resident priest at Pleasant Point. The next day, the Pastor from Eastport gave the Sisters ten dollars for food. Sister Clare sent a young Indian boy to Eastport to buy food, and he "stole half the money!" The amazing truth is that the Sisters—as in all Frances Warde's foundations—did not give up. They did not go back to Manchester. The Sisters of Mercy are still serving the Indians at Pleasant Point today.

The morning after the Sisters' arrival at their new mission, they knew that despite all the hardships that faced them, they were to live in beauty. Passamaquoddy Bay, after the rain, shone in all its summer loveliness. Curving island shores, blue skies above moving waters, white-winged gulls, drifting clouds above far-off green hills made Pleasant Point a place of breath-taking beauty. Across the blue expanse of Passamaquoddy rose the purple headlands outlining the St. Croix River, dividing Maine from New Brunswick. To the East lay the beautiful stretch of the fog-famed Bay of Fundy.

Pleasant Point village, however, was irregular in construction, completely unpaved, extreme in its disorder. The huts were poorly built and consistently dirty. The little Church of St. Ann adjoined the Sisters' hut. In 1861, the former house of Father Edmond Demillier had been razed and a school built in its place.[13]

Since the Passamaquoddies were more given to hunting and

fishing than the Penobscots, who had adopted more of the white man's style of life, the Sisters at Pleasant Point at first faced problems different from those of the Sisters at Indian Island. The Passamaquoddies were more difficult to instruct in the ordinary school subjects. Yet they clung with unbelievable tenacity to the Catholic faith brought to them by Jesuits 200 years before. The children were lovable and loving. They gradually became willing to learn reading, writing, and arithmetic. The difficulties of the Sisters were complicated because their little charges washed rarely and combed still more rarely. Girls under twelve smoked and chewed tobacco, and the handkerchief was unknown. In time, the children learned to follow instructions in making their school and their little homes more livable.

The Passamaquoddies at Pleasant Point did not have the Celebration of the Eucharist in their own church on Sundays. A priest came from Eastport on Monday nights, and on Tuesday mornings, all of the Indians participated at Mass. On Sundays, however, they held their own services at St. Ann's Church, led by elders of the tribe. Though the Sisters were at first surprised at the Sunday service, it illustrated a spiritual response discovered consistently by Europeans visiting the Maine Indians in the eighteenth and nineteenth centuries. When John de Cheverus, later the first Bishop of Boston, came to Maine as an exile of the French Revolution in 1797, he found that the Indians he visited, although they had lacked the service of a priest for forty years, prayed faithfully together every Sunday. They were even able to sing a Requiem Mass exactly as it was sung in France, chanting the *Kyrie* and the Preface in Latin![14] The Sisters of Mercy at Pleasant Point found the Indians reciting Vespers and singing hymns on Sundays in their own language. Their fathers had been taught to pray thus generations before by their Jesuit friends. The Indians had never forgotten. They preferred melody to harmony, Gregorian Chant to figured song.[15]

Frances Warde's third foundation among the Maine Indians was at Peter Dana Point (once called Louis Island), near Princeton, on the Schoodic Lakes. Owing to a disagreement over the election of their Governor, a band of Passamaquoddies had left Pleasant Point fifty years before the arrival of the Sisters of Mercy and settled at Dana Point. The Sisters from Pleasant Point served the Indians at Dana Point for four months each year, from the latter part of August until November. They saw their new mission for the first time in 1879 in the full glory of Indian Summer. They were fascinated with the pines and hemlocks, the willows and maples, the slender birches casting their reflections on the calm waters of the Schoodic Lakes. The scenery was scarcely less lovely in winter than in summer. Because of mosquitoes and large black flies, the Sisters were unable to serve at Dana Point during the hot months. A tiny modern convent was built for them adjoining small St. Ann's Church. In front of the Church was a little cemetery. Nearby was Long Lake with its woodland boundaries, and in the distance towered purple-gray mountains. From the convent on the brow of a hill, the Sisters could see the far-flung chain of Schoodic Lakes, studded with countless tiny islands.

The Indians at Dana Point were more nomadic than their tribesmen at Pleasant Point. Their spirit of wandering and their dislike for planting were obstacles to their material advancement.[16] Their huts were dirty and ill-kept. They greased their bodies and kept fires burning continually as protection against mosquitoes and flies. Since the children usually accompanied their parents in their roaming, they made little progress in school. It was disappointing to the Sisters to discover that, on arriving each fall at Dana Point, they found much undone of the work they had accomplished the previous year. Today, however, the Convent and the school at Dana Point are open during the entire school year. The number of students, however, is only about sixty. Dana Point is now part of a large Indian Township near Princeton.

The early *Annals* of the Sisters at Dana Point record that the Indians, despite their primitive way of life, still knew the prayers of the Mass and Vespers translated years before by Jesuit missionaries into the Abnaki language. Like their brothers at Pleasant Point, they still practiced beautiful rituals passed down to them by their ancestors. On New Year's Day, for example, they visited one another to offer the Kiss of Peace. On Good Friday, they bathed their feet in the Schoodic Lakes and then went to their little church to adore. When one of their members died, they placed a white resurrection veil on the corpse and sang hymns throughout the night. On Easter Sunday, the oldest woman of the tribe placed a symbolic sign on the forehead of every member.[17]

Frances Warde loved the Indians of Maine and was awed by their simple faith. They returned her love and called her their "Great White Mother." True to her promise, she visited her Indian missions in late summer of 1879, a month after her Sisters left Manchester for Pleasant Point.[18] Since Pleasant Point is eighty miles farther east than Old Town, Frances visited Indian Island first. When she arrived, the warm summer day was magnificent, and the waters of the Penobscot sparkled in the sun. As soon as she and her companions reached the right bank of the river, Chief Stockvesin Swassin crossed in his own canoe to welcome her. The birch bark canoe had a frail appearance, and Frances was doubtful about so romantic a journey. The Chief at once produced a small boat to row her to Indian Island. All the Penobscots of the Island awaited her at the shore, and the children sang Abnaki songs of welcome. It was a great fiesta day for all! Frances went first to St. Ann's Church to offer a prayer of thanksgiving. Then, as she walked toward the wigwam convent she exclaimed, "How happy Catherine McAuley would be had she lived to see this day!" The Indians came individually to thank her for sending her Sisters to live among them. She gave them medals as gifts, and they gave her baskets they themselves had woven. Then, they presented their babies for the "Great Mother's" blessings. Frances placed her hand upon the head of each child with a prayer. When she was ready to leave, Chief Stockvesin Swassin and his braves escorted her to Old Town and saw her off to Bangor.

From 1879 until the year of her death, Frances visited her Indian missions at least once a year. She sent her loved Indians gifts for their altars, and they sent her their own handiwork. Their reverence for the "Great White Mother" was known throughout Maine. The three missions continued to prosper with the help of the Sisters. Many of the Penobscots and Passamaquoddies, after attending high school in Eastport or Bangor, left their reservations to seek a new life. Sometimes they returned when old to die among their own people.

New homes, schools, and convents have been built at the Indian missions over the years. At Pleasant Point, for example, a new brick Church and Chapel of St. Ann with an adjoining Convent of Mercy was completed in 1928. But the love of the past is still felt everywhere in the Indian missions. On the ground floor of the convent at Pleasant Point, one can still see—on the spot that was once part of the church built in 1835—two simple slabs that mark the graves of Fathers Edmond Demillier and Kenneth Kennedy, pioneer Jesuit missionaries to the Abnakis. Sylvester Gabriel, an old Indian Chief from Pleasant Point, still has tales to tell of Mercy Sisters and their service to the Abnakis long ago.[19]

The Indian schools taught by the Sisters now operate under

the Government of the State of Maine. A Committee on Indian Affairs occasionally visits the reservations. The schools, called Contract Schools, are not actually State schools. The Sisters' salaries are paid by State funds, however, while improvements on school property are provided by tribal funds. Today the Sisters sometimes suffer frustration at Indian Island, Pleasant Point, and Dana Point. The Indians lack incentive and opportunities. Leaders among them are wanting because the most capable of them have rejected the poor living conditions on their reservations to join the White World beyond. Sylvester Gabriel laments a social welfare system which he believes has led his people to apathetic "living on the government."

From the beginning, some State government officials have attempted to banish the Sisters from the reservations. Reports of the visiting Committees on Indian Affairs, however, have always been favorable toward the work of the Sisters.[20] The Indians, moreover, have never tolerated any suggestion that the Sisters withdraw from their reservations. In the Archives of the Sisters of Mercy in Portland is a copy of a petition to Mother M. Eugenia, former Superior of the Portland Sisters, begging her to retain her Sisters at Indian Island despite efforts of government officials to remove them on the plea of "separation of Church and State." Signed by Chief Louis Nicholas, Governor of the Indian Reservation, and his Council, it reads as follows:

> Indian Island
> Old Town, Maine
> November 16, 1932

Reverend Mother Eugenia:

We the undersigned, residents of the Penobscot Indian Reservation, in appreciation of their considerate and consistent work, do hereby apply to you not to remove the Sisters of Mercy from our Reservation. We promise to give them our support, consideration, and respect.

For fifty-four years, the Sisters of Mercy, who know no home but the Heart of Our Lord, have labored untiringly among the Penobscot Indians. Many sacrifices were made by them for the education of our children. From the first, the Sisters' work was not confined to secular studies, but many weary hours were spent visiting the sick and the dying.

Since 1881, State Officials appointed by the Government to investigate the conditions of the Maine Indians have been unanimous in their high praise and appreciation of the labors of the Sisters among the Indians. As late as 1930, that praise was heard through a statement issued by Mr. W. O. Chase, Superintendent of the Old Town and Orono School Department concerning the Indian children who came from the Island to the Old Town Schools:

"I have carefully examined the records of every Indian child attending the Old Town Junior and Senior High Schools. I find that in their work they have maintained standards somewhat above the average of the schools as a whole. I also have carefully examined the records which they made during the first year after their transfer to the Old Town schools. Not one of the pupils now in school failed in his work during the first year."

Considering the facts stated herein, we hope you will grant us our request.

It is now almost one hundred years since Frances Warde made her three foundations at Indian Island, Pleasant Point, and Dana Point. The Indians still speak of the love the "Great Mother" had for them. Her Sisters, despite all obstacles, are still serving in the apostolate to the Indians to which she sent them. Life on the reservations is no longer at the peak of development experienced between 1880 and 1930. The majority of the Maine Indians have mingled with the white communities of the State. But the Sisters of Mercy, from 1878 until the present, have continued to labor among the Indians who, like the Blacks, have been deprived because of the color of their skin. While most of the white population of Maine has had little interest in and less care for the Abnakis (a Maine newspaper editorial declared a few years ago that many people of the State were even unaware of the existence of the Indian Reservations), Frances Warde's Sisters have remained faithful.

Catherine McAuley once said to Frances Warde that when God institutes a religious congregation, he gives at the same time the grace that is necessary for such a congregation. Each community of religious receives a grace particularly adapted to the duties they are called to perform. It would seem that Frances Warde's apostolate of announcing the Word of God to the American Indians was especially graced in the State of Maine.

20

Petition to Rome Once More and Moral Victory; A Celebration

DURING the later part of her life, Frances Warde, worn out from long years in the Mercy apostolate, suffered from ill health which she seems to have accepted so quietly that little was made of it in the *Annals* of the Sisters of Mercy. References to Frances' illness are found in the *Diary* of Bishop Healy,[1] who referred frequently to his visits to Mount St. Mary's at Manchester, New Hampshire, and in the correspondence of Kent Stone.[2] Frances was threatened with pneumonia in January of 1877. In July of the following year, she was again seriously ill, but nevertheless accompanied her Sisters in late summer on the foundation of St. Paul's Convent and School in Princeton, New Jersey. Again, in June of 1879, she "was by no means well,"[3] so that she was unable to go personally on the foundation of St. Ann's Convent and School at Pleasant Point, Maine. Characteristically, she recovered sufficiently to visit her Indian Missions in late summer of the same year. Like Saint Frances Cabrini, Frances Warde did not allow ill health to interfere with her apostolate.

Personal sorrow, too, came to Frances during the late seventies. On December 15, 1879, her well loved sister, Mother Josephine Warde, died at St. Maries of the Isle in Cork, Ireland. Since their childhood days at Bellbrook, Frances and her sister had been very close to each other. Sarah Warde had entered the Convent of Mercy at Baggot Street, Dublin, the year that Frances was professed. She had been sent on the Mercy foundation to Cork in 1837 and appointed Superior there in 1839, pending the return of Sister Clare Moore from Catherine McAuley's first British foundation in Bermondsey, England. When Sister Clare was again sent to London in 1841, Josephine was once more appointed Superior at the Cork Convent of Mercy. Most of the remaining years of her life were spent as leader of the Sisters of St. Maries of the Isle. Josephine established Convents of Mercy at Passage West, Bantry, Templemore, Queenstown (Cobh), and Sunderland in Yorkshire. She was one of the first Mercy Superiors to respond to the petition of Cardinal Henry Edward Manning in 1854 for Sisters to serve as nurses in the Crimean War. But her favorite apostolate was to send young girls to enter the Convents of Mercy established by Frances Warde in the United States. Josephine did not live to realize a project dear to her, the founding of a College for Women— similar to the Missionary College for men at All Hallows, Dublin—in which young ladies would be trained for the American missions. Back in 1845, when Frances Warde returned to Ireland from Pittsburgh, she had visited her sister in Cork. If the American founder ever again saw her sister, there is no record of the meeting. Yet the two were as close in spirit at Josephine's death in 1879 as they had been during the eighteen-thirties in Carlow and in Dublin.

Frances' old friend, Kent Stone, now Father Fidelis of the Passionist Congregation, had returned to Mount St. Mary's to preach a retreat for the Sisters there in August of 1878. He was at SS. Giovanni e Paolo in Rome in 1879 when he heard of Josephine's death through his and Frances' friend, Father Edmund Hill. Stone hastened to write to Frances, revealing the same beautiful faith he had expressed to her nine years earlier when his little girl, Ethel Xavier, had died at Manchester:

Dear Rev. Mother,

I have received a letter from Father Edmund, in which he tells me that you have lost your dear . . . sister, Mother Josephine, of Cork. I have used the wrong word, for how can we call such a blessed death a "loss"? I confess I feel something like envy when I hear of such a happy ending of a well-spent life . . . Such a death always makes me exclaim in my heart, *Deo gratias* . . . Yet I know what an affectionate and generous heart you have, my dear Rev. Mother, and how keenly you feel the severance of earthly ties, and I know that our human nature cannot help feeling the pain of that which is to mere nature a blow and a loss. And so I send you at the same time my sympathy and my congratulations.

I am sure you haven't forgotten me, and I hope you still pray for me sometimes.[4]

None understood better than Kent Stone the suffering of loss experienced by Frances, and none knew better than she the anguish he expressed in words so guarded as to be almost cliché: "I know . . . how keenly you feel the severance of earthly ties . . ." Though neither now spoke in their letters of the children of Kent Stone, both knew too well the long pain of separation.

From Ireland came a letter of Denis M. Bradley, Chancellor of the Diocese of Portland, who was visiting in Cork and present at Josephine's funeral. Bradley was a Manchester boy, he had been prepared for Confirmation at St. Ann's by Frances Warde, and he had been a young priest-protegé of William McDonald. He assured Frances that Josephine had died peacefully, loved by her Sisters and by everyone in Cork. The Sisters in Manchester feared the effect that Josephine's death might have upon Frances. But they need not have feared. Like Catherine McAuley, Frances could have said that "the grave was always open in her regard." Over and over again through the years, she had accepted with faith both separation and death. In Pittsburgh, during the typhoid plague, she had experienced the deep grief of the deaths of four of her young Sisters within a month. Indeed, after the early loss of Edward Nolan in Carlow in 1837, Frances had never again given way to excessive grief.

The year 1879 brought to Frances another cause for personal grief, in this case followed by deep joy. Frances' grandniece, Mary Agnes Warde, aged eleven, was then living with her mother, Margaret Keogh Warde, in Pittsburgh. John Warde, favorite nephew of Mother Frances and father of the little girl, had died at Mercy Hospital in Pittsburgh in 1868, a few months before Mary Agnes was born. He had served in the Fifth Regiment of the Excelsior Brigade during the Civil War and had been honorably discharged in 1862 because of rheumatic fever. After her husband's death, Margaret Warde had opened "Mrs. Warde's Select Academy" in Pittsburgh. She was a popular novelist, a poet, and an admired teacher. Her brother, Father James Keogh, was a man of remarkable intellect who at the age of sixteen had been sent by Bishop Michael O'Connor to study at the College of the Propaganda in Rome. Because of his extraordinary scholarship, he was made a Doctor of Divinity at eighteen and was presented with a mosaic by Pope Pius IX. Margaret Keogh Warde's health had always been frail, and in the early months of 1879 she became seriously ill with tuberculosis. With her usual kindness, Frances Warde offered to care for her grandniece at Mount St. Mary's until the child's mother became well again. Although Frances had seen Mary Agnes but seldom, she was very fond of the little girl. After her visit

427

to the Convent of Mercy in Pittsburgh at the time of her Philadelphia foundation in 1861, Frances seems to have gone back to her first American foundation only once again. Sometime around 1872, she visited St. Mary's Convent, Webster Avenue—the Convent that she herself had planned with Michael O'Connor more than twenty years earlier. Years later, Mary Agnes Warde recalled that she had there met Mother Frances for the first time and loved her.[5]

Frances' grandniece arrived at Mount St. Mary's in February, 1879, and was enrolled as a resident student. In early summer, she returned temporarily to her home in Pittsburgh. Margaret Keogh Warde died in October, 1879, and Mary Agnes again journeyed to Manchester, this time to remain permanently under Mother Frances' care. The little girl's brother, Sylvie, four years older than she, went to live in Southern Illinois with his Aunt Jennie, Frances Warde's niece, Jane Warde Hight. So the sorrow of Margaret Warde's death brought with it joy for Mother Frances in having her little grandniece with her in Manchester.

Mary Agnes Warde proved to be a talented girl. She was a fair writer, an artist, and a musician who played the harp magnificently. Her talents were developed well at Mount St. Mary's. In June, 1884, shortly before her sixteenth birthday, she was graduated from the Academy at Manchester. And in July she entered the Congregation of Mercy there just two months before the death of Frances Warde. Mary Agnes was received as a Novice in January, 1885 with the name Sister Paul Xavier. When she died in 1955, she had served the Manchester community for seventy years.

The *Mount St. Mary Journal*, a monthly magazine published at the Manchester academy for several years, contains a number of articles written by Sister Paul Xavier.[6] In these essays is evident once more a curious phenomenon concerning the relationship of Frances Warde with those she loved. It has been pointed out that Frances, sensitive to the greatness of Catherine McAuley, saved her letters carefully for posterity. Yet Frances' correspondence with Catherine was not preserved at Baggot Street. Again, Frances scrupulously filed away the letters of Kent Stone, recognizing their importance even as he wrote them to her. Yet Stone did not save Frances' letters to him. "Hundreds" of other documents that Frances treasured carefully for the *Annals* of the Sisters of Mercy, moreover, were destroyed after the death of Mother Austin Carroll in Mobile, Alabama. The small number of Frances Warde's own letters that have been preserved seem to have survived almost by happy accident. Bishop James O'Connor of Omaha, for example, saved all his correspondence, so that Frances' letters to him were preserved by accident among hundreds of other epistles.

It is obvious that if others had manifested the same awareness and sensitivity concerning Frances' letters that she demonstrated with regard to their correspondence, a broader vision of her life and work and that of all the Sisters of Mercy in America would have been possible.[7]

Perhaps this somewhat puzzling and yet not willful want of thoughtfulness is explained best in a statement made fifty years ago by Paul L. Blakely of the staff of *America*. "It is somewhat curious," he wrote, "that a woman who did so much for the Church and for social and educational progress [Frances Warde] should be so little known in this part of the world. But perhaps we . . . are so blinded by our own greatness that we have no eyes for the work of others."[8]

One would expect that Sister Paul Xavier Warde, who not only loved her great-aunt but recognized clearly her spiritual greatness, would have written for posterity a significant account of the remarkable woman whom even her contemporaries viewed as a genius. At the request of other Sisters of Mercy,[9] Mary Agnes Warde did write in later years an appreciation of her aunt's character,[10] but only in very general terms, emphasizing qualities of personality already recorded elsewhere. "In all my conversations with her," she wrote of Frances Warde, "she never once told me of the great things she had accomplished or the hardships she had endured in the past." Sister Paul Xavier had to learn of Frances Warde's heroism from other Sisters of Mercy. Yet Mary Agnes lived with her aunt for six years, between the ages of eleven and sixteen, impressionable years during which she must have observed and heard much that a writer of her ability could later incorporate into a meaningful biographical monograph of Mother Frances. But the curious truth is that Sister Paul Xavier's informal essays in the *Mount St. Mary Journal* deal chiefly with her own experiences. Her longest series of articles, written when she was thirty, relates to her schoolgirl adventures as a resident student. Yet she had shared the day-to-day life of one of America's great women, and she would have been the first to insist upon Frances' greatness.[11]

On the day that Frances Warde would be buried, James Healy was to remark upon the rare quality of her self-effacement. Wherever she served the people of God, Frances Warde centered attention upon her apostolic work, not upon herself. Perhaps one of the most significant differences between Frances and many of the servants of Christ who were her contemporaries was her sense of history. She seemed to know almost intuitively what to preserve for posterity. Foresight is a rare gift; hindsight is common.

After the deaths of Josephine Warde and Margaret Keogh Warde, Frances turned her thoughts typically to a new venture. She had received a request to establish a Convent of Mercy and a school at Laconia, New Hampshire. Though she had led foundations from Manchester to six states—to Pennsylvania, Nebraska, Maine, California, Vermont, and New Jersey—she had yet to establish a branch house in New Hampshire itself. Before she could set out for Laconia, however, it was time for the 1880 election of the Mother Superior at Manchester.

As in the case of the election of 1877, Bishop James Healy's *Diary* again reveals his unnecessary involvement in the election of the Sisters. An entry in the *Diary* for July 15, 1880, states that "Rev. Mother seems determined to hold the superiority if she can—and Father McDonald is intensely and bitterly opposed to any succession." Then Healy adds, referring to himself, "The Bishop is determined to adhere to the Rule unless Rome make an exception." Bishop Healy's implicit suggestion that Rome might *not* make an exception is difficult to understand. Only a simple request from the Bishop or the Sisters was needed to validate the American founder's continuation in office by election if her Sisters so desired.

The next entry in Healy's *Diary* is dated August 18. He writes that Sister Mary Catherine Clifford was elected Superior, Mother Frances Warde was made First Assistant, and Mother Xavier Leeson Mistress of Novices. No indication is given as to whether the Sisters desired to re-elect Mother Frances as Superior. The election itself was, in a sense, indicative of the judgment of the Sisters. Since they were not permitted to elect Frances Warde, they chose her for the second office in the Congregation, while they named her two close co-workers and friends, Catherine Clifford and Xavier Leeson, as leaders of the Congregation with her. On August 22, Bishop Healy stated in his *Diary* that he had "received a telegram from Rome empowering him to confirm the Rev. Mother for one year if elected." And on September 2 he wrote in his journal: "The Bishop learns today that a rescript from Rome would allow Rev. Mother Warde to be Superior again if elected by a two-thirds vote. Too late now."

Much more revealing of what actually happened at Manchester in the election of 1880 are letters extant in the Portland Diocesan Archives and in the Irish College in Rome. Weeks before the election, Bishop Healy busied himself concerning the internal affairs of the Congregation of Mercy. On July 9, 1880, he wrote to Mother Frances as follows: "I made it my duty to ask each and every one [of the Sisters] whether their desire was that I should apply to Rome that you might be again eligible as Mother Superior." He continued: "The number of those who desire that the Rule should be observed is so considerable that Rome would certainly not grant the permission . . . I think the simple and good way is for you to write me a letter requesting me not to write to Rome."[12] One can imagine the tension created among the Manchester Sisters by Healy's interviews, especially since he based his interrogation on the question of whether or not "the Rule should be observed."

To be sure, the Sisters were well aware that Bishop Healy had refused to request permission from Rome for Mother Frances' re-election in 1877. They themselves had requested and received papal approval. They knew that the same approval would be available without difficulty in 1880. Healy's dogmatic statement that "Rome would certainly not grant the permission" was probably not known to the Sisters. Mother Frances would not share Healy's offensive letter to her with the Congregation at large.

In any case, a petition *was* sent to Rome, asking that Frances Warde might be eligible to be re-elected as Superior. The letter is not extant in Roman Archives, but the probability is that it was similar to the petition of 1877. Evidently, the letter was forwarded to Rome through Father William Mc-

Donald. As in the case of the petition of 1877, the answer received by Bishop Healy in Manchester on September 2, 1880, was affirmative. In the Archives of the Irish College at Rome is a letter written by Frances Warde on September 13, 1880, to Dr. Tobias Kirby, Rector of the Irish College. It was customary in the second half of the nineteenth century for Irish-American clergy and religious to forward letters to the Pope through the Rector of the Irish College. Approval of France Warde's eligibility for re-election was sent to Manchester by Monsignor Kirby. Following is Frances Warde's letter[13] to him:

> Mount St. Mary's
> Manchester
> New Hampshire
> America

Very Revd. and dear Father:

Some ten days since our saintly Pastor [William McDonald] received your most welcome letter containing your highly prized letter to myself and the rescript of His Holiness for my re-election. I thank you so much for such great kindness. I remember having had the pleasure of seeing you with our sainted Foundress in Baggot Street Convent, and again in Carlow. The memories of the past are filled with saintly associations.

We all feel most grateful for the interest you have evinced in our Community. We have one hundred and thirty Sisters teaching in this Diocese, thirteen hundred children in our schools in this city, large numbers in Portland and other towns in Maine, two orphan homes, one here with a house for the aged and infirm, three Indian settlements, etc., etc.

I could not describe the untiring zeal of our holy Pastor. Surely it is all for God with him. I heard the late Bishop [Bacon] say in presence of many that the fact was "that everything Father McDonald put his hand to was blessed by God." But now, most venerated Father and friend, our present Bishop is fond of changes. He would not permit the election to wait longer than the 18th of last month—to hear from Rome. The letters did not come, as you know, so in consequence he would not allow my name to be mentioned, and another Sister was that day elected. The Community were obliged to vote for another. When your valued letters arrived with the rescript and were sent to the Bishop, he said that "it would be too late now to have another election" . . .

Thanking you again and again, most Revd. and dear Father, asking your prayers and your blessing for myself and dear Sisters, I am

> Most gratefully and respectfully
> Yours in Ct,
> Sr. Mary Frances Xavier Warde

Place this little prayer in your breviary. It will remind you to pray for your early friend.

Convent of Our Lady of Mercy
September 13, 1880

So ended the Manchester Mercy election of 1880. Bishop Healy had his way, but the victory was not his.

Since Frances Warde had already planned the opening of a convent and school in Laconia, New Hampshire, before the election of August 18, she continued the venture and was ready to leave for Laconia before the end of August. Sister Bernard McDonald was named Superior of the new mission. Two newly professed Sisters were also appointed. William McDonald accompanied them to their new Convent.

Laconia is a lovely town nestled among the lakes of central New Hampshire at the gateway to the White Mountains. The natural beauty of the scenery is so exquisite that a local bard once exclaimed:

> *We've seen the prairies and the flowers*
> *Beside their sparkling rills,*
> *But nothing ever gladdens us*
> *Like old New Hampshire hills.*

434

Though the population of Laconia was dominantly Puritan, the Sisters of Mercy were invited to live and teach there by Father John Lambert Schakers, who had come in 1873 as a missionary to America from Holland.[14] He had arrived in Laconia in 1878, just in time to help his parishioners to rebuild St. Joseph's Church, which had been demolished by fire. He was carpenter, painter, plasterer, plumber, and gardener. He planted trees and laid out beautiful landscapes. Then he urged the Catholic children of the town to come to St. Joseph's to school. He even composed his own unique catechism for them. When all was in readiness, he sent an invitation to Frances Warde to bring her Sisters to his parish.

At Laconia, Frances opened not only St. Joseph's Parochial School with 165 students but a night school for the young men and women who worked all day in the local hosiery mills. The Sisters also visited and cared for the sick in their homes. When the works of mercy were well established, Mother Frances and Father McDonald returned to Manchester.

The year 1881 was to bring unforgettable experiences, both happy and sad, to Frances Warde. The Sisters of Mercy throughout the world celebrated their Golden Jubilee on December 12, the anniversary of Catherine McAuley's profession and the foundation of the Congregation of Mercy in Dublin. Eucharistic Celebrations were offered in glad thanksgiving in Ireland, England, Scotland, Australia, New Zealand, North America, and South America. The growth of the Congregation from its small beginnings in Baggot Street was seemingly miraculous. But nowhere had the apostolate of Mercy spread more rapidly than in the United States. During only thirty-eight years, from the time of the Pittsburgh foundation in 1843 until the Mercy Jubilee Day in 1881, over 200 convents with 10,000 Sisters had sprung up in the United States. No one was more personally involved in the realization of Catherine McAuley's dream than Frances

435

Warde. And no one would have taken less credit to herself. Like Catherine McAuley, she had always insisted that the Mercy apostolate was God's work, not hers. Of the original seven who came from Carlow to Pittsburgh in 1843, only Frances and her dear friend, Elizabeth Strange, lived to celebrate the fifty years of service.

In October, 1881, the Sisters of Mercy of Manchester marked the Jubilee by petitioning Pope Leo XIII for his "blessing and prayers for ourselves, our Community, all our works of Mercy, orphans, sick, poor, students, and converts . . ."[15] The blessing of the Pope was sent to Mercy Sisters throughout the world on November 17, 1881. Frances Warde joyfully celebrated the anniversary with all the younger Sisters of her Congregation. But, in a sense, they could never know as she did the meaning and the price of the vision fulfilled. They had never lived and prayed and planned with Catherine McAuley at Baggot Street, Carlow, Naas, and Wexford. They had not loved and worked and suffered as Frances had in Pittsburgh, Chicago, Loretto, Providence, Hartford, New Haven, Newport, Rochester, Philadephia, Omaha, Bangor, Yreka, North Whitefield, St. Johnsbury, Burlington, Jersey City, Portland, Indian Island, Pleasant Point, Dana Point, Bordentown, Princeton . . . Frances' foundations of Mercy were endless, and each was unique in its joy and pain as the Holy Spirit breathed upon its Sisters. Only Frances Warde had shared in all.

Frances was growing old. She had celebrated her seventy-first birthday. She was becoming aware that her time of service was limited, and she was eager that Sisters of Mercy who would come after her would know the glorious history of their Congregation. She felt obliged to contribute to that history an account of those events which only she could relate from experience. In January, 1882, one month after the

Golden Jubilee celebration, she sat down to write to Mother Austin Carroll, compiler of the four-volume *Annals* of the Sisters of Mercy.[16] Her letter indicates that she was spending long hours dictating the history of her foundations to Mother Gonzaga O'Brien, her Assistant:

Dearest Sister M. Austin,

. . . I have been sitting beside Sister Mary Gonzaga for many days giving her all the information of our first days in Pittsburgh, our six weeks' previous journey across the Atlantic, our safe arrival in New York, and many incidents . . . about our crossing the Allegheny Mountains to get to our dusky home in Pittsburgh, our reception, and our first Mission, Chicago, and the wonders of my homeward journey night and day across the Prairies . . .

Then our Hospital, [as] soon as I was a little rested. The Day and Boarding Schools . . . St. Xavier's . . . the number of our Sisters dying in our Hospital on Penn Street, our moving to the Bishop's new house near the Cathedral.

When I had given much time and attention to these matters, Sr. M. G. says that she thinks you know all about them; if so, it is useless to repeat them. We will have the [accounts of the] Indian Settlements all ready, [as] soon as you need them.

I would like to tell something about Providence and its commencement. Now send me a line and say if you would like to see what we have written. Sister has fifteen of our Holy Foundress' [letters] written out for you—she continues writing them.

Did you not remember that last Monday the 23rd. was the anniversary (50th) of my Reception, the first Sister who received the Holy Habit of the Order of Mercy in our first Convent in Baggot Street, and Tuesday the 24th. was the 49th anniversary of my Holy Profession, the first professed. How full of joys and deep sorrows my life has been, none can tell. It is a long time in which much good could have been accomplished, and I fear much *neglected*.

I got letters from Carlow and Cork; they seem to remember

me, and my length of time in Religion . . . The memory of the
past is filled with humbling reflections for me.

> Pray often for your dear Sister in Ch.,
> M. M. F. Xavier

Even now, however, Frances Warde was not to divorce
herself from the immediate apostolates of the Congregation
of Mercy. True, Catherine Clifford was now Superior at
Manchester, but Frances was her Assistant. And Mother
Catherine's deference for Frances was such that she considered her own office an accident of election. "Mother
Xavier Warde was her highest earthly ideal, and notwithstanding their different temperaments, she imbibed her spirit
with many of her principles of government."[17] Whatever was
to happen during Catherine Clifford's term of office, Frances
Warde would be involved in both the decision and the action.

For a few years prior to 1882, rumors had circulated that
Bishop James Healy desired a division of the Diocese of
Portland. The States of Maine and New Hampshire were
said to be too large a territory for one Bishop to manage. In
June, 1880, Healy had appointed his Chancellor, Denis M.
Bradley, as Pastor of St. Joseph Church in Manchester. This
assignment led to speculation that Manchester might become
the Episcopal See of a new Diocese covering the entire State
of New Hampshire. Bishop Healy had also intimated to
Frances Warde that, unlike Bishop Bacon who wished to
establish a mother house in Portland for the Mercy Sisters
of both New Hampshire and Maine, he desired to divide the
Congregation by establishing a separate mother house in Portland.

Healy took his first step toward his design for the Sisters of
Mercy in 1881 when he invited Frances Warde and Catherine
Clifford to Portland to discuss the possible establishment of a

new boarding academy for young ladies in Portland. He had already chosen an ideal site near the "Deering Oaks" made famous by Henry Wadsworth Longfellow's poem, "My Lost Youth." The property, called "Forest Home," was part of the former estate of F. O. J. Smith, Portland publisher, lawyer, and giant in the financial and civic affairs of Maine during the middle and late sixties. It had been a beautiful spot, with flower gardens, a trout pond, and an enclosure for small deer. After the death of Smith, much of his property came into the possession of James P. Baxter of Portland, so that it was called "Baxter's Woods."

Frances Warde and Catherine Clifford agreed to establish St. Joseph's Academy at Deering. Accounts of Bishop Healy's life indicate that he "gave the Sisters full possession and control of the large and valuable property he purchased at Deering,"[18] and that he envisaged a mother house for the Sisters of Mercy there. The truth is that the money with which the property was purchased was the dowry of Fannie King of Boston, who entered the Manchester Congregation in 1881. A sum of $20,000 was given to Healy by the Sisters in 1884 in exchange for St. Elizabeth's Convent in Portland and the property in Deering Oaks.[19] When Bishop Healy died in 1900, the Portland Sisters still had their center at St. Elizabeth's Convent on Free Street, which had been successively Bishop Bacon's residence, St. Elizabeth's Convent and Orphan Asylum, and St. Elizabeth's Mother House and Academy. The new Mercy mother house at Deering, called St. Joseph's Convent, was not begun until Louis Sebastian Walsh was appointed Bishop of Portland in 1906. It was dedicated in 1909.

Few people today are aware of the complicated relationship of Baxter's Woods (the site of Deering Oaks) to the invention of the telegraph, the founding of Western Union, and the creation of Cornell University.[20] A tinge of romance surrounds Baxter's Woods and the former farm home of financier F. O. J. Smith in Deering. One day, while sailing up the Hudson River, Smith noticed on deck a downcast young man who seemed to be in great trouble. He engaged the stranger in conversation and discovered that he was Samuel F. B. Morse, artist and inventor. The youth was depressed because he had invented a method of transmitting messages by means of copper wire, but he had no money to demonstrate his invention and make it workable. The two men became friends, and Smith offered to help to finance Morse's project. The younger man experimented on Smith's estate. He was known to the residents of the Deering area as a "crazy man" who wandered around the woods stringing wire to trees to prove the efficiency of his mad invention. Smith entertained Morse at his home, sometimes called "the Castle," and continued to encourage the inventor in his project. Eventually, the United States Congress was persuaded to appropriate money for a trial telegraph line between Baltimore and Washington. Morse and Smith had concluded that the most practical method of transmission would be by underground lines. But installation of such lines by hand would be too expensive. They grappled with the problem of an installation machine.

One day a plow salesman named Ezra Cornell made a routine call upon Smith, who published *The Maine Farmer*. Cornell found Smith on his knees, with a plow moldboard at his side, as he sketched with a piece of chalk. Smith explained that he wanted to design a machine that would dig a ditch and deposit the upturned soil on each side of it. Then, he added, the soil could be replaced with a second machine. Cornell thought that *one* machine could do the whole job. Smith was dubious of Cornell's idea, but he was convinced finally and engaged Cornell to construct the projected machine. Finally, with Smith and Morse watching, Cornell demonstrated his machine, harnessed to eight oxen, on Smith's estate. The experiment was successful. At first, Cornell was reluctant to give up his plow business. But convinced at last of the marvelous potentialities of the telegraph, he began in 1843 to lay the pipe for the telegraph wire between Baltimore and Washington along the route of the Baltimore and Ohio Railroad. The rest is history. On May 24, 1844, Morse sent his famous message, "What hath God wrought." Cornell became one of the founders of Western Union in 1855. He amassed a fortune with which he built Cornell University.

A plaque on an oak tree in Baxter's Woods commemorated the spot where Morse carried on his original experiments. The plaque has now disappeared, but the trees on the grounds of St. Joseph's Convent and Academy mark the site of Morse's invention. It seems fitting that Frances Warde made her last foundation in Maine on this historic spot. She came to the United States in the same year that the telegraph was invented. Morse and Cornell were pioneer geniuses in industrial America; Frances Warde was a spiritual genius.

To be sure, long before the Sisters of Mercy established their Convent and Academy in Deering, the flourishing days of F. O. J. Smith's Castle had passed. Smith had built a three-story brick building on the grounds of his estate which he disposed of in his will as a "Home for Indigent Females." In the seventies, however, the house was considered to be too far from the city to be used as a home for the aged. There were also two small wooden structures on the property. Bishop Healy, Frances Warde, and Catherine Clifford decided to convert the brick building into St. Joseph's Convent and Academy, and one of the smaller buildings into St. Joseph's Home for aged women.

The Sisters of Mercy, with Sister Petronilla O'Grady as

Superior and Director of the Academy, moved into their new home in Deering on March 19, 1882.[21] Sister Petronilla was one of Frances Warde's closest friends. As a young woman of beauty and wit, she had come to Manchester from Galway, Ireland, in 1869, on the appeal of Mother Frances. She was destined to be the second Mother Superior of the Congregation of Mercy in Portland after its separation from the Manchester community. On September 1, 1882, the Sisters from Manchester took charge of St. Joseph's Home for aged women at Deering, the Superior being Sister Mary Jane Doyle, who as a young novice had been a pioneer at St. Elizabeth's Convent and Orphanage in Portland.

Deering was the last site for a Mercy mother house founded by Frances Warde. She returned to Manchester from Deering in the fall of 1882, her mind occupied with many decisions that she must make during the following year. The proposed division of her Congregation at Manchester required much thought and diplomacy if she was to keep her Sisters happy. Division meant that difficult choices would have to be made, friends would be separated, loved convents would be left forever, loneliness would have to be endured. Frances Warde knew too well the meaning of these experiences. She would know how to lessen the suffering of her Sisters.

21

A Cause to Rejoice; Final Election and Final Mission

On January 8, 1883, Sister Catherine Clifford of Manchester wrote the following letter[1] to the Superiors of Convents of Mercy throughout the world, announcing the Golden Jubilee of Frances Warde's profession as a Sister of Mercy:

Will you accept the warmest invitation for yourself and Sisters . . . to the Golden Jubilee of our venerated and loved Rev. Mother, Wednesday, Jan. 24th?

From her numerous spiritual children and each community of our Sisters throughout the world, we solicit a union of prayer to the Mother of Mercy to obtain every blessing for one who has done so much to extend the greater glory of God by saving souls . . .

You will rejoice to hear that our loved Mother is wonderfully well, actually zealous as ever . . . .

Yours affectionately in Christ,
S. M. Catherine Clifford

Surprisingly, Frances was "wonderfully well" during the early months of 1883. It seemed that Providence granted her special energy for the happy celebration of her Jubilee. Almost immediately came a response to Catherine Clifford's letter from Frances' cousin, Mother Catherine Maher, in

Carlow: "What a world of good our Mother Warde achieved in her fifty years!" Catherine Maher recalled a beautiful legend concerning a monk at prayer that Frances had told her novices "long, long ago" at St. Leo's. Now, the Carlow Sisters reminded Mother Frances, she herself was experiencing the joy of that monk like:

> *The sudden singing of a bird*
> *So sweet, and clear, and loud*
> *It seemed a thousand harp-strings ringing.*

Probably the most revealing tributes in their reverence for Frances were the letters written by those unable to attend the Jubilee celebration.[2] Since they could not go personally to Manchester, they put their devotion into words. The Sisters of Frances' loved Convent in Westport, her first Mount Saint Mary's, greeted her in verse from across the sea:

> *May the white-winged bright angels, those spirits sublime,*
> *Who enraptured keep watch round the throne,*
> *Bear all our fond greetings from Erin's green Isle*
> *To that land which you now call your own. . . .*

> *If we seek cherished spots in our dear Island Home*
> *Where the seedlings of Mercy you cast,*
> *Carlow, Westport, and Wexford, and Naas will recall*
> *Brightest moments beloved of the past. . . .*

Of all the greetings from Ireland, however, the one that filled Frances Warde's eyes with tears was that which came from the Convent of Mercy in Downpatrick with a shamrock from the grave of St. Patrick and the blessing of Catherine McAuley:

> No brilliant dye
> To charm your eye,
> No fragrance to impart,
> Has our shamrock got,
> Yet shall it not
> Be dear to your Celtic heart?
> A type of the love
> Of our Mother above
> For the child of her cherished "First Seven,"
> As green as our spray
> For your Jubilee day,
> With her smile and her blessing from Heaven.

From Geelong, Australia, Sister Gabriel Sherlock, who had met Frances Warde at Baggot Street years before, wrote that the Australian Sisters were praying for "the beloved Mother whom we all revere, and whose dear name is so familiar to us." And she added, "I would like to kneel at her feet and receive her blessing."

The Sisters of St. Xavier's Convent in Chicago, Frances' first American foundation from Pittsburgh, wrote to remind her both of their own beginnings and of her days of joy and sorrow as the companion of Catherine McAuley:

Glancing back on the years that have flown, you will think of our small convent on the lake shore. The seed you cast on this prairie has been blessed by God, and has produced fruit for eternity a hundredfold. Grateful memories of you, dear Mother, still linger here . . . . The gentle spirit of our Holy Foundress will rejoice in your joy and obtain blessings not only for the companion of her early trials but also for those who have the honor and happiness of being numbered among her children.

Tributes from Bishops, priests, religious, and friends poured into Mount St. Mary's at Manchester. Abbot Boniface Wimmer, O.S.B., founder of St. Vincent Archabbey, Latrobe, the first Benedictine Archabbey in the United States, on the original site of Mount Saint Vincent's Academy (later St. Xavier), founded by Frances Warde in 1845, wrote to Frances: "I find myself seventy-five years of age— fifty years a Benedictine and fifty-one years a priest, therefore too old to travel, despite the pleasure it would give me to be present at the ceremonies to take place on this joyful occasion in the sight of heaven and earth." A long-time friend, Father Edmund of the Passionists, questioned Frances in his greetings: "Do you not feel like holy Simeon when he sang his *Nunc Dimittis?* Could you not use his beautiful words as you look back on the past, so filled with mercies? God bless and keep you always, my very dear friend." Michael O'Connor, now a Jesuit, wrote from Boston College, in the name of his confreres, a promise of prayers to the Master for whom Frances "had labored so long and so well."

Frances' close friend, Mother Catherine Seton of the Sisters of Mercy of New York, daughter of Elizabeth Seton, founder of the Sisters of Charity, was too old and feeble to go to Manchester. She declared to Frances, "How I wish some angel of Mercy could descend to earth and bear me to your side, that with a warm embrace I could congratulate you . . . ." And Emily Harper, friend of forty years, offered Frances "devoted and grateful love for all the affection you have given me through so many years since we first met. Would that I had the same record in my state of life as you have sent before you!"

Perhaps three tributes from Bishops and religious are outstanding among the many received with joy by the Manchester Sisters. They express best the meaning of Frances Warde's contribution to the Church in America.

Father Alfred Young of the Paulists wrote from New York in behalf of himself and Father Isaac Hecker, founder of

446

the Paulists. Both were too ill to attend the Jubilee celebra tion. Young, a long-time friend of Frances, was able to state simply and directly the feeling of the clergy of the United States for her:

As Very Rev. Father Hecker and I have been promoted to the rank of General Invalid, it will be quite impossible for either of us to make the journey to Manchester . . .

Therefore, we are going to make an act of virtue out of this unwelcome necessity, and do that which costs us the most while this joyous festivity is being celebrated—which is, to stay at home. Indeed we would both rejoice to show you, as you are most worthy to receive, our fraternal respect and heartfelt congratulations. In what I am saying to interpret the directions of Very Rev. Father Hecker, and as expression of my own feelings, I am repeating as well the sentiments entertained by all our community. I add for myself (and no doubt with the willing assent of everybody) *that, if we of the clergy do not strengthen your soul by prayers at God's Altar, then we are little deserving of having had such a woman and such a religious in our day and generation.* It is to be hoped that in fifty years' time of service to the servants of God, you have managed to acquire enough humility to bear a little praise to your face.

Bishop Thomas Francis Hendricken of Providence, Rhode Island, had known Frances Warde for many years. In 1872, when the Diocese of Providence was separated from that of Hartford, he had been appointed its first Bishop. Hendricken's appreciation for Mother Frances revealed a lucid realization of her status in the American Church as well as an awareness of her very close relationship with Catherine McAuley:

I entertain for Rev. Mother Warde sentiments of the deepest affection . . . and send a thousand blessings. She is a grand historical character. Her works are a benediction to the Church.

447

The Community which she almost founded continues to pour its streams of charity on God's poor and to fill heaven with holy souls.

Tradition relates that, of all the Jubilee greetings received at Manchester, Frances loved best the poem sent by Father Edmund Hill of the Passionists (quoted above). An English convert and author, he was a close friend of Kent Stone, Father Fidelis of the Passionists. The two were equally devoted to Frances. The verses seem sentimental today, to be sure, but the eighties were a sentimental decade in America. What is important is that Father Edmund knew the thoughts and the memories that would most delight Frances Warde at the age of seventy-three:

'Twas a jubilee day, our first Mother's first daughter,
When setting your face towards the Western afar,
You braved the long leagues of the storm-haunted water,
To follow the shining of Mary, the Star.

On toiled the good ship, bringing nearer each morrow,
Its message of Mercy, its burden of love;
Seven offerings of faith from the "Island of Sorrow,"
A mystical band with the seal of the Dove.

But you were the chief in that virginal Seven,
And lo, when their feet touched America's shore,
'Twas the day your Saint Xavier landed in Heaven,
And the blessing he gave you abides evermore.

Rejoice, 'tis a jubilee day, dearest Mother!
Your daughters stand up in this home of the free,
And bid today echo the joy of another
Which dawned ere you followed the Star of the Sea.

'Twas the morn of your bridal; the troth you then plighted,
How faithfully kept we your children attest.
You may count us by scores, and we greet you united
With happier scores who have gone to their rest.

This Jubilee spousal—this calm Golden Wedding—
Lights up like a sunset the grace-fruited past,
And we hail in the peace its sweet radiance is shedding
A pledge of the glory that shall crown you at last.

Long before ten o'clock on the morning of Frances Warde's Jubilee Day, the streets leading to St. Anne's Church in Manchester were filled with townspeople eager to participate in the Solemn Pontifical Eucharistic Celebration. They watched the Jubilee procession led by seventy Sisters and fifty priests who preceded the officers of the Mass clad in festive gold vestments. Then came Bishop Healy, the Celebrant, followed by the Bishops of Burlington, Springfield, and Hartford, and the Archbishop of Boston.

It was a special joy for Frances that her friend, Bishop Louis de Goesbriand of Vermont, preached the sermon. He chose as his text, "My soul magnifies the Lord, and my spirit rejoices in God my Saviour because He Who is mighty has done great things in me, and holy is His Name." De Goesbriand read Frances' vows of religion to all assembled, and then he told them what he knew of her life. He spoke warmly of her pioneering adventures at the time of her Chicago foundation and of his own unforgettable encounter with her in Toledo when both were young. He enlarged upon the great services of Frances to her fellow men for the sake of Christ, and he ended by declaring that her best title to fame was that of "Sister of Mercy."

Archbishop John Joseph Williams rose at the close of the Eucharistic Celebration to ask all present to thank God for the works He had accomplished through Mother Frances. Williams then intoned the "Te Deum." He did not know that the closing lines of the hymn expressed the motto that Frances Warde had chosen long ago to be engraved in the ring she had received at her profession: "In You, O Lord, I have hoped; I shall not be confounded."

Bishop Healy, meanwhile, was determined to do all in his power to honor the Jubilarian. If he and Mother Frances had not always agreed on methods of carrying out her apostolate, he nevertheless made it clear to all that he revered her for her heroism and for her unselfish labor in the Church of Maine and New Hampshire. Healy refused to sit at table for the Jubilee dinner. Rather, he donned a white apron and served Frances and her Sisters. Later, the guests viewed the gifts that had been sent to Frances from all over the world: a silver cross with relics from Pittsburgh; Vermont marble statues from Burlington; a treasure chest from the "Isle of Rhodes" from Providence; a handmade basket with fifty tiny canoes from the Indian Missions in Maine; a herbarium of native ferns from New Zealand. Bishop Healy himself presented an album with pictures of all the Convents founded by Mother Frances.

Until her death, this Jubilee Day was to be a happy memory for Frances. But now apostolic work was still to be done. No definite word had yet been received from Bishop Healy concerning the proposed division of the Diocese of Portland or the separation of the Sisters of Mercy of Maine from those of New Hampshire. Early in 1883, the Manchester Sisters had a request from Father Daniel Murphy, Pastor of St. Mary's Church in Dover, New Hampshire, for Sisters of Mercy to teach 400 children in the new St. Mary's School he proposed to have ready for occupation in September. Frances Warde felt an apostolic kinship with Father Murphy, whose zeal she well understood. For over twenty years he had traveled through Maine and New Hampshire building churches and schools. When he had completed his building project in one parish, he was invariably sent to another. Seemingly, he never grew tired. Murphy had established a parochial school in Portsmouth, New Hampshire, in 1865, and Mother Frances had sent Sisters to teach there. When Mother Catherine Clifford now attempted to send Sisters to Dover, however, she immediately met opposition from the Bishop of Portland.

Bishop Healy had already decided upon the imminent division of the Sisters of Mercy and had applied to Rome for the division of the Diocese of Portland when Catherine Clifford attempted to establish a Mercy Convent and School in Dover. It soon became evident that a minor tug-of-war would ensue between Bishop Healy and Mother Catherine. The core of the struggle lay in the fact that, when division of the Sisters of Mercy would be finally announced, the Sisters residing in New Hampshire would become the Manchester Congregation while the Sisters living in Maine would become the new Portland Congregation. Bishop Healy's aim was to establish a strong Portland community of Sisters which would be directly under his authority; Catherine Clifford's goal was to maintain a strong Manchester community. The latter Congregation had consistently flourished in numbers since 1858; the future of the Maine Congregation would be problematic. In 1882, for example, eight Sisters had been professed and eight had received the religious habit at Mount St. Mary's. In 1884, only one Sister was to be professed in Portland. The Maine community would require time for growth. In his usual methodical manner, therefore, Bishop Healy seems to have set about the task of increasing the number of Sisters at the branch houses in Maine before declaring them to be separated from the Manchester mother house.

451

On March 19, 1883, Healy wrote to Catherine Clifford,[3] declaring that he could see "no hope" for the possibility of opening a Mercy Convent and School in Dover. The reason he gave was that Mother Catherine had been recently unwilling to send Sisters to Portland to teach in a school of 1,000 children. Since eight Sisters were required to teach 400 children in Dover, however, a school of 1000 would have required twenty Sisters. Healy was demanding a great deal in asking for twenty active Sisters to teach in Maine just before the division of the Mercy Congregation. In his letter to Mother Catherine, he also asked for a complete list of the Sisters in the Manchester Congregation. Evidently Catherine Clifford had sent him a roster beginning with the young women who had entered the Congregation in 1881. The Bishop insisted on a listing of those who had entered in 1880 to make his roster complete.

On April 3, 1883, Bishop Healy again wrote to Catherine Clifford, "requiring under most strict obedience" a list of the Sisters who had entered Mount St. Mary's in 1880. Rumors of the impending division of the Manchester Sisters, meanwhile, were heard everywhere in Maine and New Hampshire. Gossip was intensified when, in early spring, workmen began to repair and renovate St. Elizabeth's Convent in Portland. Obviously, a Mercy mother house was to be established soon in Maine.

Finally, on June 29, 1883, Bishop Healy published a Decree declaring the division of the Sisters of Mercy of the Portland Diocese into two Congregations. He wrote to Catherine Clifford: "From the date of this letter, no changes can be made without an exchange of Sisters; and this must be made after the new Mother is elected in Portland." The Bishop also declared that a Mother Superior should be elected in Manchester on August 2 and in Portland on August 4. At Mount St. Mary's there were now only twenty-six professed Sisters and, as Healy stated in his *Diary,* "a numerous novitiate." In Portland there were forty-two professed Sisters. The Bishop had succeeded in increasing the number of Sisters in Maine. To be sure, the Dover foundation was delayed.

As decreed, the election of the Mother Superior in Manchester took place August 2, 1883. Frances Warde's health was now failing rapidly. She was also beginning to lose her sight. Her Sisters feared that they would not have her among them for long. They wished that she would die as "the Reverend Mother." They elected her as Mother Superior unanimously for the last time in the first election of the new Manchester Congregation. If Bishop Healy was surprised at the decision of the Sisters, he gave no indication of puzzlement. He simply recorded the election in his *Diary,* adding that Sister Gonzaga O'Brien was chosen as Mother Assistant and Sister Catherine Clifford as Director of Novices.

Two days after the election, Frances Warde began her annual spiritual retreat. On August 12, she wrote in her *Journal*:

May the Cross of Christ be about us! O good Cross, that makes us rejoice in the holy Will of God. Close to God, all is peace and contentment in Him. They tell me I am growing strong again; they try to hope it is so, but I feel old age is here, and I realize that very soon I am to stand before the Throne to render an account of my stewardship. It is an awful responsibility to sit in the chair of a Superior—awful possibilities of being careless and failing in the binding duties attached, and awful opportunities of rejoicing the Sacred Heart by making every circumstance fruitful for God's greater glory . . . I put myself without reserve in God's Hands.[4]

The election at the Portland Convent of Mercy, held on August 4, 1883, brought joy to Frances Warde. Chosen as first Mother Superior of the Maine Congregation was Sister Theresa Pickersgill. Theresa was one of Frances' converts to the Catholic faith. She was born in Wales to English Protestant parents who migrated to Lowell, Massachusetts, in 1850. Her father, Frederick Richard Pickersgill, was a well-known artist. She studied at St. Mary's Hall, an Episcopalian Academy in Burlington, Vermont. After the death of her mother, her father established a business in Manchester. Theresa became a member of the first graduating class of Mount St. Mary's Academy. A beautiful girl, she was called "Queen of the Ice" because of her skill in winter sports. Her father at first refused to allow her to join the Catholic Church. But she was eventually baptized by Father McDonald at Mount St. Mary's, where she entered the novitiate in 1864. She took the name of Theresa Xavier in honor of Frances Warde. The author of the Portland Sisters' *Annals* wrote of her that "until the day she died, every word and act of Mother Theresa showed the spirit of her beloved and first Superior, Mother Xavier Warde."[5] Two other loved friends of Frances Warde, Sister Clare Leeson and Sister Petronilla O'Grady, were elected to the General Council of the Portland Sisters. Indeed, Bishop Healy could have no doubt now of Frances' influence upon her Sisters.

Though her physical health was rapidly declining, no decline of zeal was evident in the life of Frances Warde. Before the month of August was over, she completed the foundation of St. Mary's Convent and School in Dover! Bishop Healy raised no objections. He was anticipating approval from Rome of the division of the Diocese of Portland. When the Decree would arrive, the Manchester Sisters of Mercy would be no longer under his jurisdiction. In any case, he would no longer oppose Frances Warde, whom he now openly venerated and whose life was already a heroic legend in New England.

St. Mary's Convent in Dover was the last foundation of Frances Warde. She chose her namesake, Sister Frances Xavier Leeson, as first Superior of the Dover Convent of Mercy. Frances Leeson was destined to be elected Mother Superior in Manchester after Frances Warde's own death. Seven Sisters accompanied their Superior to the new mission. Unable to make the journey to Dover herself, Frances sent Catherine Clifford to accompany the pioneers. As she said goodbye to them at the door of Mount St. Mary's, Frances knew without a doubt that Dover marked the end of nearly fifty years of Mercy foundations for her. The apostolic journey was nearing its end. The joy Frances felt in her heart as she sent out her last missionary band to spread the Good News of Christ was stronger and deeper, though perhaps less spontaneous, than her happiness on that April day forty-six years earlier when she set out on her first foundation from Dublin to Carlow with Catherine McAuley at her side.

Frances would have enjoyed the first days of her Sisters in Dover. When Father Daniel Murphy stopped their carriages at the corner of Central and Church Streets in Dover on that first August day, all were thrilled to see a neat cross over the door of a one-time hotel and the inscription, "Convent of Mercy." St. Mary's Convent was especially blessed. The spirit of union among the Sisters at Dover was unusual. "Mother Frances [Leeson]," wrote one of the Sisters, "must have imbibed the spirit of our American foundress, she was so kind. She did not govern with an iron hand but in a spirit of gentleness, like steel that bends, owing to her understanding of the spirit of our Rule."[6] Together the Sisters at St. Mary's dusted and cleaned their old hotel and turned it into a happy convent home. "If God will only make this one of His chosen places for blessing children, it will be perfect in loveliness," one of the Sisters wrote home to

455

Frances Warde in Manchester. On September 3, 1883, the Sisters at St. Mary's opened Sacred Heart School to 400 children of the town. The Dover mission brought rare joy to Frances Warde.

As Mother Frances surveyed the apostolic works accomplished by her Sisters in New England, she was often filled with awe. She watched her followers as they spread the Word of God throughout Rhode Island, Connecticut, Vermont, Maine, and her best loved New Hampshire. "When I offered myself to God . . . to help spread the works of our Institute in the American mission," she once said in her later years, "I did not dream of the good to be done in educating the grand, sturdy New England character."[7] This statement referred undoubtedly to the hundreds of non-Catholics, children and adults, that she and her Sisters taught and influenced in New England from the time of her arrival in Providence in 1851 until her last years. Frances continued until the end of her life to teach Christian Doctrine and to bring converts to the Catholic faith. When she was no longer able to walk alone, in her last months, she asked her Sisters to help her to the Convent parlor so that she might continue her instruction of "the sturdy New England character."

To be sure, the children in the schools that Frances Warde founded were dominantly the children of poor immigrants. As she observed the service of her Sisters in these schools, in the homes of the poor and the sick, in hospitals and orphanages, Frances witnessed miracles before her eyes. Closest to her heart in her last years were the apostolic works of the Manchester and the Portland Sisters. Could she have looked ahead seventy-five years, she would have been amazed to see 500 Sisters in her Manchester Congregation, teaching in thirty-eight elementary and high schools in New Hampshire, Massachusetts, South Carolina, and even far-away

California. She would have been thrilled to see her loved Mount St. Mary's expanded to become a liberal arts college in Hooksett, New Hampshire, as well as an Academy in Nashua. Most of all, she would have been happy to know that the original Mount St. Mary's in Manchester still exists, that those who love her memory can still journey to Manchester and stand at the entrance to Mount St. Mary's precisely where she stood in the summer of 1858 when Father William McDonald first suggested the name for the Convent of "Martha's Vision"—the same name that she had loved long before at Westport, Ireland. The new mother house of the Manchester Sisters in Windham, New Hampshire, would be a vision fulfilled for Frances Warde, but her heart would linger with the loved old mother house at St. Anne's.

As for Portland, Mother Frances would have been no less amazed could she have looked ahead seventy-five years. She would have seen 400 of her Sisters serving the people of God throughout the State of Maine in thirty-three parochial schools and nearly as many Mercy Convents, in two hospitals, nurses' training schools, academies, orphanages, homes for the aged, and a liberal arts college. The geographical scroll would include such cities and towns as Bangor, Calais, Biddeford, Lewiston, Brunswick, Orono, Bar Harbor, Benedicta, Houlton, Augusta, and a host of others, including Frances' loved Indian Missions at Old Town, Pleasant Point, and Peter Dana Point. Frances would have smiled, perhaps, if she remembered her disappointment at Bishop Healy's decision to erect the Kavanagh School in Portland in place of Bishop Bacon's proposed Mercy mother house. St. Joseph's Mother House at Deering, dedicated in 1909, would have surpassed all her dreams for a Portland Convent. Finally, though Frances would have been delighted with all the visible proofs of the apostolic services of her Sisters, she would have realized that the value of the contribution to the people of God of the Institute of Mercy can never be measured by the staggering statistics of the numbers of children and adults educated, the numbers cared for in hospitals, orphanages, and homes, or by the numbers of cumulative years of missionary service of successive generations of Sisters of Mercy. Like Catherine McAuley, Frances Warde knew that the apostolic work of the Institute of Mercy was not hers but God's, that He alone can measure the spiritual and human impact upon the hundreds of thousands of His people whose lives have been touched by the Sisters of Mercy.

22

Death of Frances Warde

DURING the last years of her life, Frances Warde often
expressed regret that Catherine McAuley was not alive to
see how her Sisters had spread the Good News of Christ
through their services to the people of God all over the
world. Frances felt privileged to be able to see with her own
eyes all the good that had been accomplished through the
Institute of Mercy. She contemplated the Providence of God
which had directed the beginnings of the Mercy apostolate
at the house on Baggot Street and developed it miraculously
over fifty years. There was no purely human explanation
for the flowering of the tiny seed of the Christian apostolate
that Catherine and Frances had tended so carefully in Dublin long ago.

Often Frances meditated on the unusual circumstances of
her own life. A Power beyond herself had always guided
her. She recalled that she might never have gone to Dublin
as a young girl of seventeen if her father had not lost his
lovely home at Bellbrook in County Laois. She might never
have met Catherine McAuley! And Catherine might never
have sent her to Carlow if the Irish founder had not resolved to let no purely human consideration influence her
decisions concerning the apostolate of Mercy. Frances remembered, too, how a British Bishop had prevented her own
foundation of a Mercy Convent in Liverpool. How different
her life would have been if she had carried the Mercy apos-

tolate to England instead of to America! Again, Frances herself had nothing to do with the decision to establish a Mercy foundation in Pittsburgh from Carlow. She had not even considered going to the United States. The strong triumvirate of Michael O'Connor, Francis Haly, and James Maher had chosen her as the founder of the American apostolate of the Sisters of Mercy. She had acquiesced to the Will of God. And Frances' amazingly widespread mission in the United States seemed also to have been directed by the Spirit to which she had always surrendered so completely. She had received a call from Pittsburgh to Providence and from Providence to Manchester. From each of these three cities as apostolic centers, she had responded to calls to establish the Institute of Mercy in innumerable cities and towns throughout the United States. Her response had always been positive. True, she had made decisions of her own. She had drawn upon the human wisdom with which the Spirit had blessed her. But she saw herself always as an instrument. Her work was in God's Hands. Frances Warde lived always in two worlds: for her, the things that are seen could never be separated from the things that are not seen. The divine and the human were one. The direction of her life had come from God. Her whole life had been an answer to His call. No woman ever lived who was more completely an apostle of Christ.

After her establishment of her last Mercy Convent in Dover, New Hampshire, in August, 1883, Frances still continued her apostolate at Manchester. Her strength was failing perceptibly. Yet she continued to give instructions, particularly to adults as always, at Mount St. Mary's. She continued to read the Holy Scripture daily. As her sight failed gradually, Father McDonald brought her a Bible with especially large print. It is still preserved at Windham, New Hampshire, well-worn from continual use. In January, 1884,

Frances was able to be present in the Chapel at Mount St. Mary's when six young girls were received into the Manchester Congregation and five made their vows as Sisters of Mercy. In late March, Frances contracted pneumonia. Her health failed so rapidly that Mother Gonzaga O'Brien sent out pleas for prayers to Mercy Convents in New England. For a time, Frances' health seemed to improve. "You would be charmed," wrote Mother Gonzaga to a friend, "with her tranquil, cheerful patience in this severe trial. Not a single complaint."[1]

On April 15, 1884, a telegram from Rome confirmed the division of the Portland Diocese and the creation of a new Diocese with Manchester as its center. Denis Bradley, whom Frances had taught Christian Doctrine as a child and who had received his First Communion from Father McDonald at St. Anne's, was named the first Bishop of Manchester. It was difficult to say whether Frances Warde or William McDonald was the happier at Bradley's appointment. He was the spiritual child of both.

On April 20, Bishop Healy came to Manchester to offer the Celebration of the Eucharist at Mount St. Mary's and to say goodbye to the Sisters of Mercy there. The Bishop had mellowed somewhat during the last few years of his jurisdiction over them. He was to become dear to the Mercy Sisters in Portland. Indeed, perhaps his greatest fault in dealing with the Sisters at Manchester had been his sense of proprietorship: he had wanted them to be *his* Sisters.

Denis Bradley was consecrated Bishop of Manchester on June 11, 1884. Frances Warde had asked her Sisters to design and make the episcopal vestments of her old student. She herself had supervised, with almost sightless eyes, this loving labor. When the day of the consecration arrived, however, she was too feeble to attend the ceremony.

During the following summer months, Mother Gonzaga

sent messages to the Mercy Convents in New England, asking the Sisters to come to Manchester to receive Frances Warde's final blessing. The Sisters came—from Hartford and Providence and Burlington and Portland. Though Frances could not recognize them at once with her failed sight, she greeted them warmly and blessed them individually. She told them freely that she knew that her death was near.

Frances' last official function as Mother Superior occurred on August 6, 1884, when she attempted to go to the parlor to welcome the Jesuit priest who came to conduct the annual August Retreat of the Sisters. Frances became ill and had to return to her bed. The Sisters coaxed her to go to the Convent infirmary, but she preferred her own bed in the corner of a dormitory she had long shared with several other Sisters. Frances had never had a room of her own—only a bed, a wash-stand, and a chair in the simple dormitory. There she now remained, sitting up for a short time each day, praying, and counseling her Sisters.

Frances Warde had been a witness to the living Christ since her childhood days at Bellbrook House. Now she would be a witness to the dying Christ.[2] Father McDonald, her spiritual adviser and friend of twenty-six years, was her firm support to the end. On September 14, with the Sisters of Mount St. Mary's kneeling at her bedside, Frances received the Sacrament of Extreme Unction. She remained calm and peaceful, praying continually. With a presentiment of the day of her death, she said often, "Next Wednesday." And a few times she exclaimed, "My long and stormy life is coming to an end."

At ten o'clock on the evening of Tuesday, September 16, all at Mount St. Mary's knew that Frances' death was very near. She asked her Sisters to come to her to say goodbye. She spoke to each one in turn. Mother Gonzaga, her companion of thirty years, leaned over her and pleaded, "Darling Mother, bless me, your old child . . . and this Community . . . and your children of the Order of Mercy scattered throughout the world." Frances raised her arm, made the Sign of the Cross, and said distinctly, "God love and bless you forever." Then she asked Father McDonald, Mother Gonzaga, and Catherine Clifford to care for her grandniece, Mary Agnes Warde, who had entered the Manchester Congregation two months earlier. Frances fumbled for her watch, gave it to Mary Agnes, and asked the girl to pray always for her Aunt who loved her dearly. Then, thoughtful of others like Catherine McAuley, who asked on her death bed that her Sisters would have a warm cup of tea after she had gone, Frances sent her Sisters off to rest. When Mother Gonzaga, who had watched so long with her, hesitated to go, Frances said, "Go to rest, my dear. I need nothing . . . just your prayers." And then she gave Mother Gonzaga her last blessing. It was the same simple blessing which Catherine McAuley knew that Frances Warde loved best, the benediction that Catherine had sent to her in 1841 in her last letter from Dublin to Carlow: "May God Almighty bless you."

The two Sisters who remained with Frances, Philomena McQuade and Regina Blake, noted a change in her a few hours after midnight. They called Mother Gonzaga and Catherine Clifford. Father McDonald came to give Frances his last blessing. She spoke the names of Jesus and Mary and whispered repeatedly, "O God, be merciful to me, a sinner." Just before daybreak, the Convent bell at Mount St. Mary's announced to the town that Frances Warde was dying. At seven o'clock on the morning of Wednesday, September 17, 1884, as the Sulpician Abbé John Baptist Hogan, President of St. John's Seminary, Boston, celebrated the Eucharist in the Convent Chapel for her, Frances Warde died. William McDonald rose from his knees at her bedside to go to St. Anne's Church and offer the Celebration of the Eucharist for his friend's entrance into eternal life.

The Sisters at Mount St. Mary's lovingly dressed Frances in her religious habit and placed her on the narrow iron bed on which she had died. Returning from St. Anne's, Father McDonald stood over Frances' lifeless body and recalled the rude hut in which her patron, Francis Xavier, had died. The priest's eyes rested on the simple cot, the wash-stand, the straight chair, and the crucifix that Thomas Cullen had given to Frances long ago in November 1843, as she sailed from Liverpool on the *Queen of the West*. The vows which she had signed with her own hand fifty-two years before, with Catherine McAuley at her side, had been placed in her hands. "She kept them," said Father McDonald, "God knows she kept them."

No one knew better than William McDonald the spiritual odyssey of Frances Warde. He was reputed to be a saint. But he was a quiet man who spoke little. As he left Mount St. Mary's on the morning of September 17, he met a parishioner who loved Frances Warde. She held up before him a rosary that Frances had given her, saying that now she would prize it more highly than ever. "If you had only one bead that belonged to Mother Warde," Father McDonald answered, "it would be enough. She was a holy woman."

Frances Warde had requested on her death bed that she be given a simple burial. However, Bishop Bradley, Father McDonald, and her Sisters thought that all those who loved Mother Frances should not be deprived of participating in the funeral of "the woman who had done more good for humanity, perhaps, than any other woman on the American continent."[3] The burial would be simple, but no one would be refused attendance.

All during the day of September 17, the Manchester Sisters prayed beside the body of Mother Frances in the simple dormitory where she had died. In the evening, she was placed in a simple pine coffin and taken to Mount St. Mary's Chapel, where her Sisters kept prayerful watch until Saturday, September 20. From daybreak on Saturday morning, Bishops and priests offered a continuous Celebration of the Eucharist in the tiny Chapel that Frances had loved.

At nine o'clock a funeral procession such as Manchester had never seen began to form at the entrance to Mount St. Mary's. Hundreds of people from New Hampshire and other parts of New England and beyond lined Laurel and Union Streets leading to St. Anne's Church. The young girls of Mount St. Mary's and the children of St. Patrick's Orphanage formed a guard of honor at the church steps. One hundred Sisters of Mercy were led by Mothers Gonzaga O'Brien and Catherine Clifford, Sister Mary Agnes Warde and Emily Harper. One hundred priests, representing the diocesan and religious clergy of New England, were preceded by six priest pallbearers, friends of Frances Warde from New England parishes. Five other friends of Frances were officers of the Mass, and Father McDonald was Master of Ceremonies. Bishop Denis Bradley, the Celebrant, was followed by Bishops Thomas F. Hendricksen of Providence, Patrick T. O'Reilly of Springfield, Lawrence S. McMahon of Hartford, Louis de Goesbriand of Burlington, and James Healy of Portland. The Sisters' Choir of Manchester sang the Mass.

At the close of the Celebration of the Eucharist, Bishop Healy preached, taking as his text, "A woman strong of heart, whose price is from the uttermost coasts" (Proverbs, 31: 10). The man who had worked closely with Frances Warde for nine years, in both union and conflict, only to recognize clearly in the end the profound mystery of grace in her life, now freely told the world of her greatness. The lan-

465

guage in which Bishop Healy spoke of Frances revealed his humility before his vision of her life:

While warmth of devotion and strength of heart are by no means rare in woman, there was in this woman's life a sacrifice and a fortitude which man can never fathom. Mother Xavier Warde was eminently strong of heart. One could never enter her presence without feeling the dignity, the almost majesty, which was inseparable from her . . . Yet there was about her a gentle charm which rarely failed to attract . . . Rise up and testify, you who have been associated with her. Testify to her spirit of sacrifice, her courage, her strength. As Mother M. Frances Xavier, she established for herself and her Order convent after convent in Ireland and then in our United States. She was always and everywhere the same; she left one home after another, whenever God called, as though home were not home . . . One who was admired, one who was everywhere respected, and one who won the affection of all who knew her. Her character was beautiful and her fidelity was never surpassed. She was always the religious seeking seclusion. Yet her works and she were known, I might say, almost from the Atlantic to the Pacific Ocean and from our northern frontier to the shores of the Gulf of Mexico. . . .

Mother Warde's praises can be properly sung only by the hundreds of the poor whom she has helped; the children to whom she has sent teachers of both earthly and heavenly wisdom; the sick she has comforted; the souls she has rescued by her own fervent words or those of her daughters . . .

Mother Xavier has passed away from her devoted Sisters, who will miss each day her experience, her kind advice, her wise government. The never-wearying care, the love, the grand religious presence can never come back, but she is living the true life. She will continue to be the guide and protector of this Community, whose glory she will ever be in that heaven which, by God's grace, her life of prayer and good works have merited for her.[4]

It was fitting that Frances Warde's old friend, Bishop Louis de Goesbriand, gave the solemn absolution, "Enter not into judgment with your servant . . ." Then the procession of closed carriages, followed by hundreds of townspeople, moved through the streets of Manchester to St. Joseph's Cemetery. On that warm September day, the beginning of a New England fall, all of the residents of Manchester had left their homes to honor Frances Warde. Parents took their children to Frances' funeral so that, years later, they might remember their presence at that historic event. A long-time resident of Manchester, Burt P. Moran, recalled as late as 1966 that at the age of five he stood at the corner of Laurel and Union Streets, holding his mother's hand as Frances Warde's coffin was carried from St. Anne's Church. His mother, who had once attended Mount St. Mary's Convent School in Westport, Ireland, said to him, "A great woman is buried today—Mother Xavier Warde."[5]

In the center of the small plot of the Sisters of Mercy in St. Joseph Cemetery, surrounded by evergreens and cedar trees, with the hills of New Hampshire beyond, Frances Warde was buried. Denis Bradley and Louis de Goesbriand stood at the head of her coffin as William McDonald offered final prayers for her entrance into eternity. A few weeks later, her Sisters erected a marble cross over Frances' grave with the inscription:

> Reverend Mother M. Xavier Warde,
> Foundress of the Order of Mercy
> in the United States, December 21,
> 1843, and of Mount Saint Mary
> Convent, Manchester, New Hampshire,
> July 16, 1858. Died September 17,
> 1884, in the 74th year of her age

and the 53rd of her Religious
Profession. Grant to her, O Lord,
Eternal Rest.

To this spot the Sisters of Mercy of the United States today go on pilgrimage to pray at the grave of "the revered, long-to-be-remembered Mother Frances Xavier Warde."[6]

23

Flowering of a Century and a Half

THE growth of the Sisters of Mercy throughout the world since their foundation by Catherine McAuley in Dublin less than 150 years ago has been characterized as a modern miracle. In a comparatively brief historical period, the Congregation of Mercy increased to 25,000 members with 1,500 convents in North and South America, Europe, Asia, Africa, and Australia.[1] It is the largest English-speaking Congregation of religious women in the world. The Sisters conduct colleges, secondary schools, elementary schools, academies, and business schools; hospitals and schools of nursing; social service centers; child care centers; homes for the aged; residences for women; retreat houses and night refuges; catechetical centers; and numerous individual apostolates rapidly expanding beyond the traditional service areas of education, health, and welfare.

The phenomenal development of the apostolates of the Sisters of Mercy has been nowhere more evident than in the United States. There are more Convents of Mercy in America than in all other countries in the world combined. The remarkable growth of the Congregation in the United States owes its origin to Frances Warde, the American founder, for the majority of American Convents of Mercy trace their origin directly or indirectly to Mother Frances.[2]

The life of Frances Warde offers for contemplation one of the greatest women not only in the history of the Catholic

Church but in the history of the United States. No woman in the record of the Church surpassed her in the pioneering spirit of the apostle. No woman founded personally more convents and institutions for the service of the poor, the sick, the illiterate, and all those in need. No woman led more non-believers to the Christian faith. Perhaps no woman ministered more to suffering humanity in America.

Frances Warde's personality had the unique qualities of a woman of genius. Indeed, there was an enigmatic profundity to her character that challenges complete definition. She was unlike Catherine McAuley, who was a woman somehow transparent in her holiness. Catherine's response to life was profoundly simple. Her inner and her external life were united in a happy harmony that presented no difficulty of interpretation to those who knew her. In short, though she was a woman of great spiritual depth, she was not hard to understand. Her personality had a luminous quality that helped to define her holiness. She was universally loved. Frances Warde, the woman closest to Catherine McAuley, was quite different from her in personality. Perhaps this very difference was a reason for their lasting friendship. They complemented each other.

Frances was a more complex personality than Catherine. She was more inward in her response to reality, more enigmatic in her relationships with others. Her holiness had a translucent, rather than a transparent, quality. She was not easy to understand. She did not reveal herself to many. Only those who knew her longest and most intimately, like Catherine McAuley in Ireland or William McDonald in America, were fully aware of the depth of her faith and love. The sanctity of those who were closest to her is perhaps a good index to her own holiness of life.

Probably the first thing her contemporaries noted about

Frances Warde was the charm of her person. It was said of her that "she could charm the birds from the trees."[3] She was tall and attractive, blue-eyed, "straight as a reed, a real grandee."[4] The Sisters who knew her remarked often concerning the loveliness of her smile. Her protégée, Sister Frances Xavier Leeson, once said that she was "stern looking, but with a beautiful smile."[5] And Sister Austin Carroll, Mercy annalist, wrote often of Frances' pleasant personality, "especially when she smiled."[6] An amusing story, traditional in the New England Mercy communities, relates that Mother Frances once appeared unexpectedly at the Convent of Mercy in Hartford, wearing a navy blue suit and bonnet.[7] The young novice who answered the door did not know that Frances was a Sister. When the older woman passed directly into the Convent and up the front stairway, the girl was chagrined. But Frances turned at the top of the stairs and flashed her brilliant smile—at the same moment that the Superior of the Convent appeared to redeem the situation.[8] No one enjoyed a humorous situation more than Frances. Stern she might sometimes appear, but she was basically benign.

Frances Warde's delight in all that was beautiful was completely spontaneous. She loved trees and fields and the gardens she created wherever she went—in Pittsburgh, Providence, Manchester, or Bordentown. There she walked and talked and prayed with her Sisters, fascinated with the simple joy of being alive. Frances was fond of music and of beautiful voices in choir. She passionately loved her family, her friends, her spiritual Sisters, and her God. Yet her expression of her response to the beauty of life was not always understood.

The term "queenly" is one that appears over and over again in references to Frances' character. Her grandniece,

Mary Agnes Warde, once wrote in a memoir that Mother Frances "appeared at the doorway with all the majesty of three Queen Victorias."[9] And after Frances' death, a Pittsburgh Sister, reminiscing, reminded Bishop James O'Connor of the early days at St. Xavier's Academy, Latrobe, when Mother Frances "was a Queen among these wilds—as well as in Pittsburgh."[10] This characteristic queenliness illustrates well the ambivalent impression created in some of Frances Warde's acquaintances by her physical bearing. She was "aristocratic, always dignified, even as a young woman,"[11] a quality very pleasing to her friends. But to some persons, this same quality appeared as haughtiness; to them, Frances had "a strong sense of caste," she "might irritate you, but you got the over-all impression that she was a lady."[12] Yet Frances was "reserved and strict, but not severe."[13] Because of her dignity, sometimes interpreted as dominance, she was not loved by *all* as Catherine McAuley was. Yet everyone, even those who would have preferred her to be less "haughty," found in her a loving compassion. She always forgave immediately and forgot the offense forever. No matter what the delinquency of a novice, a simple apology restored her at once to Frances' affection. It would seem, too, that the American founder's "queenliness" of manner, noted by Catherine McAuley the first time she met Frances as a "dignity" which always attracted the Irish founder, was indeed an inherited characteristic. John Warde, Frances' father, was usually described as a "dignified gentleman." If Frances' manner seemed haughty to some of her acquaintances, it was attractive to most of them.

Her charm at recreation became proverbial. "We never knew anyone to surpass her as a conversationalist," wrote one of her Sisters.[14] And another asked, "Where is the person in America or anywhere else who could converse like her and show such stores of general information?"[15] Frances' letters—those that are extant—reveal the same charm as her conversation. She often used her gifts as speaker and writer to draw others to Christ. She never offended by preaching, however, but often used humor to drive home a point that in the conversation of a less sensitive woman would have emerged as heavy or dull.

Frances' sharp sense of the ridiculous frequently prompted her to contagious laughter that won over everyone in her presence.[16] When the occasion was right, she could tell one witty story after another until the tears rolled down her cheeks. One of her favorites concerned the well-loved Andrew Fitzgerald, once President of Carlow College and dear friend of Catherine McAuley, who sometimes reacted like a small boy when he fancied he had been hurt. After giving a beautiful gift of table silver to the Carlow Sisters, Fitzgerald felt injured one day because he did not receive an invitation to a Feast Day celebration at St. Leo's. He therefore appeared suddenly at the festive board to demand back his silver just as the Sisters were about to sit down to dinner! No one could embellish the account of so ridiculous a situation as Frances could. And she would quickly turn to fun the tragi-comedy of a Sister who exaggerated the importance of a minor calamity of convent life. Best of all, the vision of the unhappy Sister herself was turned toward laughter.

Mother Frances' generosity to the poor was legendary. Senior Sisters at Manchester, reminiscing at the turn of the century, recalled a day long before when a person in great want came to Mount St. Mary's to ask for help. Frances listened to the sad story of the beggar and then went to a drawer, took out all the money she had, and put it in the hand of the needy one. Before evening, a large sum of money was brought suddenly to the Sisters from a completely unexpected source.[17] The Sisters believed that Frances' care for the poor brought them many blessings.

The liberality with which Frances gave of her own person, moreover, was unequaled. Her whole life was a service to others. Even in her old age, she visited the sick in Manchester regularly, taking with her hot soup and soda bread. But her greatest offering of herself was in the back-breaking service of her foundations and the near-sacrifice of her life—once on her unforgettable return journey from her Chicago mission, and again during the fatal typhoid plague of 1848 in Pittsburgh. From the time of her middle years, Frances' bodily strength was never equal to the strength of her will to serve God's people. Yet she continued to labor, despite physical weakness, almost until the day she died. It was said of her at the time of her burial that her energy in serving others was not exceeded by that of the youngest Sister in her Congregation.

The American founder's love for the people of God led her, like Saint Paul to whom she was sometimes compared, to be all things to all men. Whether she was serving the rough rivermen who came up the Ohio River to Pittsburgh for instruction in Christian Doctrine; factory hands in the Iron City or inmates in its penitentiary; Abnaki Indians on their reservations; or a Russian Princess whom she taught at Newport, Rhode Island, Frances was able to adapt her own personality to that of the individual who sought her help—not with condescension, but with sincere friendliness.

This same love and liberality toward others was the source of what some of Frances' acquaintances regarded as her chief faults: she trusted people too much. She trusted to the point of folly, so that her acts of kindness occasionally boomeranged, to her own decided disadvantage. She sometimes embarrassed her friends by associating with publicans and outcasts. Frances was not a calculating person. Therefore the individuals she served deceived her at times.[18] More frequently, her liberal judgments of others brought help and support to persons in real distress. Frances had the grace and good fortune not to be critical of the weaknesses of human nature. Again like St. Paul, she was so aware of her own need for the grace of God that she would have considered it irrational—and un-Christian —to judge others. On her death bed, she repeated over and over again the words of the tax collector, "O God, be merciful to me, a sinner." Though strongly aware of her own faults, she developed a habit of always seeing good in others. She always lived, according to her view, in the most delightful city, in the happiest religious community, with the most agreeable persons. "All her geese were swans." Her universal charity and her sincere interest in each person she met minimized her own defects in the eyes of others and won her numerous friendships. When she visited her convents, she talked to each Sister with so personal a concern that each believed that Frances had a special affection for her. In truth, she did. When dealing with children, particularly, Frances insisted upon loving care for each individual. She would not tolerate severe correction. Rather, she counseled her Sisters to win the children in their classes to right action not by punishment but by love and by well-timed praise.[19]

Frances Warde's universal love did not preclude warm personal love for the many friends she won during her long and eventful life. Possessing a genius for friendship, she maintained a permanent loyalty toward those fortunate enough to win her special regard. In the matter of friendship, she actually seemed to transcend her mortality. She chose her friends unerringly and bound herself to them forever. She did not permit time nor distance nor death to subtract one iota from her devotion to Catherine McAuley. In all of her friendships—for Edward Nolan, James Maher, Agatha O'Brien, Cecilia Maher, Gonzaga O'Brien, Catherine Clifford, Teresa Pickersgill, William McDonald, Catherine Seton, Emily Harper, Louis de Goesbriand, and others—a complete mutual trust existed.

The response of Frances Warde to friendship was one aspect of a quality of her personality that her friends and associates stressed most profoundly at the time of her death. All who knew her—from the youngest Sister to the oldest friend to Bishops and priests to contemporary journalists pointed out the unique womanly *strength* of the American founder of the Sisters of Mercy. She was considered by all to be "a strong woman raised up by God to do a great work for Him."[20] Many religious women of the nineteenth century were women of prayer. But Frances Warde was a strong woman of both prayer and action. She was literally a pioneer in striking a trail across the United States, establishing the apostolate of Mercy wherever she went. Her apostolate demanded extraordinary spiritual strength. When James Maher, Frances Haly, and Michael O'Connor chose her in 1848 as the one woman capable of the suffering and hardship necessary to open the way across mid-nineteenth-century America for thousands of Sisters of Mercy in the wake of thousands of European immigrants, they acted with wisdom and grace. Like Frances herself, they were unaware of all that her future in America would demand of her. But they knew that the apostolate of Mercy in the United States would require heroic strength. Frances' journey from Chicago to Pittsburgh in 1846 in a Conestoga wagon was a realistic symbol of her spiritual odyssey in the New World.

Her reputation as a woman who accomplished what she set out to do preceded her and followed her. Therefore the Bishops of the United States, between 1843 and 1883, continually sought her leadership in establishing Convents of Mercy, schools, hospitals, and homes for all those in need. They knew that Frances' Sisters would persevere. Suffer they did, but they never abandoned their missions. Frances' leadership somehow inspired the young women she trained to become greater than they were. Their youth and inexperience sometimes seemed to be assets rather than handicaps to their spiritual and social accomplishments. Sister Agatha O'Brien, for example, was only twenty-two when, with the help of a few novices younger than herself, she established the Congregation of Mercy in the frontier town of Chicago under Frances Warde's guidance. The Chicago Congregation and its work developed almost miraculously. Agatha O'Brien was typical of the first Superiors of many of Mother Frances' foundations. True, many of them sacrificed their youthful lives in the service of God's people, but not before they had laid solid foundations for enduring centers of Mercy.

Like Catherine McAuley, Frances would have laughed at any reference to her own "success." However, it was said of her that "the administrative genius of Mother Warde made the spread of the Sisters of Mercy to the West possible. Yet the difficulties of winning a way in the new unsettled West were little in comparison with those of breaking a path into Puritan New England."[21] As a spiritual and psychological pioneer, Frances crossed greater frontiers than geographical ones. In her administrative innovations, she modeled her government on the policies of Catherine McAuley, who understood the type of religious government demanded by nineteenth-century culture. In establishing Convents and in training her Sisters, one of Frances' familiar remarks was "Mother Catherine would do it this way" or "Mother Catherine would not do that." As leaders, however, these two women spontaneously revealed their own personality traits.

Catherine was said to be gentle and docile. Frances possessed a certain assertiveness that Catherine did not. She could exert a wholesome aggressiveness when her apostolate demanded it. This quality was, indeed, essential to a religious founder in a pioneer society like that of America in the forties, fifties, and sixties. Docility would not have served Frances well, for example, in the early days of her Providence foundation when she was forced to face a mob of Know-Nothings at her convent door. The situations she encountered sometimes demanded that she assert her rights boldly and fight for justice for her Sisters and the people she served.

Frances was equal to the demands of her apostolate. When she was persecuted, she maintained a calm dignity, tolerance, and self-composure that never failed to impress the fanatics who attacked her. Through her peacemaking efforts, both by word and by example, she often changed mutual distrust to mutual regard among Catholics and Protestants in many towns of New England. She was actually able to bring order and friendliness out of chaos.[22] In her dealings with the hierarchy of the Church, she sometimes encountered resistance to her projects of mercy that required not only firm insistence on her rights but extreme diplomacy. Bishop Healy, for example, ruled the Diocese of Portland like "a monarch."[23] Frances endured hard times at his hands. Yet she contrived eventually to establish a real friendship with him. He finally regarded her, in her last years, with even exaggerated admiration.

The diplomacy practiced by Frances Warde did not smack of pretension or even subtle artfulness. Those with whom she dealt knew precisely what her judgment was in a given situation. But in negotiating her plans for her Mercy apostolates, she had a real gift for forestalling hostility. In matters of indifference, she yielded. In matters of importance, when she could not persuade by peaceful means, she withdrew only to initiate at once new Mercy projects in new areas. Or, if she hoped that her work would prosper even under frustration, she accepted resistance calmly. Frances once wrote to a Bishop who thought he understood her apostolate better than she did: "Since we cannot have things as we desire, we will adopt your views, trusting in God to make all conduce to His Glory."[24]

To be sure, Frances was a woman of innovative ideas with a mind of her own. She sometimes aroused opposition among a number of Sisters of Mercy because she believed in adapting certain Mercy customs to suit the American environment, which she found to differ in many aspects from that of Ireland. When she encountered opposition to her progressive ideas, she explained her position calmly and patiently. But she did not become unduly depressed or frustrated under opposition. Frances was a "free spirit" before her time.[25] Her apostolate awaited her everywhere in America. She did not have to seek missions for the many young women who joined her. The leaders of the American Catholic Church sought her out, and she responded in freedom, choosing those apostolates in which she and her Sisters could best fulfill the goals of the Congregation of Mercy. Her insight in making decisions concerning her apostolates is proverbial. She had a "spiritual sixth sense" in choosing both the works and the geographical areas in which to pursue them that resulted in seemingly miraculous growth. Yet her new establishments almost always originated in poverty and difficult circumstances. Like Catherine McAuley, she was actually suspicious of auspicious beginnings. Frances' personal insight in proclaiming the Word of God, when considered realistically against the background of her expansion of the Congregation of Mercy from Maine to California, is awe-inspiring.

The uniform success of Frances' ventures often led her contemporaries to believe that she did not experience the suffering and spiritual purgation that normally accompanies the heroic efforts of religious founders. These judgments could not have been more false. Eleven years after Frances' death, Mother Teresa Austin Carroll wrote of her:

Persons brought into close contact with Mother Warde, especially in her later years, seeing only her marvelous success and the honors that fell thick and fast about her, were sometimes tempted to think that her life had been all sunshine. In point of fact, however, no originator of great enterprises ever experienced more thwarting, more contradictions, more ingratitude, more persecution even from those to whom she naturally looked for assistance and encouragement, than did this distinguished and extraordinary woman. And the fact that during her worst experiences of the vanity, the folly, the narrowness, the jealousies of some with whom she had close relations, she looked on poor human nature more in sorrow than in anger is perhaps the best eulogy of her noble heart.[26]

No doubt Frances Warde was a saintly woman.[27] Testimony to her holiness is not difficult to find.[28] Bishops, priests, religious, the people of God who knew her told of her goodness. She was indubitably a woman closely united with Christ. Her constant word to her Sisters was: "Keep your thought buried in Divinity, and busy yourselves in spreading God's kingdom in the hearts of men." Her frequent aspirations were, "O Jesus, be my strength. I have no hope but in You," and "Let all be lost, provided God is not lost." Frances' life both within the Congregation of Mercy and within the total Church was witness to her complete commitment to Christian unity in Jesus. Like Catherine McAuley, she sought "unity and charity" above all. She was rightly called the "head and the heart" of the Mercy Congregation, the "flower of the flock" of Catherine McAuley. Within the Church of Christ, she offered superhuman testimony to zeal for the Kingdom of

God. Her witness has received public memorial. Church and chapel windows, in traditional fashion, are dedicated to the memory of her fervor for Christ and care for his people: at Mount Mary's Chapel, Manchester, New Hampshire; at St. Joseph's Convent of Mercy, Deering, Maine; at Mount St. Rita Chapel, Providence, Rhode Island; at St. Ann's Chapel, Indian Island, Maine. At the Shrine of the Immaculate Conception, Washington, is a beautiful window dedicated to Our Lady of Mercy with Catherine McAuley and Frances Warde at her feet, as well as a monument to Michael O'Connor and the "First Seven" of Pittsburgh.

Such public testimony to Frances Warde's holiness is only a recognition of human awareness of her union with Christ and all men in love and service. Like Catherine McAuley, her early ideal, Frances did not confide to others—with the possible exception of William McDonald—the depth of her life with Christ in God. Hints of her inner life exist in the meager number of her written words which remain today. It is certain that she transcended great suffering through the joy of her union with Christ. Her grandniece, Sister Paul Xavier Warde, recalled a rare statement of Frances concerning her spiritual gifts. Sister Mary Agnes wrote:

We are not surprised to learn that a long and serious illness followed her arrival in Pittsburgh from Chicago, for her bodily strength did not equal her great will. In speaking of this most trying journey afterward, Mother Warde seemed to have forgotten the sufferings in the memory of her religious privileges at Toledo, "blessed then as I was with more consolation from the good God than I deserved."[29]

The statement is brief. Frances seldom spoke of herself. Her friends were aware, however, of the extraordinary spiritual discernment she had revealed even as a child. Her life in Christ was grounded in Holy Scripture which, unlike many of her contemporaries, she read daily throughout her life. Her reverence in prayer was noteworthy. Even the tone of her voice as she prayed touched all who heard her.

Founded on Scripture, Frances' spiritual life of love was based on the faith and hope which she expressed in her motto at profession: "In You, O Lord, I have hoped. I shall not be confounded." Frances' faith was as simple at her death as it was when she first came to Baggot Street as a novice. Experience, especially the purification of pain, deepened her faith but never changed its profound simplicity. Frances was known to become actually angry with Sisters who failed to place their trust in God.[30] Her faith was undoubtedly the source of her close associations with non-Catholics. She was a "general favorite" among them. "Perhaps no woman ever brought so many adults to membership in the Catholic Church."[31] Though she initiated and developed spiritual and corporal works of mercy of all types, Frances' greatest personal apostolic gift was the spiritual instruction of non-Catholic adults. Her own gift of faith was so brilliantly lucid that it literally lighted up the lives of the adults she served.[32]

One of the most revealing commentaries on Frances Warde's holiness of life comes from Sister Austin Carroll, compiler of the four-volume *Annals* of the Sisters of Mercy. Mother Austin knew Frances for years, and her testimony is the more significant because she was not one who was always warmly responsive to Frances' personality. As annalist, she realized the central importance of the American founder's work to the history of the Sisters of Mercy. Yet the complexity of Frances' personality puzzled her. A series of letters, written between 1862 and 1889 reveals the gradual and beautiful metamorphosis of Mother Austin's attitude toward Frances Warde.[33]

On March 3, 1882, as Austin Carroll planned the fourth

volume of the Mercy *Annals,* she wrote to her friend, Bishop James O'Connor, in Omaha: "Would you mind telling me confidentially what you think of M. Frances Warde?" The writer expressed a doubt that Frances was "fit for canonization. And yet I believe she is very holy in her own way—she puzzles me." In a sense, Mother Austin's puzzlement was a compliment to Frances. The American founder could in no sense be characterized by easy nineteenth-century formulae for holiness. She was no "plaster saint." A perusal of Mother Austin's *Annals,* on the other hand, uncovers frequent conventional, stereotyped descriptions of sanctity. It is a truism that lives of the saints written by many of Frances Warde's contemporaries revealed little of their humanity. These hagiographies were often molded according to preconceived patterns which demanded a sterile type of "perfection" in every detail of the saints' lives. A Passionist who was a companion of Frances' friend, James Kent Stone (Father Fidelis of the Cross), during his apostolic service in Panama and Buenos Aires, was once asked to write down his impressions of Father Fidelis' heroism. He wrote the following:

Since heroism in the evangelical virtues is the supreme test applied by Mother Church in calculating the merit of her saints, rather than the absence of human traits, Father Fidelis should rank high on this score. Faults he had. It could not be said of him, as Disraeli in fine sarcasm said of Gladstone, "The man has not a single redeeming fault!" Father Fidelis was adorned with his full quota. Like Liguori, Patrick, Augustine, Paul, he was intensely human in his faults. There are some persons so weak mentally or spiritually that they take offense at the human in God's great servants. They cannot bear to know the whole truth about even an Apostle. But those who best knew the human in Father Fidelis admired the heroic in him all the more. His heroic love of God, and of perishing souls, flamed forth more gloriously from the human setting of his faults. It was intensely real in an intense human being. We who have no experience and scarcely an understanding of his sacrifice, we must all bow to his heroism.[34]

It is doubtful that Mother Austin would have understood completely the above definition of holiness. Frances Warde, to be sure, was not Kent Stone. But she was closer to St. Paul in the humanity and intensity of her holiness than to any pre-fabricated saint's life. When she declared on her death bed, "My long and stormy life is coming to an end," she spoke the truth. If the kingdom of heaven suffers violence, Frances Warde was one of the violent who bear it away.

James O'Connor's response to Mother Austin's inquiry concerning Frances Warde is not extant, but his judgment of the sanctity of the First Seven is recorded in the Carlow *Annals*. Visiting the Convent community room at St. Leo's in 1885, he declared: "When I look around this room and think that these holy women [the seven Pittsburgh founders] once occupied it, I feel that I am visiting the shrine of saints."[35] Perhaps James O'Connor helped Mother Austin to form a just judgment concerning Frances Warde. Early in 1884, she wrote again to James O'Connor, declaring that Mother Frances "had fine qualities after all" and that she was now "leading a most holy life and preparing like a saint for the near end. Pray that I may do the same." On the death of Frances six months later, Mother Austin wrote to Sister Gonzaga O'Brien in Manchester, asking for "some mementoes of her which I shall treasure sacredly" and claiming that Mother Frances "loved me better than anyone now living except yourself." And in a letter to O'Connor dated May 14, 1886, Sister Austin indicated that she had solved her puzzle concerning Frances' holiness completely. She was engaged in compiling the *Annals* of the early Mercy days in Pittsburgh, and she confided to Bishop O'Connor: "Jane Warde sent me many of the letters her Aunt wrote when young. They give me a higher idea of Mother Warde than I had before. They show her to have been really holy and most zealous." Finally, in a letter dated May 5, 1899, Sister Austin, speaking of the need for religious leaders in New Orleans, echoed James O'Connor: "Would that we could get seven like the first seven in Pittsburgh!"

The ultimate proof of Mother Austin's final judgment concerning the holiness of Frances Warde is found, to be sure, in the two chapters devoted to Mother Frances in the fourth and last volume of the Mercy *Annals,* published in 1895. Here Sister Austin acknowledged Frances Warde's spiritual greatness without reservation. Like other Sisters of Mercy, Mother Austin was now completely aware that "the mustard seed sowed by [Frances Warde] and her little band from Carlow had sprung up into a wonderful tree spreading its branches everywhere."[36] Writing of the American founder whom she now called "the Great Mother," Sister Austin declared unequivocally, "The name of Mother Warde is illustrious among the distinguished servants of God and man and as such will be in eternal remembrance."

The testimony of Sister Austin Carroll is recorded as a special witness to Frances Warde's holiness because it originated in a lack of comprehension of the nature of Frances' sanctity and developed over a number of years into a full flowering of discernment. The hundreds who loved Frances present a simple and less complicated testimony.[37] In a sense, every holy man or woman is unique in sanctity. Frances Warde added a new dimension to the mystery of God's saints. It does not increase Frances' spiritual stature to quote innumerable witnesses to her spiritual genius. She was "the flower of the flock" of Catherine McAuley, "the first of all

485

the blessings of the Sisters of Mercy in America." It is probable that "no woman has lived to whom the Church in the United States owes more than it does to her." She was "one of the most extraordinary women in all the long list of founders of religious congregations. To unusual gifts of mind and character, she added zeal for God's glory and a burning desire to help the unfortunate which made failure impossible . . . The spirit of her Sisters has never flagged or grown weary." Superlative tributes to Frances Warde might be multiplied endlessly.

To her and to Catherine McAuley, such praises would have been unimportant. They both believed firmly that the Congregation of Mercy was the work of God, not of the Sisters to whom He gave the grace to proclaim His Word and to spread His Kingdom. No one should claim honor for herself. All their lives, these two holy women dreamed dreams and, despite seemingly insuperable sufferings and frustrations, made their vision become reality. They were ir. God's hands. Because of Frances Warde's faith, hope, and love, her life transcended limitations. There was more human grandeur in a few moments of her self-sacrifice than in a whole life of self-aggrandizement. Her call was from Jesus Christ. The fulfillment of her ministry to America was the work of God, not her own: Christ lived in Frances Warde.

Notes

1

1. The name of Frances Warde's mother has been stated erroneously as Jane Maher by early biographers. Although Frances Warde's birth and baptismal certificates are not available, convent records concerning both Frances and her sister, Sarah, in Dublin, Carlow, and Cork, as well as Pittsburgh, Providence, and Manchester, all indicate that the mother of Frances Warde was Mary Maher. The wife of Frances' uncle, John Maher of Freshford, Kilkenny, was named Jane. Evidently the name of Frances' aunt was confused with that of her mother.

2. Five deeds, dated as follows, in the Registry of Deeds, Dublin, refer to Bellbrook and the lease of John Warde: 30 April 1798; 28 February 1799; 28 May 1819 (two deeds); 21 November 1822.

3. Paul Cardinal Cullen's uncle, Thomas Maher, was the father of James Maher, who also became Rector of the Irish College in Rome. Another uncle, Patrick Maher of Kilrush, was the father of Mother Teresa, Sisters of Mercy, Carlow and later Athy; Mother Catherine, Sisters of Mercy, Carlow; and Mother Michael, Sisters of Mercy, Athy and later Callan. Cullen's aunt, Judith Maher Cullen of Craan, was the mother of Mother Paula, first Superior, Sisters of Mercy, Westport; Mother Josephine, Sisters of Mercy, Pittsburgh; and a second Mother Josephine, Sisters of Mercy, Carlow. Two aunts of Cullen, Johanna Maher and Elinor Maher, became Presentation Sisters. Altogether, Cardinal Cullen had two aunts and eighteen first cousins in convents, most of them Sisters of Mercy.

4. Sister M. Catherine Garety, *Reverend Mother M. Xavier Warde*, p. 10.

5. *Ibid.*, p. 13.
6. *Ibid.*, p. 5. See also Mother Teresa Austin Carroll, *Annals of the Sisters of Mercy,* I, pp. 255–56.
7. Both Garety and Carroll state that Frances Warde and her sister, Sarah, lived in Mountrath. Carroll indicates that Sarah lived with her uncle, William Maher, (I, 257). Further evidence that the girls lived with their Uncle William lies in the fact that Francis Haly, administrator of the mensal parish of Mountrath and later Bishop of Kildare and Leighlin, was a frequent visitor to Frances Warde's home when she was a girl (Carroll, III, 48) and was a close friend of her Uncle William Maher (Carroll, I, 191). Killeany, home of William Maher, was part of the mensal parish of Mountrath.
8. Garety, pp. 8–9.
9. Maynooth College records list the following: "John Ward, Diocese of Kildare, Matriculated in Humanities, February 15, 1819." Under the column indicating date of ordination, John Ward's name is followed by the simple statement, *"Nil aliud."* His death is indicated in Carroll, *Annals,* I, 255 and Garety, p. 4.
10. Garety, p. 6.
11. Carroll, I, 256.

2

1. Garety, p. 15.
2. Sister Clare Augustine Moore, *Memoir of Mother McAuley.*
3. See Sister Bertrand Degnan, *Mercy Unto Thousands,* pp. 23–26.
4. Mother M. Clare Moore, *Derry S Manuscript* (Bermondsey Annals).
5. *Derry L Manuscript.*
6. *Ibid.*

3

1. *Derry L Manuscript.*
2. Mother M. Clare Moore, *Derry S Manuscript.*
3. See Degnan, *Mercy Unto Thousands,* pp. 79–80.
4. *Derry L Manuscript.*
5. M. C. McAuley to Sister Elizabeth Moore, January 13, 1839.
6. Sister Clare Augustine Moore, *Memoir of Mother McAuley.*
7. *Derry L Manuscript.*

8. Frances Warde did not use one signature consistently throughout her life. She was consistent, however, in always using the feminine form of "Frances." In the Baggot Street register, she is listed as "Mary Frances Teresa"; in Carlow, "Mary Frances Xavier"; in Pittsburgh, "Mary Frances" and "Mary Frances Xavier." In Pittsburgh account books, she used the signature, "Sister Mary Frances Warde" from 1846 until 1850. In the year 1850, she used "Sister Mary Frances Xavier" occasionally. In Manchester account books, which she maintained without a break from 1858 until 1880, she used as signatures both "Sister Mary Frances Xavier" and "Sister Mary Frances Xavier Teresa." In Manchester property deeds, which may have varied signatures for legal reasons, we find the following: "Frances Theresa Ward"; "Frances T. Ward"; "Maria Theresa F. X. Warde"; "Maria Theresa Frances X. Warde"; and "Frances Teresa Warde." Only "es" in "Frances" never varies.
9. Mother Catherine McAuley, "Treatise on the Mercy Spirit," Bermondsey, England.
10. Garety, pp. 20–21.
11. Carroll, *Annals*, I, 257–58.
12. Roland Burke Savage, *Catherine McAuley*, pp. 196–97.
13. Mother M. Clare Moore to Sister Clare Augustine Moore, August 25, 1845.
14. *Acta*, Pon., I, 1835, Fol. 58, Propaganda Fide Archives, Rome.
15. Carroll, *Annals*, I, 87.
16. *Ibid.*, p. 134.

4

1. M. Comerford, *Collections Relating to the Dioceses of Kildare and Leighlin*, II, 46.
2. Comerford, I, 165–70.
3. Judgment of Bishop James Doyle, the famous "J.K.L." of Kildare and Leighlin. Quoted in Carroll, *Annals*, I, 168.
4. Carroll, *Annals*, I, 180.
5. Among many sources, the Carlow *Annals* alone list Sister Xavier O'Connell as a member of the party. If Sister Xavier accompanied the Sisters to Carlow, she did so as a postulant, Jane O'Connell, for she did not receive the habit at Baggot Street until July 1, 1837.

6. William John Fitzpatrick, *The Life, Times, and Correspondence of the Right Rev. Dr. Doyle, Bishop of Kildare and Leighlin,* I, 417.

7. *Maries,* the old genitive form, is correctly written without an apostrophe and is pronounced *Mary's.*

8. Carroll, *Annals,* I, 175.

9. Carlow *Annals.*

10. M. C. McAuley to M. Frances Warde, August, 1837.

11. Carroll, *Annals,* I, 187.

12. Mary C. McAuley to Sister Mary Teresa White, October 17, 1837.

13. M. C. McAuley to M. Frances Warde, October 23, 1837.

14. M. C. McAuley to M. Frances Warde, December 29, 1837.

15. M. C. McAuley to M. Frances Warde, February 17, 1838.

16. The letters written by Frances Warde to Catherine McAuley were destroyed at Baggot Street. Many of Mother Frances' American letters, collected by Mother Austin Carroll, were destroyed in Mobile, Alabama, on the death of Mother Austin in 1909. In her *Annals,* III, 390, Mother Austin had stated that she had "hundreds" of Mother Warde's letters in her possession.

17. Mary C. McAuley to Sister M. Teresa White, November 1. 1838.

18. M. C. McAuley to M. Frances Warde, June 16, 1838.

19. See M. C. McAuley to M. Frances Warde, March 24, 1838; April 9, 1838; June 16, 1838; August 23, 1838; October 25, 1838; November 17, 1838.

20. Mary C. McAuley to Very Reverend Doctor Andrew Fitzgerald, July 3, 1838.

21. Carroll, *Annals,* I, 204.

22. *Ibid.,* 205.

23. The Sisters of Mercy under Frances Warde did not open a "poor school" in Carlow, as the Presentation Sisters had been conducting a school for poor children there since 1809. See Carroll, *Annals,* I, 395.

5

1. M. C. McAuley to Rev. Gerald Doyle, September 5, 1836.

2. M. C. McAuley to Sister M. Elizabeth Moore, January 13, 1839.

3. M. C. McAuley to M. Frances Warde, August 23, 1838.

4. M. C. McAuley to M. Frances Warde, February, 1839. Original in Convent of Mercy, Windham, New Hampshire.
5. M. C. McAuley to M. Frances Warde, September, 1839.
6. Carlow Convent *Annals*, September, 1839.
7. *Foundation of St. Mary's Convent of Naas*, Dollard Printing House, Dublin, 1889.
8. M. C. McAuley to S. Josephine Warde, October 18, 1839.
9. M. C. McAuley to M. Frances Warde, May 28, 1841; July 19, 1841.
10. M. C. McAuley to M. Frances Warde, January, 1839.
11. Carlow Convent *Annals*, December 25, 1839.
12. *Ibid.,* January, 1840.
13. M. C. McAuley to M. Frances Warde, June 6, 1840.
14. Original in Convent of Mercy, Windham, New Hampshire.
15. *Annals,* St. Maries of the Isle, Cork.
16. M. C. McAuley to M. Frances Warde, October 26, 1840.
17. Carlow Convent *Annals*, November 16, 1840.
18. M. C. McAuley to M. Frances Warde, November 24, 1840.
19. M. C. McAuley to M. Frances Warde, November 30, 1840.
20. M. C. McAuley to M. Frances Warde, December 15, 1840.
21. Carroll, *Annals*, I, 404.
22. M. C. McAuley to S. M. de Sales White, January 20, 1841.
23. Carroll, *Annals*, I, 404.
24. M. C. McAuley to M. Frances Warde, December 17, 1840.
25. M. C. McAuley to S. Teresa Carton, January 19, 1841.
26. M. C. McAuley to M. Frances Warde, Easter Saturday, 1841.
27. M. C. McAuley to S. M. de Sales White, December 7, 1840.

6

1. A third manuscript preserved at Naas and inscribed with Frances Warde's handwriting is a 212-page copy of a spiritual book called *The Perfect Religious,* translated from the French. Evidently Mother Frances used it for spiritual lecture. With the flamboyance sometimes characteristic of her, she placed the following signature on the flyleaf: Sister Mary Frances Teresa Xavier Warde.
2. This notebook was given to Sister Kathleen Healy, Pittsburgh, by Mother Joseph Boyle, St. Mary's Convent, Naas, March 16, 1969.

3. Quotations are from *The Jerusalem Bible,* Doubleday and Company, Inc., New York, 1966.
4. Sister Paul Xavier Warde, "A Few Leaves from the Book of My Remembrance," Manchester, New Hampshire.
5. *Ibid.*
6. This part of the *Spiritual Maxims* is found in the Wexford Manuscript, an enlargement of the Naas manuscript.
7. M. C. McAuley to M. Frances Warde, July 26, 1841.

7

1. M. C. McAuley to M. Frances Warde, August 4, 1841.
2. Carlow Convent *Annals,* June, 1841.
3. Carroll, *Annals,* III, 390.
4. See Mary Ellen Evans, *The Spirit Is Mercy,* p. 301. Miss Evans states that Sister Teresa Austin's "papers were deliberately burned after her death."
5. *Acta,* 20 July 1840, Fols. 206–229; *Scritturi Riferite nelle Congregazioni Generali,* Fols. 270–322, 1840; Archives, Propaganda Fide, Rome.
6. *Scritturi non Riferite Nei Congressi,* Vol. 27 (1839–42), Irlanda, 340–43.
7. *Ibid.,* p. 498. Changes in the *Rule* proposed by the consultor to the Sacred Congregation, 20 November 1840, may be found on pp. 366–75.
8. Thomas Cullen, Liverpool, to his brother, Paul Cullen, Rector, Irish College at Rome, July 30, 1841. Archives, Irish College, Rome.
9. Carlow Convent *Annals,* April 2, 1874.
10. Sister di Pazzi Delaney suffered from epilepsy, which subjected her to unusual temperamental responses.
11. Carroll, *Life of Catherine McAuley,* p. 433.
12. Roland Burke Savage, *Catherine McAuley,* Dublin, N. H., Gill and Son Ltd., 1949, p. 376.
13. John MacErlean, S.J., who devoted years of research to the life of Catherine McAuley, expressed a similar judgment in a letter to Mother M. Raphael, St. Maries of the Isle, Cork, May, 1941: "We would have been in a poor way if Frances Warde had not preserved so many letters of Mother McAuley."
14. Sister M. Paul Xavier Warde to Mother M. Carmelita Hart-

mann, Baltimore, April 18, 1941. Archives, Sisters of Mercy, Bethesda, Maryland.

15. Sister M. Paul Xavier Warde to Sister M. Hieronyme McCaffery, Pittsburgh, June 16, 1949. Archives, Sisters of Mercy, Pittsburgh, Pennsylvania.
16. Carlow Convent *Annals,* June 16, 1842.
17. Carroll, *Annals,* III, p. 48.
18. Carlow Convent *Annals,* February 22, 1843.
19. Carroll, *Annals,* I, 364.
20. Quoted in Patrick L. Madden, *St. Patrick's Holy Mountain,* Sign of the Three Candles, Fleet St., Dublin, 1929, p. 5.
21. Westport Convent *Annals,* February 2, 1843.
22. Daniel Murray, Archbishop of Dublin, to Francis Haly, Bishop of Kildare and Leighlin, April 1, 1843. Carlow Diocesan Archives, Braganza House, Carlow.
23. William David Coyne, *Venerable Archdeacon Cavanagh,* Knock Shrine Society 1953, pp. 23–24.

8

1. In 1943 there were 861 Mercy Convents in the United States. In Ireland, England, Wales, Scotland, the Channel Islands, Isle of Man, Newfoundland, Australia, New Zealand, South America, Central America, the West Indies, and South Africa combined, there were 648 convents.
2. "Michael O'Connor," *Woodstock Letters,* I–II, 1872–73. Woodstock College, Woodstock, Maryland.
3. See, for example, Michael O'Connor, Marseilles, to Paul Cullen, Rome, April 1, 1843. Archives, Irish College, Rome.
4. Carroll, *Annals,* III, 45.
5. Carlow Convent *Annals,* October 5, 1843.
6. Margaret Cullen, Prospect, Ireland, to her brother, Paul Cullen, Irish College in Rome, December 5, 1843. Archives, Irish College, Rome.
7. Carlow Convent *Annals,* 1885.
8. Carroll, *Annals,* III, 58.
9. Because of anti-Catholic persecution in Ireland, the professed among the early Sisters of Mercy were addressed as "Mrs." and novices were called "Miss."
10. Thomas Cullen, Liverpool, to Paul Cullen, Irish College in

Rome, November 15, 1843. Mary was Thomas Cullen's small daughter. Archives, Irish College, Rome.

11. Michael O'Connor, Liverpool, to Paul Cullen, Irish College, Rome, November 10, 1843. Archives, Irish College, Rome.

12. Carroll, *Annals,* III, 63.

13. See Rev. J. T. Dean, Curate at St. Paul's Church, Pittsburgh, to Rev. Thomas Heyden, Bedford, Pennsylvania, December 15, 1843. Pittsburgh Diocesan Archives. See also Carroll, *Annals,* III, 66.

14. Sister Pierre Jones, *Memoirs of the Pittsburgh Sisters of Mercy,* p. 33.

15. Elizabeth Strange, "The First Years in Pittsburgh." Unpublished Manuscript. Archives, Sisters of Mercy, Pittsburgh.

16. Michael O'Connor, on board the "Great Western," per French Packet via Marseilles, to James O'Connor, Seminarian at the Propaganda, Rome, August 10, 1845. Omaha Diocesan Archives, Omaha.

17. Carlow Convent *Annals,* August 1845.

18. *Ibid.*

9

1. See Carroll, *Annals,* III, 227–34, Archives, Sisters of Mercy, Chicago; "Sisters of Mercy," *Illinois Catholic Historical Review,* III (April, 1921), 339–70.

2. *The Pittsburgh Catholic,* September 18, 1846.

3. See Letters of Bishop William Quarter, Chicago, to the President of the Society for the Progagation of the Faith, Lyons, France, March 15, November 28, December 12, 1844; January 1, 1846; October 1, 1847; January 12, 1848. Archives, Sisters of Mercy, Chicago. See also John E. McGirr, *Life of the Right Reverend William Quarter,* New York, D. and J. Sadlier, 1850.

4. See Francis J. Epstein, "History in the Annals of the Leopoldine Association," *Illinois Catholic Historical Review,* I (1918–19), 225–33.

5. Garety, *Mother M. Xavier Warde,* pp. 142–43.

6. *The Pittsburgh Catholic,* October 24, 1846.

7. Sister Agatha O'Brien, Chicago, to Sister Elizabeth Strange, Pittsburgh, October 26, 1851. Archives, Sisters of Mercy, Chicago.

8. Garety, *Mother M. Xavier Warde,* p. 146.
9. The account of Frances Warde's journey from Chicago to Pittsburgh is traditional among Mercy congregations in the United States. It has been written and told hundreds of times.
10. See Sister Cornelius Meerwald, *History of the Pittsburgh Mercy Hospital,* pp. 51–54.
11. *Memoirs of the Pittsburgh Sisters of Mercy,* p. 55.
12. See *The Pittsburgh Catholic,* August 8, 1846; July 31, 1847; July 19, 1848; July 28, 1849; July 27, 1851; July 24, 1852.

10

1. Stephen Badin, the first to be ordained a priest in the United States, received minor orders in France.
2. Carroll, *Annals,* III, 470.
3. Mt. Aloysius Convent *Annals.* Archives, Sisters of Mercy, Cresson, Pennsylvania.
4. Mother M. Agatha O'Brien, St. Xavier's Convent, Chicago, to the President of the Propagation of the Faith, Lyons, France, December 4, 1847. Reply, January 20, 1848. Archives, Sisters of Mercy, Chicago.
5. See Rev. Walter Quarter, New York, to the Cardinal Prefect of the Propaganda de Fide, Rome, September 28, 1856. *Congressi, America Centrale,* XVII (1855–57), Fols. 1280r to 1282r. Archives, Propaganda Fide, Rome.
6. M. Frances Warde, Providence, to Rev. James O'Connor, Pittsburgh, 1856. Archives, Diocese of Omaha, Nebraska.
7. See Sister Fidelis Convey, *Notes.* Archives, Sisters of Mercy, Chicago.
8. Sister Cecilia Maher, Carlow, to Revd. Mother, Convent of Mercy, Dublin, 1847. Archives, Sisters of Mercy, Carysfort Park, Dublin.
9. Sister Cecilia Maher, Carlow, to M. Frances Warde, Pittsburgh, August 4, 1849. Archives, Sisters of Mercy, Chicago.
10. Carroll, *Annals,* II, 598.
11. Carroll, *Annals,* II, 613.
12. S. M. Aloysia Strange, Pittsburgh, to M. M. Cecilia Maher, Carlow, Feast of the Sacred Heart, 1844. Archives, Convent of Mercy, Carlow.
13. M. Frances Warde, Pittsburgh, to James O'Connor, Charleston,

South Carolina, February 14, 1850. Archives, Diocese of Omaha, Nebraska.

14. M. Frances Warde, Pittsburgh, to James O'Connor, Latrobe, Spring, 1850. Archives, Diocese of Omaha, Nebraska.

15. Interview with Sister Cornelius Meerwald, former Archivist, Pittsburgh Sisters of Mercy, 1968.

16. James O'Connor, Latrobe, to Propaganda Fide, Rome, April 7, 1852, *Congressi, America Centrale* XVI (1852–54), Fols. 81rv and 82rv; October 28, 1854, Fol. 1176r; September 28, 1856, XVII (1855–57), Fols. 716rv and 717rv. Archives, Propaganda Fide, Rome.

17. The precise role of the "Major Superior" is not clear. The title seems not be interchangeable with that of "Vicar for Religious" since the office related only to the Mercy Congregation.

18. Chapter Book, Pittsburgh Sisters of Mercy, January 15, 1852, pp. 10–12.

19. *Ibid.*, p. 16.

20. See *Scritture Riferite nelli Congregazione Generali,* July–December 1877, Vol. 1007, pp. 1–725; *Acta,* Pon., July 17, 1877, Fol. 129, Vol. 245, pp. 129–140; *Congressi, America Centrale,* XXVIII (1877), Fols. 524–533. Archives, Propaganda Fide, Rome.

21. While she was in Pittsburgh, and afterward, the Sisters adopted the custom of calling Frances Warde either "Mother Xavier" or "Mother Warde."

22. Sister Josphine Cullen, Pittsburgh, to Father James O'Connor, Latrobe, Spring, 1950. Archives, Diocese of Omaha, Nebraska.

23. *Ibid.*

24. Michael O'Connor, Pittsburgh, to James O'Connor, Latrobe, Spring, 1852. Archives, Diocese of Omaha, Nebraska.

25. See *The Pittsburgh Catholic,* June 29, 1850.

26. Sister Antonio Gallagher, Latrobe, to Bishop James O'Connor, Omaha, January 8, 1885.

11

1. Carroll, *Annals,* III, 388.

2. Sister Camillus Byrne, New York, to Mother Mary Ann Doyle, Feast of the Resurrection, 1851. Archives, Convent of Mercy, Derry, Ireland.

3. Sister Agatha O'Brien, Chicago, to Sister Elizabeth Strange, Pittsburgh, October 26, 1851. Archives, Convent of Mercy, Chicago.
4. Mother Frances Warde, Providence, to Bishop Michael O'Connor, Pittsburgh. Quoted in Carroll, *Annals*, III, 390.
5. Garety, *Mother Xavier Warde*, pp. 158–60.
6. Quoted in Garety, *Mother Xavier Warde*, p. 177. Like most of her letters, Frances Warde's journal is lost.
7. See "In Memoriam, Miss Emily Harper," *Mount St. Mary's Record*, Manchester, New Hampshire, May, 1892, p. 4.
8. Sister M. Catherine Morgan, *A Sketch of the Work of the Sisters of Mercy in Providence*, Rhode Island, p. 24.
9. Carroll, *Annals*, III, 396.
10. Kirby Letters. Archives, Irish College, Rome.
11. Unpublished Manuscript, p. 19. Archives, Convent of Mercy, Carysfort Park, Dublin.
12. *Udienze-America Centrale*, Vol. 116, Fol. 2047 rv, 1852; *Lettere*, Fol. 1086, 1852. Archives, Propaganda Fide, Rome.
13. Carroll, *Annals*, I, 153.
14. *Congressi, America Centrale*, XXVI (1875), Fols. 72 rv to 177 rv. Archives, Propaganda Fide, Rome.
15. See Sister Mary Austin Carroll, New Orleans, to Bishop James O'Connor, Omaha, quoting Roman letters, December 12, 1883. Archives, Diocese of Omaha.
16. Annals, Convent of Mercy, Burlingame, California, December 18, 1859, pp. 164–69.
17. *Ibid.*, July 26, 1861, pp. 204–208.
18. *Ibid.*, August 15, 1861, pp. 208–11.
19. *Ibid.*, September 24, 1862, pp. 241–45.
20. *Annals,* Convent of Mercy, Limerick, II, 80–85.
21. To Sister Mary Clare McNamara, Limerick, Spring, 1864.
22. *Annals,* Convent of Mercy, Limerick, II, 201.
23. *Guide for Religious Called Sisters of Mercy*, 1866, p. 14.
24. Mother Frances Warde, Providence, to Reverend James O'Connor, Pittsburgh, March 1857. Archives, Diocese of Omaha.

12
1. Sister M. Florence Sullivan, *Memoirs, Rochester Sisters of Mercy*, p. 5.

2. Sister M. Gerald, *Annals,* Convent of Mercy, Buffalo, New York, p. 17.
3. Bishop John Timon, *Diary,* May 16, 1857. Archives, Diocese of Rochester, St. Bernard Seminary, Rochester.
4. The Pittsburgh Sisters were the "second founders" of the Buffalo Congregation when they sent a contingent of Sisters to Buffalo in 1860. Many Pittsburgh girls also entered the Hazleton Convent in its early days.
5. Bishop David William Bacon, *Diary.* Archives, Diocese of Portland, Maine.
6. M. H. Dowd, *The Life of Denis M. Bradley,* p. 43.
7. Carroll, *Annals,* IV, 159.
8. O'Connor, *Mercy Marks the Century,* p. 105.
9. David William Bacon to Francis Patrick McFarland, July 15, 1858. Archives, Convent of Mercy, Windham, New Hampshire.
10. Carroll, *Annals,* IV, 161.
11. Morgan, *Sketch of the Work of the Sisters of Mercy in Providence, Rhode Island, 1851–1893,* pp. 41, 42.
12. Carroll, *Annals,* IV, 180–81.
13. Doherty, *The First Hundred Years of the Manchester Sisters of Mercy,* p. 21.
14. Garety, *Mother M. Xavier Warde,* pp. 208–9.
15. See Lucey, *The Catholic Church in Maine,* pp. 191–4.
16. *Ibid.,* p. 189.
17. *Manchester Daily Mirror,* August 21, 1865.
18. *Manchester Union Leader,* July 8, 1863.
19. E. G. P. to Hattie Dix, March 13, 1865. Archives, Convent of Mercy, Windham, New Hampshire.

13
1. Carroll, *Annals,* IV, 189.
2. Heuser, *Mother Mary Patricia Waldron,* p. 14.
3. *Annals,* Convent of Mercy, Dobbs Ferry, New York, pp. 149–51.
4. *Philadelphia Catholic Herald and Visitor,* September 7, 1861.
5. *Ibid.,* August 30, 1862.
6. Heuser, *Mother Mary Patricia Waldron,* p. 15.
7. Interview with Mother M. Bernadette, Mater Misericordia Hospital, Philadelphia, September 30, 1968.

8. See M. Frances Warde to James O'Connor, October 28, 1861. Copy is in Archives, Convent of Mercy, Omaha.
9. *Annals,* St. Joseph Convent of Mercy, Broad Street and Columbia Avenue, Philadelphia, September 26, 1861.
10. Sister Cornelius Meerwald, Pittsburgh, to Sister Henrietta Connelly, Philadelphia, July 9, 1950. Archives, Convent of Mercy, Merion, Pennsylvania.
11. Carroll, *Annals,* IV, 190.
12. Archives, Convent of Mercy, Omaha.
13. Carroll, *Annals,* III, 92–93.
14. *Annals,* St. Joseph Convent of Mercy, Broad Street and Columbia Avenue, Philadelphia, October, 1861.
15. *Annals,* Convent of Mercy, Dobbs Ferry, New York, 1862–1871.
16. *Annals,* St. Joseph Convent of Mercy, Broad Street and Columbia Avenue, Philadelphia, pp. 12–13.
17. John S. Warde's Discharge from the Union Army is preserved at Mount St. Agnes Convent of Mercy, Baltimore, to which it was given by Sister Paul Xavier Warde, his daughter. Fanny Warde, his sister, died of tuberculosis in Pittsburgh at an early age. Jane Warde entered the Mercy Convent in Providence, Rhode Island, but left before her profession. She married later, and her little girl, Josie Warde Hight, attended Mount St. Mary's in Manchester during Frances Warde's life time.

14

1. See Sister M. Edmund Croghan, *Sisters of Mercy in Nebraska, 1864–1910,* p. 20.
2. M. Frances Warde, Manchester, to Bishop James Myles O'Gorman, Omaha, July, 1864. Diocesan Archives, Omaha.
3. M. Frances Warde, Rochester, to Bishop James Myles O'Gorman, Omaha, August 12, 1864. Diocesan Archives, Omaha.
4. *Cincinnati Telegraph,* February, 1865. See also Casper, *The Church on the Fading Frontier,* 1864–1900, p. 78.
5. Carroll, *Annals,* IV, pp. 206–7.
6. Mother Gonzaga O'Brien, quoted in Carroll, *Annals,* IV, 207.
7. See, for example, Carroll, *Annals,* IV, pp. 202–6, 251–58.
8. Fifteen of Mary Anne O'Connor's letters to her brother, Bishop James O'Connor, are extant in the Diocesan Archives, Omaha.

9. M. Frances Warde, Manchester, to James O'Connor. Diocesan Archives, Omaha, n.d.
10. Mary Anne O'Connor Davis, St. Louis, to James O'Connor, Holmesburg, June 12, 1875. Diocesan Archives, Omaha.

15

1. Kent Stone, *The Invitation Heeded*, pp. 23–31.
2. Kent Stone to Mary Kent Stone, October 9, 1869, in Smith and Smith, *Fidelis of the Cross*, p. 143.
3. *The Invitation Heeded*, p. 30.
4. Francis Patrick Kenrick, Baltimore, to Michael O'Connor, Pittsburgh, August 13, 1858. Archives, Diocese of Omaha.
5. Michael O'Connor, Pittsburgh, to Francis Patrick Kenrick, Baltimore, November 4, 1858. Cathedral Archives, Baltimore.
6. Sister Evangelist Kinsella, Pittsburgh, to James O'Connor, Omaha, October 27, 1878. Archives, Diocese of Omaha.
7. The letters of Kent Stone to Frances Warde are preserved in the Archives of the Convent of Mercy, Windham, New Hampshire.
8. Archives, Convent of Mercy, Windham, New Hampshire.
9. Quoted in Smith and Smith, *Fidelis of the Cross*, pp. 216–17.
10. Archives, Convent of Mercy, Windham, New Hampshire.
11. *Ibid.*
12. *Ibid.*
13. Quoted in Smith and Smith, *Fidelis of the Cross*, p. 289.
14. Fidelis Stone to Edmund Hill, quoted in *Ibid.*, p. 300.
15. Fidelis Stone to Walter George Smith, quoted in *Ibid.*, p. 297.
16. Smith and Smith, *Fidelis of the Cross*, pp. 419–21.

16

1. Carroll, *Annals,* IV, 470.
2. Henry Walsh, *Hallowed Were the Gold Dust Trails.* University of Santa Clara Press, Santa Clara, California, 1946, p. 397.
3. Carroll, *Annals,* IV, 228.
4. Mother Frances Dunphy, *Annals,* Sisters of Mercy, Red Bluff, California.
5. Carroll, *Annals,* IV, 471.
6. *Annals,* Sisters of Mercy, Dobbs Ferry, New York, February, 1871.

Notes

7. Catherine McAuley, in Manuscript preserved in Convent of Mercy, Bermondsey, England.
8. Louis de Goesbriand to Martin John Spalding, November 4, 1864. Cathedral Archives, Archdiocese of Baltimore.
9. Quoted in Carroll, *Annals*, IV, p. 245.
10. *Diary of Louis de Goesbriand*, August 16, 1872; August 20, 1872. Diocesan Archives, Burlington, Vermont.
11. *Ibid*, September 13, 1874.
12. *History and Corporation Meetings, 1872–1956*, Convent of Mercy, Burlington, Vermont, June 4, 1876.
13. M. Frances Warde to M. Stanislaus O'Malley, Archives, Convent of Mercy, Burlington, Vermont.

17

1. Archives, Convent of Mercy, Plainfield, New Jersey.
2. See *Letter Book* of James Roosevelt Bayley and Michael A. Corrigan, October 4, 1873, and April 13, 1874. Archives, Archdiocese of Newark, New Jersey.
3. Sister Ignatius Hogan, *Annals*, Convent of Mercy, Plainfield, New Jersey.
4. Bishop Michael A. Corrigan, *Diary*, June, 1877. Archives, Archdiocese of Newark, New Jersey.
5. Sister Ignatius Hogan, *Like a Waterwheel of God*. Archives, Sisters of Mercy, Plainfield, New Jersey.
6. Interview with Sister M. Bernard, age 96, Motherhouse, Sisters of Mercy, Plainfield, New Jersey, October 20, 1968.
7. Edwin V. Sullivan, *Annotated Diary of Bishop James Roosevelt Bayley*, Newark, New Jersey, Vol. II, p. 195.
8. Joseph M. Flynn, *The Catholic Church in New Jersey*, Norristown, New Jersey, 1904.
9. Quoted in *St. Paul's Centennial (1844–1944)*, St. Paul's Church, Princeton, New Jersey, 1944.
10. Frederick A. Childs, *History of St. Mary's Church, Bordentown, New Jersey*.

18

1. Carroll, *Annals*, IV, 284.
2. *Ibid.*, II, 620.
3. *Ibid.*, IV, 285.

4. *Ibid.,* IV, 284.
5. Sister M. Catherine Garety, *M. Xavier Warde,* Boston, 1902, pp. 227–28.
6. Sister Mary Xaveria Toohey, *Memories of Mercy,* Unpublished Manuscript, 1931. Archives, Sisters of Mercy, Portland, Maine.
7. *Ibid.*
8. David William Bacon to Frances Warde, July 23, 1873, in Carroll, IV, 22.
9. William Leo Lucey, *The Catholic Church in Maine,* New Hampshire, 1957, p. 197.
10. *Ibid.,* pp. 192–93.
11. Sister M. Benigna Doherty, *The First Hundred Years,* Manchester, Sisters of Mercy, 1968, p. 54.
12. Albert S. Foley, *Bishop Healy: Beloved Outcast,* New York, 1954, pp. 4–13.
13. Lucey, *The Catholic Church in Maine,* pp. 223–24.
14. *Ibid.,* p. 225.
15. James Augustine Healy, *Episcopal Diary* (*1875–1885*), April 19, 1875. Diocesan Archives, Portland, Maine.
16. Foley, *Bishop Healy,* p. 183.
17. Carroll, *Annals,* IV, 181.
18. Healy, *Diary,* July 6, 1875.
19. *Ibid.,* November 13, 1875.
20. *Ibid.,* January 1, 1876.
21. *Annals,* Sisters of Mercy, Portland, Maine, in *The Maine Historical Magazine,* August, 1923, p. 86.
22. Frances Warde, Manchester, to Mother Catherine Maher, Carlow, September 6, 1876, in Garety, *M. Xavier Warde,* p. 244.
23. Healy, *Diary,* May 14, June 30, July 7, 1877.
24. *Udienze,* 1878, Vol. 190, Fol. 1266 r. and v., Propaganda Fide, Rome.
25. *Udienze, America Centrale,* 1877, Vol. 186, Fol. 897 r. and v., Propaganda Fide, Rome.
26. Foley, *Bishop Healy,* p. 179.
27. Carroll, *Annals,* IV, p. 181.

19

1. See Eugene Vetromile, *The Abnakis and Their History,* New York, James B. Kirker, 1866.

Notes

2. See *Annals,* Sisters of Mercy, Peter Dana Point, Maine.
3. Archives, Sisters of Mercy, Peter Dana Point, Maine.
4. Eugene Vetromile, *Indian Good Book,* New York, Edward Dunigan and Brothers, 1856.
5. *Annals,* Sisters of Mercy, Portland, Maine.
6. See James Healy, *Diary,* October 31, 1877.
7. See Toohey, *Memories of Mercy.* Archives, Sisters of Mercy, Portland, Maine.
8. *Annals,* Sisters of Mercy, Portland, Maine.
9. Sister M. Agnes, Indian Island, Maine, to Mother Frances Warde, Manchester, December 2, 1881. Archives, Sisters of Mercy, Manchester, New Hampshire.
10. See "An Indian Relic," by a Sister of Mercy. Archives, Sisters of Mercy, Portland, Maine.
11. See James Healy, *Diary,* February 16, 1879; June 15, 1879.
12. For an account of the Sisters' arrival at Pleasant Point, see Toohey, *Memories of Mercy.* Archives, Sisters of Mercy, Portland, Maine.
13. Archives, Diocese of Portland, Maine.
14. Doherty, *The First Hundred Years,* p. 57.
15. See Eugene Vetromile, ed., *The Prayer Song,* New York, Edward Dunigan and Brothers, 1858.
16. Carroll, *Annals,* IV, 239.
17. Archives, Sisters of Mercy, Peter Dana Point, Maine.
18. Doherty, *The First Hundred Years,* p. 63.
19. Interview with Sylvester Gabriel, Portland, Maine, January, 1969.
20. See, for example, W. O. Chase, School Departments, Old Town and Orono, to William Lem, Indian Island, Old Town, Maine, April 3, 1931.

20

1. See Healy, *Diary,* January 12, 1877; July 2, 1878; June 1, 1879.
2. J. M. Stone, Lake George, New York, to Frances Warde, Manchester, October 5, 1875.
3. Healy, *Diary,* June 1, 1879.
4. Fidelis Stone, SS. Giovanni e Paolo, Rome, to Frances Warde, Manchester, March 11, 1880.
5. Interview with Sister Hieronyme McCaffrey, who knew Sister Paul Xavier Warde personally. Pittsburgh, May, 1967.

6. See *Mount St. Mary Journal*, VI (February 1898), 99–100; VI (March 1898), 109–10; VI (May 1898), 133–34; VII (June, 1898), 1–2; VII (July 1898), 17–18.

7. In addition to the letters of Frances Warde quoted in Mother Austin Carroll's *Annals*, the author of the present work, in a thorough search of Mercy and Diocesan Archives throughout the United States and Ireland, has been able to discover only twenty-two letters of Frances Warde.

8. Paul L. Blakely, S.J., New York, to the Reverend Mother, Manchester, New Hampshire, January 24, 1921.

9. Mother M. Carmelita Hartman, first Mother General of the Sisters of Mercy of the Union in the United States, who had a magnificent sense of history, urged Sister Paul Xavier to write what she knew of Frances Warde's life and background. Sister Paul Xavier had strong tendencies toward procrastination.

10. See "A Few Leaves from the Book of My Remembrance," Unpublished Manuscript, Sisters of Mercy, Manchester, New Hampshire.

11. Sisters M. Arnoldine, Magdalen, Gabriel, Theodora, and Bertha of the Manchester Sisters of Mercy, interviewed in 1968, and Sister M. Louise of the Providence Congregation, interviewed in 1967, all testified to Sister Paul Xavier's admiration for and devotion to Frances Warde. These Sisters all knew Mary Agnes Warde personally.

12. Bishop James Healy, Portland, to Mother Frances Warde, Manchester, July 9, 1880. Diocesan Archives, Portland, Maine.

13. Frances Warde, Manchester, to Msgr. Tobias Kirby, Irish College at Rome, September 13, 1880. Kirby Letters, Irish College, Rome.

14. See Doherty, *The First Hundred Years*, pp. 76–78.

15. See Papal Blessing, November 17, 1881. Archives, Sisters of Mercy, Manchester.

16. Frances Warde, Manchester, to Mother Austin Carroll, Mobile, Alabama, January 27, 1882. This letter was preserved in St. Michael's Convent, Wexford, Ireland. It was probably given to the Wexford Congregation by Mother Austin Carroll.

17. Obituary of Mother Catherine Clifford, *Mount St. Mary Record*, Manchester, January, 1913, p. 83.

18. See Foley, *Bishop Healy: Beloved Outcast*, pp. 176–77.

19. See Toohey, *Memories of Mercy*. Archives, Sisters of Mercy, Portland.
20. Several accounts of the fascinating history of the property upon which St. Joseph's Convent and Academy in Deering were built are in the Archives of the Sisters of Mercy, Portland.
21. For an account of St. Joseph's Convent and Academy and St. Joseph's Home for the Aged at Deering, see Archives, Sisters of Mercy, Windham and Portland. Also, Toohey, *Memories*, Portland Archives.

21

1. Copies of Sister Catherine Clifford's letter are preserved in the Archives of the Sisters of Mercy, Windham, N.H., and in Carlow, Ireland.
2. Tributes to Frances Warde on her Golden Jubilee are preserved in the Archives of the Sisters of Mercy, Windham, N.H. See also Carroll, *Annals*, IV, 263–70; Doherty, *The First Hundred Years*, pp. 84–85; and Garety, *Mother M. Xavier Warde*, pp. 251–65.
3. See Letters of Bishop James Healy to Mother Catherine Clifford, March 19, March 26, April 3, June 27, and June 29, 1883. Diocesan Archives, Portland, Maine.
4. Quoted in Doherty, *The First Hundred Years*, pp. 88–89.
5. Toohey, *Memories of Mercy*. Archives, Sisters of Mercy, Portland, Maine.
6. Sister Mary Lawrence, in a signed statement. Archives, Sisters of Mercy, Windham, N.H.
7. Archives, Sisters of Mercy, Windham, N.H.

22

1. Carroll, *Annals*, IV, 273.
2. For accounts of Frances Warde's death, see Garety, *Mother M. Xavier Warde*, pp. 274–83; Carroll, *Annals*, IV, 274–77; Doherty, *The First Hundred Years*, pp. 93–98.
3. Garety, *Mother M. Xavier Warde*, p. 279.
4. Bishop Healy's eulogy of Frances Warde is preserved in the Archives of the Sisters of Mercy, Windham, N.H. It was quoted in numerous publications in September, 1884, including the *Manchester Mirror and American*.

5. Burt P. Moran to Mother M. Damian, 1966. Archives, Sisters of Mercy, Windham, N.H.
6. Bishop Denis M. Bradley, Sermon preached at Mount St. Mary's Convent, on the fiftieth anniversary of the American foundation of the Sisters of Mercy, December 21, 1893.

23

1. Convents of Mercy are established in England, Ireland, Scotland, Wales, Channel Islands, Isle of Wight, Isle of Man; United States, Canada, Newfoundland, Central America, South America, West Indies; Australia, New Guinea, New Zealand; India, Philippine Islands, Guam; South and East Africa.
2. Other foundations of Sisters of Mercy in the United States were made from Dublin to New York in 1846 by Mother Mary Agnes O'Connor; from Kinsale to San Francisco in 1854 by Mother Baptist Russell and to Cincinnati in 1858 by Mother Teresa Maher; from Naas to Little Rock, Arkansas, in 1851 by Mother Teresa O'Farrell; and from Ennis to Middletown and Meriden, Connecticut, in 1872 by Mother Mary Agnes Healy and Mother Teresa Perry. The Little Rock Congregation thus owed its origin to Frances Warde by way of Naas, founded from Carlow. The Middletown and Meriden Congregations amalgamated in 1911 with the Hartford Congregation founded by Frances Warde. The New York, San Francisco, and Cincinnati Congregations were phenomenal in their growth like Mother Frances' foundations in Pittsburgh, Chicago, Loretto (Dallas), Providence, Hartford, Rochester, Manchester, Philadelphia, Omaha, Portland, Burlington, and Bordentown (Plainfield).
3. Interview with Sister M. Gabriel, Manchester, New Hampshire, January, 1968.
4. Manuscript, Archives, Sisters of Mercy, Hartford, Connecticut.
5. Interview with Sister M. Euphrasia, Windham, New Hampshire, January, 1968.
6. Carroll, *Annals,* IV, 282.
7. Frances Warde sometimes traveled in secular dress because of bigotry in New England and for convenience when she traveled alone.
8. The story was related during an interview with Sister M. Louise, St. Xavier's Convent, Providence, Rhode Island, November, 1967.

Notes

9. Sister Paul Xavier Warde, "A Backward Glance—III," *Mount St. Mary's Record*, Manchester, New Hampshire, May, 1898.

10. Sister M. Antonio Gallagher, St. Xavier's Academy, Latrobe, to Bishop James O'Connor, Omaha, October 12, 1884. Diocesan Archives, Omaha.

11. Interview with Sister M. Magdalen, Windham, New Hampshire, January, 1968. See also Sister M. Cecelia, *Hartford Catholic Transcript*, 1902.

12. Interview with Sister M. Theodora, Hooksett, New Hampshire, quoting Mother M. Bertha, Manchester, New Hampshire, January, 1968.

13. Mother M. Arnoldine, Manchester, New Hampshire, January, 1968.

14. Carroll, *Annals*, IV, 283.

15. Sister Juliana Purcell. Quoted in Carroll, *Annals*, IV, 283.

16. *Ibid.*, 282.

17. Garety, *Mother M. Xavier Warde*, p. 286.

18. See Sister M. Cecelia, *Hartford Catholic Transcript*, 1902. Archives, Manchester Sisters of Mercy.

19. Testimony of Sister M. Bennet Ward, Providence, Rhode Island, 1878. Manuscript, Archives, Sisters of Mercy, Providence.

20. The phrasing is that of Sister M. Magdalen, Windham, New Hampshire, a contemporary of Sister Paul Xavier Warde.

21. Review of Garety, *Mother M. Xavier Warde, New York Sun,* 1903.

22. See William P. Clancy, "Address on the Unveiling of the Portraits of Mother McAuley and Mother Warde," *Mount St. Mary's Record*, XXXIX (December 1931–February 1932), 46–56.

23. Interview with Sister M. Magdalen, Windham, New Hampshire, January, 1968. Sister Magdalen's father was a friend of Bishop Healy.

24. Carroll, *Annals*, IV, 261.

25. Interview with Sister M. Louise, St. Xavier Convent, Providence, Rhode Island, November, 1967.

26. Carroll, *Annals*, IV, 260–61.

27. See William A. Hickey, Bishop of Providence, Sermon on the Diamond Jubilee of the Founding of the Providence Sisters of Mercy, *Providence Visitor*, March 13, 1926.

28. See, for example, Bishop James O'Connor, Omaha, quoted in *Annals,* Carlow Sisters of Mercy, 1885; Sister Elizabeth Strange, Pittsburgh, to Bishop James O'Connor, Omaha, September 24, 1884, Diocesan Archives, Omaha; and Mother M. Bernard, Bayview, Rhode Island, quoted in the *Mount St. Mary's Record,* XI (March 1903), 7: "Her bright example has done much to help me over many rugged and hard circumstances, and the thought that she is in heaven and understands and knows the efforts and struggles it often causes to work for God alone, has consoled and encouraged me to bear and endure many things which I know would meet her approval."

29. Sister Paul Xavier Warde, "A Chapter of Incidents," *Mount St. Mary's Record,* II (January, 1894). 15–17.

30. Interview with Sister M. Elizabeth, Hooksett, New Hampshire, January, 1968.

31. Sister M. Cecelia, *Hartford Catholic Transcript,* 1902. Archives, Sisters of Mercy, Hartford, Connecticut.

32. See "My Conversion," *Mount St. Mary's Journal,* I (July 1892), 37–39.

33. See Mother Austin Carroll, Mobile, to Bishop James O'Connor, Omaha, March 6, 1880; March 3, 1882; February 29, 1884; October 1, 1884; May 14, 1886; May 5, 1889. Diocesan Archives, Omaha. See also Mother Austin Carroll to Mother M. Gonzaga, September 18, 1884. Archives, Sisters of Mercy, Windham, N.H.

34. Quoted in Walter George Smith and Helen Grace Smith, *Fidelis of the Cross,* New York: G. P. Putnam's Sons, 1926, p. 308.

35. *Annals,* Carlow Sisters of Mercy, 1885.

36. Sister M. Antonio Gallagher, Latrobe, to Bishop James O'Connor, Omaha, Epiphany, 1883. Diocesan Archives, Omaha.

37. See, for example, Editorial, *America,* December 12, 1931; *Providence Visitor,* March 5, 1926; Jeremiah S. Buckley, Sermon, August 17, 1930, Archives, Sisters of Mercy, Manchester; Denis M. Bradley, Sermon, December 2, 1893, Archives, Sisters of Mercy, Windham, N.H.; William P. Clancy, Address, *Mount St. Mary's Record,* XXXIX, 45–56.

Selected Bibliography

BOOKS AND PERIODICALS

Bernard, Mother M. *The Story of the Sisters of Mercy in Mississippi, 1860–1930*. New York: P. J. Kenedy & Sons, 1931.

Bolster, Evelyn. *The Sisters of Mercy in the Crimean War*. Cork: The Mercer Press, 1964.

Bowen, Sister M. Neri, McGirr, Sister M. Camillus, and Meerwald, Sister M. Cornelius, Compilers. *History of the Pittsburgh Sisters of Mercy, 1843–1943*. Privately Reproduced. Pittsburgh, Sisters of Mercy, 1946.

Burton, Katherine. *His Mercy Endureth Forever*. Tarrytown, New York: Sisters of Mercy, 1946.

Carroll, Mother M. Teresa Austin. *Leaves from the Annals of the Sisters of Mercy*, 4 Vols. New York: P. O'Shea, Publisher, 1881, 1883, 1888, 1895.

Carroll, Mother M. Teresa Austin. *Life of Catherine McAuley*. New York: D. and J. Sadlier and Co., 1866.

Casper, Henry W., S.J. *The Church on the Fading Frontier*. Vol. II of *The Catholic Church in Nebraska*. 3 Vols. Milwaukee: The Bruce Publishing Co., 1966.

"Centenary of the Sisters of Mercy." Editorial. *America*, December 12, 1931.

A Century of Mercy, 1861–1961. Philadelphia: Sisters of Mercy, 1961. Privately Printed.

Childs, Frederick A., Compiler. *History of St. Mary's Church, Bordentown, N.J.* Bordentown, N.J.: St. Mary's Church, 1945.

Clancy, William P. "Address on the Unveiling of the Portraits of Mother McAuley and Mother Warde," *Mount St. Mary's Record*, XXXIX (1931–32), 46–56.

Clifford, Mother Catherine: Obituary. *Mount St. Mary Record*, XX (1913), 83.

Comerford, M. *Collections Relating to the Dioceses of Kildare and Leighlin.* 3 Vols. Dublin: James Duffy and Sons, 1886.

Costello, Sister Mary Loretto. *The Sisters of Mercy of Maryland, 1855–1930.* St. Louis: B. Herder Book Co., 1931.

Coyne, William David. *Venerable Archdeacon Cavanagh.* Knock Shrine Society, 1953.

Cram, Hal. "Catholic Church in Portland," *Maine Catholic Historical Magazine*, III (1914), 25–28.

Croghan, Sister M. Edmund. *Sisters of Mercy in Nebraska, 1864–1910.* Ph.D. Dissertation. Washington, D.C.: Catholic University of America, 1942.

Cullen, Thomas F. *The Catholic Church in Rhode Island.* Providence, R.I.: Franciscan Missionaries of Mary, 1936.

Customs and Minor Regulations of the Religious Called Sisters of Mercy in the Parent House, Baggot Street, and Its Branch Houses. Dublin: J. M. O'Toole and Son, 1869.

Degnan, Sister M. Bertrand, R.S.M. *Mercy Unto Thousands.* Westminster, Maryland: The Newman Press, 1957.

Doherty, Sister M. Benigna. *The First Hundred Years of the Manchester Sisters of Mercy.* Privately Printed. Manchester, New Hampshire, 1968.

Donworth, Sister Margaret Mary. *The Golden Jubilee: Saint Francis Xavier's Convent of Mercy, Providence, R.I., 1851–1901.* Privately Printed. Providence, R.I., 1901.

Dowd, Mary H. *The Life of Denis M. Bradley.* Manchester, N.H.: Guidon Publishing Co., 1905.

Epstein, Francis J. "History in the Annals of the Leopoldine Association," *Illinois Catholic Historical Review*, I (1918–19), 225–33.

Evans, Mary Ellen. *The Spirit Is Mercy.* The Story of the Sisters of Mercy in the Archdiocese of Cincinnati. New York: Newman Press, 1959.

Fitzgerald, Sister Mary Innocentia. *A Historical Sketch of the Sisters of Mercy in the Diocese of Buffalo, 1857–1942.* Buffalo, N.Y.: Mount Mercy Academy, 1942.

Fitzpatrick, William John. *The Life, Times, and Correspondence of the Right Rev. Dr. Doyle, Bishop of Kildare and Leighlin.* 2 Vols. Dublin: James Duffy, 7 Wellington Quay, 1861.

Flynn, Joseph M. *The Catholic Church in New Jersey*. Norristown, New Jersey, 1904.

Foley, Albert S., S.J. *Bishop Healy, Beloved Outcast*. New York: Farrar, Straus and Young, 1954.

Garety, Sister M. Catherine. *Rev. Mother M. Xavier Warde*. Boston: Marlier and Co., Ltd., 1902.

Garraghan, Gilbert J., S.J. *The Catholic Church in Chicago, 1673–1871*. Chicago, Ill.: Loyola University Press, 1921.

Gately, Sister M. Josephine. *Seventy-Five Years in the Passing, The Sisters of Mercy, Providence, R.I., 1851–1926*. Providence, R.I.: The Providence Visitor Press, 1926.

Golden Jubilee Celebration: Foundation of St. Mary's Convent of Mercy, Naas, September 24, 1889. Dublin: Dollard Printing House, 1889.

The Golden Jubilee, St. Francis Xavier Convent, Providence, R.I., 1851–1901. Privately Printed. Providence, R.I., 1901.

The Golden Milestone, 1846–1896. Fifty Years of Labor by the Sisters of Mercy of New York City. New York: Benziger Brothers, 1896.

Hartnett, Sister M. Vincent. *The Life of Rev. Mother Catherine McAuley*. With an Introduction by Ven. Richard Baptist O'Brien, D.D. Dublin: John F. Fowler, 3 Crow St., 1864.

Heuser, Herman J. *Reverend Mother Mary Patricia Waldron*. Philadelphia: Dolphin Press, 1916.

Historical Records and Studies, United States Catholic Historical Society. Papers Relating to the Sisters of Mercy in the United States. III, Pt. 1, 254; IV, 210–12; VII, 283–388; VIII, 151, 195–240, 294–329; 450–512; IX, 1–34, 80, 399–421; XXXII, 8, 151–76; XXXV, 357–402; XXXVI, 155–87, 254–84; XXXIX, 271–346; LXXXVII, 104–192.

Holland, Sister Mary Ildephonse. *Lengthened Shadows: A History of the Sisters of Mercy, Cedar Rapids, Iowa*. New York: Bookman Associates, 1952.

Hyde, Sister Mary Antonia. *Mercy*. Rochester, N.Y.: George P. Burns Press, Inc., 1932.

Jones, Sister M. Pierre, Compiler. *Memoirs of the Pittsburgh Sisters of Mercy*. Compiled from Various Sources, 1843–1917. New York: The Devin-Adair Co., 1918.

Lambing, A. A. *A History of the Catholic Church in the Dioceses of Pittsburg and Allegheny.* New York: Benziger Brothers, 1880.

Leahy, Walter T. *The Catholic Church in the Diocese of Trenton.* Princeton, N.J.: Princeton University Press, 1906.

Lennon, Sister Mary Isidore. *Milestones of Mercy. Story of the Sisters of Mercy in St. Louis, 1856–1956.* Milwaukee: Bruce Press, 1956.

Lucey, William Leo, S.J. *The Catholic Church in Maine.* Francestown, N.H.: Marshall Jones Co., 1957.

McEntee, Sister Mary Veronica. *The Sisters of Mercy of Harrisburg, 1869–1939.* Philadelphia: The Dolphin Press, 1939.

McGirr, John E. *Life of Right Rev. William Quarter.* New York: D. and J. Sadlier, 1850.

MacSuibhne, Peadar. *Paul Cullen and His Contemporaries.* 3 Vols. Naas, Kildare, Ireland: Leinster Leader, Ltd., 1961, 1962, 1965.

Madden, Patrick L. *St. Patrick's Holy Mountin.* Dublin: Sign of the Three Candles, Fleet St., 1929.

Meagher, Rev. William. *Notices of the Life and Character of Most Rev. Daniel Murray.* Dublin: Gerald Bellew, 79 Grafton Street, 1853.

Meerwald, Sister M. Cornelius, Compiler. *History of the Pittsburgh Mercy Hospital, 1847–1959.* Privately Reproduced. Pittsburgh, Pa.: Sisters of Mercy, 1959.

Memoir of Mother Mary Gonzaga O'Brien. Manchester, N.H.: The Magnificat Press, 1920.

Moran, Patrick Francis, ed. *The Letters of Rev. James Maher, with a Memoir.* Dublin: Browne and Nolan, 1877.

Morgan, Sister M. Catherine. *A Little Sketch of the Work of the Sisters of Mercy in Providence, Rhode Island, from 1851 to 1893.* Providence, R.I.: J. A. and R. A. Reid, Printers, 1893.

Morgan, Sister Mary Evangelist. *Mercy, Generation to Generation.* History of the First Century of the Sisters of Mercy, Sacramento, California. San Francisco: Fearon Publishers, 1957.

"My Conversion," *Mount St. Mary Journal*, I (July, 1892), 37–39.

Neumann, Sister Mary Ignatia, ed. *Letters of Catherine McAuley.* Baltimore: Helicon Press, Inc., 1969.

O'Brien, Sister M. Gabriel. *Reminiscences of Seventy Years (1846–1916).* Chicago: Fred J. Ringley Co., 1916.

O'Connor, Sister Mary Loretto. *Mercy Marks the Century.* Privately Printed. Providence, R.I.: Sisters of Mercy, 1951.

O'Connor, Mary J. "St. Francis Xavier," *Mount St. Mary Record,* I (December, 1892), 64.

O. F., "Indian Island in the Penobscot," *Fordham Monthly,* XXVII (1908), 2–5.

O'Hanlon, John Canon and O'Leary, Edward. *History of the Queen's County.* 2 Vols. Dublin: Sealy, Bryers, and Walker, 1907.

One Hundred Years of Mercy Unto Generations. Privately Printed. Omaha, Nebraska: Sisters of Mercy, 1964.

One Hundred Years of Sanctuary (1855–1955). Centenary Publication of Sisters of Mercy of Baltimore.

O'Reilly, Sister Mary Cecilia. *Sisters of Mercy in the Diocese of Hartford.* Privately Printed. Hartford, Conn., 1931.

Russell, Matthew. *The Life of Mother Mary Baptist Russell.* New York: The Apostleship of Prayer, 1901.

Russell, Matthew. *The Three Sisters of Lord Russell of Killowen.* New York: Longmans, Green and Co., 1912.

St. Paul's Centennial (1844–1944). St. Paul's Church, Princeton, N.J., 1944.

Savage, Roland Burke, S.J. *Catherine McAuley: The First Sister of Mercy.* Dublin: M. H. Gill and Son Ltd., 1950.

"Sermon Delivered by the Rt. Rev. D. M. Bradley, Dec. 21, 1893," *Mount St. Mary Record,* II (January, 1894), 193–94.

Serving God and Humanity in Chicago 100 Years, 1846–1946. Privately Printed. Chicago: Sisters of Mercy, 1946.

A Sister of Mercy. *Memoir of Reverend William McDonald.* Privately Printed. Manchester, N.H.: Mount St. Mary, 1909.

"Sisters of Mercy in Burlington, Vermont, 1872–1922," Golden Jubilee Number, *Mount Saint Mary Journal,* Burlington, Vermont, 1922.

"Sisters of Mercy in Burlington, Vermont, 1872–1947," Diamond Jubilee Number, *Mount Saint Mary Journal,* Burlington,, Vermont, April, 1947.

"The Sisters of Mercy," *Illinois Catholic Historical Review,* III (April 1921), 339–70.

The Sisters of Mercy Centennial in the Diocese of Providence, 1851–1951. Privately Printed, 1951.

Sisters of Mercy, 1831–1931. Privately Printed. Sisters of Mercy, Province of Omaha, December 12, 1931.

Sisters of Mercy, Philadelphia. *A Century of Mercy, 1861–1961.* Privately Printed. Philadelphia, Pa., 1961.

"Sisters of Mercy in Portland," Golden Jubilee Number, *The Maine Catholic Historical Magazine*, VIII (August, 1923), 75–141.

Sixty Years: Mother Mary Francis Xavier [Leeson]. Manchester, N.H.: The Magnificat Press, 1929.

Smith, Walter George and Smith, Helen Grace. *Fidelis of the Cross, James Kent Stone*. New York: G. P. Putnam's Sons, 1926.

Souvenir of Loretto Centenary, 1799–1899. Cresson, Pa.: Swope Brothers, Printers, 1899.

Stone, James Kent (Fidelis of the Cross, C.P.). *An Awakening and What Followed*, 1920. Revision of *The Invitation Heeded*. New York: Christian Press Association Publishing Co., 1869.

Sullivan, Edwin V. *Annotated Diary of Bishop James Roosevelt Bayley*. 2 Vols. Newark, N.J.

Vetromile, Eugene, S.J. *The Abnakis and Their History*. New York: James B. Kirker, 1866.

Vetromile, Eugene, S.J. *Indian Good Book*. New York: Edward Dunigan and Brother, 1856.

Vetromile, Eugene, S.J. *The Prayer Song*. New York: Edward Dunigan and Brother, 1858.

Walsh, Henry. *Hallowed Were the Gold Dust Trails*. Santa Clara, California: University of Santa Clara Press, 1946.

Warde, Sister M. Paul Xavier. *Mount St. Mary Record*, "A Backward Glance—II," VI (March, 1898), 109; "A Backward Glance —III," VI (May, 1898), 133–34.

Warde, Sister M. Paul Xavier. "A Chapter of Incidents," *Mount St. Mary Record*, II (January, 1894), 15–17.

Warde, Sister M. Paul Xavier. "In Memorian, Miss Emily Harper," *Mount St. Mary Record*, (May, 1892), 4.

Woodstock Letters, I, II, 1872–73. Woodstock College, Woodstock, Maryland.

ANNALS, ARCHIVAL COLLECTIONS, DIARIES, DOCUMENTS, LETTERS, NEWSPAPERS, REGISTRIES, UNPUBLISHED MANUSCRIPTS

Annals, Archival Collections, and Letters, Sisters of Mercy:
  Ireland: Convents of Mercy—Carlow, Cork, Derry, Dublin, Limerick, Naas, Westport, Wexford.
  Rome: Archives, Irish College; Archives, Propaganda Fide.

United States: Convents of Mercy—Albany; Baltimore; Bangor, Me.; Bethesda, Md.; Buffalo; Burlingame, Calif.; Burlington, Vt.; Chicago; Cresson, Pa.; Dallas, Pa.; Dobbs Ferry, N.Y.; Hartford; Indian Island, Me.; Latrobe, Pa.; Mobile, Ala.; Nashua, N.H.; New Orleans, La.; Newport, R.I.; North Plainfield, N.J.; Omaha; Peter Dana Point, Me.; Philadelphia; Pittsburgh, Pa.; Portland, Me.; Providence, R.I.; Red Bluff, Calif.; Rochester, N.Y.; Sacramento, California; Towanda, Pa.; Wilkes-Barre, Pa.; Windham (Manchester), N.H.

Archival Collections and Letters, Diocesan Archives:
Ireland: Carlow, Braganza House.
United States: Baltimore, Cathedral Archives; Buffalo; Burlington, Vt.; Cincinnati; Chicago: Mundelein Seminary and Notre Dame University Archives; Hartford; Newark, N.J.; Omaha; Philadelphia: Diocesan Archives and St. Charles Borromeo Seminary Archives; Pittsburgh, Pa.; Portland, Me.; Providence, R.I.; Rochester, N.Y.: St. Bernard Seminary; Trenton, N.J.

Bacon, Bishop David William. *Episcopal Diary.* Diocesan Archives, Portland, Me.

Bayley, Bishop James Roosevelt. *Episcopal Diary, 1853–72.* Diocesan Archives, Newark, N.J.

Bayley, Bishop James Roosevelt. *Memorandum Book, 1842–76.* A Little Diary, Supplement to His *Episcopal Diary, 1872–77.* Cathedral Archives, Archdiocese of Baltimore.

Bayley, Bishop James Roosevelt and Corrigan, Bishop Michael Augustine. *Letter Book.* Diocesan Archives, Newark, N.J.

Canevin, Bishop J. F. Regis. "Outline of the History of the Diocese of Pittsburgh, 1794–1915." Unpublished Manuscript. Diocesan Archives, Pittsburgh.

Connelly, Sister Mary Henrietta. *History of the Sisters of Mercy of Philadelphia.* M. A. Thesis. Villanova University, 1953.

Convey, Sister M. Fidelis. *Mother Agatha O'Brien and the Pioneers.* M. A. Thesis. Loyola University, Chicago, 1929.

Corrigan, Bishop Michael Augustine. *Episcopal Diary, 1873–80.* Diocesan Archives, Newark, N.J.

de Goesbriand, Bishop Louis. *Diary.* Diocesan Archives, Burlington, Vt.

Derry L[arge] Manuscript. "Notes on the Life of Mother Catherine McAuley" by a Sister of Mercy. Written Prior to 15 May 1847.

Unpublished Manuscript. Archives, Convent of Mercy, Derry, Ireland.

Derry S[mall] Manuscript. "The Life of Our Holy Foundress, Her Birth and Early Education," by a Sister of Mercy. Written c. 1849–50. Unpublished Manuscript. Archives, Convent of Mercy, Derry, Ireland. (Integral Part of *Annals,* Sisters of Mercy, Bermondsey, England.)

Documents and Letters, Archives, Propaganda Fide, Rome: *Acta; Congressi, America Centrale; Lettere; Scritturi non Riferite Nei Congressi; Scrituri Riferite nelle Congregazioni Generali; Udienze, America Centrale.* 1835–1884.

The Guide or Advice to a Superior. Unpublished Manuscript. Archives, Sisters of Mercy, Cork. (Manuscript overlaps in part the *Spiritual Maxims of Mary Frances Warde.*)

Healy, Bishop James Augustine. *Episcopal Diary* (1875–85). Diocesan Archives, Portland, Me.

Healy, Bishop James Augustine. *Letter Book.* 3 Vols. Diocesan Archives, Portland, Me.

Hogan, Sister Mary Ignatius. *Like a Waterwheel of God,* Chronicles of Early Mission Days, Sisters of Mercy in New Jersey, 1873–1895. Revised by Sister Marie LaSalle O'Hara, 1895–1946. Unpublished Manuscript. Archives, Sisters of Mercy, North Plainfield, N.J.

Letters of Father Fidelis of the Cross (Kent Stone) to Frances Warde. Archives, Sisters of Mercy, Manchester, N.H.

Letters, Irish College, Rome: Cardinal Paul Cullen Collection; Tobias Kirby Collection.

McAuley, Catherine. *The Bermondsey Manuscript.* Unpublished Manuscript on the Spirit of the Sisters of Mercy. Archives, Sisters of Mercy, Bermondsey, England.

Moore, Sister M. Clare Augustine. *Memoir of the Foundress, M. C. McAuley,* 1864. Unpublished Manuscript. Archives, Sisters of Mercy, Carysfort Park, Dublin.

Morris, Sister M. Mercedes. *Sisters of Mercy of Oklahoma, 1844–1944.* M. A. Thesis. Catholic University of America, 1947.

Newspapers:
Bordentown Register, Bordentown, N.J., 1932; *Boston Globe,* 1875–84; *Boston Pilot,* 1931, 1958; *Church World,* Portland, Me., 1948, 1955, 1965; *Cincinnati Telegraph,* 1865; *Daily*

True American, Trenton, N.J., 1885; *Hartford Catholic Transcript,* 1902; *Manchester Free Press,* 1963; *Manchester Daily Mirror,* 1858, 1859, 1860, 1861, 1865, 1884; *Manchester Mirror and American,* 1884; *Manchester Union Leader,* 1863, 1958; *Philadelphia Catholic Herald and Visitor,* 1861; *Pittsburgh Catholic,* 1843–1885; *Pittsburgh Commercial Journal,* 1846–1847; *Portland Press Herald,* 1965; *Portland Sunday Telegraph,* 1957; *Providence Journal,* 1855; *Providence Visitor,* 1926.

O'Donohue, Sister M. Aquinas. *Sisters of Mercy in Texas, 1875– 1945.* M. A. Thesis. Catholic University of America, 1948.

Parish Registries, Ireland:

Abbeyleix, Port Laoise—Parochial House and Vicarage; Freshford, Kilkenny; Mountrath, Port Laoise.

Pierce, Sister M. Gerald. *Annals of the Sisters of Mercy, Diocese of Buffalo, 1858–1958.* 2 Vols. Unpublished Manuscript. Archives, Sisters of Mercy, Buffalo, N.Y.

Records, Genealogical Office, Dublin Castle, Dublin.

Registry, St. Patrick's College, Maynooth, Ireland.

Registry of Deeds, Dublin. Five Deeds, Bellbrook House, Abbeyleix, Laoise.

Spiritual Maxims of Mary Frances Warde. Carlow, February 2, 1839. Unpublished Manuscript. Archives, Convent of Mercy, Naas.

Strange, Mother Elizabeth. "The First Years in Pittsburgh." Unpublished Manuscript. Archives, Sisters of Mercy, Pittsburgh.

Sullivan, Sister M. Florence. *Memoirs of Rochester Sisters of Mercy.* M. A. Thesis, Canisius College, 1928.

Timon, Bishop John. *Episcopal Diary* (1855–1867). Diocesan Archives, Buffalo.

Toohey, Sister Mary Xaveria. *Memories of Mercy.* Unpublished Manuscript. 150 pp. Sisters of Mercy, Portland, Me., 1931.

Warde, Frances, Compiler. *Book of Private Prayer.* Carlow, June 16, 1837. Unpublished Manuscript. Given to Sister Kathleen Healy, Pittsburgh, by Mother M. Joseph Boyle, Naas, March 16, 1969.

Warde, Sister M. Paul Xavier. "A Few Leaves from the Book of My Remembrance," Manchester, N.H. Unpublished Manuscript. Archives, Sisters of Mercy, Windham, N.H. 1947. 9 pp.

Institutions of Mercy Founded by Frances Warde

FRANCES WARDE founded personally perhaps more convents, schools, hospitals, and institutions of social welfare than any other religious leader of the Western World. Following are the Institutions of Mercy she established. Religious foundations which were mother houses, or centers which maintained novitiates and expanded their apostolates to new institutions, are marked with the asterisk. Though circumstances prevented Frances Warde's presence at the opening of her missions to Loretto, Omaha, Yreka, the Indian Missions, and Dover, she was nevertheless their founder. The Carlow Institute of Mercy was established, strictly speaking, by Catherine McAuley, while Frances Warde was its first Superior. It is listed, however, because Frances Warde was so closely associated with its institution that she is often called its founder.

*Carlow	1837	St. Leo Convent
"	1839	St. Leo Pension School
"	1840	House of Mercy
*Naas	1839	St. Mary Convent
"	1839	St. Mary Pension School
"	1839	St. Mary Free School
*Wexford	1840	St. Michael Convent
"	1841	House of Mercy
"	1841	Orphan Home (St. Michael)
*Westport	1842	Mount St. Mary Convent
"	1842	St. Mary Free School
"	1843	St. Mary Pension School
*Pittsburgh, Pa.	1843	St. Mary Convent

"	1844	St. Mary Academy (Our Lady of Mercy Academy, 1894)
"	1845	St. Paul Cathedral School
"	1846	Orphan Asylum (St. Paul)
"	1846	St. Patrick School
"	1847	Mercy Hospital
Latrobe, Pa.	1845	Mount St. Vincent Convent
"	1845	Mount St. Vincent Academy (St. Xavier Academy, 1847)
"	1845	St. Vincent School
*Chicago	1846	St. Mary Convent
"	1846	St. Mary School
"	1846	St. Xavier Academy
*Loretto	1848	St. Aloysius Convent (Cresson, 1879)
*Providence, R. I.	1851	St. Xavier Convent
"	1851	St. Xavier Academy
"	1851	St. Peter and Paul Cathedral School (Tyler School)
"	1851	St. Patrick School
"	1851	Orphan Home
"	1854	St. Joseph School
*Hartford, Conn.	1852	St. Catherine Convent (Independent, 1872)
"	1852	St. Patrick School
"	1853	St. Catherine Academy
"	1853	St. Catherine Orphanage (St. James)
New Haven, Conn.	1852	St. Mary Convent (Affiliated Hartford, 1872)
"	1852	St. Mary Orphan Home (St. Francis, 1855)
"	1852	St. Mary Academy
"	1852	St. Mary School
"	1854	St. Patrick School
Newport, R. I.	1854	St. Mary of the Isle Convent
"	1854	St. Mary of the Isle School
*Rochester, N. Y.	1857	St. Mary Convent
"	1857	St. Mary School

"	1857	Academy of the Immaculate Conception
*Manchester, N. H.	1858	Mount St. Mary Convent
"	1858	St. Anne School (St. Agnes, 1882; McDonald, 1893)
"	1858	Mount St. Mary Academy
"	1858	Union Street School (Evening School for Young Ladies)
"	1860	Park Street School
"	1865	St. Mary Orphanage (St. Patrick, 1874)
"	1869	Lowell Street School (St. Joseph, 1870)
"	1874	Home for Aged Ladies
*Philadelphia	1861	Convent of the Assumption
"	1861	Assumption School
"	1861	Academy of the Sisters of Mercy
"	1861	Night School, Parish of the Assumption
*Omaha	1864	St. Mary Convent
"	1864	Mount St. Mary Academy
"	1864	Holy Angels School
Bangor, Me.	1865	St. Xavier Convent
"	1865	St. Xavier Academy
"	1865	St. John School
"	1865	St. John Night School
Portsmouth, N. H.	1865	St. Patrick Convent
"	1865	St. Patrick School
*Yreka, Calif.	1871	Convent of Mercy
"	1871	St. Joseph Academy
North Whitefield, Me.	1871	Convent of Mercy
"	1871	Academy of Mercy
"	1871	Orphan Home for Girls
St. Johnsbury, Vt.	1872	Convent of Mercy
"	1872	Notre Dame des Victoires School

*Burlington, Vt	1874	St. Patrick Convent of Mercy (Independent, 1876)
"	1874	St. Mary Cathedral School
"	1875	St. Mary Night School
Jersey City, N. J.	1872	St. Patrick Convent
"	1872	St. Patrick School
"	1872	Academy of Mercy
*Bordentown, N. J.	1873	St. Mary Convent (North Plainfield, 1908)
"	1873	St. Mary School
"	1873	St. Joseph Academy
Princeton, N. J.	1878	St. Paul Convent
"	1878	St. Paul School
"	1878	Academy of Mercy (St. Scholastica, 1880)
*Portland, Me.	1873	St. Elizabeth Convent (Independent, 1883)
"	1873	St. Elizabeth Orphan Home (Deering, 1909)
"	1873	St. Elizabeth Academy
"	1873	St. Elizabeth Night School
"	1873	St. Aloysius School
"	1873	St. Dominic School
"	1877	Kavanagh School (Cathedral)
"	1882	St. Joseph Academy (Deering)
"	1882	St. Joseph Home for Aged (Deering)
Indian Island, Old Town, Me.	1878	St. Ann Convent
"	1878	St. Ann School
"	1878	Night School for Young Men
"	1878	Sewing School for Young Women
Pleasant Point, Perry, Me.	1879	St. Ann Convent
"	1879	St. Ann School
Peter Dana Point, Princeton, Me.	1879	St. Ann Convent

Laconia, N. H.	1880	St. Joseph Convent
"	1880	St. Joseph School
"	1880	Night School for Young Men and Women
Dover, N. H.	1883	St. Mary Convent
"	1883	Sacred Heart School

Index

529

SEC. 364. LARCENY FROM LIBRARIES--
ANY PERSON WHO SHALL PROCURE, OR
TAKE IN ANY WAY FROM ANY PUBLIC
LIBRARY OR THE LIBRARY OF ANY
LITERARY, SCIENTIFIC, HISTORICAL
OR LIBRARY SOCIETY OR ASSOCIATION,
WHETHER INCORPORATED OR UNINCOR-
PORATED, ANY BOOK, PAMPHLET, MAP,
CHART, PAINTING, PICTURE, PHOTO-
GRAPH, PERIODICAL, NEWSPAPER,
MAGAZINE, MANUSCRIPT OR EXHIBIT
OR ANY PART THEREOF, WITH INTENT
TO CONVERT THE SAME TO HIS OWN
USE, OR WITH INTENT TO DEFRAUD
THE OWNER THEREOF, OR WHO HAVING
PROCURED OR TAKEN ANY SUCH BOOK,
PAMPHLET, MAP, CHART, PAINTING,
PICTURE, PHOTOGRAPH, PERIODICAL,
NEWSPAPER, MAGAZINE, MANUSCRIPT
OR EXHIBIT OR ANY PART THEREOF,
SHALL THEREAFTER CONVERT THE SAME
TO HIS OWN USE OR FRAUDULENTLY
DEPRIVE THE OWNER THEREOF, SHALL
BE GUILTY OF A MISDEMEANOR.

MICHIGAN COMPILED LAWS.